POLICY AND PARTY COMPETITION

POLICY AND PARTY COMPETITION

MICHAEL LAVER AND W. BEN HUNT

ROUTLEDGE • NEW YORK & LONDON

Published in 1992 by

Routledge
An imprint of Routledge, Chapman and Hall, Inc.
29 West 35th Street
New York, NY 10001

Published in Great Britain by

Routledge
11 New Fetter Lane
London EC4P 4EE

Library of Congress Cataloging-in-Publication Data

Laver, Michael, 1949–
    Policy and party competition / Michael Laver, W. Ben Hunt.
        p.   cm.
    Includes index.
    ISBN 0-415-90219-3
    1. Political parties. I. Hunt, W. Ben. II. Title.
JF2049.:L298   1992
324.2—dc20   91-35563
                                                            CIP

British Library of Congress data also available.

Contents

Acknowledgments

Many of our colleagues have helped to shape our thinking over the years. Quite a few of these people might well be happy to disown any responsibility for this, but we thank them all anyway. We do have some very specific debts to acknowledge, however. Both Ken Shepsle and Norman Schofield, on whose ideas we extensively rely, have been great sources of intellectual stimulation, advice and encouragement. Jim Alt did much to make the expert survey possible in the first place. The U.S. National Science Foundation provided the grant (SES-8822307) that supported the entire project. Our deepest thanks go to all of these.

Michael Laver, University College Galway.
W. Ben Hunt, Harvard University.

Introduction

The operation of "free" elections is taken as a key element in most working definitions of western-style liberal democracy. Real competition between two or more political parties is typically taken as a key element in most working definitions of free elections. Party competition is thus one of the central concerns of western political science.

Rather less attention is given to what it is that parties are competing *about*. In general terms, the conventional view is that they are competing to get into government on the basis of promises about what they will do if they get there. Most of the promises that political parties make, it tends to be assumed, have to do with the public policies that they will enact if they are given the chance to do so. The actual substance of the policies that are promised tends to be of less concern to many who write about party competition and democratic elections; the process of competition is assumed to ensure that the policies promised, whatever these might be, will reflect the wishes of the electorate.

This book looks in detail at the role of policy in the process of party competition. We consider this from two interacting perspectives, one theoretical, one empirical. We review a range of theoretical arguments about the role of policy in party competition and we illustrate these arguments with a completely new data set, one assembled especially for the book and published in full in a long appendix. Our central purpose is to consider how much light theories of party competition throw on the practice of party competition in the twenty four parliamentary democracies that form the core of our study.

In subsequent chapters we describe our empirical work, before going on to deal with various aspects of the role of policy in party competition. Before we get down to business, however, we must be quite clear about what we mean by policy and what we mean by party competition. We begin with the latter, which is the easier to define.

What is Party Competition?

In practice, party competition is a continuous process with no beginning and no end. In order to begin to understand it, however, we must start somewhere. Logically and ideologically, we take party competition to begin with an electorate, each member of which has preferences about alternative states of the world. Periodically, elections are held. In these, each member of the electorate, on the basis of his or her preferences, chooses between several possible courses of action. These actions involve voting in favor of some outcome or another or, of course, not voting. Once votes have been cast, an electoral law transforms the collection of votes cast into an election result. While election results may relate to local or to international organizations, or to referendums on specific policy decisions, the election results that we shall be concerned with in this book concern the allocation of seats in a national legislature. These seats are allocated to particular politicians belonging to particular political parties. During the electoral phase, therefore, party competition comprises a contest for legislative seats between party politicians, each of whom is trying to attract the votes of electors.

Once the election result has been declared, the electorate plays no formal role in the process of party competition until the next election. It continues to play an informal role, however, in the sense that politicians develop their strategies in anticipation of the behavior of the electorate at subsequent elections. They do certain things because they expect these to win votes; they avoid actions that they expect to lose votes. The fact that politicians anticipate the results of future elections means that changes in the preferences of the electorate are reflected in the strategies of political parties, even after the electoral phase is over.

The substance of party competition in any particular setting, of course, depends upon the powers of the legislature with which it is concerned. One power of most legislatures is the power to legislate—the power to pass bills into law. A second power concerns the obligation to select and support an executive. This is the preserve of all legislatures which operate under the system of "parliamentary government", in other words of most European legislatures. The most notable western legislature that does not operate under the system of parliamentary government is of course the United States Congress, which the USA Constitution keeps formally quite separate from the executive.

In theory, parties in a typical legislature compete with each other over the passing of bills and the supporting of governments. In parliamentary government systems, however, executive control over the legislative agenda means that the most important practical feature of party competition has to do with the maintenance of the government. If a government controls a legislative majority it can, in most European countries, effectively legislate at will.

After the legislative phase of party competition, another election is held. The cycle repeats itself continuously and indefinitely, and we take its starting point to be electoral competition, partly as a convenience and partly because it is the electoral phase of party competition that is typically taken, ideologically, to define the type of "democratic" political system with which our empirical analysis is concerned.

What is Policy?

The second basic matter that we must be quite clear about before we can usefully proceed concerns what we mean by "policy". This is a much more tricky business, and one that is surrounded by considerable ambiguity in the literature.

The logical starting point in our own interpretation of the role of policy in party competition has to do with the preferences of voters. We can take some of these preferences as being "intrinsic", not in the sense that they are genetically or biologically determined—we leave this question entirely open—but in the more practical sense that the source of "intrinsic" preferences is exogenous to the process of party competition. We will follow conventional usage and refer to such intrinsic preferences as "tastes."

As we shall see in the next chapter, the assumption that tastes are exogenous to party competition is not the only one that we could have made. A quite considerable body of literature assumes, in contrast, that electoral tastes are fashioned by party competition. The acceptance of one or other of these assumptions—or indeed of both—seems to us to be an act of faith as much as anything else. We make no bones about putting our faith in the assumption that tastes are exogenous to party competition.

Particular courses of action are instrumental in bringing about particular states of the world. Proposed programs of action explicitly intended to bring about particular states of the world can be thought of as "policies." People's tastes lead them to prefer some states of the world to others, thus voters have preferences for policies based on their tastes.

The theories that we will be using to give shape to our accounts of party competition are unified by their general view of voting as a purposeful rather than as a purely emotional act. They thus assume that individuals can compare any two possible states of the world in terms either of preference or indifference— each individual prefers one state to the other, or does not care at all which comes into being. Most theorists go further than this and assume that there is at least some limited internal coherence in the preferences of individuals, a coherence that enables individuals to rank different policies. The policy preferred by an individual to all others can be thought of as this person's "ideal" policy.

While this general approach to what is meant by "policy" seems neat enough on the face of things, it does not get to the heart of what most people have in mind when they talk about policy in the context of party competition. One particular example that illustrates this quite clearly has to do with the tastes we might ascribe to politicians. Some people may become politicians, having tastes just like those of typical voters, because they wish to promote particular policies that have implications for the electorate at large. Others may become politicians because they have a taste for the trappings of politics—the power, the notoriety and the opportunities for personal profit. If a politician adopts a purposeful course of action designed to further these latter objectives, bribing voters in order to win elections for example, then this would be a "policy" according to our general definition. Yet a politician would be referred to as "having a policy of bribing voters" only with a heavy dose of irony. In general usage, therefore, which we will follow in this book, "policy" tends to mean "public policy", that is, policy with potential implications for sections of the electorate as a whole rather than just for particular individuals.

Policy and Party Competition: Overview

Over the past thirty years or so, a rapidly expanding literature has developed to deal with the role of policy in party competition. This literature is usually traced back to a seminal book, *An Economic Theory of Democracy,* published by Anthony Downs in 1957, though Downs himself refers to a number of other authors who considered the matter before him. Branches of this literature deal with a number of aspects of the role of policy in party competition, notably with elections, intra-party politics, legislative behavior, and government formation. The number of articles and books that have by now been published within this tradition is simply immense. It is not our intention to review them here. Indeed, as the reader will quickly notice, we have deliberately been very sparing in our discussion of the literature throughout this book. We wanted to concentrate on a few basic issues that apply across the board, and to avoid getting caught up in a thicket of detail. Thus, we select a theme that is common to all of this analysis, the description of party systems in terms of configurations of actors in "policy spaces", and explore this theme from a number of different perspectives.

Spatial representations of the arena in which voting and party competition take place have become pervasive in recent years, and are practically the only way in which theorists characterize the preferences of the relevant actors. Waving a magic wand and assuming a policy space into being is an easy thing to do—and a body of powerful and suggestive theory has been based upon such assumptions. There tends to be a further, more dubious, and certainly unstated, assumption underlying such approaches, however. This is that describing the actual positions of key actors on the dimensions that define policy spaces presents no more than technical estimation problems. Such estimates may in practice be imprecise and unreliable, it is assumed, but there is in some sense an underlying reality to which they refer.

Quite a few authors have estimated party positions on the widely-used "left-right" ideological dimension for a range of democratic political systems. As we shall see, when more than one such estimate has been made for a given country, even on the basis of quite different types of data, there is usually a high level of consistency between them. This certainly suggests that some underlying variable is reliably being captured.

Empirical estimates of policy spaces have not kept pace with an ever-more sophisticated body of theory, however. Increasingly, theoretical accounts have dealt with multidimensional policy spaces, yet empirical estimates of party positions in these spaces are both much thinner on the ground and much more problematic. Certain authors have estimated party policy positions in certain countries on several different policy dimensions. But the selection of dimensions involved in these studies is much more idiosyncratic. More seriously, almost every empirical analysis has ignored a range of important matters concerning how party positions on several different dimensions can be combined into a configuration of parties in a multidimensional policy space. Factors that must be considered include the different weights that different parties give to different policy dimensions, and the manner in which actors trade off distances on one policy dimension against distances on another. Both of these matters have to do with crucial parameters, not relevant for one-dimensional models, but not estimated in most multidimensional spatial analyses.

In the chapters that follow, we elaborate theoretical treatments of the relationship between policy and party competition in multidimensional policy spaces, using an extensive new data set on party policy positions in twenty four democracies. This data set, based on an expert survey, not only estimates party positions on a large number of policy dimensions, it also estimates for the first time a range of other parameters that are essential to the representation of party competition in multidimensional policy spaces.

As the reader will quickly appreciate, this book is more about the process of empirical elaboration than about the theories themselves, on which much has already been written. We feel very strongly, however, that the process of empirical elaboration is no mere technical problem of estimation. As we shall argue at several points in the subsequent discussions, it is only when a serious attempt is made to operationalize many of the key concepts in the spatial approach that we see several aspects of this approach that are typically rather vague and underspecified. Developing a full-blooded empirical elaboration of these theories is not just an afterthought or an activity fit only for research assistants—it is a central part of the business of theorizing.

In the first chapter, therefore, we discuss a range of theoretical matters that must be cleared up before we can set about estimating party positions in multidimensional policy spaces, and a range of other parameters related to the role of policy in party competition. In the second chapter we describe our expert survey which we believe to be, by some considerable measure, the largest and most comprehensive to have been conducted within this theoretical tradition. In the third chapter we describe the the policy spaces that we estimated and the party configurations that we found in these. In the fourth chapter we discuss other key parameters of party competition, concentrating especially on the trade-off between office and policy payoffs, the different ways in which different parties rate the importance of the same policy dimensions, and the identity of key decision makers within political parties. In the final chapter, we put these discussions to work in the elaboration of a range of theoretical treatments of one of the most vital aspects of the process of party competition, the business of forming a government.

When all is said and done, however, our central purpose in this book has to do neither with the theory of party competition nor with its empirical description. It has to do with the relationship between these two intellectual endeavors. Above all, we hope to encourage those who are interested in theories of party competition to take a more lively interest in the empirical elaboration of these. In this context, we regard a vital and integral part of this book to be Appendix B, in which we report in full our estimates of all relevant parameters for all parties in all countries in our study. Appendix B is not exactly bedtime reading, but it is definitely something for theorists to play around with during office hours. It is our steadfast conviction that there is no better way to understand particular theory than to get out a pencil and paper and start running some through some real data—by hand. If we can't get a theory to make sense of the data when we do this, then we have misunderstood the theory, misapplied it, or simply chosen a bad one. Whatever the explanation, it is something that we need to get to the bottom of before we go on. Confronting theory with data is, quite simply, an invaluable learning experience for anybody. And that, we hope, is the main value of this book.

1

The Structure of Electoral Policy Preferences

As we said in the introduction, we take the logical and ideological starting point of party competition to be the tastes of the electorate. We thus begin our discussion of the role of policy in party competition by considering possible sources of structure in electoral tastes. We then discuss how to describe possible structures of preference in the electorate, whatever their source. In particular, we consider spatial representations of the structure of tastes, since these have become ubiquitous in recent times.

We make no apology for dwelling on these basic issues, which have tended to be rather neglected in many accounts of the role of policy in party competition. While spatial metaphors have become the *lingua franca* of theorists of party competition, in the wake of the seminal work of authors such as Black and Downs, spatial "models" are often deployed rather uncritically, without much thought being given to precisely what is implied by them. As we shall see, while spatial representations of the structure of tastes in a group of political actors can be powerfully suggestive, their use is not always as straightforward as might appear at first sight. Whether this is done explicitly or implicitly, the use of spatial representations involves making rather complex assumptions about how individuals view the political world, assumptions whose validity is far from self evident.

Sources of Structure in Policy Preferences

The central question that concerns us in this chapter is whether there are sufficient regularities in the policy preferences of voters for there to be some sort of structure in the process of competition between politicians. If there are not such regularities, then political competition should be chaotic and disorganised.

Structures in electoral policy preferences manifest themselves as relationships between voters. These relationships are expressed in terms of similarities and differences in the tastes of pairs of voters in relation to the range of policies that could conceivably be promoted. Different views about the possible sources of structure in electoral preferences tend to define different theories of voting and party competition.

The main differences between theories have to do with whether sources of structure in party competition derive from exogenously given patterns in the "intrinsic" tastes of voters, or whether structure emerges endogenously as a result of the process of party competition itself. Thus it may be the case that electoral preferences are exogenously structured because groups of voters have similar intrinsic tastes, for some reason or another that has nothing at all to do with party competition. Or it may be the case that electoral preferences are endogenously structured by party competition itself. This may happen because politicians choose a particular method of allocating responsibilities to government departments, for example, or of holding elections, which "artificially" restricts the range of choices available to voters and thereby conditions their preferences. Theorists are rarely explicit about the sources of structure in electoral preferences that they have in mind, but it is not difficult to find examples of alternative interpretations in the literature.

Theorists of party competition who have followed in the tradition of Downs, for example, almost invariably assume that the fundamental source of structure in party competition is a set of electoral tastes. They further assume, albeit implicitly, that the source of these tastes is quite exogenous to party competition. Exploring the impact of different sets of electoral tastes on party competition is a large part of what Downsian theorists do. Indeed, one of the things that attracted such widespread interest in the work of Downs in the first place was his argument that, in one-dimensional party systems (see below), the pattern of electoral preferences makes little difference to the pattern of party competition (Downs, 1957).

People working within this tradition never consider the impact of different patterns of party competition on the structure of electoral tastes. Changes in the structure of these tastes are seen as being the result either of foreseeable developments in technology, society and the economy, or of unforeseeable "shocks" to the system. Sources of shock may be entirely exogenous—a nuclear accident in another country, for example—they may be endogenous random events—the discovery of oil in the North Sea had a major impact on British politics, for example—or they may be deterministic but essentially unknowable— for example the unpredictable chaotic outcomes of complex nonlinear interactions between clusters of variables. Public concern about famine in a particular Third World country, for example, may suddenly "take off" and result in major pressures on politicians because of a powerful but very obscure interaction of factors, despite that fact that other more serious Third World famines arising in only slightly different conditions have previously had little impact on public opinion.

A superior being might be able to predict this interaction effect, but it appears as a shock to mere mortals.

The key feature of the Downsian approach to party competition, therefore, is that the electorate is autonomous. The structure of electoral preferences does not depend on party competition itself, so that describing patterns of party competition fundamentally requires being able to describe patterns in the tastes of the electorate. More or less everything else can be deduced from these patterns.

An alternative approach is to see the political system itself as the source of structure in electoral tastes, and thus in party competition. One very important endogenous source of structure, for example, is political socialization. This is the mechanism whereby the political elite "educates" voters into a set of views about which policies are, and which are not, feasible and/or desirable. The process of socialization may also be concerned with relationships between different policies, as voters "learn" that you can do this, or you can do that, but you can't do both. Voters may also "learn" that certain policies promote the interests of certain types of voter, while other policies promote the interests of other types of voter.

One influential version of this general approach can be found in the "party identification" models of the Michigan School, exemplified by the well-known work of Campbell, Converse, Miller and Stokes. This sees party choice by voters as the product of an enduring set of partisan attitudes developed within each individual, made coherent by the development of a sense of identification with a particular political party. Party identification "is a psychological identification, which can persist without legal recognition or evidence of formal membership and even without a consistent record of party support . . . the strength and direction of party identification are facts of central importance in accounting for attitude and behavior" (Campbell, Converse, Miller, and Stokes, 1964: 67–8). Thus voters, it is assumed, come to regard themselves as Democrats, Republicans, Conservatives, Christian Democrats, or whatever. Such bonds are formed over a long process of socialization and are changed only by major events.

Voters' preferences in relation to particular policies are assumed by party identification theorists to derive from their urge to reduce their overall level of cognitive dissonance, making all of their attitudes as consistent as possible with one another. Given the "role of enduring partisan commitments in shaping attitudes" (Campbell, *et al.*, 1964: 78), voters come to prefer policy positions that are consistent with those put forward by the party with which they identify. In this important sense, while fundamental tastes may be exogenous to party competition, particular policy preferences cannot be "read off" directly from tastes, but are conditioned strongly by party identification. This means that the actual structure of policy preferences is endogenous to party competition.

Another important source of structure in policy preferences has to do with public administration, the process by which policy decisions taken within the political system are implemented. Obviously, there is considerable specialization and division of labor between government departments. Different departments have responsibility for different policy areas. Thus "policy jurisdictions" emerge which, because of the complexity, technical detail and expertise involved in each, give considerable autonomy over policy outputs to those who control them. Those politicians and public administrators involved with the government department responsible for telecommunications, for example, are far better placed than anybody else to determine the choices that the public are offered on telecommunications policy. The particular set of policy jurisdictions found in a given political system thus provides a very important source of structure in party competition, a matter that forms the basis of recent work by Laver and Shepsle and Austen-Smith and Banks (Austen-Smith and Banks, 1990; Laver and Shepsle, 1990a, b).

Policy jurisdictions are at least partially endogenous, since politicians can and do try to reorganize the responsibilities of government departments, for example. Yet we also note that very similar sets of government departments tend to operate in a range of very different political systems. No matter which country you look at, there is almost always a department of finance, a department of foreign affairs, a department of justice or internal affairs, a department of health, a department of education, a department of agriculture, and so on. This suggests that there might be at least some intrinsic logic to the grouping of particular sets of policy responsibilities in particular ways, and hence to the structuring of policy in general.

The matter of whether the most important sources of structure in electoral policy preferences are exogenous or endogenous to party competition may or may not be important to the models that are developed, depending upon what each sets out to explain. If the aims of the theorist are relatively modest, relating to patterns observed at a particular election or to a short sequence of elections, then the structure of electoral preferences may be taken as a given. It may not be necessary to go too deeply into how this has been given. (Such an approach amounts, of course, to treating the structure of electoral preferences as exogenously imposed and unchanging.) If the aims of the theorist are more grandiose, as they sometimes are, relating perhaps to the evolution of the party system in a particular country or to differences between party systems in different countries, then it is difficult to ignore the sources of structure in electoral policy preferences. Obviously, it will otherwise be impossible to determine whether differences over time or between countries are a result of differences in the exogenous structuring of electoral preferences, or a result of the endogenous development of the party system itself.

We state our position on this matter quite clearly and unashamedly. Our aims in this book are for the most part rather modest, so that the precise source of structure in electoral policy preferences does not matter to us. We will, however, be looking at broad differences between party systems. When it does make a difference, we take the source of structure in electoral tastes to be exogenous to party competition. At no stage in this book do we develop a psychological theory that deals with how developments in party competition affect the tastes of voters, or a theory of how politicians fashion the institutions of public administration to constrain choices in such a way as to suit their own ends. This implies that we view differences between party systems across space and time as resulting either from different decisions taken by different key actors faced with similar alternatives, or from exogenous differences in the structure of electoral tastes.

Describing the Structure of Policy Preferences: Policy Spaces

Thus the structure of electoral tastes may be the product of exogenous similarities in the physical, social and economic circumstances of different voters, or it may be the product of an endogenous restriction on the range of political alternatives on offer, the result of forces within the political system itself. Either way, most theorists accept that electoral preferences are structured in some way. The question that then arises is one of how this structure should be described. Typically, it is described in spatial terms. There is no particularly deep theoretical reason for the use of the spatial analogy, which is a consequence of historical accident, ease of visualization and, by now, convention.

The historical source of the spatial analogy is usually cited as the evolution of seating arrangements in the post-revolutionary French Constituent Assembly of 1789. This evolution is described eloquently by Thomas Carlyle, even discounting his trenchant ideological views. First, he describes a political system without structure:

> . . . there are Twelve Hundred miscellaneous individuals; not a unit of whom but has his own thinking-apparatus, his own speaking-apparatus! In every unit of them is some belief and wish, different for each, both that France should be regenerated, and also that he individually should do it. Twelve Hundred separate Forces, yolked miscellaneously to any object, miscellaneously to all sides of it; and bidden to pull for life! . . . (Carlyle, 1871: 189).

> For the present, if we glance into that Assembly-Hall of theirs, it will be found, as is natural, 'most irregular.' As many as 'a hundred members are on their feet at once;' no rule in making motions, or only commencements of a rule; Spectators' gallery allowed to applaud, and even to hiss; President, appointed once a fortnight, raising many times no serene head above the waves (Carlyle, 1871: 192).

Then Carlyle describes the emergence of structure:

> Nevertheless, as in all human Assemblages, like does begin arranging itself to like; . . . There is a Right Side (Coté Droit), a Left Side (Coté Gauche); sitting

on M. le President's right hand, or on his left: the Coté Droit conservative; the
Coté Gauche destructive (Carlyle, 1871: 192).

The actual physical clustering of like-minded individuals in legislative chambers, in particular the self-placement of conservatives to the right of the Chair and radicals to the left, is thus a potent image that has been used to describe the structure of preferences among legislators. The left-right analogy can be extended to the structure of preferences among voters, if it is assumed that the policies promoted by legislators accurately reflect the policies desired by voters.

Between left and right is the center. Some legislative chambers—the British House of Commons for example—are arranged in a way that prevents deputies from placing themselves physically in the center. The center in such cases has only conceptual meaning. Most chambers, however, follow the example of the French Assemblé National, with seating arrangements in the form of a semicircle or horseshoe. This creates a curved line, running from left to right, which does in fact have a physical center. It has become traditional in most of these countries for deputies who are neither conservative nor radical to seat themselves in the center.

The general ideological structure of these seating arrangements is illustrated in Figure 1.1. It is interesting to note that, while all legislative chambers do of course have a physical existence in three dimensions, seating arrangements within them tend to have *ideological* significance only in one dimension. A second physical dimension may be used to designate political seniority, as in the distinction between frontbenchers and backbenchers in Britain, while ventures into the third dimension typically signify no more than overexcitement. The important point to be noted is that seating arrangements in a three-dimensional legislative chamber could certainly evolve so as to allow for a physical manifestation of policy similarities and differences in two independent dimensions. This almost never happens, however. The ideological structure of legislative seating arrangements is almost invariably one-dimensional.

When all is said and done, the confrontation between a left pole and a right pole is a pervasive method of describing differences in the political tastes of individuals. While there are many substantive interpretations of left and right in politics, the left pole has in general become associated with policies designed to bring about the redistribution of resources from those with more to those with less, and with the promotion of social rights that apply to groups of individuals taken as a whole even at the expense of individual members of those groups. The right pole has become associated with the promotion of individual rights, including the right not to have personal resources expropriated for redistribution by the state, even at the expense of social inequality and of poverty among worse off social groups.

Moreover it has become common to think of leftness and rightness as being matters of degree. Just as there is a physical center between left and right in many

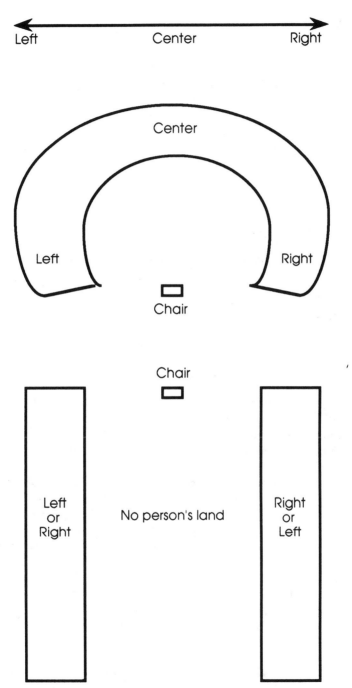

Figure 1.1 Westminster and "Continental" arrangements of left and right in legislatures.

legislative chambers, there is an ideological center between left and right in most groups of legislators. This is conventionally taken to imply that most policy preferences can be described as having a particular position on a line, or dimension, joining the two ideological poles. Thus, in Figure 1.2, the left and right poles are points L and R. They are joined by a line or dimension, LR. Point M is the precise midpoint of the dimension. Point A, to the left of this midpoint, is closer to point L than it is to point R. Point B, to the right of the midpoint, is closer to R than to L. This is not of course to say that everything that is politically salient about a policy preference can be described in terms of its position on this left-right dimension. But it does imply that most individuals will have politically salient policy preferences that can be described as having, among other things, a position on this dimension.

The precise political meaning of these positions on the left-right dimension (or indeed on any other ideological dimension) is often glossed over by those who write about such things. Spatial representations of policy positions have become part of the common currency of political argument, and writers often tend to assume that everyone knows what is implied by them. It is worth taking a moment, however, to consider the matter, since an interlocking set of definitions is involved.

Policy dimensions, it should be remembered, have no absolute meaning. They are ways of describing certain types of structure in the tastes of a group of individuals. The pervasiveness of the left-right dimension in accounts of party politics is thus an empirical phenomenon. It reflects the fact that preferences of groups of individuals in a wide range of political settings do tend, for one reason or another, to be structured according to the same general tendencies. However, precise policy positions on these dimensions have meaning only in terms of the tastes of actual or conceivable individuals within the political system in question. When we talk about the extreme left pole of the left-right dimension, therefore, we are talking about the position of a policy such that it is not possible to conceive of an actor who would prefer a more left-wing policy. The equivalent meaning applies to the extreme right-wing pole.

Such interpretations are not difficult to deal with. What, however, of point A in Figure 1.2? While it is clear that point A is at neither extreme of the scale, and is thus between L and R, what does it mean to say that it is closer to L than to R? Since the dimension has no absolute meaning. but rather describes a structure of preference, it might on the face of it seem reasonable to say that A is closer to L if, faced with a choice between only L and R as alternative policies, a person whose ideal policy was at point A would choose L. But what does it *really mean* to say that a person's ideal policy is at A?

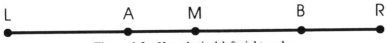

Figure 1.2 Hypothetical left-right scale.

We can approach this question by considering the meaning of the midpoint, M, of the dimension. We do have a sense of the meanings of the two extreme poles of the dimension. Given these, we can say that M describes the policy preferences of a person who is perfectly indifferent between L and R, if forced to choose between only these alternative policies. This gives a meaning to M, in terms of the policy preferences of a real or at least a conceivable individual. Of course, it is possible to give a meaning to any point on the dimension in the same way. This can be done by continually bisecting sectors of the dimension. For example, the midpoint M_{lm} of the sector between L and M (M now has a meaning) can be found, and the process can continue until a sufficiently detailed set of scale positions has been defined. Returning to point A, having described the meaning of the point in terms of a set of indifference relations, it is of course true that, faced with a choice between only L and R as alternative policies, a person whose ideal policy was at point A would choose L. This is a *consequence* of having an ideal policy at point A, however, not a *definition* of the meaning of the point.

Thus the fact that a policy dimension has only relative meaning is reflected in the fact that the meaning of every point on the dimension is described in terms of a set of indifference relations between other points in the system. The scale is anchored in reality by the assumption that we can give some sort of substantive interpretation to at least two points in the system.

All of this may seem to be using a sledgehammer to crack a nut, but it is very important to be quite clear about the proper interpretation of the policy spaces that we shall be using throughout the rest of this book. This is because political scientists have become increasingly cavalier in the manner in which they brandish the concept of a policy space, and there is some danger that it may lose much of its meaning.

Multidimensional Policy Spaces

The use of a single ideological dimension to describe the structure underlying the splendid complexity of tastes in any real political system is obviously a gross oversimplification. In particular, it is easy to think of other ideological dimensions that are quite independent of the left-right dimension, in the sense that it is not possible to predict a person's position on the other dimension by knowing their position on the left-right dimension. For example, consider an "urban-rural" dimension that reflects the interests of urban voters at one end of the scale and the interests of rural voters at the other. It is quite possible for someone to be simultaneously at the left end of the left-right scale and to be pro-urban, or to be on the left and pro-rural. Similarly a person could easily be right-wing and pro-urban, or right-wing and pro-rural.

Figure 1.3 shows two independent dimensions, a left-right dimension and a rural-urban dimension. Consider a person, Y, whose ideal policy on the left-right dimension is quite close to the left-wing pole of the scale, and whose ideal policy on the rural-urban dimension is slightly to the urban side of the center of the scale. The top part of Figure 1.3 shows the two policy dimensions taken one at a time. If we consider how Y feels about the policy L, we know from the preceding argument that Y is indifferent between L and L', where L and L' are the same distance from Y in opposite directions on the left-right dimension. Furthermore, Y would prefer any policy that was closer to Y than L, that is any policy on the segment of the left-right dimension between L and L'. By the same token, considering only the rural-urban dimension and how Y feels about policy T, Y would prefer any policy closer to Y than T, that is, any policy on the segment TT'.

When two or more independent dimensions structure political tastes it is customary, though by no means necessary, to present these as if they were orthogonal dimensions in a multidimensional physical space. This is convenient since it allows an ideal policy that has meaning in terms of, say, two dimensions (a left-wing, pro-rural, policy for example) to be given a single position in a two-dimensional space spanned by the dimensions in question. Just as with a single dimension, it is important to consider the meaning of policy positions in such multidimensional "policy spaces".

It is of course a simple matter of algebra or geometry to add extra policy dimensions to any space and political scientists have a tendency to do this in a rather profligate manner. But the actual meaning of policy positions in multidimensional spaces has an additional layer of complexity, being based on a very sweeping assumption that is typically unstated.

For example, a policy that implies L on the left-right dimension and T on the urban rural dimension can be described as having the position LT in the two dimensional policy space drawn in the lower part of Figure 1.3. In the same way, the policy positions of person Y on the two policy dimensions can be described by using a single point, Y, in the two-dimensional space. The question that must now be addressed concerns how person Y feels about policy LT. The logic that was deployed when we looked at each dimension in isolation suggests that Y will prefer to LT any policy located within the rectangle bounded by the broken lines running through L, L', T and T'. Such policies lie simultaneously between L and L' *and* between T and T'.

While it seems very plausible to argue that policies within this rectangle will be preferred by Y to LT, it is possible, however, that policies outside the rectangle will also be preferred. Consider how person Y feels about a policy at Z, which is well outside the rectangle because, taking into account only the left-right dimension, Z is much further away from Y than is L. However, Z is very close to Y's ideal policy on the urban-rural dimension. Is it possible that Z will be preferred by Y to LT because its closeness on the urban-rural dimension more

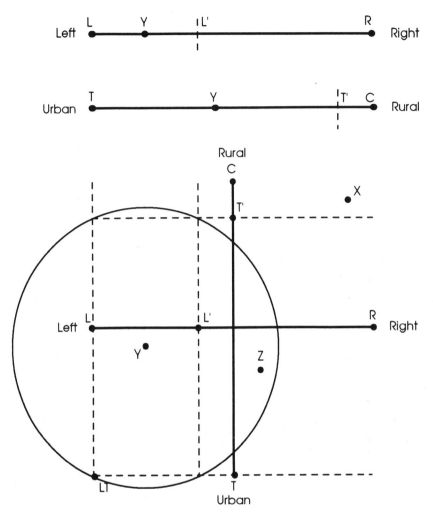

Figure 1.3 The relationship between two policy dimensions.

than compensates for its distance on the left-right dimension? Does Y trade off closeness on one dimension against distance on another when evaluating the various policies on offer?

Ultimately, of course, the answer to such a question is empirical. Theorists, however, invariably make very strong explicit or implicit assumptions about such trade-offs between policy dimensions. They do this when they use a single measure of the "distance" between one policy position and another in multidimensional policy spaces. We must remind ourselves once more, however, that policy spaces have only relative meaning, in the sense that they describe structures in the preferences of actual or at least conceivable people. This means that assumptions about the relationship between dimensions are assumptions about the preferences of individuals in the system, not assumptions about the system itself.

The first sweeping assumption that tends to be made by many theorists is that every individual in the system trades off the various policy dimensions in the same way. This does not mean that it is assumed that all individuals weigh all dimensions equally, but rather that they all agree on both the relative weight of each dimension and how these are traded off against each other. This assumption is very convenient, however implausible, since it allows us to draw and analyse a single spatial "map" of the structure of policy preferences of a particular group of individuals. If we do not make such an assumption, then there are as many different maps of the system as there are sets of relative weights of the dimensions and manners of trading these off—ultimately as many different maps as there are individuals.

In the empirical discussions that follow, we present strong evidence that different actors do in fact attach different weights to different ideological dimensions. This suggests that the use of a single spatial map of any policy system is a considerable oversimplification. We attempt to take theoretical account of this possibility below, when discussing coalition bargaining between parties but, as we shall see, this does present complex problems of analysis and interpretation. Assuming a single spatial map, however inadequate, certainly is convenient.

The second sweeping assumption that tends to be made when people use multidimensional policy spaces has to do with the manner in which individuals trade off distance from their ideal policy on one dimension against distance from their ideal policy on another, to derive an overall indication of the "policy distance" between two points in the space. Overwhelmingly the most common assumption is that distances on different policy dimensions are traded off in a manner that is directly analogous to the trading off of distances in physical space. In other words it is assumed that individuals view the interaction between policy dimensions in Euclidean terms, though this is but one of many plausible possibilities.

Figure 1.4 describes three plausible yet very different ways of looking at the manner in which individuals trade off gains or losses on one policy dimension, X, against gains or losses on another, Y. The figure deals with how a single individual at B feels about a policy at A. The individual at B perceives the distance from policy A on dimension X as being BC, and the distance from A on dimension Y as being AC. In this particular example, the ratio of BC to CA is perceived as 4:3.

Thinking in Euclidean terms, points A, B and C describe the classic 3:4:5 triangle of Pythagoras. The Euclidean distance between A and B is thus 5, given $BC = 4$ and $CA = 3$. ($AB^2 = BC^2 + CA^2$). More generally, consider any two points in a two dimensional space, say A_{xy} and $B_{x'y'}$, where x, x' and y, y' are coordinates on dimensions X and Y respectively. The Euclidean distance between

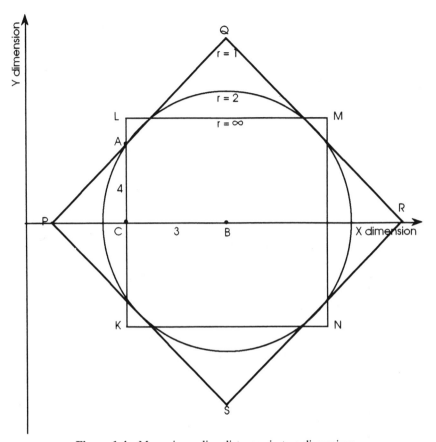

Figure 1.4 Measuring policy distances in two dimensions.

A and B is $((x-x')^2 + (y-y')^2)^{1/2}$, the square root of the sum of the squares of the distances between the points on each dimension. This assumption about how individuals trade off their evaluations of policy on two different dimensions is chosen more for its mathematical tractability than for its empirical realism, though several generations of microeconomic theory have been based on versions of the assumption of Euclidean preferences and have managed at least to survive in the same world as the economic agents about whom the assumption is made.

The great advantage of the assumption of Euclidean preferences is that it allows policy spaces to be described and analysed in terms of a familiar geometry. Returning to Figure 1.3, for example, it allows us to describe how person Y feels about policy LT in terms of the circular "indifference curve" centred on Y and passing through LT. Everything inside the curve is preferred by Y to LT. Thus, if the two dimensions are equally important and Y's preference structure is Euclidean, then Y prefers Z to LT. The fact that it is closer to Y on the rural-urban dimension more than outweighs, given the Euclidean trade-off assumption, the fact that it is further away on the left-right dimension. In the same way, in Figure 1.4, the way in which B feels about A is described by the circular indifference curve centred on B and passing through A. Every policy located inside this indifference curve is preferred by B to policy A.

The Euclidean distance between two points in a space with any number of dimensions can be conceived of in a very straightforward manner. This distance remains the square root of the sum of the squares of the distances between the points on each dimension. Thus the distance d_{ab} between points A and B is given by

$$d_{ab} = (\sum_{i=1,n} | x_{ia} - x_{ib} |^2)^{1/2}$$

where n is the number of dimensions and x_{ia}, x_{ib} are the coordinates of A and B on dimension i. Obviously, the geometric representation of this quickly becomes very complex. Indifference contours which, as we saw, are circles in two dimensions, become spheres in three dimensions and hyperspheres in four or more dimensions. But all this means is that algebra becomes a more convenient way of handling the analysis than geometry as the dimensionality of the space under consideration moves above two. The logic of the approach is, however, the same.

While the assumption of Euclidean trade-offs is by now very commonplace in descriptions of the structure of an individual's policy preferences, it is far from being the only one that can be made. Figure 1.4 also describes two of the infinite number of alternatives to the assumption of Euclidean trade-offs. The first and perhaps the most obvious alternative is to assume that the distance between two points is simply the sum of the distances between them on each policy dimension. If two dimensions have equal salience, then this amounts to assuming that an individual always feels compensated for losing one unit on one dimension by gaining one unit on the other dimension.

This assumption about trade-offs implies measuring the distance between two policy points using the "City Block" metric, so-called because the effective distance between two points in a city must be measured in terms of movement that can take place only along the "dimensions" defined by the alignment of the city blocks. Since diagonal movement is not possible given city blocks, the Euclidean metric makes misleading estimates of the effective distance between two points in a city. The general formula for the City Block distance between the two points A and B in a space of n dimensions is

$$d_{ab} = \sum_{i=1,n} | x_{ia} - x_{ib} |$$

Returning to Figure 1.4, we see that using the City Block metric to measure the distance between A and B implies that we must use an alternative indifference contour to describe how a person at B feels about a policy at A. If the distance

BC is 4 units and CA is 3 units as before, then the City Block distance AB is 7 units. This implies that B feels the same way about A as about policy points that have B's ideal policy on one dimension but which are 7 units removed from B's ideal policy on the other dimension—points P, Q R, and S in Figure 1.4. In fact, the contour joining all points that have a City Block distance of 7 from B is the rotated square defined by P, Q, R and S. Everything inside this indifference contour is preferred to policy A by an individual with an ideal policy at B and City Block preferences.

Both the City Block and the Euclidean metric are special cases of a more general metric, the Minkowski metric, which defines the distance between a pair of points in terms of the distances between the coordinates of these points on salient dimensions. The distance d_{ab} between two points A and B, measured using the Minkowski metric, is

$$d_{ab} = (\sum_{i=1,n} | x_{ia} - x_{ib} |^r)^{1/r}$$

where all of the other terms are defined as before, and r is the order of the metric. As can be seen from the equations above, the City Block and Euclidean metrics are Minkowski metrics of order one and two respectively. Thus they are labelled in Figure 1.4 as $r = 1$ and $r = 2$.

Obviously, r can be varied to define an infinite number of possible metrics, each of which describes some manner in which distance on one dimension is traded off against distance on another. Any one of these is a potentially plausible account of the structure of an individual's preferences. This can be seen by looking at the limiting case represented by the highest order Minkowski metric— this is the Infinity metric. Inspection of the equation for the Minkowski metric to see what happens as r approaches infinity shows that the Infinity metric defines the distance between two points to be the distance between their coordinates on the dimension on which they are furthest apart. Returning to Figure 1.4, for example, this suggests that the distance between B and A is 4, the distance between them on the X dimension, the dimension on which they are furthest apart. Indeed, all points that are 4 units from B on the X dimension, and are closer than 4 units to B on the Y dimension, are described by the Infinity metric as being at a distance of 4 from from B. This gives rise to the indifference contour described by the two vertical lines cutting the X dimension, and the two horizontal lines cutting the Y dimension, at a distance of 4 from B. (Any point north of the line LM or south of the line KN is such that its distance from B on dimension Y is greater than its distance of dimension X, and this distance is greater than 4.) The indifference contour generated by the Infinity metric is the square KLMN, labelled "$r = \infty$" in Figure 1.4. This indifference contour describes the preferences of an individual who evaluates a policy package only in terms of the particular policy dimension on which the package is least satisfactory—which after all seems a rather reasonable assumption about how someone might feel about things.

This discussion of the various metrics that might be used to measure the distance between two policy points serves to illustrate the argument that the assumption of Euclidean preferences that is typically made, whether explicitly or implicitly, by those who analyse policy spaces is but one of a wide range of plausible possibilities. As we have indicated, the selection of the most appropriate metric should in the last analysis be an empirical issue, based on the preference structures of real political actors. It is our understanding that almost no empirical work has been done on this matter, however. Thus the choice of metrics has been driven largely by theoretical criteria, conditioned largely by the better-understood mathematical properties of, and the intuitively more appealing visualisations offered by, Euclidean spaces.

We ourselves cannot be too high and mighty about this, since we offer no evidence on the most appropriate metric to be used and follow convention for most of the discussions that follow. We will assume for the most part that all relevant actors use the same, Euclidean, metric to measure policy distances. Nonetheless, we feel that it is important that alternative metrics be considered. We therefore present our raw data on party policy positions on a dimension-by-dimension basis and make no assumptions about a metric in estimating these, so as to allow others to analyse the relevant policy spaces using different metrics, as might seem appropriate.

Which Policy Dimensions are "Salient"?

In an abstract theoretical sense, the structure of policy preferences in any political system can only be described completely by using a policy space of very high dimensionality, spanned by all potential policy dimensions. In practice, analysts usually confine themselves to policy spaces defined by a small set of "salient" policy dimensions. Typically, the dimensions deemed salient can be counted on the fingers of one hand, though noncircular definitions of the salient "dimensionality" of a policy space are, as we shall see, quite hard to come by.

As with the preceding discussion of metrics, the problems that arise when we attempt to assess the dimensionality of particular policy spaces arise from a rather awkward interplay of theoretical and empirical considerations. Most theorists are apt to fix the dimensionality of the policy spaces that they use in their analyses by *fiat*. They typically declare that such and such a space is one-dimensional, two-dimensional, or whatever—and agonize not at all over whether the dimensionality of any particular policy space is known, knowable or even meaningful as a concept. Yet, as seminal work by McKelvey and Schofield has shown, the dimensionality of a policy space has a fundamental impact on theoretical analyses of the stability of the political system concerned (McKelvey, 1976, 1979; McKelvey and Schofield, 1987; Schofield, 1983, 1986).

While the theorist can wave a magic wand and declare a policy system to be one-, two-, or three-dimensional, the empirical analyst dealing with a particular case is left with no hint as to how to determine the actual dimensionality of the space in question. And this empirical problem is not one of mere operationalisation. The problem is best illustrated by an example, such as that in Figure 1.5, which shows a policy space in which two dimensions of policy are deemed to be important, both on *a priori* and empirical grounds. Dimension X is economic policy, specifically the degree of economic redistribution that ought to be engaged in by government. Dimension Y is social or moral policy, specifically the degree of proper state involvement in matters such as abortion, divorce and sexual relations. These are theoretically quite independent dimensions of policy, since it is easily possible to conceive of individuals who might favor state intervention in the economy but not in personal life, others who might favour state intervention in both, and so on. Empirically, furthermore, surveys might show that political actors generally consider both policy dimensions to be salient.

If the positions of political actors on these dimensions are perfectly correlated, then the position of an actor on one dimension can be perfectly predicted from his or her position on the other. The positions of five actors in the system, A, B, C, D, and E, are given in Figure 1.5—they all have ideal policy positions arrayed on the broken diagonal line. Should this policy space be seen as one- or two-dimensional?

The argument in favor of a one dimensional representation is that the empirical locations of the actors in the system demonstrate that a superficially plausible *a priori* two-dimensional description has turned out in practice to be an artifact. The empirical analysis shows that the economic and the social policy dimensions are actually different manifestations of the same underlying dimension, which which might think of as a "socio-economic left-right dimension". This is drawn as Dimension Q in Figure 1.5, and the important point about Dimension Q is that this single dimension is all that is required for a complete empirical description of the positions of every actor in the policy space in question. With enough ingenuity, we could probably come up with a hundred different-sounding ways of describing the meaning of Dimension Q, of which Dimension X and Dimension Y are but two, but this would not make the policy space one-hundred-dimensional. This argument boils down to the assertion that the assessment of the dimensionality of any given policy space is of its essence an empirical matter.

The argument that the policy space in Figure 1.5 is not one-dimensional is essentially counterfactual, though it is no less potent for that. Whatever might be said about the particular empirical clustering of particular actors in particular parts of the space, it can be argued that the *potential* for actors to take up policy positions in different parts of the space is self-evident, and that it is this potential that conditions the strategies of the various actors. On this account, the clustering of the actors along so-called Dimension Q is no more than an empirical observation to be explained—an effect, not a cause, of what is going on. If the clustering of the actors on a line is very strong, it might be argued, then there is a clear

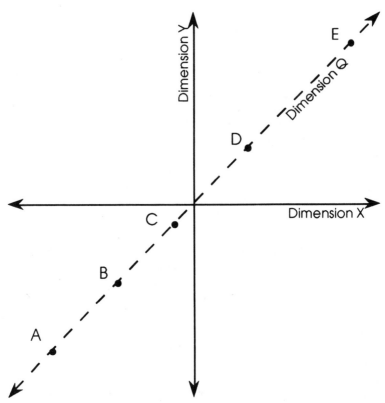

Figure 1.5   The ambiguous dimensionality of policy spaces.

intellectual challenge to explain why large sections of the space are uninhabited. But the answer is not to assume that, because they are uninhabited, they do not exist.

This dilemma takes us back to our initial consideration of the sources of structure in the preferences of political actors. If we assume that the sources of structure are entirely exogenous to political competition, then the argument in favor of using purely empirical estimators of the dimensionality of policy spaces is a strong one. After all, if preferences are structured exogenously, and if every actor in the system has preferences that can be described using only Dimension Q, then the probability that this has happened by chance is so tiny that it can be discounted. Dimension Q is your only man, and Dimensions X and Y are almost certainly artifacts.

However, if the preferences of political actors are structured endogenously, as a result of the processes of political competition itself, then their arrangement in a particular way, along Dimension Q for example, becomes one of the things that we ought to be interested in explaining. Furthermore, there is a clear possibility that this structure will change as a result of developments in political competition. So-called Dimension Q merely represents a particular alignment of actors in what is "really" a multidimensional space.

The trouble with this latter account is that we are left with no hint as to how to estimate the "real" dimensionality of a particular policy space, since empirical estimators are inevitably conditioned by the particular state of political competition. Furthermore, empirical estimators self-evidently cannot deal in counterfactuals.

For this reason, it seems to us that the most feasible way forward is to work with purely empirical notions of the dimensionality of policy spaces. This, as we have just argued, requires making the assumption that the fundamental sources of structure in the policy preferences of political actors are exogenous to political competition. This may seem on the face of it to be a relatively uncontroversial approach to take, though it seems so mainly because such matters have largely been ignored by both pure theorists and empirical researchers. The methodological implications, however, are rather radical.

Most theories of party competition do depend upon making *a priori* assumptions about the dimensionality of particular policy spaces, and developing arguments that depend upon the possibility that any point in the space might be inhabited by at least one individual with the appropriate preferences. According to the argument that we have just made, however, these theories cannot be tested empirically, since we have no proper basis for estimating the dimensionality of a particular policy space.

In our terms, such "theories" should be seen more as toolkits for building particular analytical methods and techniques that can be used as aids in the interpretation of political competition in particular countries. If the methods and techniques prove useful aids to interpretation, then we can continue to use them, but this does not necessarily imply that the general theories from which they are derived have been scientifically validated. This means that the essential purpose of empirical analysis, on this view, is the substantive interpretation of actual political competition in particular systems, not the testing of formal theories. What the formal theories do is to provide us with the analytic tools that enable our substantive interpretations to be more systematic.

Conclusions

Spatial representations of the structure of political interaction are, when all is said and done, no more than a set of conventions that have been adopted by political scientists to communicate with each other when describing particular types of regularity in the preferences of political actors. However spatial representations have become extremely influential conventions in recent years, as political scientists have constructed a quite detailed image of the political world in spatial terms, and have proceeded to subject this spatial image to logical and empirical analyses of increasing complexity and sophistication.

It is not, of course, necessary for us to rummage around in the entrails of a convention every time that we want to use it. Conventions, after all, typically involve shared assumptions that do not need to be spelled out whenever they are deployed. Conventional acceptance of spatial descriptions of politics thus allows theorists to set up problems quickly and efficiently, in the reasonable expectation that everyone who needs to do so understands what they are talking about.

Our central purpose in this particular book, however, is empirical. It has been our contention in this chapter that insufficient attention has been given, in empirical applications of the spatial approach, to the fact that policy spaces are no more than conventions. There is no sense in which a policy space is an underlying intrinsic reality, essentially knowable if we could overcome technical estimation problems. The reason for such weaknesses in empirical applications of spatial models has been that the driving forces behind the whole approach have been theoretical rather than empirical. This account of politics has been developed by theorists who have been at liberty to assume a policy space with such and such dimensions, voters with such and such preferences, political parties with such and such policy positions. The basic validating criteria of these theorists, furthermore, have been logical rather than empirical. As a consequence, once we roll up our sleeves and get on with the business of operationalization, certain theoretical constructs tend, if not to come apart completely in our hands, then certainly to be less sturdy than we might have hoped, when we put them to work in the real world. In other cases, fundamental difficulties that emerge in attempts to operationalize certain concepts suggest inherent theoretical ambiguities in the concepts themselves.

All of this implies that the process of operationalization, such an important feature of theoretical development in general, has not progressed far enough in relation to theories of party competition. In creating the technology to apply the science, we often identify points at which the science needs a little more thought. Our basic contention in this chapter is that, while there is plenty of science behind spatial representations of party competition, there is not yet enough technology to allow these representations to be as practically useful as they might be.

For this reason we make no apology for taking some time in this chapter to do at least a little rummaging around in the entrails of the spatial approach, and our discussion of the "dimensionality" of policy spaces illustrates quite clearly the justification for doing this. The number of salient dimensions in a policy space is a very important variable in spatial accounts of the structure of political competition. The theorist has the freedom to assume any number of dimensions and the mathematics to enable these to be analysed. The empirical analyst can estimate the positions of specified political actors on the x "most salient" policy dimensions in a given system without too much difficulty (though undoubtedly not without controversy), provided that "x" is given. The empirical analyst can therefore provide the theorist with a one- two- three- or any-dimensional estimation of a particular policy space—the problems involved are huge but merely technical. Estimating x, however, the "real" salient dimensionality of the policy space involved, is quite another matter. The main reason for this is that we need to know quite clearly what "x" really means before we can make a sensible attempt to estimate it.

There are, of course, empirical techniques for extracting a small number of underlying dimensions from complex multidimensional data sets. And there are techniques within these approaches for settling upon a particular set of dimensions as the basis of the most efficient low-dimensional representation of the data. But it is clear that this is not what theorists have in mind when they talk of the "dimensionality" of a particular policy space. As we saw, if the preferences of key political actors with respect to two salient policy dimensions are perfectly correlated, then almost any empirical technique for dimensional analysis will present the data as if it is one-dimensional. External intervention from those with a theoretical interest in the data is necessary if we are to be provided with a meaning for the dimensionality of the space within which we represent these preferences, if this is to reflect more than mere correlations between variables. Yet, if we go back to the theorists and ask them what they have in mind when they talk about the dimensionality of a policy space, it is difficult to get helpful answers. This suggests that a good deal more theoretical consideration needs to be given to this important matter.

The dimensionality of policy spaces is not the only subject shrouded in some ambiguity. Another has to do with the assumptions that are made about how people trade off distance from their ideal point on one dimension against equivalent distances on other dimensions. This shows up empirically as a decision that must be taken over the metric to be used when measuring how a given individual perceives the policy distances between two points in a multidimensional policy space. Again, theorists are free to assume whatever they wish, though in practice they almost invariably assume Euclidean distances. Again, the empirical analyst, in trying to decide which metric to use and why, can find theoretical justifications for particular decisions rather sparse.

Overall, there is no doubt that the spatial account of voting and party competition has added immensely to our understanding of politics. Our argument here does nothing to gainsay this. The point that we wish to make is not only that the operationalization of this approach is a more complex task than many have hitherto realised, but that it also points to fundamental theoretical ambiguities that have thus far been swept under the carpet in the set of conventions that have been accepted. The lessons that we take from this discussion, therefore, have to do with identifying certain theoretical issues that we take to be still effectively open. In collecting data in order to estimate policy spaces, we have tried to close as few of these issues as possible. Thus we make no final judgement on the dimensionality of the spaces concerned, though we do obviously only estimate a finite (and rather small) number of policy dimensions for each country. And we make no final judgment on the metric to be used in constructing the spaces. While we do some empirical analysis of multidimensional policy spaces in conventional terms, using a Euclidean metric, we present the data in a form that permits their reanalysis using other metrics. Above all, indeed, we present all of the basic data in a large appendix to this book, since our ultimate aim is to facilitate the exploration of the issues that we have raised in this chapter rather than ultimately to resolve them.

2

An Expert Survey

As we saw in the previous chapter, theoretical analyses of voting and party competition are often based on spatial representations of the preferred policy positions of the various actors. Empirical applications of these approaches, however, are typically forced to depend on low-grade information about these policy positions. The result is often that a rather sophisticated theory is applied to a somewhat rough-and-ready data set. This creates problems for the evaluation of the theories concerned, as Franklin and Mackie (1984) have clearly demonstrated for theories of coalition formation. Apparently innocuous differences between different low grade data sets go a long way towards explaining different evaluations of the same theories by different authors—and the same argument could doubtless be made for other aspects of the theory of party competition. The level of empirical research in this general field, in short, falls far short of its level of theoretical sophistication. A worrying consequence of this is that the empirical element in state-of-the-art theoretical analyses of voting and party competition is as often as not rather unsatisfactory. A surprising number of well-regarded theoretical arguments turn, for their empirical component, on the use of selected and limited data sets to demonstrate the virtues of particular theories, in a process akin more to rhetoric than to science.

Obviously, in an ideal world, these theories would be subjected to a comprehensive empirical examination, yet individual theorists cannot be expected to collect their own primary data sets at every turn, especially given the limited research funds available to the social sciences. If we are dealing with national party politics, furthermore, the population of cases is rather small. A limited number of countries, each with a limited number of political parties, have had a limited number of elections in recent history, resulting in the formation of a limited number of governments. This has two important consequences. First, it is simply not good sense for research assistants to be continually going out and collecting these data as if no one had ever collected them before. Second, it is simply not good science for theorists to be continually analyzing these "new" data as if no

29

one had ever analyzed them before. Country-level data on elections and party competition provide one of the most thoroughly picked-over heaps of information in the entire field of social sciences. The shape of this heap is by now very well-known and has obviously informed the theorists who subsequently use bits of it to test their work. Continually to re-use the same data in order to conduct "scientific" tests of new theories is dubious enough; to do so in a selective and unsystematic manner is quite beyond the pale.

In the long term, at least some aspects of these problems can be resolved. The ultimate aim of the political science community should be to build a comprehensive data base on all issues related to voting and party competition. If this data base was accepted by scholars as providing the set of benchmarks against which their theories could sensibly be measured, then at least one source of ambiguity would be removed. This would go a long way towards resolving the type of problem that Franklin and Mackie highlight, with many of the apparent empirical contradictions in the field potentially the result of using different data sets collected by different people in different ways. While it would not and could not resolve the "stale data" problem, it would at least remove any excuse that theorists might have for demonstrating the virtues of their work using only selected parts of the very well-known data on voting and party competition in western democracies.

In order to build such a data base, what is needed is to draw together, organize, reanalyze and synthesize the scattered but considerable empirical work that has already been done in the field, supplementing this with original primary research where necessary. The research that we describe in this book is intended as a contribution to the initial phase of this research program, and is designed to map out the basic territory to be covered.

What we report here are the results of a large-scale survey of country specialists designed to collect the information necessary to estimate a wide range of parameters associated with the spatial representation of party competition in as many as possible of those western countries with a tradition of free elections. The information that we present includes "expert" estimates of the positions of key political actors on a number of substantive policy scales, each of which has been identified on an *ad hoc* basis by a range of authors as being important, but most of which have not previously been the subject of comprehensive cross-national research. We have also collected information on the differences between the policy positions of party leaders and party voters; on party-specific weights assigned by party leaders to policy dimensions; on the dimensionality of the resultant policy spaces; on the extent to which leaders trade off the desire to get into office against the desire to affect policy outputs; and on various other aspects of the role of policy in political decision-making.

Most of this chapter elaborates the details of our expert survey. Before this, however, we deal briefly with the current state of empirical research on party policy positions.

Empirical Policy Spaces: The Story So Far

Essentially four methods have been used to estimate the positions of political actors on particular policy dimensions. The first relies on the content analysis of policy documents, the second on the analysis of mass survey data, the third locates government policy on the basis of actual expenditure flows and the fourth relies on expert judgements.

Content Analysis of Policy Documents

One obvious method of estimating party policy positions is to read what parties write about these. This can be done in a systematic way by analyzing their official policy documents. Since voters do not publish policy documents, this approach will never to have much to tell us about the policy preferences of the electorate. But, since parties can at least in theory be held accountable for their published policy statements, these documents do provide some reasonably firm ground on which to base a description of official party policy.

A version of this approach was adopted by those involved in a major project conducted by the Manifesto Research Group, one of the research groups of the European Consortium for Political Research (ECPR). Members of the group who were fluent in the languages concerned used the techniques of content analysis to code the content of the election manifestos issued by almost every political party during the course of every election since the Second World War. The analysis was conducted for many, but not all, western European countries. These data were used to generate a multidimensional spatial representation of party policy in each of the systems studied for each election held (Budge, Robertson and Hearl, eds., 1987). This study was extended to include an equivalent coding of government policy programs and reanalyzed to generate both a single left-right dimension and a set of twenty policy dimensions common to many European coalition systems (Laver and Budge, eds., 1992).

If we are prepared to accept that what goes into party manifestos has some meaning, even if it should not necessarily be taken at face value, then the content analysis of policy documents obviously has much to tell us about party policy at the elite level. The main problem with this approach has to do with the rather ambiguous methodological status of the coding scheme that is required before the analyst can code each sentence or column centimeter of the document concerned into one of a limited set of categories. The trouble is that the design of the coding scheme obviously strongly conditions the precise empirical description of the manifesto. While this technique has considerable potential, we feel that it is likely to be more effective once a broader consensus has emerged as to the way in which a content analysis coding scheme should span the range of potential contents of policy documents. And this consensus in turn awaits agreement on the set of policy dimensions that are needed for a valid description of party politics in the countries under consideration.

Analyses of Mass Survey Data

The most direct way to get information about the overt policy preferences of voters is to ask the voters themselves. Survey research is thus one of the main sources of data about electoral policy positions. Inglehart and Klingemann (1986), for example, report their reanalysis of a series of Eurobarometer surveys in which respondents were asked to indicate their own position on a left-right scale. The mean scores of different groups of party identifiers can be used to locate the "party in the electorate" on a left-right dimension. Sani and Sartori (1983) apply a broadly similar strategy to a different selection of countries. Bruneau and Macleod (1986), reporting on Portugal, for which no comparable scales are available, asked survey respondents to locate parties rather than themselves on a left-right scale and report mean scores for all parties derived from all respondents, rather than from supporters of the party in question.

As survey research extends its reach, there is an ever-expanding portfolio of studies that report estimated positions of voters on left-right scales for an ever-larger selection of party systems. At present, however, their comparative value is somewhat undermined by significant methodological variations in how these estimates are derived. A comprehensive reanalysis of this large pool of data, according to a set of common methodological guidelines, is clearly a high intellectual priority.

Even after this, however, systematically comparable results will, for the most part, deal only with electoral preferences on the ubiquitous left-right dimension. While surveys of electoral opinion typically deal with quite a wide range of policy issues, the particular issues treated tend to vary from system to system. The centrally coordinated set of surveys in the Eurobarometer series do deal, for the countries studied, with a more unified set of issues. Even for these surveys, however, performance does not always live up to promise, as particular questions often get dropped, for one reason or another, from surveys conducted in particular countries.

In the last analysis, it is obviously only mass survey research that can provide a comprehensive description of the policy preferences of mass electorates. Comprehensive reanalysis of collections of national studies, according to guidelines designed to generate broadly comparable policy scales, is clearly one way forward. Furthermore, Eurobarometer data offer a much underanalyzed resource for a more limited subset of countries. There is no getting away from the fact, however, that the research tasks involved are both huge and relatively unglamorous. We may therefore have to wait quite some time for the results.

Analyses of Government Expenditure Flows

An alternative way of estimating the policy positions of politicians is to look not at what they say in their manifestos but at what they actually do if and when elected to office. One very clear set of traces that politicians leave on the public record has to do with public expenditure. The actual flow of public expenditure into particular policy areas can be used as an indicator of government policy in relation to these areas. Such expenditure is an unambiguous indicator of *party* policy only in those countries for which one-party government is endemic and then, of course, only for those parties that get into office.

In all other countries, public expenditure flows are the outcome of bargaining between coalition partners. In these cases, they can only usefully used as indicators of *government* outputs, measures of policy "payoffs" that can be compared with the policy preferences and bargaining strengths of the various actors. Preliminary analyses of the impact of government membership on spending flows in the USA (Budge and Hofferbert, 1990), Germany (Hofferbert and Klingemann, 1989), Ireland (Laver and Mitchell, 1989), the Netherlands (Keman, 1989), and Sweden (Bergman and Strom, 1989) suggest that there are some quite strong relationships between government spending and the published policies of government parties in particular policy areas. There is clearly considerable potential in the development of this line of inquiry, since public expenditure is obviously quite a "hard" source of data on public policy. The problem here is that it is not a comprehensive data source. As parties move into and out of government, public expenditure provides hard information on policy positions only for certain political actors, and then only in certain circumstances.

Expert judgments

Another way to gather data on the policy positions of key political actors is to survey people who are expert on the country in question. Early tests of coalition theories relied almost entirely on policy scales that were derived from expert judgments. Scales used by De Swaan (1973), Dodd (1976), and Taylor and Laver (1973) fall into this category—each involves the collation of information from a listed range of published sources. Building on these approaches, Browne and Dreijmanis (1982) asked commissioned country specialists, in chapters on various coalition systems, to use their own best judgment to construct a two-dimensional representation of the policy space that they were dealing with. By far the most systematic analyses of expert judgments of positions on a left-right scale, however, can be found in the work of Morgan (1976), and of Castles and Mair (1984). Castles and Mair asked "leading political scientists" to locate parties in "their" systems on a left-right scale ranging from "ultra-left" to "ultra-right". They averaged these results to generate a set of interval level left-right scales. Morgan asked a named list of about 120 political scientists a more complex set of questions, dealing with the location of parties on up to three scales, as well as with the relative weights of these scales, though he actually reports data only for one dimension of policy.

As we have seen, much of the information on party policy that is central to our interests can be derived from the more "objective" sources discussed above— published policy documents, mass surveys and government expenditure flows.

Certainly, published party manifestos and audited national accounts are in some senses closer to political reality than expert surveys, but they are also incomplete. As we have also seen, none of these types of source is comprehensive in the sense that it deals with all actors and policy areas that we might be interested in, and does so on a comparable basis for all countries that we need to know about.

One great advantage of the expert survey as a source of information is that, properly designed, it can be comprehensive. First, this means that identical questions, all calibrated in the same basic terms, can be posed for as many systems as experts can be found to give advice on. A second and methodologically more interesting advantage of this technique is that it is the only one available for collecting information on many key parameters relating to policy-based analyses of voting and party competition. Many of these parameters do not manifest themselves in ways that can be calibrated using harder data sources. These parameters include party-specific weightings of the policy dimensions, differences between the policy positions of party politicians and party voters, and the extent to which politicians trade off the desire to get into government against the desire to enact specific policies.

Expert estimates of such parameters may not keep the most picky of purists happy but are very much better than no estimates at all. And doing nothing, the effective alternative to conducting an expert survey in many cases, is the solution implicitly adopted by those whose simply ignore key parameters for which there are no estimates.

The research reported in this book involves an extension of earlier expert surveys on the role of policy in party competition. We asked a larger universe of experts to locate parties on a more extensive set of named scales; we broke the traditional left-right scale into four clearly distinct component parts; experts were given the chance to specify additional scales if they felt these were necessary; all scales were assigned weights on a party-specific basis and judgments were collated on other matters relevant to policy bargaining.

When selecting the expert survey technique, one important factor was the exploratory status of our study. As we said at the outset, the main aim of our current work is to sketch out the basic territory, in the expectation that this will be triangulated more precisely where possible using harder data sources. As we have just indicated, there are important parameters for which no other type of estimate may ever be available. But many parameters may be estimated by other means. In these cases, the expert survey fulfills two quite distinct roles. First, it provides preliminary estimates of these parameters, to be replaced when better estimates are available but to serve in the meantime as a working resource. Second, it provides some sort of indicator of the policy dimensions and other matters that experts within the profession regard as important. We argued above that the lack of a commonly accepted data set was one obstacle to progress in this general area. One of the things that we hope the expert survey may help to achieve is to give some sense of the shape that a commonly accepted data set might take.

Our Expert Survey

The Countries Studied

Our intention was to collect information for all First World countries that currently hold free elections. We thus set out to cover all of Western Europe, plus Canada, the USA, Australia, New Zealand, Japan and Israel—a total of twenty five political systems. We achieved this objective, with varying degrees of success, for all countries except for Switzerland, which the almost unanimous nonresponse of our experts unfortunately forced us to abandon. The complete list of countries can be found in any of the tables that follow. One welcome consequence of the range of responses that we received is that we managed to put together systematic data on the role of policy in a number of countries that have hitherto been rather neglected by comparative researchers—Malta, New Zealand and Portugal are obvious examples.

The Experts

Our experts were political scientists. Our questionnaire, described below, was sent in the first instance to indigenous political scientists with a professional interest in the country in question. In other words, for Norway, we contacted Norwegian political scientists working on party politics or public policy in Norway, and we did the same for the other countries. We used four key directories to draw up our initial mailing list. For Western Europe, we used *Political Science in Europe,* the directory of member departments of the European Consortium for Political Research (ECPR). For North America, we used the *Biographical Directory* of the American Political Science Association (APSA). Both of these directories list individuals' self-descriptions of their academic interests, on which we based our selection. For Iceland, Malta, Israel and Japan, we used the *Social Sciences Citation Index* to identify those who had published on these countries in the previous five years, supplementing this with the listing of overseas members in the APSA *Biographical Directory.* For Australia, New Zealand and for Malta once again, we used the *Commonwealth Universities Yearbook.*

Our aim was to contact the full universe of indigenous country specialists, as identified above, for each of the countries in the study apart from the USA. With so many of the world's political scientists working in and on the USA, we chose a sample of 100, taken from the set of those who had published most recently on USA politics, according to the *Social Sciences Citation Index.*

For three countries, Iceland, Luxembourg and Malta, the very small number of indigenous political scientists meant that even the full universe of experts was too small, and an alternative approach was adopted. In Malta, all members of the Faculty of Arts at the University were approached, which gave us a total of eighteen target respondents. In Iceland and Luxembourg the net was cast much wider, to include the chairs of the main political parties, trade unions and employers' federations and the editors of the national newspapers. This gave a total of thirty to forty targets in each case, though the response rate in these much more general populations was very low.

For a few countries, notably Spain, Portugal, Italy, Israel and Japan, early response rates among indigenous academics were so low that the population was extended to include non-indigenous political scientists identified by the *Social Sciences Citation Index* as publishing on the countries in question. These were based mainly in the USA and Britain.

In all, 1228 "experts" were approached for judgments on the twenty five countries in the study. The distribution of targets between countries can be seen in Table A1 in Appendix A. The initial mailing took place in February 1989. We sent a postcard reminder to non-respondents six weeks later, which significantly boosted the response rate. European colleagues were put under further pressure with an offer by Michael Laver to meet them at the 1989 annual meeting of the European Consortium of Political Research in Paris, and quite a few targets were sufficiently concerned to avoid this possibility that they eventually completed their questionnaires. As a final small incentive, we offered respondents a personal copy of all of the estimated scale positions for "their" countries, as soon as these were available, and the vast majority of those who did reply indicated that they wanted this. Altogether 355 completed questionnaires were received, a response rate of around thirty percent. This is typical for postal surveys but, considering that the questionnaire was in English, was administered mainly to non-native English speakers and took about two hours to complete, this must be considered a very good level of response.

A small number of our targets, ten or so, refused explicitly to respond and wrote to tell us why. The most common reason was that the person concerned did not feel expert in the country in question—the product of what were often rather vague descriptions of specializations in our source directories or of the fact that, for some countries with small professions that we did not know very well (Portugal, for example), we defined our target population very widely. It may well be that many of our other non-responses fell into this category too.

There were three refusals on explicit methodological grounds. The first, from an American, was on the basis of a long and detailed list of suggestions for the improvement of our entire study. The second was from a group of Danes who had discussed the project collectively and decided that none would respond since they felt that the results would inevitably be biased. The third was from a New Zealander who denounced our attempt to "quantify the unquantifiable". The most startling refusal was from a Maltese academic, who wished us well but said that it was "his policy not to discuss Maltese politics with non-Maltese."

At a far more prosaic level, about sixty of our initial letters were returned by the US post office. In most cases this was because the addressees had moved away since the directories we used were published (though these were always the most up-to-date-editions) and, for one reason or another, our letters had not been forwarded. The staleness of even the most up-to-date directories may well, of course, account for far more non-responses than this—certainly for those professions that we knew well, we were able from our own knowledge to identify and correct many errors before the initial mailing. (These errors for the most part concerned people who had been left on the books of institutions from which they had departed, and had not been added to the books of institutions that they had joined, presumably because they had failed to fill out questionnaires!)

As Table A1 in Appendix A shows, the response rate varied considerably from country to country. The highest response rate by far, at 72 percent, was from Irish political scientists. This is not surprising since Ireland is the permanent base of Michael Laver and has a small but tightly knit profession—almost all of the fifty targets were personally known to him. The second highest response rate was from Canada, where we had almost no personal contacts. In general, above average response rates came from the English-speaking countries and Scandinavia (most Scandinavian countries have active political science professions and high levels of English language skills.) The lowest response rates came from southern Europe, Switzerland and Japan. Starting from a relatively small base, this meant that we received only three replies from Switzerland. While Castles and Mair (1984) published estimates of scale positions that were based on the judgments of three experts, we felt that this was too small a number, and therefore reluctantly excluded Switzerland from the rest of the study.

We set ourselves a minimum goal of five experts before including a country in the subsequent analysis. Though obviously we would have liked far more, we were forced to settle for this minimum number in the cases of Greece, Iceland, Luxembourg and Spain. Since these are all countries for which relatively little cross-nationally comparable data is available, we felt that having at least imprecise estimates of policy positions in these systems was better than having no estimates at all, and therefore included these countries in the analyses that follow. Since at no stage do we present results based on the pooling of data from all countries included in the analysis, others who may wish to impose stricter criteria when selecting countries for inclusion can do so on the basis of Table A1.

We promised our respondents that we would maintain complete confidentiality, and clarified in correspondence with several who were concerned about this matter that we would publish no final list of their names. Nonetheless we must record our very sincere thanks to all who replied—they certainly know who they are! Many respondents did far more than simply filling out our lengthy questionnaire. Some sent us newspaper cuttings, offprints of articles, even books, as well as long letters elaborating on aspects of their responses. While revealing no names, we should also record that we are also very pleased that those who cooperated came from right across the board of the profession. Many very senior country specialists are included among our respondents, as well as many young academics whose careers are just starting. Overall, we were extremely satisfied with the professional balance of our experts.

The Questionnaire

The questionnaire that we sent to target respondents was sixteen pages long and very onerous to complete. Quite a lot of general information about the role of policy in party competition already existed for many of the countries being studied. Thus our main aim in this study was to supplement existing data with a body of detailed information about policy positions on a wide range of dimensions for all significant parties in each system. Our respondents, as we have seen, were professional political scientists. Since survey research is one of their standard research tools, we assumed, rightly or wrongly, that political scientists would have a higher tolerance for completing a long and complex questionnaire than other human beings. We therefore took the strategic decision to go for detail, even at some cost in terms of the lower response rate that would be likely to result from the use of more complex and time-consuming questionnaire. In order to make a significant move towards a shorter and simpler questionnaire, we would have been forced to deal with fewer parties and fewer policy dimensions. In our judgment this would have added less to our stock of knowledge, even with a higher response rate. Since, as we have already indicated, our long-term objective is to find alternative "harder" sources for as much of the information in this data set as possible, we felt that potential problems with the response rate were a price worth paying for being able to gather information on hitherto unresearched matters.

One consequence of our decision to go for detail was that we asked respondents to locate virtually all parties in each system on our policy scales. We included every national party that won seats in the national legislature at the most recent election, and all parties that won more than one percent of the vote nationally. In addition, we included significant regional parties. (A number of Canadian respondents objected strongly to our inclusion, under the latter provision, of the Partie Quebequois, refusing to locate it on our scales. In this single case we have therefore been forced by our respondents to drop this party from the analysis.)

These criteria often generated quite a long list of parties, up to fourteen in some countries. The reason we wanted this information is that it is quite common for even very small legislative parties to have a major role in government formation and other aspects of party competition in certain delicately balanced situations. As often as not, such parties have been neglected in previous empirical analyses. The result of this neglect is that, when these situations come up for consideration, researchers have been forced to make rather sweeping *ad hoc* assumptions about the policy positions of key actors in order to complete their analyses of what are often the most intriguing bargaining situations.

A consequence of this decision was that the scales we offered respondents had to be "big" enough to cope with the positions of up to fourteen parties. While conventional psychometric analysis tends to favour the use of five- or seven-point scales in order to reduce measurement error, such scales typically apply to the attitudes of respondents on single issues. The respondent completes the scale by selecting one scale position and leaving (say) six blank. We were asking our respondents to locate maybe fourteen separate stimulus points simultaneously on the same scale. Indeed it was part of the very essence of our technique that respondents gave us a *juxtaposition* of all parties in the system on the same scale. We did not find much help on this matter in the literature. Accordingly, and given that our respondents were professional political scientists who should not have been totally unfamiliar with such things, we decided to use a twenty-point scale for party positions on the main policy dimensions. We did this on the grounds that, in a fourteen-party system, this would enable respondents to rank order all parties, as well as leaving them six blank scale positions so as to give them scope to provide us with at least a limited amount of interval level information. A consequence of this is that, in the rare two party systems in our study (the USA and Malta), the twenty-point scales were probably "too big", a comment made to us by two US respondents. It is interesting to note as it turns out, however, that there was if anything less variation between respondents in the location of the USA parties on our scales than there was in most of the other systems. In general, we found no relationship between the number of parties in the system and the level of variation in the judgments of respondents, which leads us to conclude that the design of the scales to accommodate the "big" party systems has not prejudiced estimates of scale positions in the "small" ones.

Respondents were asked to locate the policy positions of both leaders of and voters for all parties in their countries at a particular point on each of a series of policy scales, listed in detail in Table A2 in Appendix A. Each scale was identified both by a title and by a more precise pair of interpretations, defining the two endpoints, in order to reduce as far as possible any ambiguity about its meaning.

Turning to the substance of the scales, the conventional left-right dimension was broken into what were taken *a priori* to be four distinct component parts. These related to the public finances, to public ownership, to social or "moral" policy and to foreign policy. In addition, we used scales to capture rural-urban, clerical-anticlerical and environmental policy, and policy on decentralisation, each identified by several authors as being critical in at least some of the countries to be studied. Respondents were also given the chance to define two additional scales that were of particular importance in their countries. In addition, respondents were asked to assess the importance—*for each of the parties in the study*—of each of the policy dimensions under consideration . The collection of information on party-specific weightings of the various policy dimensions is a good example of the particular benefits of using an expert survey over other techniques. Party-specific weights are almost impossible to estimate using other means, yet are vital to the description of the policy-based party competition. As far as we are aware, systematic estimates of party-specific weights of policy dimensions have not previously been attempted by comparative researchers.

Our second set of questions dealt with the role of policy in the internal politics of particular parties. Respondents were asked to place three sections of each party (leaders, legislators and activists) on scales that dealt with the level of influence that each section has over the formation of party policy; the level of influence that each has over participation in government; and how far into the future each section looks when making decisions about government membership. Respondents were also asked to make judgments on the extent to which party leaders trade off policy objectives against getting into office when bargaining over government formation, and the extent to which party leaders can rely on outside groups when bargaining in the legislature. These parameters have been discussed informally by several authors, and are central in particular to accounts of minority and surplus majority government. As far as we are aware, however, no serious attempt has previously been made to estimate them for a range of party systems, and an expert survey is probably the only way that this can be done in a comprehensive manner.

One final party-specific question asked respondents to estimate, taking all aspects of party policy into consideration, how close each of the parties was to their own personal viewpoint. The main purpose of this question was to check the respondents' other judgments for bias. Using answers to this question, we ran a long series of bias checks, reported in Appendix A. These were designed to assess whether our respondents' placement of any given party on any given scale could be predicted from their views about the party in question. If we had found evidence of systematic bias, we had a series of techniques up our sleeves with which we would have attempted to unscramble this. However, as the analysis reported in the data appendix shows, the evidence suggests that there was very little biasing of our expert judgments by the personal views of our experts. It was only very rarely possible to predict judgments about the scale positions of parties from respondents' personal views. Accordingly, we make no attempt to reprocess what our experts told us in the empirical discussions that follow.

The final set of questions that we asked had to do with the role of policy in party competition in the system as a whole. We asked about the impact of opposition parties on government policy; about the proportion of governments falling as a result of policy disputes; about the relative evaluation of a cabinet portfolio as a reward of office or as a means to affect policy; about the publicization of internal cabinet policy disputes; about the level of ministerial autonomy in policy-making; and about the frequency of cabinet reshuffles. We also asked about the ranking of cabinet portfolios in government formation negotiations, and about the control of cabinet portfolios over key policy dimensions.

Overall, the questionnaire involved making a very large number of judgments, particularly for the large party systems. About sixty variables were involved, many estimated for each party in the system. For a ten party system in which all dimensions had some salience, completing the questionnaire involved making some 440 judgments. Our draft questionnaire had been even longer, but was reduced in volume as a result of cries for mercy from a group of twenty respondents whom we subjected to a pre-test of the draft. The final version was, to be quite frank, as long as we decently felt we could get away with. Viewed in this light, it is a testament to the patience and goodwill of the profession that the response rate was as good as it was, and that most of our long-suffering colleagues are still speaking to us.

Analysis of Face Validity

Having collected the data, our next task was to check their face validity. The most obvious way to do this would have been to compare our estimated scales with other published scales but, since there were no published scales dealing with most of the variables in our expert survey, this was not possible. However, we feel strongly that the general credibility of these data among both country specialists and political theorists is one of their most vital characteristics, so that the issue of face validity is an important one. We tackled this problem in two ways.

First, we circulated all of our provisional estimates of scale positions and other parameters back to all country specialists who had completed the survey. This allowed us to fulfill our promise to make the data available as soon as possible to our experts, but it also allowed us to ask them to comment on the face validity of all estimates. We received quite a few replies, mostly commenting on a detail here and a detail there, as well as offering other general comments on the study, further offprints of articles, newspaper cuttings and so on, together with several requests for the data on other countries in the study. While we were pleased by the very positive feedback that we received, it is of course possible that those who disagreed with us were so disgusted that they threw our material into the nearest trash can, so this cannot be taken as a definitive check of face validity.

We thus used a second face validity check, at least in relation to the conventional left-right descriptions of political ideology. We contrasted party positions on the scale dealing with policies on public ownership, which we took *a priori* to be the closest to conventional definitions of a left-right scale, with three published left-right scales. These were the two most comprehensive previous sets of expert judgements, assembled by Castles and Mair (1984), and by Morgan (1976), and the left-right scale based on the content analysis of party manifestos, derived by Laver and Budge (1992). The results of this comparison are reported, for those countries for which the published scales in question are available, in Table A3 in Appendix A. They show that the rank ordering of parties on our public ownership scale corresponds very closely with the rank ordering of parties on the previously published scales for individual countries. Correlations between our scale positions and positions on each of the other three scales, for the same parties, were very high—we found a correlation of 0.93 between our scale and the Castles-Mair scale; 0.91 with the Morgan scale; and 0.85 with the Laver-Budge scale. (In general, the three expert scales correlated more closely with each other than any of them correlated with the scale based upon the content analysis of party manifestos and derived from a quite different data source.)

While this analysis of face validity of course conclusively proves nothing, it is nonetheless quite gratifying. The validity of many of our other parameter estimates cannot be checked in such a direct manner; however, the fact that our left-right scales do appear to be valid adds to our confidence in the validity of the other data.

The Estimates

Our estimates of all of the parameters outlined above, for each party in each of the twenty four countries studied, are published in full in the tables in Appendix B. These tables report, for each party in each country in the study, the means and standard deviations of the raw scores returned by the set of country experts for each variable. They also report the mean z-score for each party. The latter of course contains no new information, but is provided to give an instant readout of where a given party fits into the overall configuration of parties on the dimension in question.

These data are put to work in the various substantive discussions that can be found in the chapters that follow. Overall, however, it is fitting to note at this stage that there is a consistency and coherence about the results of the empirical discussions that counteracted many of our initial misgivings about the potential usefulness of the data. If we are brutally honest with ourselves, of course, we must concede that this consistency may be the result of no more than a consistency in the prejudices of our political scientists. Nonetheless, it should be remembered that the estimates are based on the views of quite independent sets of political scientists for each country. Many of these were not particularly sympathetic to this style of analysis and none were able to have any idea of potential results in other countries, or indeed of other expert judgments in their own country.

Of course, all dimensional analyses of party competition, whether they are based on deductions from *a priori* assumptions or on inductions from empirical data, are artificial constructs. They are designed in the last analysis to provide us with a conceptual vocabulary with which to describe a subtle and complex set of human interactions. In this sense, the proof of the pudding must always be in the eating. If we feel that we have added to our understanding of the political world by using this vocabulary, then it is a useful resource. If we do not, then we should look for something else. This particular data set by its nature lies somewhere in between pure theory and arms-length empirical reality. For ourselves, we feel that it does add something to our understanding of party competition. Obviously, readers will feel free to make up their own minds on the matter.

3

Patterns in the Party System

The essential features of the approach to party competition that we rely on in subsequent discussions are:

—that voters have policy preferences, derived from some source or another;

—that politicians, typically members of political parties, make policy promises to voters. They do this so as to maximize the benefits of contesting elections, whatever these benefits might be;

—that party competition is the manifestation of a conflict of interest between politicians. Voters have an impact on this conflict during elections that take place at more or less predictable intervals.

A series of crucial empirical questions must be answered before we can develop this approach any further.

First, as we saw in Chapter One, it is conventional to describe the policy preferences of political actors in terms of "spaces" spanned by sets of policy dimensions. In order to discuss politics in any particular country in these terms, therefore, it is necessary to settle upon an appropriate set of dimensions to span the policy space in question. We must settle upon the qualitative meaning of the dimensions to be used and their relative importance, bearing in mind that the relative importance of each dimension is likely to be weighted differently by each actor. Second, we must locate relevant actors in the space by describing their preferences in terms of policy positions on the dimensions that we identify as being important. The third major empirical task is to provide a description of the relationship between the policy preferences of voters and the policy positions that are promoted by politicians. Elections are fought on the basis of this relationship, which is thus crucial to party competition in any country.

Which Policy Dimensions Are Salient?

Methodological Issues

Perhaps the most fundamental task involved in any empirical description of the role of policy in party competition within a particular country is to select a set of dimensions that give meaning to the relevant policy space. There have traditionally been three basic methods of doing this.

The first is an extension of the *a priori* approach of the deductive theorist. The analyst in effect assumes a set of underlying policy dimensions and attempts to operationalize these. Decisions about which dimensions are important are taken on "a priori" grounds, in the sense that the selection of dimensions is not systematically justified in empirical terms. This technique, for all intents and purposes, involves the analyst in reading as much as possible about politics in the country in question and emerging from this task having experienced some kind of revelation about what the important dimensions of policy actually are. The main disadvantage of this approach is that the dimensionality of the policy space in a given country, and the substantive interpretation of its particular policy dimensions, are both assumed and fixed. Little progress can be made in developing empirical descriptions of party competition that depend upon treating these matters as important independent variables.

The second basic technique for identifying the salient policy dimensions in a given country involves listening to the actors themselves. This is most obviously relevant in the case of the left-right dimension, which is of course part of the common currency of debate among practising politicians. Most politicians and some voters can, and often do, define themselves as being on the left, on the right, or in the center of the political spectrum. They often describe others as being to the left, or to the right, of themselves. Thus, while the left-right dimension "really" exists only in the imagination, as do all other policy dimensions, it has the advantage for these purposes that it exists, at least in some form or another, in the imaginations of politicians and voters as well as in those of political scientists.

Whether or not these different political actors have the same thing in mind when they talk about left and right, of course, is another matter entirely. Indeed, it is highly likely that they do not. For example, those who are described by other people as being on the extreme left, or the extreme right, rarely describe themselves in this way. Rather, they tend to think of themselves as being on the "center-left" or the "center-right," and to see others as the extremists.

Another source of ambiguity arising from using actors' self-placements on the left-right scale has to do with the fact that the scale itself has a large number both of major components and of more minor nuances, some of which may be stressed by some actors in their interpretation of left and right, while others are stressed by other actors. Thus a person who has very right-wing economic policy preferences may nonetheless see herself as being on the center-left, given her liberal preferences on moral issues which she rates as highly salient. Another person with the same basic preferences may rate economic policy as being more salient, and thus identify herself as being on the right. All ideological self-placements risk ambiguity of this sort.

The third basic method of identifying salient policy dimensions is more fundamentally inductive. It involves taking a rich and complex (that is, a very high-dimensional) set of data on the policy preferences of the various actors in a particular system and attempting to reduce this, using data presentation techniques such as factor analysis and multidimensional scaling, to a low dimensional representation of the policy space that also seems capable of "fitting" the data without too much stress. The dimensionality of the policy space is thereby determined empirically, after which the particular dimensions generated are given substantive interpretations on the basis of the manner in which the original substantive variables relate to the derived dimensions. If the same set of parties is given the same set of scores on an economic policy and a foreign policy dimension, as we saw in the previous chapter, then these dimensions may be assumed to be manifestations of a single underlying dimension. The dimensionality of the space is then reduced by one and a composite dimension combining the two is constructed and interpreted.

The disadvantage of this technique is that, while it is geared to provide at least some estimate of the minimum dimensionality of policy spaces, it provides no independent method of "fixing" the substantively important dimensions in a particular policy space. Inductively generated policy spaces such as these are typically "rotated" until a particular configuration of actors is found which allows the dimensions to be interpreted in a plausible manner. The particular set of dimensions which is used is in a sense arbitrary—any set of dimensions that span the same space would do the same job.

Yet, certain theoretical treatments of party competition set considerable store by the substance rather than merely the number of these key dimensions. Shepsle's structure-induced equilibrium approach, for example, looks at political competition in terms of policy dimensions whose substantive meaning is institutionally determined by the jurisdictions of congressional committees (Shepsle, 1979; Shepsle and Weingast, 1981, 1987). Thus, even if the relative positions of all parties on economic policy are the same as the relative positions of the same parties on foreign policy, the policy space cannot be reduced to a single dimension for the purposes of this approach, since real political decision making can only take place in the context of the dimensions defined by committee jurisdictions. Real decisions cannot be implemented in terms of some imaginary dimension. This general set of ideas has recently been extended to the analysis of government formation in multiparty systems (Laver and Shepsle, 1990a, b). Actual government policy decisions are policed by cabinet portfolios—thus the policy jurisdictions of key cabinet portfolios institutionally determine the substantive meaning of the dimensions of the effective policy space. It does not make sense, in terms of this approach, to derive these dimensions using purely inductive data-reduction techniques.

In the light of the clear possibility that we may be interested in the substantive interpretation of the main dimensions of party policy, the method that we use in what follows comes closest to the pure *a priori* technique, though it spreads the risks associated with this by using as large a number of experts as possible for any given country. Experts were offered, for every country in the study, the same basic set of eight *a priori* policy dimensions, defined quite precisely. If a particular dimension was considered not to be important, then experts were asked to ignore it. In addition, they were asked to rate the importance of each dimension for each party and to define and add additional policy dimensions if they felt that these were important. Thus the initial list of eight dimensions that we offered could be added to and subtracted from, but the basic policy dimensions, as well as their specific interpretations, were provided by us, *a priori*. In identifying these dimensions, as we saw in the previous chapter, we attempted to capture the main policy dimensions discussed in connection with party competition in the parliamentary democracies that form the basis of our study.

While the basic set of eight *a priori* dimensions formed the backbone of our questionnaire, many respondents suggested additional policy dimensions in particular instances. There was quite a wide variation in the extra dimensions suggested for most countries, but there were six countries in which there was a clear pattern in the dimensions that our experts wished to add. The six countries for which the experts converged in recommending particular additional dimensions were Britain, Canada, France, Ireland, the Netherlands and New Zealand. In three of these—Britain, the Netherlands and New Zealand—the additional dimension had to do with support for, or opposition to, nuclear weapons and/or power. In Ireland, the dimension had to do with support for, or opposition to, a British withdrawal from Northern Ireland. In both France and Canada, two additional dimensions were suggested. In Canada, one had to do with support for the extension of the role of the French language, the other had to do with support for, or opposition to, the development of closer links with the USA. In France, one additional dimension had to do with attitudes to immigration, the other had to do with attitudes towards the European Community. Respondents were asked to provide their own interpretation of the endpoints of these scales. Obviously it was often the case that, while two experts agreed on the general interpretation of the scales, they differed on the precise interpretation of their endpoints. As a consequence, there is inevitably more ambiguity in these "user supplied" scales than there is in those scales for which all respondents were confronted with precisely the same endpoints.

Empirical Results on the Salience of Policy Dimensions

Respondents were asked to rate the salience of each policy dimension for each party and the basic results of this can be found in Appendix B. If the reader runs

Table 3.1 The salience of foreign policy in Britain, by party.
(1 = lowest; 20 = highest)

Party	Salience
Conservative	17.5
Labour	14.7
Social & Liberal Democrats	12.4
Scottish Nationalists	10.4
Plaid Cymru	9.4

an eye down these figures, it will immediately be clear that there are major differences between different parties in the same country over the perceived salience of the main policy dimensions. To take a couple of examples at random from the mass of data reported in the Appendix, (which is difficult to summarize since the essence of these data is their diversity), consider the salience of the foreign policy dimension in Britain and the religious dimension in the Netherlands, described in Tables 3.1 and 3.2 respectively.

As Table 3.1 shows, there is widespread disagreement between British parties over the importance of foreign policy in party competition. The Conservative Party is judged to rate foreign policy as being almost twice as important as do the nationalist parties, and as being quite a bit more important than do any of the other parties.

Table 3.2 shows that there was an even greater divergence between the parties in the Netherlands over their rating of the salience of the religious dimension. The fundamentalist Protestant parties (SGP, RPF and GPV) rated religion as being very salient indeed. The Christian Democrats (CDA) rated religion as being moderately salient. The other parties rated the religious dimension as being much less salient.

These variations between actors in perceptions of the relative importance of different policy dimensions are vital for many spatial analyses of party competition. They imply that different parties see what might appear on the face of it to be the same basic policy space in a range of quite different ways. And the pervasive impression that can be gained from reviewing the information on this matter reported in Appendix B is that there are large variations in party-specific saliency weights in virtually every country studied. This implies that every uniform spatial "map" of these systems that might be presented, either here or elsewhere, is a rather crude approximation. Each is an amalgam of several different spatial maps of the same party system, as this is perceived differently by different key actors. *This diversity in actors' perceptions of the importance of the main policy dimensions, is one of the more important empirical conclusions from this phase of our analysis, and indeed from our analysis as a whole.*

While, as we have just seen, each party does appear to view the policy space in which it operates in different terms from its rivals, it is nonetheless conventional

Table 3.2 The Salience of the Religious
dimension in the Netherlands,
by Party.
(1 = lowest; 20 = highest)

Party	Salience
SGP	18.9
RPF	18.6
GPV	17.8
CDA	12.7
PPR	7.1
PvdA	6.0
D'66	5.8
VVD	5.6
CPN	5.6
PSP	5.2

to generate uniform spatial maps of particular party systems, based on the assumption that it makes at least some sort of sense to talk about the "overall" salience of a given policy dimension for a given party system, as if all parties agreed on this. Above all else, there is certainly no getting away from the fact that a uniform spatial map is an awfully convenient way of presenting a lot of information about a given party system.

We thus derive a general estimate of the salience of particular policy dimensions in particular countries. Obviously, simply to average the salience accorded to each dimension by each party in the country concerned would be a rather peculiar way to summarize the relative salience of important policy dimensions. If we did this, the salience given to particular dimensions by particular tiny parties—the fundamentalist Protestant parties in the Netherlands, for example—would weight equally with the salience given these by much larger and more mainstream parties, thereby distorting the results. Therefore, when we average the saliency scores assigned to each dimension by each party, we weight each score by the share of legislative seats controlled by the party in question. (Note that the saliency scores themselves represent the views of party leaders, so the entire set of saliency weights captures legislative, rather than electoral, party configurations.) Having thus computed a weighted mean score for each dimension, the final saliency score for a given dimension is then expressed as a proportion of the average weighted mean score of all policy dimensions in the country concerned. This yields an index of the relative salience of the dimension in question, taken across all parties, in which relatively more salient dimensions in a given country receive scores of more than 1.00, while relatively less salient dimensions receive scores of less than 1.00.

These general estimates of the relative salience of different policy dimensions in different countries, taking the views of all parties in each country together in proportion to their legislative strength, are reported in Table 3.3. They show that two particular dimensions, viewed in these terms, tended to be among the most salient in most countries. These were the "tax cuts versus public spending" dimension and the "social policy" dimension. The religious dimension and the urban-rural dimension, in contrast, tended to be among the the least salient in most countries. (For France and Canada, only the more salient of the "user-supplied" dimensions is listed, in each case the salience of the other dimension is low.)

The Dimensionality of Policy Spaces

As Table 3.3 shows, respondents were prepared to identify quite a wide range of policy dimensions as being salient. There is no country in which only one or two dimensions were identified as being very much more salient than all others. Assessed in terms of the number of *a priori* dimensions that experts are prepared to identify as being important in party competition, therefore, all of the party systems we studied are distinctly multidimensional.

We set out to explore this conclusion further with a more inductive dimensional analysis of our data. Such analyses proceed on the basis of the assumption that, if the relative observed positions of a set of actors on two policy dimensions are identical, then both dimensions are "really" manifestations of a single underlying policy dimension. In effect, observed policy positions are taken as indicators of underlying and unobservable policy dimensions. The task of the empirical researcher is then to estimate the latter using the former.

A common approach in the literature has been to take a large set of policy variables relating to a given set of actors, and to attempt to reduce these to a much smaller number of underlying dimensions using principle components analysis. This technique essentially identifies sets of highly intercorrelated variables and estimates a single artificial variable, or factor, which can be substituted for them while continuing to explain most of the variance in the data. The set of variables which contribute to the definition of the factor is then used to interpret its meaning. (See Budge, *et al.*, 1987, for a description of the application of this method to policy data assembled from the content analysis of party manifestos.)

Table 3.4 shows the results, for each country, of a principle components analysis of expert judgments of party positions on our eight *a priori* policy dimensions. (Each expert's placement of a single party on each of eight scales was taken as the unit of analysis.) Variable loadings for components with eigenvalues greater than one are reported, together with the percentage of the variance in the data accounted for by each component. Variable loadings of more than 0.5 are highlighted in bold, unless the variable in question had a higher loading on another dimension.

Table 3.4 shows that, for nearly every country, the policy dimensions that we assumed *a priori* to be facets of a general left-right scale (these are taxes versus services, foreign policy, public ownership, social policy and anticlericalism) tend to load strongly on a single underlying factor. This is especially true for those

Table 3.3 Weighted Mean Saliency Score, by Dimension, as Proportion of Mean Weighted Saliency Scores for all Dimensions, by Country.

	Taxes versus spending	Social policy	Foreign policy	Public ownership	Environment	Centralisation	Urban versus rural	Religious dimension	Most salient local dimension	
Australia	1.27	1.10	0.86	1.10	1.09	0.99	1.00	0.58		
Austria	1.17	1.06	0.90	1.08	1.14	0.73	1.04	0.88		
Belgium	1.26	1.18	1.02	0.98	0.78	1.13	0.82	0.82		
Britain	1.35	1.08	1.10	1.25	0.98	1.01	0.81	0.43	1.37	Nuclr.
Canada	1.20	1.13	1.04	1.18	0.98	1.06	0.83	0.58	1.60	US rel.
Denmark	1.31	1.03	1.28	1.06	1.01	0.85	0.92	0.56		
Finland	1.11	1.03	0.94	1.01	0.97	0.95	1.14	0.85		
France	1.18	1.18	0.94	1.15	0.76	1.06	0.80	0.93	0.85	Europe
Germany	1.10	1.15	1.05	0.95	1.16	0.89	0.94	0.76		
Greece	1.16	0.61	1.56	1.18	0.79	1.17	0.69	0.83		
Iceland	1.08	1.16	1.17	1.13	1.25	0.90	1.18	0.14		
Ireland	1.42	1.21	0.80	1.18	0.75	0.55	1.05	1.04	1.46	N. Irl.
Italy	0.91	1.15	1.08	1.02	0.95	0.97	0.77	1.17		
Japan	1.28	0.90	1.17	0.76	0.76	1.02	1.08	1.04		
Luxembourg	1.22	1.33	1.18	0.82	1.26	0.48	0.89	0.81		
Malta	0.98	1.09	1.09	1.01	1.15	0.82	0.71	1.14		
Netherlands	1.28	1.32	1.09	0.95	1.29	0.64	0.65	0.77	1.17	Nuclr.
Norway	1.13	1.20	0.99	1.09	0.98	0.91	0.93	0.78		
New Zealand	1.33	1.14	0.99	1.06	0.98	0.95	1.11	0.44	1.21	Nuclr.
Portugal	1.04	1.17	0.95	1.28	0.94	1.13	0.82	0.66		
Spain	1.21	1.17	1.11	1.03	0.85	1.26	0.67	0.68		
Sweden	1.24	1.09	0.96	1.16	1.08	0.98	0.82	0.66		
USA	1.37	1.44	1.19	0.56	1.21	0.93	0.72	0.59		
Mean	1.20	1.13	1.06	1.04	1.00	0.93	0.89	0.75		

Note: In this and the following table, Israel has not been included because the diverse Israeli "liberal" parties were aggregated under a single party label when data were collected. This made weighting procedures ambiguous.

Table 3.4 Dimensional Analysis of Policy Spaces.

Country		Taxes versus services	Foreign policy	Public ownership	Social policy	Religious dimension	Urban versus rural	Centralisation	Environment	% variance explained
Australia	Dim 1	.89	.76	.76	.95	.86	.82	-.17	.90	63.9
Australia	Dim 2	.13	-.34	-.15	.10	.15	-.02	.96	.23	14.5
Austria	Dim 1	.87	.69	.86	.79	.55	.71	-.46	.57	49.1
Austria	Dim 2	.13	-.06	.07	.30	-.10	-.51	.81	.75	19.9
Belgium	Dim 1	.69	.81	.92	.88	.88	.50	-.07	-.08	47.8
Belgium	Dim 2	-.18	.35	.26	.14	.02	-.59	.86	.98	28.5
Britain	Dim 1	.96	.92	.89	.86	.02	.31	.80	.80	58.3
Britain	Dim 2	.13	.06	.17	.03	.72	.74	-.39	-.34	17.2
Canada	Dim 1	.85	.81	.77	.95	.75	.79	-.63	.85	64.6
Denmark	Dim 1	.79	.84	.90	.83	.79	.74	-.01	.49	53.1
Denmark	Dim 2	-.11	.12	-.22	.34	.04	-.60	.94	.67	23.6
Finland	Dim 1	.81	.54	.78	.84	.90	.52	.08	.55	45.3
Finland	Dim 2	-.18	-.37	-.22	.16	.04	-.18	.88	.68	18.8
Finland	Dim 3	.23	.49	.30	-.24	-.18	-.75	.14	.11	13.3
France	Dim 1	.93	.83	.88	.86	.85	.63	.67	.44	60.1
France	Dim 2	.15	.18	.35	-.33	.19	.40	-.54	-.81	17.7
Germany	Dim 1	.74	.79	.71	.82	.74	.47	.56	.83	51.2
Germany	Dim 2	.52	-.10	.55	-.39	-.51	-.69	.18	.25	19.7
Greece	Dim 1	.90	.70	.85	.60	.92	.42	.35	.76	51.2
Greece	Dim 2	.03	.48	.41	-.70	.07	.33	-.82	-.26	21.6
Greece	Dim 3	.21	-.05	.29	.23	.26	-.75	-.19	-.52	14.1
Ireland	Dim 1	.88	.74	.81	.77	.84	.74	.41	.41	52.1
Ireland	Dim 2	.08	.08	.10	.07	.07	.38	-.72	-.76	16.0
Ireland	Dim 3	.33	.45	.48	-.51	-.36	-.36	.04	-.15	13.6
Israel	Dim 1	.46	.90	.81	.89	.87	-.32	.00	.74	48.4
Israel	Dim 2	-.72	-.09	-.51	.31	.47	.65	.98	.46	33.4

Table 3.4 Continued

Country		Taxes versus services	Foreign policy	Public ownership	Social policy	Religious dimension	Urban versus rural	Centralisation	Environment	% variance explained
Italy	Dim 1	**.77**	**.74**	**.69**	**.82**	**.78**	**.64**	**.76**	**.82**	56.8
Italy	Dim 2	**.56**	.00	**.52**	-.44	-.41	-.59	.10	.24	17.0
Japan	Dim 1	**.97**	**.86**	**.99**		**.80**	**.98**	-.46	**.97**	77.3
Japan	Dim 2	.17	.45	-.02		-.14	-.15	**.86**	.13	14.8
Luxembourg	Dim 1	**.79**	.47	**.89**	**.77**	**.87**	**.84**	.26	.14	47.3
Luxembourg	Dim 2	.25	**.77**	.01	-.47	-.13	.32	-**.92**	-**.93**	34.1
Malta	Dim 1	**.96**	**.68**	.10	**.89**	**.85**	.00	-**.72**	-.28	43.9
Malta	Dim 2	.11	.20	-**.96**	-.01	.29	-**.86**	.44	.27	25.7
Malta	Dim 3	-.22	.30	-.08	.03	.03	.43	-.06	**.91**	14.8
Netherlands	Dim1	**.89**	**.93**	**.93**	**.91**	**.89**	**.95**	-.09	**.67**	68.6
Netherlands	Dim 2	-.27	.00	-.22	.22	.12	.04	**.97**	.29	15.3
Norway	Dim 1	**.91**	**.90**	**.91**	**.53**	.36	-.42	.12	**.75**	45.5
Norway	Dim 2	-.07	.06	.02	**.73**	**.81**	**.80**	-.46	-.38	27.5
New Zealand	Dim 1	-.32	**.70**	-.33	**.91**	**.78**	**.89**	**.77**	.27	44.7
New Zealand	Dim 2	**.85**	**.51**	**.88**	-.15	-.05	.20	.03	**.65**	28.1
Portugal	Dim 1	**.91**	**.85**	**.98**	**.98**	**.97**	**.85**	.20	**.88**	74.3
Portugal	Dim 2	-.19	.18	.06	.07	.06	-.01	-**.97**	.05	12.8
Spain	Dim 1	**.76**	**.90**	**.90**	**.96**	**.84**	**.70**	**.56**	**.81**	65.9
Spain	Dim 2	.43	-.14	.07	.08	.14	.46	-**.60**	-.54	13.7
Sweden	Dim 1	**.92**	**.85**	**.92**	**.72**	**.85**	.11	.27	.54	50.1
Sweden	Dim 2	.02	-.17	.02	-.28	-.27	-**.92**	**.82**	**.77**	28.7
USA	Dim 1	**.96**	**.65**	**.92**	**.97**	**.83**	**.91**	-.50	**.90**	71.1
USA	Dim 2	.03	.64	.10	-.04	.06	.07	**.78**	-.24	13.6

Note 1: Variable loadings of more than 0.5 are highlighted in bold, unless the variable has a higher loading on another dimension.

Note 2: Insufficient data to complete analysis for Iceland.

systems in which the first component explains far more variation in the data than any other—Australia, Canada, France, Japan, the Netherlands, Portugal, Spain and the USA. (In each of these systems, a single underlying component explained over 60 percent of the variance in the experts' scoring of party positions on the eight policy variables.) Viewed in purely inductive terms, these might seem to be the most "uni-dimensional" party systems.

The *a priori* policy dimension that most systematically failed to load inductively with the left-right variables was "centralization of decision-making." Centralization loaded on, and often defined, the second principle component in fifteen of the twenty three countries for which this analysis could be performed (Iceland had to be omitted as its data continually generated singularity problems).

The Interpretation of Policy Dimensions

While this dimensional analysis describes in a convenient manner the intercorrelation between the scale positions of parties on different *a priori* policy dimensions, it should be treated very cautiously as an inductive estimation of "underlying" policy dimensions and thereby of the "dimensionality" of the policy space in question. The reasons for this have to do with the substantive interpretation of the policy spaces that are thereby generated.

An example of the problems that can arise can be seen in Figure 3.1, which shows a view of the Dutch policy space generated by party positions on the taxation and the social policy dimensions. Table 3.4 shows that both of these *a priori* dimensions load very heavily on the main principle component in the Netherlands, which explains most of the variance in expert judgments of Dutch party policy positions. Figure 3.1 shows why this is the case. Most of the parties are located close to a line that runs at roughly a 45-degree angle between the two substantive dimensions. This line might be thought of as an "underlying" left-right dimension. An analyst who merely looked at the results of the principle components analysis, and failed to look at the plot of party positions in Figure 3.1, might be tempted to collapse the two *a priori* dimensions into one. There are just a couple of "outliers," in the shape of the VVD and D'66.

The fundamental problem with this solution is that the VVD in particular is a vital element in Dutch politics. It is central in almost all coalition negotiations since the Second World War. Furthermore, the fact that the VVD distinguishes itself strongly in policy terms from the other "right-wing" party, the CDA, is perhaps the single most important element in any description of the Dutch policy space. Dutch politics is quintessentially characterized by competition between a clerical and a secular right, distinguished by their positions on the social and moral policy dimension.

If a purely inductive technique is used to determine that the Dutch policy space is "really" one-dimensional, then the position of the VVD might be found by projecting it orthogonally onto the principle component that reflects the derived "underlying" policy dimension. This would place the VVD between the other

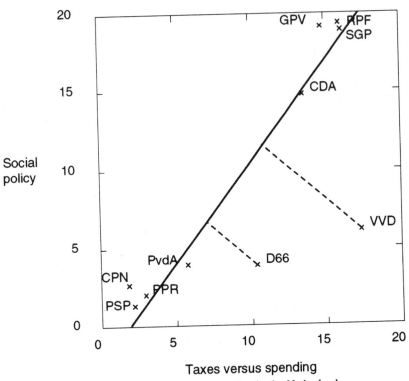

Figure 3.1 Two dimensions of policy in the Netherlands.

two large Dutch parties, the PvdA and the CDA. An alternative method would be to avoid derived dimensions altogether. Since the two component parts are closely intercorrelated, either one or the other might be taken as an "indicator" of the underlying dimension. As Figure 3.1 shows, however, the matter of which dimension is selected makes a huge difference to our interpretation of the role of the VVD in Dutch politics. If the "tax cuts versus public spending" dimension is selected, and this is the more salient according to Table 3.3, then the VVD appears to the right of the CDA. This is the position in which Dutch country specialists typically put the VVD in one dimensional spatial representations. If the social policy dimension is selected, then the CDA appears as the more right-wing party of the two.

What this example shows quite clearly, of course, is that any reduction of the two-dimensional picture of the party system that can be seen in Figure 3.1 destroys vital information and puts us at risk of missing most of the point of Dutch politics. Statistically, the VVD may appear as an outlier. Substantively, however, it is clear that the very outlying position of this party is what gives perspective to our picture of the Dutch party system. This outlying position underlines the fact that economic policy and social policy in the Netherlands are not perfectly correlated and that, furthermore, this lack of correlation is what makes sense of competition between the two main right-wing parties, the CDA and the VVD.

Bearing in mind the very serious problems that can emerge as a result of settling the dimensionality of a policy space by the rigid application of data presentation techniques, we repeat our warning that the results in Table 3.4 should be used with great care. What they do seem to show quite clearly, however, is the strong intercorrelation of the policy dimensions that are typically associated with the left-right dimension. And they identify some systems in which this association is much stronger than others. A secondary finding is that the "centralization" dimension seems to be quite independent of left and right in most of the countries in the study. This suggests that, where this dimension is salient (most notably in Belgium, Greece and Spain) it may form the basis of a dimension that cuts very clearly across all others.

What all of this means, of course, is that there is no single obvious method for estimating the dimensionality of any given policy space. Our experts, as we have seen, were prepared to identify a large number of dimensions as being salient in any given country. Many of these dimensions are interrelated. But, as we have seen in one case and we shall soon see in others, it is as often as not the precise positioning of outlying parties on correlated sets of policy dimensions that makes the all the difference. Indeed such outliers may even define the essence of a particular party system.

Party Constellations

It should be clear above all else from the preceding discussion that selecting a set of dimensions to describe a given party system is essentially a substantive task that must be based on local knowledge of politics in the country concerned. Since we certainly do not set ourselves up as experts on the politics of 24 different countries, definitive interpretation of our data is perhaps better provided by others. Nonetheless, we at least begin the process of substantive interpretation in this section, which reviews the relative locations (or "constellations") of parties on the sets of dimensions identified by our experts as being most salient. We consider first the positions of the party leaders, and move on to look at the extent to which the positions of party voters appear to differ from these.

A series of two dimensional plots of the policy positions of party leaders can be found in the figures in Appendix B. Two plots are provided for each country. The first shows the positions of party leaders on the "tax cuts versus public spending" and "social policy" dimensions, the two dimensions that we identified as being most salient on a cross-national, cross-party, basis. This allows us to generate a spatial map of each party system using the same dimensions so as to provide some uniform perspective on the different party constellations that can be found in different countries. The second plot shows the "tax cuts versus public spending" dimension against the most salient other dimension in each country.

Our intention here is to provide a country-specific spatial representation of the party system that nonetheless retains some comparative basis. These plots between them provide a very limited set of perspectives on a varied and complex data set. Readers can, and indeed they absolutely should, use the data reported in Appendix B to generate a wide range of alternative spatial representations of party systems in which they are interested, using different combinations of the dimensions that we estimate.

Reviewing these two-dimensional plots for the 24 countries in our study, four general types of party constellation suggest themselves in an impressionistic manner. First, there is what we might think of as the "Benelux" constellation. Figure 3.1 has already shown the "common" two-dimensional map of the Dutch party system. In another closely related example, Figure 3.2 shows an equivalent two-dimensional map of the German party system. Both of these party constellations have a number of features that recur in the maps of several other party systems. As in the Netherlands, while most of the West German parties line up in more or less the same relative positions on both dimensions, giving the impression that there might be a single underlying dimension, there is a very significant exception to the pattern in the shape of the FDP, a small but important party that has held the balance of power in most post-war German legislatures. Thus the German FDP is an outlier in the same important sense as the Dutch VVD—in each case the outlying position of the party gives perspective to the party system as a whole. These two liberal parties are at the right-hand end of the scale on economic policy but are relatively progressive on social policy.

The relative position of the German FPD and the Dutch VVD give a distinctive shape to a particular type of party constellation that recurs in several European countries. The best examples of this can be found in Austria, Belgium, Luxembourg, the Netherlands and West Germany. The basic shape of the party constellation in the Netherlands can be seen in the other Benelux countries, Belgium and Luxembourg. Each party constellation is essentially triangular, with a social democratic pole, a liberal pole and a Christian democratic pole. (In the Belgian case, note that these poles comprise party "families," each of which has a Flemish and a Walloon language member.) In each of the Benelux countries, the liberal pole is distinguished from the Christian democratic pole by an outlying position on social policy—the liberals are more liberal on social policy than a one dimensional interpretation would enable us to predict from their economic policies.

The Austrian party system can also be thought of as an example of this general type of party constellation, though the key players in Austria seem to be far closer together, in relation to the other parties. The two dimensional spatial maps suggest, therefore, that the Benelux countries plus Germany and Austria have party systems that are similar in certain interesting respects. In each case, the main parties maintain a relationship with each other that is at least two-dimensional. In each case this is the result of the existence of a strategically important (if not always large) secular liberal party that distinguishes itself on the right from a

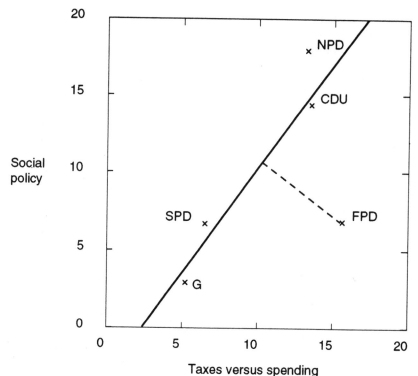

Figure 3.2 Two dimensions of policy in Germany.

large Christian democratic party by having more liberal policies on social and moral issues. In the somewhat less convincing Austrian case the role of the Christian democratic party is fulfilled by the ÖVP. (Gallagher, Laver and Mair, 1991, discuss the confrontation between Christian democracy and secular liberalism in these countries.)

A second group of party constellations that look quite similar to one another can be found among the Mediterranean countries. With the exception of Italy, these are each characterised by a large populist conservative party which has a strong nationalist appeal and which is neither anticlerical nor particularly liberal on social affairs. This group of parties includes the Gaullists (RPR) in France, New Democracy in Greece, the Nationalist Party in Malta, the Social Democrats (despite their name) in Portugal, and the Coalición Popular in Spain. In most of these countries, there is a divided left-wing pole, with a social democratic party and usually another left socialist or communist party. As the plots in Appendix B show, these Mediterranean countries do not have significant outlying liberal parties, so that the basic shape of the party constellations is bipolar rather than tripolar.

A clear example of this type of constellation can be seen in France and other examples of it can be seen in Greece and Malta (though the main left-wing pole is not divided in Malta). The underlying logic of party competition is very similar to this in Spain and Portugal, though the essential bipolarity of these systems is superficially obscured by the existence of a larger number of parties. Each of these party constellations is thus characterised by a basic opposition between a social democratic pole on the one hand and a conservative/nationalist pole that is not challenged by a strong Christian democratic party on the other. While there may well be many other parties in the system, these are not central to competition. In particular, parties that lie a significant distance away from these poles tend not to be involved in the government formation process.

Our third general type of party constellation is also bipolar, and can be seen in the English-speaking democracies, including Australia (where the poles contrast Labour and the Liberals), Britain (Labour and Conservative), New Zealand (Labour and National Party) and the USA (Democrats and Republican). There are strong similarities between the Mediterranean and the English-speaking party constellations. The right in each case is anchored in a strong nationalistic secular conservative party. On the left, however, the English-speaking systems tend to be characterised by a single social democratic party, with no communist or left socialist representation to speak of.

A fourth group of party constellations can be found in Scandinavia, where commentators have traditionally emphasised the theme of "two-bloc" politics. In this type of party constellation a medium-sized secular conservative party tends to coexist with a small, Protestant, Christian democratic party. Both of these confront a strong social democratic pole. The Scandinavian constellation differs from the strongly bipolar southern European systems, however, in that a significant middle-of-the-road liberal or agrarian party tends to bridge the gap between the conservative pole and the social democratic pole. In Denmark, for example, this role is filled by the Radical Liberals (RV), who have alternated in office as members of both social democratic and bourgeois coalitions. Norway, Sweden and Finland also conform strongly to this description, with Iceland a similar but less striking case.

The four types of constellation that we have described so far are defined in terms of the two dimensions of policy identified by our experts as being generally salient in most countries—economic and social/moral policy. In addition, it will be remembered, we identified certain other dimensions as being salient in particular countries, and the figures in Appendix B also plot party positions on these. When we review these plots, our simple classification of party constellations remains more or less constant, though there are a number of significant exceptions.

The most striking of these relate to the two countries for which the "centralization of decision-making" dimension was very salient—Belgium and Spain. In each case, the centralization dimension captures a fundamental centralist-federalist debate in party politics. It will be remembered that this dimension appeared in the factor analyses discussed above as being quite independent of the left-right dimension. It is not surprising, therefore, that using it transforms the spatial maps of the party systems involved. In both Spain and Belgium, we find a very clear-cut polarisation between the main parties in the system, arrayed from left to right in the "centralist" reaches of the space, and smaller parties representing radical decentralist or separatist positions (such as the Volksunie in Belgium, or the Basque separatist parties in Spain) which can be found in the separatist areas of the space. These two countries should clearly be considered as special cases, each requiring an additional, decentralist dimension to capture essential features of the structure of party competition.

The other main deviation from the basic constellations elaborated above concerns the impact of the environmentalist dimension in a number of the Benelux party constellations, notably Germany, Austria, Luxembourg and the Netherlands. In each of these cases, the environmental dimension is rated as being highly salient. In each case, taking account of an environmental dimension has the effect of compressing ideological differences between liberals and Christian democrats and contrasting both of these parties with the social democrats. As a result, the salience of the environmental dimension does not change the basic tripolar structure of these systems, though it does provide additional points of agreement between the two main parties of the right.

In each of the other countries studied, including the most salient additional policy dimension has the effect of shuffling the party constellations around somewhat, but it does not change their basic shape.

While most of the countries studied fit more or less neatly into one of our basic classifications, four of them do not; these are Ireland, Israel, Italy and Japan. The Irish party constellation has a weakly tripolar structure, with salient parties (Fine Gael and the Progressive Democrats) in a position rather similar to that of the liberal pole in the Benelux systems. However, in relative terms, these parties are not as far away from the Christian democratic pole (a role filled by Fianna Fáil) as their counterparts in systems with a clear cut opposition between Christian democrats and anticlerical liberals. Neither Fine Gael nor the PDs are anticlerical and Fianna Fail is not explicitly Christian democratic.

Italy is distinctive in having a strong Christian democratic party without a strong secular liberal party—the main party of the secular right being the neofascist MSI. The MSI is not anticlerical, however, occupying a position rather close to that of DC. There is a liberal party with more permissive social policies, the PLI, but it is too small to have much of an influence on politics (though it has been a "surplus" member of quite a few Italian governments). In many ways, therefore, the Italian party constellation comes closest to the Mediterranean two-bloc model, with the DC substituting for a more secular conservative nationalist party. However, the socialists and social democrats (PSI and PSDI) have regularly gone into government with the Christian democrats, so the polarisation between the two blocs is very weak.

The Japanese system looks quite unlike any in Europe, given the relatively liberal social policies ascribed by our experts to the main party of the right, the LDP. This powerful right-wing party confronts a divided cluster of left-wing rivals, and the system is certainly bipolar rather than tripolar. But the right-wing pole appears to have a substantively different meaning to that in either the Mediterranean, English speaking or Scandinavian models.

A quite distinctive feature of the Israeli party constellation concerns the role of the conservative religious parties. These occupy parts of the standard two dimensional policy space occupied by no other party in our study. They are very conservative on social/moral policy, yet middle-of-the-road on economic policy—pushing them towards the virtually uninhabited upper left quadrant of the space. Apart from these parties, the confrontation between Labour, Likud and the Liberals looks strongly tripolar—but the religious parties, often crucial in government formation, clearly add a unique element to the Israeli constellation.

Overall, of course, our classification of party constellations is highly *ad hoc* and impressionistic—representing no more than a few preliminary speculations on the shape of our data. Nonetheless, some of the patterns that emerge are at least superficially quite striking and seem to invite classification, though it is difficult to see how such shapes could ever be classified in a totally systematic manner. Obviously, the most dramatic differences in the shapes that we have been looking at are those between the tripolar Benelux systems and the others. Perhaps the most dramatic similarity between systems is that, in virtually every party constellation that we have considered, the left is anchored in a very similar position relative to the other parties. Thus it appears to be the relative position of the various major actors in the right-hand part of the policy space that gives shape to different party systems.

Patterns in the Electorate

The party constellations that we have just been discussing relate to the policy positions of *party leaders*. They are also relevant to party competition in the electorate, of course, since party policy positions will be taken into account by voters when deciding how to behave at election time. It may well be that voters take into account many more things besides the relative policy positions of the parties when deciding whether and how to vote. Nonetheless it seems plausible to suppose that the relative positions of the parties do affect election results, and that each possible constellation of party policy positions can therefore be associated with a particular "most likely" election result. If we assume, all other things being equal, that voters are more likely to vote for parties that are closer to them in policy terms, than for parties that are farther away from them, then the distribution of votes between the parties, combined with the configuration of policy positions, gives us quite a lot of information about the distribution of electoral preferences. If we further assume that party leaders are at least partially motivated by the desire to maximize votes, then a particular set of party policy positions should be associated with a particular distribution of electoral opinion.

In other words, we can assume that a particular party constellation is the result of party leaders picking a party position that is a "best response" to the positions of other party leaders, given a distribution of electoral opinion. And we can attempt to deduce things about the distribution of electoral opinion from this. As a very crude example, we might deduce, if large sectors of a particular policy space are uninhabited by any political party, in a multi-party system with low costs of entry, that relatively few voters must have ideal policies in this sector of the space. Otherwise, it is difficult to explain why some existing or new party does not take up a position designed to attract these votes.

The search for particular configurations of parties associated with particular distributions of electoral opinion is the basic project of Anthony Downs' *An Economic Theory of Democracy* and its intellectual successors (Downs, 1957). The basic requirements for a full-scale empirical elaboration of Downsian models are spatial maps of the preference structure of the electorate, which we did not assemble as part of this study since these inevitably depend upon the analysis of mass survey data. We can make some progress on the matter, however, by looking at the relationship between electoral success and the party policy positions that we have estimated. While we do not know the distribution of electoral policy preferences across the policy spaces that we have derived, we can observe whether this distribution would need to be very uneven and contrived in order to produce the election results that we actually observe. Of course, each of the spatial maps that we have derived represents no more than a very imperfect two-dimensional slice of a much more complex reality. In each country other, unobserved, dimensions may be more salient for any or all of the parties. Assuming that we are not completely wide of the mark, however, these policy spaces do enable us to make inferences about the structure of preferences in the electorate.

The two-dimensional spatial maps in Appendix B record the share of the popular vote won by each party in the general election most closely preceding 1 January 1989, when the project was commenced. Also presented in Appendix B are a set of diagrams generated from these two-dimensional pictures that divide each space into a set of regions, with each region related to one of the parties. Each point in each region, which might be thought of as the "policy domain" of some particular party, is closer to the party in question than to any other party. This region represents the area in the space within which policy-oriented voters prefer the party in question to any other party. It represents the "catchment area" of a party in the policy space. (These diagrams, which will be more familiar to hydrologists than political scientists, are technically known as Voronoi tessellations, or Thiessen diagrams.) This represents the area in the space within which policy-oriented voters prefer the party in question to any other party.

Figure 3.3 gives an example of one of these diagrams, showing party domains in Sweden, together with each party's percentage vote share in the Swedish general election of 11 September 1988. These particular results do appear to be consistent with Downsian voting on the basis of relatively uncontrived distributions of electoral opinion. If the highest densities of voters are taken to be in the center-left of the map, closer to the Social Democrats than to any other party, and if there is an even distribution of electoral opinion across the right-hand side of the map, then it is not difficult to see how the Swedish election result of 1988 was generated. The Communists and Greens were blocked by the Social Democrats from access to the vast bulk of voters, while the bourgeois parties spread themselves out to appeal to particular segments of the more diverse right-wing vote.

In contrast to this, consider the results of the Italian election of 14–15 June 1987, shown in Figure 3.4. In this case, it is necessary to imagine a more contrived distribution of electoral preferences to see how such an election result could have been generated on the basis of Downsian voting. While it is not difficult to see why the Christian Democrats (DC) were the largest party, it is necessary to envisage an intense "hotspot" of opinion in the immediate vicinity of the Communist Party to explain the fact that the Communists did so much better than the Socialists (PSI) and Social Democrats (PSDI). Of the latter

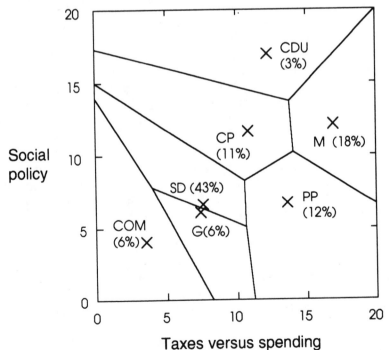

Figure 3.3 Policy domains in Sweden.

two, furthermore, the PSDI seem better placed ideologically to benefit from the concentrations of electoral opinion in the vicinity of the Christian Democrats— yet in practice they have never been able to do so. It is of course possible to come up with a distribution of electoral opinion that reconciles these voting patterns and party positions. One no-nonsense way to do this is to assume that voters are perfectly concentrated, in just the right proportions, on the precise policy positions of the parties. If we wish to assume reasonably smooth changes in the density of electoral preferences across the space, however, then it is more difficult to come up with a description of the Italian electorate that is consistent with Downsian voting on the basis of these party policy positions.

For the most part, taking the set of countries as a whole, it is not difficult to envisage distributions of electoral opinion that could generate observed election results from most of the policy positions we estimated. It is difficult to be more systematic about this, but we can make some general observations about the apparent distribution of electors in our policy spaces.

In the first place, we should note that there is very clear evidence of an uneven distribution of voters across virtually all of the policy spaces that we analysed. The Italian case shown in Figure 3.4 provides a good example of this general phenomenon. Quite a few of the party domains occupy similar areas, but the

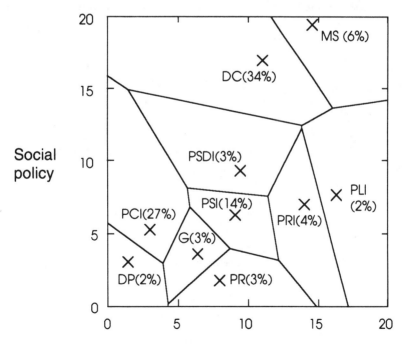

Taxes versus spending

Figure 3.4 Policy domains in Italy.

relevant parties command very different shares of the popular vote. The policy domain of the PSDI in Italy, for example, was almost as "large" as that of the Christian Democrats (DC), but the latter won more than ten times the popular vote. Such disparities are very common in the maps of party policy domains reported in Appendix B.

The comparison between the PSDI and DC also highlights a second general feature of these maps. The policy domain of the PSDI is closer to the center of the policy space than that of the DC, yet the latter won many more votes. A number of party systems have sparsely populated centres, in this sense. In addition to Italy, obvious examples include Belgium, Japan, Norway, Portugal and Spain. In other systems, the allocation of votes between policy domains is consistent with the frequently assumed uni-modal distribution of electoral preferences. Examples of this pattern include Australia, Canada, Denmark, France, Germany, Greece, Iceland, Luxembourg, New Zealand and Sweden. In two of these cases, Denmark and Sweden, the party close to the centre (in each case the social democrats) occupies a small policy domain relative to the other parties, yet wins a large share of the popular vote. Obviously, this suggests a quite steeply peaked distribution of electoral opinion, relative to the policy positions of the parties.

A further general observation that can be made on the basis of the maps of party policy domains reported in Appendix B is that there is little evidence of the pathological types of party configuration that unreconstructed Downsian analyses of spatial competition sometimes imply. We get a clear sense that parties spread themselves more or less evenly across the policy space, rather than clustering in particular parts of it. This implies that parties do take account of factors such as the threat of entry by new parties, the role of activists and party financiers, and other matters that act as brakes on the convergence of rival parties on the same small parts of the policy space.

Obviously we do not know, since this is the first study of this particular type, whether the party domains described in Appendix B are stable and enduring features of the party system in question, or whether they are in a constant state of flux. Certain configurations of parties are highly sensitive to quite small movements in party positions, which can produce large movements in the relative sizes of adjacent policy domains. These diagrams thus could be used to identify those systems whose party constellations implied greater volatility in election results. This could be done by exploring the sensitivity of the policy domains to slight perturbations in party positions, though we ourselves have not yet conducted such an exercise.

Overall, the maps of party policy domains in Appendix B, together with others like them based upon different combinations of policy dimensions, offer a powerfully suggestive way of exploring the spatial dimensions of electoral competition. They allow us almost the only consistent way to look at the policy preferences of mass electorates, while using only information on the policy positions of political parties. This seems to us to be a very useful avenue for further explanation since information on the parties themselves, of course, is much easier to assemble than information about the preferences of members of a mass electorate.

Party Leaders, Party Voters and Party Policy

The extent to which party policy is related to electoral success has to do with the preferences of voters. In the general Downsian account of party competition, a party does not necessarily maximize its vote by occupying the point in policy space preferred by the most voters. The level of a party's vote is determined by the number of voters who feel themselves closer to the party in question than to any other party, which of course depends upon the policy positions of the other parties. Indeed, on this logic, we would expect a party's precise policy position normally to differ somewhat from the policy position most preferred by those who vote for it. We note, for example, that parties are rarely in the centre of their policy domains, as these are mapped in Appendix B.

Without a set of spatial maps of the policy positions of all European voters, it is difficult to explore this matter comprehensively. However, we did make a general attempt to get a grip on it by asking experts to locate the policy positions of "party voters" as well as those of party leaders. Taking this to mean the modal policy position preferred by those who vote for the party, we can get some idea of the extent to which the policies put forward by a party differ from the policies preferred by those who vote for it. These figures are reported extensively in Appendix B.

Consider, to take the example of the British Conservative Party, the different positions of party leaders and party voters on the "tax cuts versus public services" dimension. Conservative leaders were judged to occupy a position at 17.2 on the 1 to 20 scale, while Conservative voters were judged to occupy a position of 12.9. There was thus a big gap between party leaders and party voters on this issue. In contrast, Labour leaders and Labour voters were judged to have very similar positions on this dimension, while Conservative leaders and Conservative voters were judged to have very similar positions on the foreign policy dimension. An enormous number of party-specific comparisons such as this are reported in Appendix B and, once more, readers are encouraged to roll up their sleeves and explore the implications of these data for the countries in which they have a special interest.

Some general trends are worth reporting however. The Downsian model is well-known for its implication that parties should tend, other things being equal, to converge towards the center of the policy spaces in which they compete. This is particularly true for parties on the periphery of the space, which have little to lose, and much to gain, by converging on their rivals closer to the centre. This general prediction that party leaders will tend to have policy positions closer to the centre of each policy scale than party voters can be examined very crudely by attempting to predict the positions of party leaders from those of party voters. If a simple regression model is used to do this, then the prediction is that:

$$\text{leaders' position} = a + b * (\text{voters' position}) + \varepsilon$$

where a > 0, b < 1 and (a+20b) < 20. (In other words, when party voters are at point zero on the scale, party leaders will have a score of more than zero; when party voters are at 20, party leaders will have a score of less than 20.) Table 3.5 reports the results of the simple regressions describing, for each of our experts and for each party on which they gave a judgment, the relationship between party and voter positions for each of the eight standard scales. These regressions are thus based on all of the potential maximum of 2013 pairs of expert judgments relating to party positions.

The results show clearly that there was indeed a modest but quite definite effect in the predicted direction for all policy dimensions except the religious dimension. On the religious dimension, the relationship between party leader positions and party voter positions was very weak. For each of the other dimensions, there was a strong relationship between the positions of party leaders and party voters. With the exception of the social policy dimension, on which voters were seen as being very slightly more conservative than party leaders, all regression coefficients were of the predicted sign and order of magnitude. All other constants were positive and all slopes were less than unity. This implies a tendency for party leaders to be located slightly closer to the center of each scale than party voters.

For two scales, those dealing with foreign policy and public ownership, this effect was quite marked, with a tendency for the leaders of parties at the extremes to be between two and three scale positions closer to the center. For the other scales, the order of magnitude of the effect was about one scale position at the extremes of the scale, and less for parties closer to the center.

The analysis in Table 3.5 is, of course, a very blunt instrument. It could be

Table 3.5 Regression (y=a+bx+ε) of Party Leader Policy Score (y) on Party Voter Policy Score (x).

Policy dimension	r^2	a	b	N
Taxes / services	.78	0.46	.94	1886
Foreign policy	.56	2.78	.60	1770
Pub. ownership	.70	2.45	.78	1829
Social policy	.84	−.35	.95	1856
Religious dim.	.22	9.50	.08	1446
Urban vs. rural	.83	1.06	.90	1568
Centralisation	.59	0.96	.95	1575
Environment	.75	1.16	.89	1808

repeated for every party for every country in the study, though a more useful approach in this regard is simply to inspect the mean scores reported in Appendix B for each party. The overall results, however, suggest that there is indeed a tendency for politicians to take positions rather closer to the center of the policy space than their electoral supporters.

Conclusion

What we have done in the various discussions in this chapter is to build up some pictures of the policy spaces that can be used to describe the preferences of the main political actors in each of the countries that we consider. Any particular policy space, when all is said and done, is no more than one reasonably systematic way of looking at the role of policy in structuring the relationship between the different political actors in a particular country. In an important sense, therefore, there are at least as many policy spaces as there are people interested in politics. Any of a myriad different perspectives could be just as valid, just as useful in helping us to understand party competition. One of the more important empirical findings that emerges from our survey, indeed, is that different parties appear to have very different views of the relative importance of the main ideological dimensions that structure political debate. Each, therefore, would paint a very different picture of the policy space within which politics takes place. What we have generated, therefore, is one particular set of pictures of party competition in each country, not necessarily the definitive set of pictures.

What we offer, however, is not just any old set of pictures of party competition. Based as they are on the results of our expert survey, the pictures of party competition in Appendix B are those that best reflect the views of political scientists specialising in each country, given the constraint that all specialists were forced by us to use the same basic raw materials. In a sense what we offer here is a set of received wisdoms about the role of policy in party competition, a set that has been assembled on a reasonably systematic basis and expressed in reasonably comparable terms for each country.

While noting the important finding that our experts rated large numbers of policy dimensions as salient, and judged that each party is likely to have different views about the salience of each dimension, some striking underlying patterns did emerge from our maps of the party systems.

First, it does seem plausible to classify party systems as being examples of quite a limited number of party constellations. Each of these constellations was anchored on the left by a social democratic party, the location of which, relative to the other parties, was quite remarkably consistent from country to country. None of our experts gave judgments on more than one country, while none had any idea of the judgments of other experts. Thus our findings report a very coherent received wisdom among political scientists about the location of social democratic parties in a wide range of countries.

The other key parameters in classifying party systems are the size and location of a secular liberal party, and the fragmentation of the social democratic pole. The Scandinavian and Benelux constellations are similar in having salient secular liberal parties. In the Scandinavian systems, however, the liberals bridge a gap between secular left and secular right. In the Benelux systems the policy positions of the liberals are distinctive enough to make these parties a separate ideological pole on the right—distinguished from a rival Christian democratic pole by policy on social/moral issues. The Mediterranean and Anglo-American systems are both strongly bipolar, each with a quite distinct tradition of alternation of government between poles, rather than of coalitions between poles. The two systems are distinct, however, in terms of the ideological fragmentation of the left, which tends in Anglo-American systems to be represented by a single strong social democratic party but which tends in Mediterranean systems to be ideologically split between social democrats and other parties of the left.

Second, no party constellation provides very clear evidence against the hypothesis of policy-oriented electoral behavior. While some party constellations appear to derive from more patchy distributions of electoral opinion than others, no party constellation makes sense only in terms of a very bizarre and convoluted distribution of electoral opinion. Nonetheless, we also note that, in quite a few systems, there is not a simple uni-model distribution of electoral opinion, while in no country is there a pathological arrangement of parties in the policy space that suggests unreconstructed Downsian voting.

Third, there does seem to be a quite definite tendency for politicians to take up party positions that are slightly more central than voters. While this pattern is very clear, the order of magnitude of the effect is not large. There are rather few examples of politicians taking up radically different positions from those preferred by those who support them at election time.

Finally, however, we must repeat our view that the interpretations that we provide here are inevitably very crude, since we cannot even begin to pretend that we are widely knowledgeable about politics in each of the twenty four countries under consideration. Individual country specialists should be able to use these data to generate far more subtle interpretations than we have been able to achieve here. And we very much hope that they will do so.

4

Parameters of Party Competition

The previous chapter described the policy spaces in which party competition takes place and the constellations of parties that can be found in these spaces. In this chapter we begin to look at party competition in greater detail, considering a number of matters that have to do with the motivations of political actors which are often either assumed away, or dealt with in a rather skimpy manner. We will be concerned with the motivations of politicians and in particular with the relative importance as motivating forces of the desire to get into office and the desire to affect public policy. We will also consider the time horizons of key decision-makers and the relative importance given by different parties to different dimensions of policy, the identity of key actors in the decision-making process, and the extent to which parties can rely on groups outside the legislature to help them fulfill their policy objectives. Our expert survey enables us to present detailed and party-specific empirical evidence on each of these important parameters of party competition.

The Motivations of Political Actors

The Tradeoff Between Office and Policy

It is by now conventional to classify the potential motivations of political actors as they compete with one another into one of two basic types. On one hand there is a desire for office in and for itself. On the other hand there is a desire to have an impact on public policy. As Laver and Schofield (1990) point out in an extensive review of this matter, these different motivational assumptions tend to generate quite different models of government formation.

One of the most striking differences between models concerns the role of the majority-winning criterion in accounts of government formation. If the desire to get into office at all costs is what drives politicians then governments will be "minimal winning", in the sense that they command a majority of the legislature but include no member whose legislative votes are not absolutely necessary. After all, if the government commands less than a legislative majority, then majority opposition parties who are hungry for power and nothing else should defeat the government and replace it. If the government contains parties whose legislative votes are not needed, then these "surplus" parties should be jettisoned, since they consume scarce rewards of office while contributing nothing to securing them.

If, on the other hand, what drives politicians is a desire to affect public policy, then it is clear that minority governments may survive, provided that they can satisfy the policy aspirations of the opposition. The policy motivations of politicians can be satisfied even if they never enter the government and it makes no difference to policy-motivated politicians *who* enacts the policies, just so long as they are enacted. Surplus majority governments are also be quite understandable on these assumptions since, if the rewards of office are not seen as a scarce resource, then it costs nothing to include a policy-compatible extra party in the government.

Typically, each analyst makes an assumption at the outset of a particular discussion, dealing with whether the fundamental motivating force of politicians is taken to be a desire to get into office in and for itself, or a desire to affect public policy. Subsequently discussion is heavily conditioned by this assumption, yet to our knowledge no systematic empirical evidence has been offered on its validity. As a result of our expert survey, however, we are now in a position to throw at least a little empirical light on it.

We approached the problem in two ways. Since party participation in government is typically defined in terms of party control over at least one cabinet portfolio, we need to know why politicians value cabinet portfolios. It may be that these are seen simply as rewards of office in and for themselves, intrinsically valued payoffs of the government formation game (the office-seeking motivation). Or it may be that they are seen as instrumentally necessary roles that must be filled in order to have an impact on public policy (the policy-seeking motivation). Accordingly we asked our experts, in relation to each country taken as a whole, whether cabinet portfolios are valued by politicians more as rewards of office or as the means to affect policy. The full data are reported in Appendix B and the mean scores for each country are reported in Table 4.1. A country in which political actors are concerned to the maximum possible extent with policy would score 1; a country where the actors are concerned to the maximum possible extent with office would score 9. (Obviously, there is little that we can do to check the face validity of these data. Since they deal with matters that our experts may not be used to assessing in quite these terms, readers may have less confidence in them than in our rankings of parties' ideological positions. Nonetheless, this unfamiliarity applies to all countries equally, and our main intention is to look at the *relative* positions of different countries, which we do feel to be valid.) Table 4.1 ranks countries in terms of the average score given by the relevant experts.

The patterns in Table 4.1 are quite clear-cut. The midpoint of the scale is 5,

Table 4.1 Cabinet portfolios as policy payoffs (1) or office payoffs (9).

Country	Mean Scores	Country	Mean Scores
Norway	2.75	Australia	5.81
Sweden	2.84	Portugal	5.86
Netherlands	3.20	Britain	5.94
Denmark	3.67	Belgium	6.00
Germany	4.53	Iceland	6.00
Finland	4.64	France	6.07
Spain	4.75	Austria	6.15
Luxembourg	5.00	Israel	6.44
New Zealand	5.00	Ireland	6.56
Canada	5.32	Japan	6.60
Malta	5.43	Italy	7.75
USA	5.47	Greece	8.00

from which we can see that politicians in the bulk of the countries studied were judged to value cabinet membership more as an end in itself than as a means to affect policy. The countries in which policy payoffs appear to be relatively more important can be neatly grouped—they comprise Scandinavia (minus Iceland), the Netherlands and Germany. (We should emphasise once more that experts only rated "their" countries, they did not rank order groups of countries.) The countries in which office payoffs appear to be most important are less easy to classify. They are Greece, Italy, Japan, Ireland, Israel, Austria, and France.

The suggested relationship between policy-seeking motivations and the incidence of minority and surplus majority government receives mixed support from Table 4.1. The European countries in which minority government is most common are Scandinavia (minus Iceland), Italy and Ireland (Laver and Schofield, 1990: 71). Minority government is relatively rare in the Netherlands and unheard-of in Germany. Thus, while the "Scandinavian syndrome" does juxtapose policy-seeking politicians and minority government, minority governments are also common in office-seeking Italy and Ireland and rare in policy-seeking Germany and the Netherlands. The vast bulk of European surplus majority governments can be found in policy-seeking Finland and the Netherlands, and in office-seeking Italy. Italy, therefore, appears as a significant deviant case. Experts judge Italy to have office-seeking politicians, which implies minimum winning coalitions. Yet Italy also has large numbers of minority and surplus-majority governments which we would be more inclined to expect in policy-seeking systems.

Obviously, characterising all politicians in a given system as having the same basic type of motivation is a very crude exercise. We went one stage further than this, therefore, and asked our experts to give separate scores to the leaders of each party in their countries on a twenty-point scale in terms of the following question: "Forced to make a choice, would party leaders give up policy objectives in order to get into government, or would they sacrifice a place in the government in order to maintain policy objectives?" The detailed results can be found in Appendix B. These are summarized in Table 4.2, which makes a distinction between parties taken to be interested above all in policy (with a score in the range 1.00–8.99), those taken to be interested above all in office (12.00–19.99), and those to be found in between, which appear to be balancing the two motivations (9.00–11.99).

As we might have expected, Table 4.2 shows that most countries have both office- and policy-seeking parties, though two (New Zealand and the USA) appear to have only parties that are judged to be interested above all else in office. What emerges quite clearly from a systematic review of the evidence summarized in Table 4.2, however, is that most of the key parties in the countries that we are considering are motivated primarily by the desire to get into office.

Looking beyond this broad picture, the single most pervasive pattern is for communist, left socialist, green and nationalist parties to be classified as being driven by policy-seeking motivations. Indeed, these types of party account for the vast bulk of those we can classify unambiguously in policy-seeking terms. Several communist parties are classified as balancing both motivations, however, notably those in Greece (KKE) and Italy (PCI), while the Icelandic equivalent of a communist party (PA) was classified as an office-seeking party.

Social democratic parties are the most frequent party type to be found among those balancing office- and policy-seeking motivations. The social democratic parties of Belgium (PS), Britain (Lab), Canada (ND), Germany (SPD), Malta (Lab), the Netherlands (PvdA) and Sweden (SD) fall into this category. However, most social democratic parties are classified as unambiguously office-seeking, including those of Australia (Lab), Austria (SPÖ), Denmark (SD), Finland (SDP), France (PS), Greece (Pasok), Iceland (SDP), Ireland (Lab), Israel (Lab), Italy (PSI), Luxembourg (LSAP), New Zealand (Lab) and Spain (PSOE).

Virtually all Christian democratic and secular conservative parties are classified as being driven by office-seeking motivations, with the exception of the small Protestant parties in the Netherlands and Norway, also the Liberals in Norway, the RPR and the UDF in France, and the Conservatives in Sweden.

Taken together, our estimates of the general importance of policy-seeking motivations in the system and our party-specific estimates of the willingness to trade off a place in the government against basic policy objectives, all suggest that the desire for office was judged by our experts to be a more fundamental motivation than the desire to affect public policy, at least among the mainstream parties of the countries that we are concerned with. However, as we have already argued, these data are more convincing when they are used to describe differences between countries than they are when used to make absolute judgments about the importance of policy in the group of countries taken as a whole.

It cannot be emphasised too strongly, furthermore, that to say politicians are motivated by the desire to get into office, in and for itself, is not for one minute

Table 4.2 The choice between office and policy: by party.[a]

	Parties interested most in policy (1.00–8.99)	Parties balancing office and policy (9.00–11.99)	Parties interested most in office (12.00–19.99)
Australia		Dem	Lab, Lib, Nat
Austria	KPÖ, G		FPÖ, ÖVP, SPÖ
Belgium	Aga, Eco, FB, PVV, BSP,VU	CVP, FDF, PRL, PS, PSC,	
Britain	PC, SNP	Lab	Con, Dem
Canada		ND	Con, Lib
Denmark	CC, DKP, FP, G, RF, SF, VS		CD, KF, KrF, RV, SD, V
Finland	DA, FDPL, G	FCL, P	A/C, FRP, KOK, LPP, SDP, SPP
France	FN, G, PCF	RPR, UDF	PS, MRG
Germany	G	NPD, SPD	CDU,FDP
Greece		KKE, KKEes	ND, Pasok
Iceland	WA		CP, IP, PA, PP, SDP
Ireland	DSP, SF, WP	FF, FG, Lab, PD	
Israel	Comm, Lib	Ag	Lab, Lik, NRP, Shas
Italy	DP, G, PR	PCI	DC, MSI, PLI, PRI, PSDI, PSI
Japan	Comm, SDF, Soc	CGP	DSP, LDP
Luxembourg	G, KPL		CSV, DP, LSAP
Malta		Lab	Nat
Netherlands	CPN, GPV, PPR, PSP, RPF, SGP	PvdA	CDA, D' 66, VVD
New Zealand			Dem, Lab, Nat
Norway	SF	DLF, FRP, KRF, SP, V	A, H
Portugal	G, PCP, PDC, PSR, UDP	DI, MDP	CDS, PRD, PSD, PSP
Spain	HB, IU, MUC		CDS, CIU, CP, EAJ, PRD, PSOE
Sweden	CDU, Comm, G	M, SD	CP, PP
USA			Dem, Rep

Note: Party abbreviations are elaborated in the appropriate country section in Appendix B.

to say that policy is unimportant. Rather, it is to say there is little evidence in these data to suggest that the fundamental motivating force for most politicians is an intrinsic desire to influence policy, even if this means giving up the chance of getting into office. What we can see quite clearly from data presented in this and the previous chapter is that many policy dimensions are held to be highly salient for party competition by many parties whose main concern appears to be to enjoy the benefits of getting into office. These data thus clearly suggest that the role of policy is often an instrumental means to an end, supporting the original Downsian assumption, stated so succinctly in Downs' original work, that "parties formulate policies in order to win elections, rather than win elections in order to formulate policies" (Downs, 1957: 28). This statement should be qualified by the finding that in Norway, Sweden, the Netherlands and Denmark in particular, the desire to influence public policy in and for itself seems to be a more important motivating factor than it is elsewhere.

Time Horizons

A second important feature of the motivations of political actors concerns how they feel about time. It is conventional to assume that economic actors put a lower value on future consumption than they do on present consumption. It is also conventional to assume that different actors have different preferences with regard to future consumption. Obviously, party competition is a continuous process. Elections are followed by government formations, which are followed by day-to-day legislative business, together with unanticipated shocks to the system that must be accommodated, which may followed by government resignations or defeats which may be followed by elections and so, *ad infinitum*. All of this takes time. Equally obvious, therefore, is the fact that the attitude of the various political actors to time, their "time preference" or "discount rate", is a vital strategic variable in party competition.

In bargaining over government formation, for example, it seems probable that actors who discount future benefits more steeply may be at a disadvantage relative to others, since they are less inclined to hang on in order to beat their opponents in a showdown. However, while one or two authors have had something to say about the implications of the sequence of electoral and legislative competition (Austen-Smith and Banks, 1988; Laver 1989), very little has been done to incorporate time preference into theories of party competition. Little if any empirical attention has been given, furthermore, to exploring attitudes to time among real political actors.

Accordingly, in a first exploration of this matter, we asked our experts to "assess how far into the future members of each section of each party look when making important decisions about the membership of the government." Respondents were offered a simple five point scale, running from "not at all" (scored 1) to "many years" (scored 5), and were asked to rate the attitudes to time of party leaders, party legislators and party activists. The results, for each section of each party in each country, are reported in Appendix B.

One or two general conclusions can be drawn from this preliminary empirical reconnaissance of the time horizons of party politicians. The first is that time horizons appear to be reasonably long—the modal response for most sections of most parties was "a few years". In other words, notwithstanding all of the cynical views that are so often held about the short term approach of many politicians, most of our experts regarded party politicians as calculating in a time scale longer than weeks or months when figuring party strategies on government formation.

In the second place, differences in time preference between different sections of the same party do not appear to be great, though it should be remembered that our scale was very crude. The vast bulk of respondents gave the same assessment for each section of the same party. Where there was a difference, such patterns as exist suggest that leaders and legislators have a slightly longer-term view than party activists. This is not at all a strong finding, however, and it does tend to conflict with a popular perception of party activists as being the people who are in politics for the long haul.

Differences in time horizon between different parties in the same country were sometimes quite large. In Italy, for example, the Communist Party (PCI) was judged to be calculating its government formation strategies in terms of substantial numbers of years, while some of the small parties in the long-standing five-party government coalition, the PSDI and PLI, for example, were judged to be calculating more in terms of weeks and months. In Greece, to take another example, the Communist Party (KKE) was judged to be taking a very long-term view of the government formation game, while the two main parties of government (Pasok and New Democracy) were, in contrast, judged to be operating in terms of a much shorter time scale. As a final example, the long-standing party of government in Japan, the Liberal Democrats, was judged to be calculating over a very much shorter time scale than all of the other Japanese parties.

Overall differences between systems were also quite noticeable. The Swedish parties, for example (particularly the Social Democrats and Conservatives, two main parties of government), were judged to be calculating over a much longer time-scale than the Italian parties. In the same way, Belgian politicians were generally judged to take a rather longer-term view than their opposite numbers in Portugal.

Despite the fact that there are some substantial differences between parties and between systems, however, the overall impression to be gained from looking at these data is that most politicians in most systems do take at least a medium-term view of the government formation game, calculating payoffs over a small number of years, not in weeks and months or in decades.

Of course, what we have done here is no more than to fire a ranging shot at the important problem of estimating the discount rates of politicians. We can, however, be reasonably confident from our findings that it is not justifiable to assume, along with many of the existing "myopic" theories of party competition, that politicians pay very little attention to the future. Our ranging shot suggests it is reasonable to assume that most politicians calculate their strategies at any time-point at least as far ahead as the next election and subsequent government formation. By the same token, our expert survey provides little evidence to suggest that most politicians are maximizing over a time scale of several elections, much less over an entire political career.

Beyond these very general statements it would be unwise to generalize, given the very blunt instrument at our disposal. Nonetheless, readers may care to experiment with some of the data that we present on this matter in Appendix B, exploring the impact that different views about the future might have on the business of party competition.

The Party-specific Salience of Policy Dimensions

While we looked at the general salience of policy dimensions in the previous chapter, when developing common spatial representations of party politics in different systems, we have so far said nothing of substance about the possibility that different political actors may have different views about the same policy dimensions. As we shall now see, if different actors do weight policy dimensions in different ways, then each will paint a different picture of the party constellations that characterise politics in each country.

Figure 4.1 shows a hypothetical two-dimensional party space in which three actors, A, B and C, all agree that each policy dimension is equally salient. In this particular example, the preferences of the actors are such that A is indifferent between the ideal points of B and C, B is indifferent between the ideal points of A and C, and C is indifferent between the ideal points of A and B. We have assumed in drawing this figure, in common with most others who have considered the matter, that politicians make "Euclidean" trade-offs between policy distance on one dimension and policy distance on another. We discussed in Chapter 1 the implications of assuming other types of trade-off (see especially Figure 1.4).In order to keep this discussion reasonably straightforward, however, we make the conventional assumption. This can be seen from the fact that the indifference curves drawn in Figure 4.1 are circular. The circle centred on A runs through B and C; the circle centred on B runs through A and C and so on. In Euclidean space, the actors appear to be equidistant from one another.

Imagine that, instead of weighting both dimensions equally, every one of the actors regards the vertical policy dimension as being more important than the horizontal one, and that all actors agree upon the relative importance of the two policy dimensions. In other words, imagine that the actors regarded the political impact of policy differences between actors on the vertical dimension as being more serious than the impact of policy differences on the horizontal dimension. Their indifference curves are no longer circles, but are shaped like ellipses, in such a way as to reflect the relative salience of the two dimensions. Remember, however, that the policy "spaces" that we have been using have no absolute meaning, that they are no more than representations of the relationships between the preferences of the various actors. These preferences are now represented by elliptically shaped indifference curves. Actors who share assessments of the

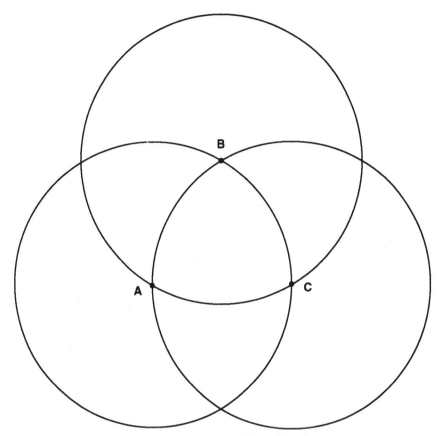

Figure 4.1 Three "equidistant" parties.

relative weighting of the policy dimensions will have indifference curves of the same basic shape.

In this case, the situation in which each of the actors is indifferent to the ideal points of the other two, for a particular agreed relative weight of the two dimensions, is shown in Figure 4.2. It appears that the actors tolerate "smaller" relative distances between points on the vertical dimension than they tolerate on the horizontal dimension. But "smaller" relative to what? There is a real sense in which, according to the indifference curves, the three actors in Figure 4.2 are *perceptually* equidistant, notwithstanding how they look on a sheet of paper. While A and C may seem further apart than A and B, for example, this is compensated by the fact that A and C have identical positions on the more important vertical dimension.

Since the space is a map of the actors' perceptions of the importance of things and nothing more, in what sense are the vertical distances "smaller" than the horizontal ones? They are smaller only with reference to the possibility that different actors assign *different* relative weights to the *same* set of dimensions.

Figure 4.3 illustrates this point. Actor A regards the vertical dimension as being more important than the horizontal dimension, and is thus prepared to tolerate smaller movements on it than actor B, who regards both dimensions as being equally important. Actor C regards the horizontal dimension as being more important than the vertical dimension, and is thus prepared to tolerate smaller movements on it than actor B. As the figure shows, as seen by B, actors A and C are equidistant—the distance BA equals the distance BC. As far as C is concerned, however, the distance CB is less than the distance CA. As far as A is concerned, AB is greater than AC. From this it is clear that the distance AB, the distance between A and B measured from the perspective of A, is different from the distance BA, the distance between A and B measured from the perspective of B. Each actor has a different spatial map of the party system. In this particular example, A and C may be seen as being equidistant from B, or A may be seen as being closer to B than is C, or C may be seen as being closer to B than is A, depending on which actor's viewpoint is taken.

The indifference curves drawn in Figure 4.3 assume that how an actor feels about the distance between two points on dimension X does not depend upon the coordinates of these points on dimension Y. Thus how an actor feels about the difference between an income tax rate of 25 percent and one of 35 percent, for example, is assumed in Figure 4.3 not to depend on the government's environmental policy. If, in contrast, an actor regards the same difference in tax rates as being less serious if the government is pro-environment than it is if the government is anti-environment, then the actor's indifference curves take a different shape.

When evaluations of distances on one dimension are independent of positions on another, then the actors' preferences are described as "separable" and the indifference curves are as in Figure 4.3. They are circles, or ellipses whose axes are parallel to the policy dimensions that form the basis of the space. When evaluations of distances on one dimension do depend upon positions on another dimension, then actors' preferences are described as "non-separable". Examples of non-separable Euclidean indifference curves can be seen in Figure 4.4. These are the elipses whose axes are rotated in relation to the basis dimensions.

It should be clear from this that to use a single spatial map of a given party

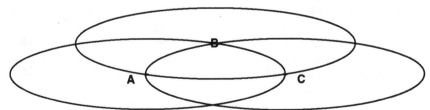

Figure 4.2 "Equidistant" parties agree on the relative salience of two dimensions.

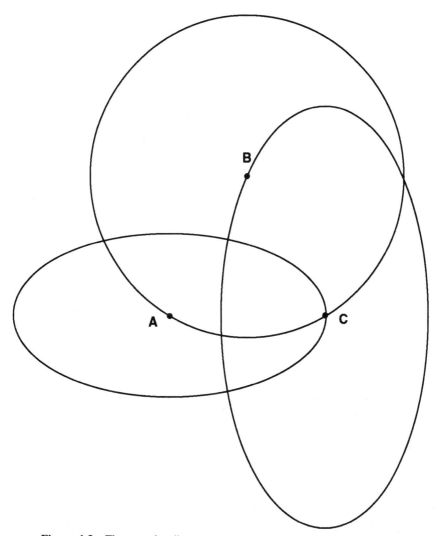

Figure 4.3 Three parties disagree on relative salience of two dimensions.

system, and to measure distances on this map using indifference curves of the same shape for every party, is to risk a very considerable loss of information. One possible solution is to use a different spatial map for each actor. This would be a very cumbersome solution to the problem, however. It is more usual, to the extent that the possibility that different actors might weight the same dimensions in different ways is considered at all, to use a single spatial map of the party system and to concentrate upon the different types of indifference curve that may apply to different types of actor, along the lines of Figures 4.3 or 4.4.

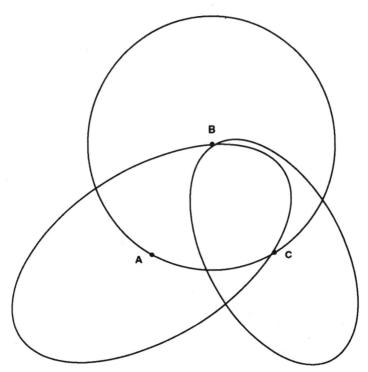

Figure 4.4 Non-separable indifference curves.

Differential assessments of the weights of the same set of policy dimensions can obviously make a huge difference to party competition. The most extreme form of this arises when one actor weights a first dimension very highly and a second not at all, while another actor weights the second dimension very highly and the first dimension not at all. In this case, the two actors might even feel there is no difference between them in policy terms. One actor pays no attention to differences on one dimension, the other pays no attention to differences on the other dimension. To all intents and purposes, they are at the same place, despite the fact that actors who gave both dimensions some weight would see them as being quite far apart. Such a structure of preference forms the basis of the classic "logrolling" deal, whereby actor A agrees to accept the ideal policy of actor B on one dimension, in exchange for actor B's agreement to accept the ideal policy of actor A on another dimension.

A much less extreme set of assumptions about separable preferences is portrayed in Figure 4.5. Actor A rates the horizontal dimension as being about three times more important than the vertical dimension, while actor B rates the vertical dimension as being just very slightly more important than the horizontal dimension. Consider how these actors might compare two policy points, X and Y. If an independent observer C rates both dimensions as being equally important, then C will view X as being exactly halfway between A and B, the point at which both A and B split their differences on both policy dimensions. Since actor A cares much less about the vertical dimension than the horizontal dimension, however, both A and B in fact agree that they prefer point Y to point X, as can be seen from the intersection of their indifference curves through X. Note that point Y is a logrolling point, which gives A its ideal policy on the dimension on which it feels most strongly, and actor B its ideal policy on the other dimension, about which it feels very slightly more strongly. In other words, a logrolling point may be preferred to a "split-the-difference" compromise even by actors who do not concern themselves exclusively with a single dimension of policy.

As our expert survey shows, such structures of preference are quite common in the real world. For example, Table 4.3 gives information on party positions and saliency weights for a number of Dutch parties, the PvdA, CDA and RPF, on the taxation and religious dimensions. Superficially, the policy of the procleri-

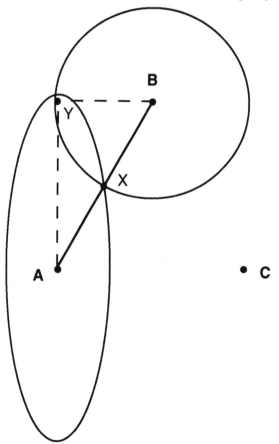

Figure 4.5 Logrolling between two parties.

cal and moderately right-wing Christian Democrats (CDA) might seem to be a compromise between the moderately left-wing and anticlerical social democrats (PvdA) and the right-wing and intensely proclerical RPF. However, the overwhelming relative concern of the PvdA for tax policy rather than religious policy, in conjunction with the overwhelming concern of the RPF for religious policy rather than tax policy, means that there is quite a large area of the policy space that both of these parties prefer to the ideal policy of the CDA. Indeed, as Figure 4.6 shows, the data indicate that PvdA and RPF might prefer a logrolling deal, whereby both parties got their ideal policy on the dimensions about which they care most, to the "compromise" position of the CDA.

The saliency weighting of each dimension by each party in each system is given in Appendix B, and can be used to calculate the relative weightings of dimensions, along the lines of the example in Table 4.3 and Figure 4.6, for any particular application in which the reader is interested.

These data are difficult to summarize, given the vast number of pair-wise comparisons that are pertinent, but one important conclusion emerges very firmly from even a casual perusal of the numbers reported in Appendix B. This is that our experts systematically told us that different parties do indeed attach different weights to the same policy dimensions. The differences in relative weights were rarely as great as those noted in Table 4.3 for the taxation and religious dimensions in the Netherlands; however, comparing a pair of dimensions for a pair of parties, differences in weighting of the order of magnitude of 2:1 in either direction were not uncommon. This is a very important general conclusion from our empirical analysis. It suggests strongly that the relative weighting of policy dimensions should not be ignored, either by theorists of party competition or by empirical analysts. This is a theme to which we will return in the next chapter, in our discussion of government formation.

The Identity of the Decision Makers

It has been customary, until recently, for most theorists of party competition to treat political parties as if they were unitary actors. Empirical specialists in the politics of any particular country, of course, have always found this assumption particularly hard to swallow. Laver and Schofield (1990) have recently reviewed

Table 4.3 Selected party positions and saliency weights in the Netherlands.

Party	Policy position Taxes	Religious	Saliency weight Taxes	Religious	Relative weight Taxes: religious
PvdA	5.8	7.3	15.1	6.0	2.5:1
CDA	13.6	15.4	18.8	12.7	1.1:1
RPF	16.2	19.7	7.9	18.6	0.4:1

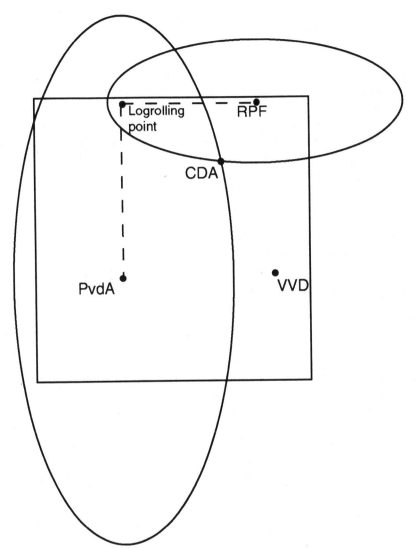

Figure 4.6 Differential saliency weights in the Netherlands.

this problem in relation to theories of government formation, while Laver and Shepsle (1990b) have presented an approach to analyzing government formation that takes account of factions within parties. What is clear from these discussions is that one of the main difficulties confronting any attempt to reconcile analyses of politics within parties with analyses of politics between parties is, as is so often the case, a lack of systematic data.

One of reasons why it is important to know precisely who is taking strategic decisions within political parties is that different sections of the same party may well have different types of motivation. In particular, party leaders, who stand to win those coveted seats at the cabinet table, may have different motivations from party legislators, who may be more concerned with the possibility of losing their seats in parliament, and from party activists, who cannot so easily consume any office payoffs and whose main motivation may be to promote particular policy objectives. Faced with the need to make policy concessions in order to get into government, leaders may be inclined to give a little more while activists may see themselves as being sold out by party bosses as a consequence. Accordingly, we asked our experts about the influence that the leaders, the legislators and the activists of each party in each system have over the formation of party policy, and over decisions about participation in government. The detailed results can be found in Appendix B. These are summarised in Tables 4.4 and 4.5, and the main patterns are quite straightforward.

Table 4.4 shows which of the three sections of the party was judged to have the greatest influence over the formation of party policy, for each party in each country in the study. Clearly, it is party leaders, rather than legislators or activists, who are judged to have the most influence. The only systematic exception to this rule involves Green parties. Many of these Green parties are decidedly anti-hierarchical in their organisational style, and party activists, rather than party leaders or legislators, usually seem to have the decisive say in party policy. Some of the "new left" parties also fit this pattern, including, for example, the Left Socialists in Denmark and Norway, and the Womens' Alliance in Iceland. Note also the very untypical position of the USA parties, in which our experts judged legislators to have the greatest say over policy, a situation with very few parallels elsewhere.

Overall, our results suggest very strongly that we should concentrate upon party leaders when looking at strategic decisions relating to the role of policy in party competition. This is not, of course, to say that the policy preferences of other sections of the party, and of voters in general, are unimportant in party competition. Rather, it is to say that it is the party leaders who are the actors with the power to take strategic decisions on the setting of party policy.

Table 4.5 shows that the position is even more clear cut when we consider strategic decisions over participation in government. With the exception of the Green parties and one or two others, virtually all such decisions are taken by party leaders, rather than legislators or activists. (This problem is not relevant in the USA, of course, which does not have a parliamentary government system.) Once more, decision making in the Green parties is more decentralized, with either activists or legislators taking key decisions on government participation.

There has been some discussion of the unitary actor status of political parties with respect to coalition bargaining. This is reviewed by Laver and Schofield (1990), who conclude that, as far as government formation is concerned, the assumption that party leaders control strategy is not unreasonable. The empirical findings reported here support and extend this conclusion. They suggest that mainstream coalition theories have not gone too far wrong in assuming that a

Table 4.4 Section of party having most influence over the formation of party policy.

	Activists	*Legislators*	*Leaders*
Australia	Dem		Rest
Austria	G		Rest
Belgium	Aga, Eco		Rest
Britain	PC, SNP		Rest
Canada			All
Denmark	G, RF, SF, VS	KrF	CC, CD, DKP, FP, KF, RV, SD, V
Finland	G		Rest
France	G	MRG, UDF	FN, PCF, PS, RPR
Germany	G		Rest
Greece			All
Iceland	WA		Rest
Ireland		Lab	Rest
Israel			All
Italy	G		Rest*
Japan			All
Luxembourg	G		Rest
Malta			All
Netherlands	CPN, PPR, PSP, PvdA		Rest
New Zealand			All
Norway	SF, V	SP	A, DLF, FRP, H, KrF,
Portugal	G		Rest
Spain	EAJ, HB	PRD	CDS, CIU, CP, IU, MUC, PSOE
Sweden	G		Rest
USA		All	

*For the PLI, PRI, PSDI, both leaders and legislators were estimated to have more or less equal influence.

single "actor" determines party strategy in the government formation game, and imply that this conclusion might be extended to other features of party politics, such as electoral competition.

It is worth reiterating strongly in this context, however, that this conclusion does not imply that the preferences of the other actors are not relevant to party competition. Thus parties must win votes in elections, and the preferences of voters are obviously relevant to this. Parties must rely on activists to mobilise their vote, and the preferences of activists are relevant to this. Leaders must face continual challenges to their position, and the preferences of all sections of the party with some influence over the leadership selection process are relevent to this. But what does seem to emerge quite strongly from our empirical findings is that it is parties' leaders who take this complex structure of party preferences into account and set party strategy accordingly. While a party does not have a single set of preferences, it may often function as a unitary actor in terms of its dealings with the outside world.

Table 4.5 Section of party having most influence over participation in government.

	Activists	Legislators	Leaders
Australia			All
Austria		G	Rest
Belgium			All
Britain			All
Canada			All
Denmark	G	SF, VS	CC, CD, DKP, FP, KF, KrF, RF, RV, SD, V
Finland		G	rest
France	G		Rest
Germany		G	Rest
Greece			All
Iceland	WA		Rest
Ireland			All
Israel			All
Italy			All
Japan			All
Luxembourg	G		Rest
Malta			All
Netherlands	CPN, PPR, PSP	PvdA	CDA, D' 66, GPV, RPF, SGP, VVD
New Zealand			All
Norway		SF	Rest
Portugal	G		Rest
Spain			All
Sweden		G	Rest

Note: Does not apply to USA.

Before we finish our discussion of the identity of the key actors in party competition, we must consider one other possibility, which is that actors outside the formal party system can also have an important impact. This matter is considered by Gregory Luebbert (1986), particularly in relation to the more corporatist decision-making regimes to be found in Scandinavia, for example. Luebbert's argument is that, in these systems, parties may well be associated with powerful interest groups, and that these interest groups are used to realize party policy objectives through the system of corporatist decision-making. He suggests this as an explanation for the frequency of minority government in Scandinavia, on the grounds that parties do not need to get into government in order to fulfill policy objectives—rather, they can fulfill these objectives from a position on the opposition benches, using their associated interest groups to exert political muscle.

Luebbert offered little systematic empirical evidence on this possibility. Accordingly, we asked our experts "how much can party leaders use groups outside the legislature to put pressure on other parties?." The full results, for each party in each country studied, can be found in Appendix B, and are summarised in

Table 4.6. This confirms Luebbert's assertion that Scandinavian parties can often rely on outside groups to apply pressure for them. Most of the important parties in Denmark, Finland, Iceland, Norway and Sweden are judged by our experts to be able to rely on group pressure. The table also confirms Luebbert's implicit contrast between Scandinavia and the more pluralist Anglo-American decision-making systems. Our experts suggested that no party can rely much on outside groups to apply pressure on other parties in Britain, Canada or the USA. In general, however, the European norm seems to be that quite a few parties can rely upon outside groups to do at least some of their dirty work, a finding that applies to countries, such as Greece or Italy, not typically thought of as being characterized by corporatist decision-making systems.

Luebbert's claim is that the ability of outside groups to affect policy outputs undermines the majority-winning criterion. This is because policy-oriented opposition parties can have an impact on policy, whether or not they are at the cabinet table. As Laver and Schofield (1990) point out, this should result in predictions not only of minority governments in these circumstances, but also of surplus majority governments, in which parties which are not necessary for a legislative majority are

Table 4.6 Parties able to use outside groups to apply pressure.
(1.00–8.99 on a scale of 1–20)

Country	Parties
Australia	Lab, Lib, Nat
Austria	G, ÖVP, SPÖ
Belgium	CVP, PRL, PS, PSC, PVV, BSP
Britain	None
Canada	None
Denmark	DKP, KF, SD, SF, V, VS
Finland	A/C, DA, FDPL, G, KOK, SDP
France	PCF
Germany	SPD
Greece	KKE, ND, Pasok
Iceland	IP, PA, PP
Ireland	FF
Israel	Ag, Lab, Lib, Lik, NRP
Italy	DC, DP, G, PCI, PLI, PR, PRI, PSDI, PSI
Japan	CGP, Comm, DSP, Soc
Luxembourg	CSV, LSAP
Malta	Lab
Netherlands	CDA, PvdA, VVD
New Zealand	Lab, Nat
Norway	A, H, KRF, SP
Portugal	PCP, PSP
Spain	CIU, CP, EAJ, HB, IU
Sweden	CP, M, SD
USA	None

included in the cabinet. Both are manifestations of a bargaining environment in which government membership is not the only way to fulfill policy objectives. Table 4.7 thus arranges the countries in our study according to how they were classified by a combination of the two relevant criteria, policy motivation and the importance of extra-parliamentary groups on policy-making. It also shows, for those countries considered by Laver and Schofield, the proportion of all governments that are either minority or surplus majority administrations.

The clustering of countries in Table 4.7 is quite striking. The combination of the two factors, policy orientation and an important role for extra-parliamentary groups, seems to identify a set of countries, essentially Scandinavia minus Iceland plus the Netherlands, in which either minority or surplus-majority governments are common. The main exceptions are office-oriented Italy and Ireland, in which minority and/or surplus governments are important, but which are classified as office-oriented systems in which the application of the minimum winning criterion ought to be more appropriate.

Conclusion

In this chapter we have taken tentative first steps towards estimating several parameters of party competition suggested as important by various theorists. In attempting to assess the validity of these estimates we are brought face to face with both the costs and the benefits of the expert survey as an empirical technique. On the benefit side, there can be no doubt that the expert survey is almost the only way to make progress towards some direct empirical judgment about even

Table 4.7 Policy orientation and the importance of extra-parliamentary groups.

Importance	*Policy oriented*	*Office oriented*
Extra-parliamentary groups important	Denmark Finland Netherlands Norway Sweden	Australia Austria Belgium Greece Iceland Israel Italy Luxembourg
Extra-parliamentary groups not important	Germany Spain	Britain Canada France Ireland Japan Malta Portugal

Note: Does not apply to USA.

the order of magnitude of the relevant parameters. Matters such as the trade-off between office and policy, the time horizons of the actors, or party-specific weightings of particular policy dimensions are clearly central to theoretical accounts of party competition, yet cannot easily be investigated by other means.

Yet this is a two-edged sword since, in the absence of other estimates, it is also difficult to assess the validity of our findings. In assessing the validity of our estimates of party policy positions, we were at least able to refer to a range of other estimates of left-right scale positions in many of the countries being studied. In assessing the validity of the parameters estimated in this chapter, we can rely only on received wisdoms. In the light of these received wisdoms, however, our results are for the most part plausible.

Politicians in Scandinavia are judged to be more policy-oriented than those elsewhere, for example. What is more, it should be remembered that each of our experts gave judgments only for a single country. This means that experts locating Scandinavian politicians on the scale relating to policy orientations had no idea of how other experts had located politicians in other countries. They were thus unable to contrive to make Scandinavian politicians appear to be more policy-oriented than others. Among the various types of party, Green parties, Communist and left socialist parties are judged to be more policy-oriented—others were judged to be more office-oriented, with the social democrats placed somewhere in between.

The estimates of party-specific dimension weightings are similarly hard to validate against other research, though they do suggest that these differential weights should be taken very seriously. The focus of strategic decision-making in each party is another important matter on which our experts made systematic judgments. Here, the clear evidence is in favor of viewing party leaders as the most important decision-makers. This suggests that unitary actor approaches to decision-making have not been as far away from the truth as some have suggested, though we must remember that party leaders must obviously take the preferences of other sections of the party into account when making their decisions.

Overall, the estimates we have presented in this chapter are derived on the basis of some very blunt instruments. Whether or not a particular analyst will feel that blunt instruments are better than no instruments at all is very much a matter of taste. If we have shown nothing else, however, we have shown that these important parameters are judged by those who ought to know about these things to vary in a noticeable and potentially very relevant way from country to country and from party to party. This suggests that people ought, at the very least, to explore the effect on accounts of party competition of varying some of these parameters. We attempt to do just this in the following chapter, which sets out to pull together a range of our empirical conclusions in relation to one aspect of the theory of party competition, the formation of cabinets in parliamentary democracies.

5

Party Policy and Government Formation

In this chapter we put some of the data that we outlined in the previous two chapters to work. We do this by elaborating a series of models that deal with the formation of governments, which we take to be one of the key political processes in the entire cycle of party competition.

Quite a few policy-based models of government formation have been developed in recent years, though most of these have been only partially elaborated in empirical terms because of a lack of systematic and comprehensive data. Such data shortages have taken three forms. First, data has not been available on a number of countries in which models of government formation could usefully be elaborated. In particular, the southern European countries of Portugal, Spain, Greece and Malta are rarely considered. In the case of the first three of these, this is probably because none was a parliamentary democracy during the period when these models were first developed, in the 1960s and early 1970s. Second, even in those countries for which data are available, party policy positions are often expressed only in terms of a single dimension of ideology. Until very recently, multidimensional data on party policy positions have been very hard to come by. Third, certain data have not been available for any country. These include estimates of party-specific saliency weightings for different ideological dimensions, trade-offs between office and policy and so on. Since our expert survey has allowed us to estimate many of these parameters, we are now in a position to present a more complete empirical elaboration of these models than has hitherto been attempted.

The approaches to the analysis of government formation that we consider converge on the same prediction in one particular circumstance. When a single party controls a legislative majority, all models predict the formation of a single-party majority government. Accordingly, we do not consider such cases. Since we can only be confident about our estimates of party policy for the period around early 1989, when our survey was conducted, we elaborate the various models of government formation in terms of the accounts that they provide for the governments in place as of 1 January 1989. This means that we did not look at government formation in Australia, Britain, Canada, Greece, Japan, Malta, New Zealand, Portugal, Spain and the USA. In each of these countries, a single party won a legislative majority in the election immediately preceding 1 January 1989. In each case, a single-party majority government was formed after the election (though in the USA it did so for reasons that had nothing to do with the institutions of parliamentary government). All theories could of course be credited with a series of successes as a result of these events, but this does not seem to be a very sensible method of proceeding. We are interested, after all, in the relative success of different approaches, in cases that distinguish between the various theories. Accordingly, we concentrate in our empirical elaborations upon government formation in the twelve countries in our study for which no party won an overall legislative majority in the preceding election—Austria, Belgium, Denmark, Finland, Germany, Iceland, Ireland, Italy, Luxembourg, the Netherlands, Norway and Sweden.[1]

We have deliberately restricted our elaboration to the time period for which we feel confident in our data. We could have dramatically extended the number of cases under consideration by looking at the formation of earlier governments, but we could not be confident that our data was valid for these time periods, since we have no real idea of how volatile the relevant parameters are. (The saliency of policy dimensions, for example, might plausibly change quite quickly. Impressionistically, at least, the environmental dimension has become salient for many parties over quite a short time period.)

In the next section we briefly describe the models of government formation that we consider in this chapter. (A more detailed exposition of all but the last of these is given by Laver and Schofield, 1990; a more detailed exposition of the last is given by Laver and Shepsle, 1990a, b.) We then use our data to elaborate the models, in order to see which can best account for the governments that actually formed, given the range of governments that possibly could have formed.

The Models

We consider several different models of policy-based government formation. While we do not of course claim to review every model of government formation that takes account of party policy, we do deal with models that illustrate a range

---

[1]We excluded Israel from the analysis, not because there is a single majority party, but because the complexity of the Israeli party system, in particular the very large number of tiny parties, made it necessary for us to group certain sets of parties (for example "liberals") before we could administer the questionnaire. This is appropriate for certian types of analysis but, given the very finely balanced arithmetic of coalition formation in Israel, means that the Israeli data are not very useful in this particular context. France was excluded for the rather different reason that its constitutional arrangements, which give the President very considerable power over the process of government formation and maintenance, take it beyond the scope of the theories with which we are concerned.

of different ways of conceptualizing the role of policy in cabinet government, ranging from the early theories of Axelrod, Leiserson and De Swaan to more recent work by Schofield, by Laver and Shepsle, and by Austen-Smith and Banks. The former models were in effect rather basic modifications to earlier coalition theories that took no account whatsoever of policy. More recent approaches are based much more fundamentally in a concern for the role of party policy.

Early Policy-Driven Models: Axelrod, Leiserson and De Swaan

Three early accounts of the government formation process that considered party policy were produced by Robert Axelrod, Michael Leiserson and Abram De Swaan (Axelrod, 1970; De Swaan, 1973; Leiserson, 1966). Axelrod was concerned with the "conflict of interest" within a potential coalition, and conceived such conflict in terms of the degree of incompatibility between the policy programs of different coalition members. In practice he did this by describing the policy programs of different actors in terms of a single left-right dimension of ideology. Conflict between actors was described simply in terms of whether actors were, or were not, adjacent to each other on this dimension. The lowest levels of internal conflict of interest were assumed to be found in coalitions in which members were adjacent to each other (or "connected") on the left-right dimension. Higher levels of conflict were assumed to be found in coalitions in which the members were not adjacent to each other.

Axelrod used a majority-winning criterion in his approach, predicting only coalitions that controlled a legislative majority, although, as we have seen, this is not strictly necessary for a theory concerned above all else with the role of party policy. Thus he constructed what became known as the "minimal connected winning" (MCW) theory. This predicts that government coalitions will be both winning, in the sense of controlling a majority in the legislature, and connected, in the sense of containing only parties adjacent to each other on the left-right scale. Minimal connected winning coalitions are thus a subset of the set of minimal winning coalitions, being minimal winning coalitions between ideologically adjacent parties.

For obvious reasons, the notion of "connectedness" loses much of its meaning for policy spaces of more than one dimension. Conceivably, there may be coalitions whose members are adjacent to each other on all relevant policy dimensions. It is often the case, however, that the configuration of parties is such that no winning coalition is possible that satisfies this quite difficult condition. In subsequent tables, we look for winning coalitions that are connected on all policy dimensions with above average salience, though it must be said that Axelrod's approach is almost never applied to multidimensional examples, and there are only four potential multidimensionally connected winning coalitions in the twelve country scenarios that we investigate.

Just because two parties are adjacent to each other on a policy dimension, of course, does not mean that they are close together in policy terms. Conversely, parties that do share similar policies may not be adjacent to each other on a policy dimension. Accordingly, Leiserson developed an account of government formation that takes account of the actual *positions* of the parties on the left-right policy dimension, rather than the *ordering* of parties on this dimension. He developed what became known as the "minimal range" theory, which predicted the formation of the minimal winning coalition with the smallest ideological range between the positions of its most extreme members (Leiserson, 1966).

De Swaan tested a number of different policy-based coalition theories in 1973, and found that an approach combining the ideas of Axelrod and Leiserson, the "closed minimal range" theory, performed much better than either theory on its own, or indeed than any other theory. The closed minimal range coalition in a particular bargaining situation is the minimal connected winning coalition with the smallest policy distance between its most "extreme" members. For the same reasons as for Axelrod's theory, it is not necessarily straightforward to generalize the minimal range approach to multidimensional policy spaces.

In the empirical elaborations that follow, we explore the approaches of both Axelrod and De Swaan, using our experts' assessments of party positions on the manifestation of the left-right dimension that was rated as most salient across the board. This was, as we have seen, the dimension contrasting high taxation and public services, on one hand, with low taxation and public services, on the other. We list all majority coalitions that contain only parties adjacent to each other on this policy dimension, and which can lose no member without ceasing to be either winning or "connected" (MCWs). We also identify the coalition in this category for which the policy distance between the two extreme members is the smallest (MRCWs). For multidimensional applications, we repeat this exercise for all policy dimensions rated by our experts as having above average salience.

An Inductive Clustering Model: Grofman

For some time, uni-dimensional models of coalition formation such as those outlined above tended to dominate the literature on government formation. In recent years, however, there has been increasing concern to interpret party competition in multidimensional policy spaces and this clearly called for an alternative approach to the analysis of government formation. Bernard Grofman has developed one such model, which is in principle capable of being used in policy spaces of any number of dimensions, though in practice he elaborated it using two-dimensional data.

Grofman built his model on the assumption that "each actor looks to form a protocoalition of himself and the actor nearest to him in N-space" (Grofman, 1982). He further assumed that once parties have joined a coalition, they cannot leave it. In other words, the government formation process is assumed to begin with a set of totally discrete parties. At the first stage, the two "closest" parties combine into a single protocoalition. At the second stage, the two parties and/or protocoalitions that are now the closest combine. And the process continues until a protocoalition forms that also satisfies some criterion for a viable government. As Laver and Schofield (1990: 138) point out, this makes the Grofman approach very close to a hierarchical clustering model of coalition building. Parties cluster into compact protocoalitions until some formation criterion (in Grofman's case, the familiar majority-winning criterion) is satisfied. For Grofman, the predicted coalition is the first majority cluster to arise as a result of this process.

While Grofman "tested" this model in a few countries for which he could get two-dimensional data, we use our set of experts' judgments to elaborate the model in all relevant countries using all policy dimensions determined by our experts to have above average salience (there were typically between four and six of these). We generate a prediction about the party membership of the government by using a cluster analysis, in which, as implicitly specified by Grofman, the measure of distance between parties is the Euclidean distance between party ideal points in the policy space selected. Although Grofman does not consider this matter, there are various ways for measuring the distance between two groups of points. The distance between all pairs of points, such that one point is in each group, can be taken. The distance between groups can be taken as the shortest such distance—or it can be taken as the longest. An alternative is to take the average of all such distances, a technique known as the "average linkage" method. A further possibility is to take the distance between group centroids. In what follows, we use the average linkage method, which takes account of all distances between pairs of points in different clusters. We do this because we assume that, while a protocoalition may function in some respects as a single unit, the individual members of the protocoalition continue to evaluate the alternatives as distinct individuals. We assume in effect that a coalition has no collective brain (Laver and Budge, 1992).

While Grofman assumes that all protocoalitions forming along the road to the final outcome are subsequently indivisible, and while we elaborate this "hierarchical" model of government-formation, we also explore an alternative possibility. This is that parties are able to use their rational foresight to anticipate the outcome of the government formation process. Specifically they will not include actors as part of the coalition-building process whose roles they can anticipate as being ultimately surplus to requirements. This means that parties which will be surplus to the legislative majority of the coalition that eventually forms do not enter the protocoalitions that mark the progress towards the final government.

An example of this general approach can be seen in Figure 5.1, which illustrates a potential process of protocoalition formation in the Netherlands after the legislative election of 21 May 1986. Four dimensions had above average overall salience in the Netherlands—the taxation, social policy, foreign affairs and environmental dimensions. Euclidean distances between party policy positions in this four-dimensional space were computed and the average linkage hierarchical clustering method applied.[2] Figure 5.1 describes the results of this analysis in the form of

---

[2]The cluster analyses were performed on a Macintosh SE using the cluster routines in the Systat 5.0 statistical package.

a tree diagram, or dendrogram. On the left hand side of the figure are the party labels and seat totals—a legislative majority requires 76 seats. The branches on the right-hand side of the figure show the clustering process. First, the new left (PPR and PSP) and the fundamentalist Protestant (RPF, SGP, GPV) parties form separate protocoalitions. The religious protocoalition is then joined by the Christian Democrats (CDA). At this stage, it is still the case that no protocoalition commands a legislative majority. Next, the Liberals (VVD) join the Christian protocoalition—the coalition that results does command a legislative majority and the relevant node is marked with a black dot on the dendrogram. This is, in effect, the Grofman prediction.

We might assume, however, that parties can anticipate this process and will not include, as part of the process of hierarchical coalition building, the small fundamentalist Protestant parties whose votes will not eventually be needed for the eventual government majority. This results in a prediction that the government which emerges will be a CDA-VVD coalition, and this is in fact the government which formed.

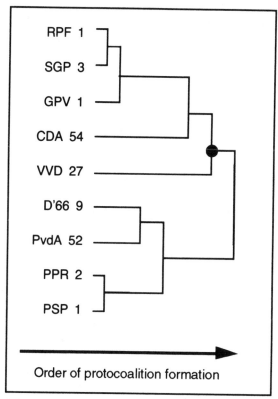

Figure 5.1 Cluster-based model of government formation in the Netherlands.

Government Formation as a Cooperative Game: Schofield

While Grofman's account of coalition formation is largely based upon an inductive generalization about what he assumes to be the strategies of politicians in coalition negotiations, Schofield has developed an account of coalition formation in multidimensional policy spaces that is based firmly within the traditions of deductive cooperative game theory. (For recent summaries of this work, see Laver and Schofield, 1990; Schofield, 1990.)

When only one dimension of ideology is salient, according to this general approach, the median legislator is boss. The party controlling the median legislator cannot rationally be defeated by its opponents, since all parties to the right of it prefer the policies of the median legislator to any policy that is more left-wing, while all parties to the left of it prefer the policies of the median legislator to any policy that is more right-wing. Since those to the left of the median legislator must be in a legislative minority, as must those to the right, it follows that there is no policy that a majority of the legislature prefers to that of the median legislator. If only one dimension of policy is salient, the median legislator is at what is described as the "core" of the government formation game. Ignoring the possibility that parties controlling exactly 50 percent of legislators are on the left of the scale, leaving parties controlling exactly 50 percent of legislators on the right, there is always a median legislator. Thus, in a one dimensional system, there is always a party controlling the median legislator, and this party should always control the government.

When more than one dimension of policy is salient and all legislators behave as undisciplined individuals, then McKelvey's famous "chaos" theorem proves that, except in very special circumstances, any point in the space is such that another point can be found that is preferred to it by a majority of the actors (McKelvey, 1976). This point can in turn be beaten by another point and so on, *ad infinitum*. There is no core, no equilibrium outcome. Coalition formation is predicted to be chaotic and unstable.

Schofield has subsequently shown that, if party discipline binds legislators together into unequal-sized units so that government formation is a weighted voting game, then the largest party can sometimes occupy a core position in a two dimensional party system. This is not necessarily the case even in a two dimensional system, and it is never the case in a three- or more dimensional system (Schofield, 1990). Consider Figure 5.2, for example, in which parties A, B and C control twenty seats each, while party D controls forty seats. The policy position of party D can be beaten by a policy at P, the midpoint of the line BC, and preferred to D by A, B, and C. That in turn could be beaten by a point Q, close to D on the line BD, preferred to P by B and D. That in turn could be beaten by point D, preferred to Q by C and D, and so the cycle continues. Once more, in this example there is no core, no equilibrium outcome. Bargaining is predicted to be chaotic and unstable.

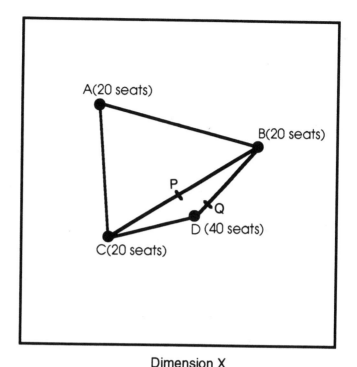

Figure 5.2 A four party system with no core.

If party D is moved slightly, however, so that it lies inside the triangle ABC, then it is in a much more powerful position. This is shown in Figure 5.3. The triangle ABC defines the "Pareto set" of the parties A, B and C, which make up the only majority coalition that excludes D. The Pareto set of a group of parties is the set of points such that it is not possible to move from any point in the set without making at least one of the parties worse off. In Figure 5.2, point D is outside the Pareto set of A, B, and C—thus at least one point, for example P, can be found such that A, B, and C all prefer P to D. In Figure 5.3, in contrast, D is in the Pareto set of A, B and C, which between them are a majority coalition. Thus A, B and C, the only majority coalition that excludes D, cannot agree on any single point that they all prefer to D, and this is the key to D's power. If the ideal point of Party D were to be the status quo, then no majority coalition could find any point preferred to D by all members. This should mean that D is in equilibrium. Schofield termed such a party a "core party". McKelvey and Schofield proved that, in two dimensions, only the largest party can be a core party (Schofield, 1986; McKelvey, 1987; see Laver and Schofield 1990 for a nontechnical exposition).

Identifying a core party in a two-dimensional system is thus straightforward. It is sufficient to check if the largest party has an ideal point that is in the Pareto

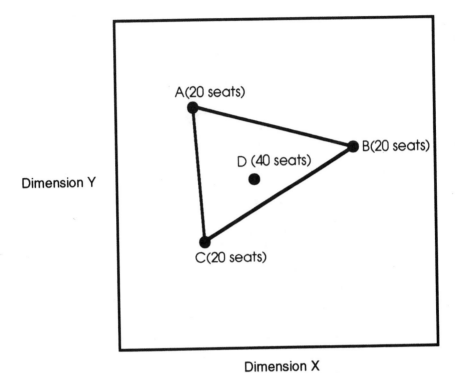

Figure 5.3 A four party system with a core party.

set of every majority coalition. Conversely, if there is a ideal point of the majority coalition such that the largest party is outside the Pareto set of the coalition, then the largest party is not a core party and, for a two-dimensional game, there can be no core party.

Figure 5.4 shows the relevant configuration of parties in Sweden, giving each party's position in a two-dimensional policy space, together with its number of seats in the legislature. We can see from this configuration why it is that the Social Democrats can be considered to be a core party in Sweden. The only winning coalition that excludes the Social Democrats must include all other parties. The ideal point of the Social Democrats lies in the Pareto set of the other parties, shown by the polygon in Figure 5.4.

We also note from Figure 5.4, however, that rather small changes in the ideal point of the Social Democrats (in a northwesterly, or southeasterly direction, for example) could destroy the party's core position by placing it outside the Pareto set of an opposing majority coalition. A small move by either the Communists or the Moderate Unity Party (M) would have the same effect. This potential instability is a product of the particular empirical configuration of the parties in the two dimensional policy space that we are using—and is a very clear-cut example of the complex issues raised by the dimensionality of policy spaces, reviewed in earlier chapters. As can be seen from the two-dimensional figures in the data appendix, many of the policy spaces that we are using are rather like the Swedish example, in the sense that they might be thought of as potentially "one-dimensional", if the precise orientation of the basic policy dimensions that define the space is not an issue (and it is not an issue in Schofield's account of government formation).

In this particular Swedish example, we could decide that the policy space in question is "really" one-dimensional, and that our two observed policy dimensions are really different indicators of a more fundamental underlying dimension. (The evidence for this would be the close correlation between party positions on the two dimensions.) In this event, movement on a second dimension has no real meaning and the Social Democrats are unequivocally a core party in a one-dimensional game.

Alternatively, we could decide that the empirical configuration of parties in Sweden was a product of the strategic calculations of the parties themselves, each of which has full freedom to move positions in a two-dimensional policy space. In this event, the core position of the Social Democrats is highly vulnerable to

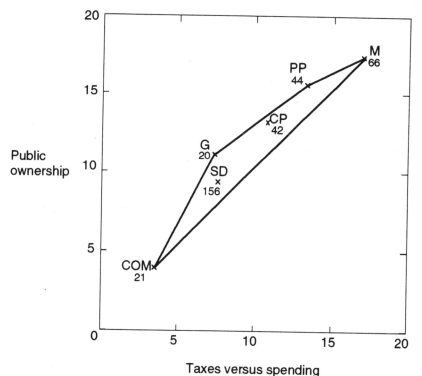

Figure 5.4 The core position of the Swedish Social Democrats.

slight shifts in party positions. These different interpretations of the same data are two quite distinct alternatives—one of them sees the party configuration under consideration as being stable, the other sees it as being unstable. Yet pure empiricism will not help us to decide between conflicting interpretations.

In more general terms, the core position of the party controlling the median legislator in a one-dimensional configuration of parties looks highly unstable once the possibility of movement on another policy dimension is admitted. If the parties were perfectly aligned along one line in a two-dimensional space, then the median party would be unstable in its core position if it controls less than a majority of seats, even if it was the largest party. The slightest movement off the line by this party would remove its core position, since the remaining parties would be a majority coalition with a Pareto set defined by the line. This makes all one dimensional solutions to the government formation game appear to be unstable, unless the possibility of movement in a second dimension is unequivocally ruled out.

More generally, of course, equilibrium outcomes of the government formation game, described in a given number of dimensions, are likely to cease to be equilibria if the possibility of movement on additional dimensions is admitted. The implication of this is that, for theoretical approaches in which the dimensionality of the policy space is a crucial independent variable, and it clearly is crucial in the weighted voting game modeled by Schofield and McKelvey, theorists must consider how the dimensionality of a policy space may be determined.

McKelvey and Schofield have proved that, when there are three or more dimensions, a core party cannot exist even in a weighted majority voting game (McKelvey and Schofield, 1986). When the policy space is one- or two-dimensional, then a core party may exist. If one does exist, then Schofield argues that this should control the government, even as a single-party minority administration. He does go further than this, indeed, using the incidence of one-party minority governments as *prima facie* evidence of the existence of a core party in the system. This in turn he takes as evidence of the relevance of no more than two dimensions of policy to party competition (Schofield, 1990). Thus, accepting the Schofield approach, the existence of dominant parties in government, and in particular of single-party minority governments, is evidence that only one or two dimensions of policy are relevant in a number of European countries. This is of course to use our data in a different way from that in which it is normally used. On this logic, the composition of governments is exploited to make statements about the dimensionality of the relevant policy space, rather than the dimensionality of the policy space being exploited to make statements about the party composition of governments.

In order to explore the empirical application of Schofield's ideas, we took the two-dimensional representation of the policy space for each party system that was most closely tailored to the country in question. That is, we took those two-dimensional figures from Appendix B that were generated by combining the standard left-right dimension with the most salient "local" dimension in each country in our study. We looked in these spaces for core parties that might be in a position to control the process of cabinet government.

Our basic results can be reported very quickly, since we unequivocally identified a core party, in Schofield's terms, in only Sweden, out of the twelve countries under consideration. In Belgium, the Christian Democrats are a core party if it is assumed that the two language wings in each of the main party "families"—socialists, liberals and Christian Democrats—will only go into and come out of government together. If it is assumed that the language wings are capable of participating in the government formation game as independent actors, then there is no core party in Belgium. In both of these cases, the core party was central to the government that actually did form. In the other ten cases, we were able to identify at least one majority coalition whose Pareto set excluded the ideal point of the largest party, and hence to determine that there was no core party.

Considering the possibility that the configuration of parties in some of the policy spaces in question might "really" be one dimensional, we also identified core parties assuming that parties were arrayed along what appeared to the the most appropriate underlying dimension. The countries concerned were Denmark, Iceland, the Netherlands and Sweden, as can be seen from the figures in Appendix B. In each case the most appropriate candidate for a single underlying dimension was taken to be a "left-right" dimension running diagonally from the bottom left to the top right of the two dimensional space in question. In Sweden, the core parties were the same as in the two-dimensional representation. In the other three countries, while there was no core party in the two-dimensional configuration, there was a core party (as there always is) in the one-dimensional representation. In Denmark this was the Radical Liberals (RV); in Iceland the Progressive Party (PP); and in the Netherlands the core party was the Christian Democratic Alliance (CDA). In each of these latter cases, the core party in one dimension participated in the government, though never as a single-party minority administration.

Overall, where the Schofield approach was able to identify a core party, this party did participate in government. In many cases, however, no core party was identified, and in this event the approach has much less to say about the party composition of the eventual government.

Government Formation as a Non-Cooperative Game: Laver and Shepsle; Austen-Smith and Banks

Alternative approaches to the analysis of government formation have recently been based upon the theory of non-cooperative games (that is, games based upon strategies that each player can enforce acting only on his or her own behalf). Often, the rules of these games are generated by particular institutions circumscribing the government formation process. Thus Laver and Shepsle (1990a, b), as well as Austen-Smith and Banks (1990), have developed accounts of government formation that focus upon mechanisms by which credible promises about future government policies can be made. The particular institution that they consider is the cabinet. Laver and Shepsle take the allocation of powerful cabinet portfolios to particular individuals with well-known policy positions to be the only credible statement about the future policies of any government. This allocation gives a particular party power to control policy within the jurisdiction of the relevant portfolio—but obviously this power must be exercised in the light of rational expectations about the actions of all other actors, a number of whom will control other portfolios and hence other policy jurisdictions. Thus both Laver and Shepsle, as well as Austen-Smith and Banks, model government formation as a non-cooperative portfolio-allocation game.

The institution of the cabinet and the need to allocate cabinet portfolios as a part of the government formation process provide a source of structure in the government formation game, structure that can be shown to constrain the potential for chaos to a quite considerable degree. Equilibrium governments are predicted very much more frequently by this general account of the government formation process than by the traditional spatial model. Furthermore, in contrast to the core party approach, the allocation of cabinet portfolios provides a source of structure that generalizes to any number of policy dimensions.

In order to get a sense of this approach to the formation of governments, consider the simple example in Figure 5.5, which shows three parties, A, B and C in two salient policy dimensions, X and Y (ignore the curves for a moment). Any two parties can combine to command a legislative majority. If one portfolio controls policy on the X dimension and another portfolio controls policy on the Y dimension, then there are nine different ways in which the two portfolios can be allocated between the three parties. If party B gets both portfolios, for example, this is represented by outcome BB. If party C gets the X portfolio and party A gets the Y portfolio, then this represents outcome CA, and so on. Each allocation of portfolios is represented by a point on the "lattice" in Figure 5.5. According to Laver and Shepsle, these are the only credible proposals that can be made about future government policies. Any other proposal can be made, of course, and even ostensibly agreed to by the parties. But it will not be not credible, since it cannot be "policed" by allocating a portfolio to a party with an incentive to enforce the policy in question. Rather, Laver and Shepsle assume, the portfolio holder in these circumstances has both the incentive and the ability to implement his or her own preferred policy.

The total set of points in the space that are preferred to BA by parties controlling a legislative majority—the set of proposals that could beat BA in a legislative vote—is known as the "winset" of BA. If the winset of BA contains no credible proposal, then BA must be a stable equilibrium; there is no credible alternative that can beat it.

Figure 5.5 shows how each of the parties feels about proposed policy BA. The area inside the indifference curve centered on A and going through BA contains the set of points preferred by A to BA. Similar interpretations apply to the

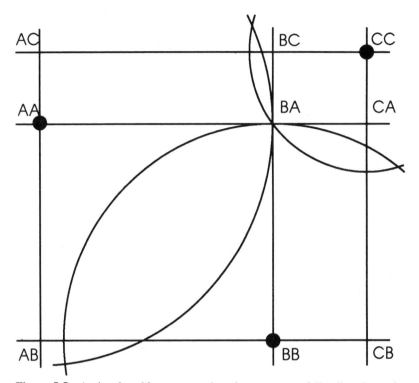

Figure 5.5   An invulnerable status quo in a three party portfolio allocation game.

indifference curves centered on other parties. The area defined by the intersection of the two indifference curves centered, respectively, on A and B thus shows the part of the policy space preferred to BA by both A and B. This area contains no credible proposal. Similarly, there is no credible proposal preferred to BA by both A and C, or by both B and C. In other words, there is no credible proposal in the winset of BA. This therefore represents a stable equilibrium government, with party B controlling the X portfolio and party A controlling the Y portfolio. Despite the fact that there are many points in the policy space preferred to BA by a legislative majority, none of these is credible in the sense of being policed by a portfolio allocation. This can be seen by the fact that there is no point on the lattice of credible proposals in the winset of BA.

A second feature of the Laver-Shepsle approach is that no party can be forced into government against its will. Every party can therefore veto any proposed government in which it controls a key portfolio. Figure 5.6 shows that the possibility of such vetoes further reduces the range of possible alternatives to any given *status quo*—it shows how parties A, B and C feel about BB, an outcome policed by giving both portfolios to party B. There are two credible alternatives that are preferred to BB by both party A and party C—these are BA and BC. Despite this, parties A and C are not collectively in a position to impose outcomes BA and BC, despite their legislative majority. This is because both of these outcomes involve the participation of party B, which can veto them by refusing to accept the relevant portfolios. Party B will clearly do this, preferring outcome BB, its ideal policy, to either alternative. A huge area of the policy space is preferred by a legislative majority to BB, but the only credible policy proposals in this area can be vetoed by party B which is a key participant in each of them.

Laver and Shepsle thus interpret the process of government formation in terms of the interaction between political actors, given a lattice of credible proposals, the preferences of the actors and the possibility that a proposal can be vetoed for strategic reasons by any or all of its participants. Because of the strategic issues involved, a full elaboration of this approach in multidimensional policy spaces is quite complex, and is due to be reported extensively in forthcoming work by Laver and Shepsle. For our present purposes, we elaborate an aspect of this approach for two-dimensional representations of the policy space in each of the countries studied. We do this by identifying potential equilibrium cabinets using the lattice of credible proposals derived from the two-dimensional policy space that our experts identified as being the most appropriate for the country in question. However, we identified the policy dimensions that are salient in the

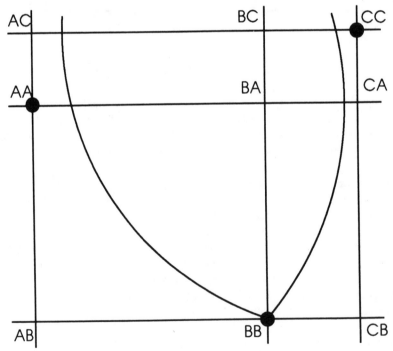

Figure 5.6 A party B minority government.

portfolio allocation game using a method that differed from the one that we used to assess the salience of policy dimensions for party competition in general.

Hitherto, we have used estimates of the salience of policy dimensions that were based upon expert responses to a series of questions about the importance of these dimensions "for party competition." Obviously, experts will have taken a range of aspects of party competition into account when giving their responses to these questions. In anticipation of the current phase of our analysis, we also asked each expert to list "in order of importance . . . the key cabinet positions that must be filled as part of the process of forming a government." We report on the mean ranking of cabinet portfolios for each country in the study in Appendix B.

Obviously, these rankings may be used to assess the value of the "portfolio payoffs" going to each party, in a more detailed version of the type of exercise engaged in by Eric Browne and his associates (Browne and Feste, 1975; Browne and Franklin, 1973; Browne and Frendreis, 1980), or by Budge and Keman (1990). For our purposes, however, we use the data as a more appropriate means to identify policy dimensions that are important in the government formation process. Because Laver and Shepsle assume that the allocation of key portfolios is a central feature of government formation, and because politicians' forecasts of subsequent government policy outputs on key dimensions are based on the identity of the individual who holds the portfolio with jurisdiction over that dimension, assessments of the importance of portfolios are also indicators of the importance of related policy dimensions. If policy is what drives the government formation process, then the salience of key cabinet portfolios will be closely related to the salience of the dimensions over which they have jurisdiction.

In reality, of course, even apparently similar portfolios can have subtly different policy jurisdictions in different countries, and certain aspects of the partitioning of the policy space into jurisdictions can differ radically from country to country. Nonetheless, similarities in the jurisdictions of key portfolios, across a range of countries, are far more striking than differences. There are almost always key portfolios for finance, foreign affairs, internal affairs, defence, agriculture, justice, and so on. This means that we can classify each of the portfolios mentioned by our respondents into a limited number of policy domains.

First, there is economic policy. This almost always includes: a very highly ranked "finance" portfolio; a somewhat less highly ranked but still very important "economic affairs" portfolio of some kind; and possibly even a third cabinet portfolio relating to finance or economic policy. Second, there is always a highly ranked "foreign affairs" portfolio. Associated with this is a "defence" portfolio, which we found in practice always to be rated below foreign affairs. Typically, finance and foreign affairs are the two top-ranked portfolios. Only in Belgium, of the countries we study here, was the top-ranked portfolio neither finance nor foreign affairs but rather, for obvious reasons to do with Belgium's communal conflict, internal affairs. In general, there are usually two internal affairs portfolios. One is typically a highly ranked portfolio designated as either "internal" or "home" affairs. A second, less highly ranked, portfolio in this area is typically designated as "justice". Three other policy areas that we found to have consistently salient portfolios are: various social welfare portfolios, including "health," "education," "social welfare," "housing," and so on; an "environment" portfolio; and an "agriculture" portfolio (or the highly ranked fisheries portfolio in Iceland).

Table 5.1 summarizes our findings on the relative importance of cabinet portfolios for the twelve countries involved in this phase of our study. The portfolios mentioned by our respondents were classified as having jurisdiction in one of the six policy domains outlined in the previous paragraph. Table 5.1 reports the policy domains of the top five ranked portfolios in each country.

Overall, the clear pattern is for economic policy to be either the first or second ranked portfolio in every system. Sometimes, economic policy is also the second ranked portfolio. In this case, we take policy to be dominated by the senior economics portfolio. Moving beyond the universal importance of the finance portfolio, each of the systems under consideration can be classified according to whether it is internal or foreign affairs that provides the top-ranked non-finance portfolio. In three countries—Austria, Belgium, and Italy—internal affairs is the more important. In the remainder—Denmark, Finland, Germany, Iceland, Ireland, Luxembourg, the Netherlands, Norway and Sweden—foreign affairs is the more important.

Table 5.1 Ranking of portfolio domains in 13 coalition systems.

Country	Top five policy domains, in order*					Two domain view	
Austria	Econ	Econ	Int	Welf	For	Econ	Int
Belgium	Int	Econ	Econ	For	Welf	Econ	Int
Denmark	Econ	For***	Int	Int	Econ	Econ	For
Finland	For	Econ	Econ	Int	Welf	Econ	For
Germany	For	Econ	Int	For	Econ	Econ	For
Iceland	Econ	For	Ag	Welf	Econ	Econ	For
Ireland	Econ	Econ	For	Ag	Int	Econ	For**
Italy	Econ	Int	For	Econ	For	Econ	Int
Luxembourg	For	Econ	Econ	Welf	Env	Econ	For
Netherlands	Econ	Welf	Econ	For	Int	Econ	For
Norway	Econ	For	Welf	Welf	Econ	Econ	For
Sweden	Econ	For	Welf	Welf	Env	Econ	For

*Policy domains are Econ = economic policy; For = foreign policy; Int = internal affairs; Welf = welfare policy; Ag = agriculture; Env = environment.

**The foreign affairs portfolio in Ireland has responsibility for Anglo-Irish affairs, within the Anglo-Irish Agreement. Given the very high salience of Northern Ireland policy, and the very low salience of other aspects of foreign policy, Northern Ireland policy was used as the indicator of party policy within the foreign affairs jurisdiction in Ireland.

***First two Danish portfolios equally-ranked.

In comparison with the general assessment of the salience of policy dimensions, the striking feature of the data reported in Table 5.1 and Appendix B is that foreign affairs appear to figure much more prominently in the portfolio allocation game in particular than in party competition in general. This suggests that estimates of the salience of policy dimensions that are not geared specifically to the government formation process may not reflect the relative importance of the different decisions that have to be taken when allocating portfolios within a cabinet. If foreign affairs is universally rated as a highly salient cabinet portfolio, then this implies that party policies on foreign policy are important in the specific context of government formation, even if they are less important in other areas of party competition. Governments, after all, cannot escape the need to take foreign policy seriously during their time in office, even if this does not arouse any great excitement among voters.

Having settled upon the policy dimensions that are salient for a simple two-dimensional government formation game, we then elaborated the Laver-Shepsle approach by identifying portfolio allocations that would form the basis of equilibrium governments. Figures 5.7 and 5.8 give an example of how this was done for the straightforward case of Germany. The Bundestag election of 25 January 1987 generated a legislature in which the arithmetic coalition structure was very simple. The Christian Democrats (CDU) could form a majority with any one of the three other parties—Social Democrats (SPD), Free Democrats (FDP) and Greens (G). The three other parties could form a majority if they all combined together. The outgoing government, and hence the status quo in government formation negotiations, was a coalition between CDU and FDP, in which the CDU controlled the Finance portfolio and the FDP controlled the Foreign Affairs portfolio. This credible point (CDU, FDP) is identified in Figure 5.7 by the intersection of respective party indifference curves. These curves show how each of the parties feels about the *status quo*, assuming Euclidean preferences. The winset of the CDU-FDP coalition is the union of four separate areas, each corresponding to a winning coalition. Each area shows the part of the policy space preferred to the *status quo* by some winning coalition. Three of these areas are defined by the intersection of the CDU indifference curve with an indifference curve relating to one of the three other parties; the fourth is defined by the intersection of the indifference curves of the three other parties.

Figure 5.7 shows instantly that each of these areas contains no credible proposal, thus the credible winset of the *status quo*, (CDU, FDP) is empty. The portfolio allocation approach treats the *status quo* as being in equilibrium, and thus predicts the reformation of the incumbent CDU-FDP coalition, with the Foreign Affairs portfolio once more going to the FDP and the Finance portfolio once more going to the CDU. This is in fact what happened in this particular case.

Figure 5.8 shows another striking aspect of this particular situation, which is that that there is an alternative equilibrium government—a CDU "minority"

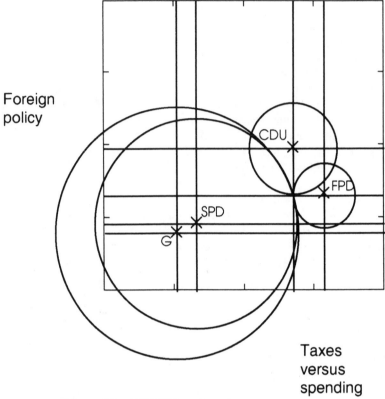

Figure 5.7 CDU-FDP coalition in Germany, 1987.

administration. The winset of the (CDU, CDU) government is shown in Figure 5.8. by the intersection of the respective indifference curves of each of the other parties. This winset contains a number of credible proposals, including the *status quo* (CDU, FDP), which we know to have an empty winset. Note also, however, that every one of these proposals involves the participation of the CDU, which can therefore veto each of them by refusing to accept the appropriate portfolio. If the CDU formed a minority government (CDU, CDU), then it would obviously refuse to go along with any counterproposal which it liked less, and in which it was a necessary participant. But Figure 5.8 shows that no proposal excluding the CDU is preferred to a (CDU, CDU) *status quo*. This implies that a minority CDU government would also be an equilibrium, and that the CDU is in a particularly powerful position in this particular government formation game, given its ability to veto every counterproposal in the winset of its ideal point.

Given a status quo of (CDU, FDP), however, the unequivocal prediction of the portfolio allocation approach in this particular German example is the

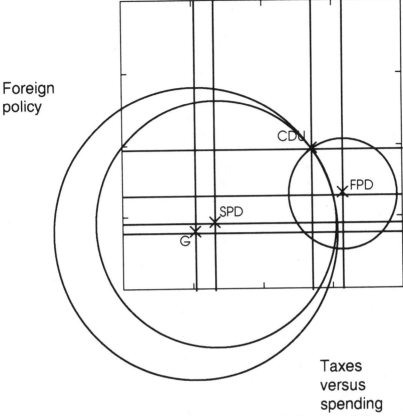

Figure 5.8 Potential CDU minority government in Germany, 1987.

continuation of the *status quo*. This is a "rich" prediction of the government that will form, in that it deals not only with the party composition of the cabinet, but also with the precise allocation of key portfolios between parties. In particular, note that an alternative coalition between the CDU and FDP, in which the portfolios were switched between parties, represents quite a different credible point (FDP, CDU), which is not in equilibrium in this case. Given the data to hand, however, we are not in a position to predict the full party membership of the cabinet, which would require information on a very large number of policy dimensions. Rather, we concentrate on the two most important portfolios, as these were identified in Appendix B. This means that, if one party is predicted to control both key portfolios in a particular setting, for example, then the portfolio allocation approach does not necessarily imply that only this party will form the government. Other portfolios, and hence formal government membership, may be distributed according to other, unmodeled, criteria.

The Models and the Data

Tables 5.2 to 5.13 set out the predictions of the various models, comparing these with the actual governments that formed, on a country-by-country basis. The performance of each of the models under consideration is summarized in Table 5.14.

In general, the early coalition formation models perform rather poorly. They do score some successes, but typically make precise predictions, that are not fulfilled, about the composition of governments. In part, this is because of the reliance of most of these models upon the majority-winning criterion. Thus MCW theory and the clustering model both predict a center-right coalition in Denmark, for example, while MCW theory can account for a center-right government in Italy. In the case of Denmark, however, the actual center-right government that

Table 5.2   Austria, 23 November 1986 (84 seats for majority).

	Socialist Party (SPÖ)	Peoples Party (ÖVP)	Freedom Party (FPÖ)	Greens
Seats	80	77	18	8
MCW	X	X		
		X	X	
5D-MCW	None			
MRCW		X	X	
5D-Cluster		X	X	
Minimal cluster		X	X	
Core	None			
Portfolio game**		X	X	
			X	
	X	X		
ACTUAL GOV	X	X		

**In this case the portfolio game account predicts a standoff between two equilibrium proposals (FPO, FPO) and (OVP, FPO), leaving the possibility that the status quo (SPO, OVP) will continue.

Table 5.3   Belgium, 13 December 1987 (107 seats for majority).

	PS/SP	Ecol/Aga	FDF	PSC/CVP	VU	VB	PRL/PVV
Seats	72	9	3	62	16	2	48
MCW	X	X	X	X			
				X	X	X	X
4D-MCW	None						
MRCW				X	X	X	X
4-d Cluster				X	X		X
Minimal cluster				X			X
Core				X			
Portfolio				X			
ACTUAL GOV	X			X	X		

Table 5.4 Denmark, 10 May 1988 (88 seats for majority).

	SF	SD	CD	RV	KrF	KF	V	FP
Seats	24	55	9	10	4	35	22	16
MCW	X	X	X					
		X	X	X	X			
		X	X	X	X	X	X	X
5D-MCW	None							
MRCW		X	X	X	X			
5D-Cluster			X	X	X	X	X	X
Minimal cluster			X	X		X	X	X
Core	None							
Portfolio		X						
		X	X					
ACTUAL GOV				X		X	X	

Table 5.5 Finland, 15–16 March 1987 (101 seats for majority).

	DA	FPDL	SDP	G	FRP	A/C	FCL	KOK	SPP
Seats	4	16	56	4	9	40	5	53	13
MCW			X	X	X	X			
					X	X	X	X	
						X	X	X	X
4D-MCW	None								
MRCW						X	X	X	X
4-D Cluster					X	X	X	X	X
Minimal cluster					X	X		X	X
Core	None								
Portfolio			X			X			
						X			
ACTUAL GOV			X		X			X	X

Table 5.6 Germany, 25 January 1987 (249 seats for a majority).

	G	SPD	CDU/CSU	FDP
Seats	42	186	223	46
MCW		X	X	
			X	X
4D-MCW			X	X
MRCW			X	X
4-D Cluster			X	X
Minimal cluster			X	X
Core	None			
Portfolio			X	X
			X	
ACTUAL GOV			X	X

Table 5.7 Iceland, 25 April 1987 (31 seats for a majority).

	PA	WA	SDP	PP	IP	CP
Seats	8	6	10	13	18	7
MCW	X	X	X	X		
				X	X	
5D-MCW	None					
MRCW				X	X	
5-D Cluster			X	X	X	X
Minimal cluster				X	X	
Core	None					
Portfolio				X		
			X	X		
ACTUAL GOV	X		X	X		

Table 5.8 Ireland, 17 February 1987 (83 seats for majority).

	WP	DSP	Lab	FF	FG	PD
Seats	4	1	12	81	51	14
MCW			X	X		
				X	X	
6D-MCW	None					
MRCW				X	X	
6-D Cluster				X	X	X
Minimal cluster				X	X	
Core	None					
Portfolio				X		
ACTUAL GOV				X		

Table 5.9 Italy, 14–15 June 1987 (316 needed for majority).

	DP	PCI	G	PR	PSI	PSDI	DC	PRI	MSI	PLI
Seats	8	177	13	13	94	17	234	21	35	11
MCW	X	X	X	X	X	X				
					X	X	X			
					X	X	X	X	X	X
4D-MCW	None									
MRCW					X	X	X			
4-D Cluster	X	X	X	X	X	X		X		
Minimal cluster	X	X			X	X		X		
Core	None									
Portfolio	None*									
ACTUAL GOV					X	X	X	X		X

*In this case the portfolio allocation approach predicts cycles.

Table 5.10 Luxembourg, 17 June 1984 (33 seats needed for majority).

	KPL	G	LSAP	CSV	DP
Seats	2	2	21	25	14
MW			X	X	
				X	X
4D-MCW				X	X
MRCW			X	X	
4-D Cluster	X	X	X	X	
Minimal cluster				X	X
Core	None				
Portfolio				X	
ACTUAL GOV			X	X	

Table 5.12 Norway, 8–9 September 1985 (79 seats needed to win).

	SF	A	KrF	SP	H	FRP
Seats	6	71	16	12	50	2
MCW		X	X			
			X	X	X	X
3D-MCW			X	X	X	X
MRCW		X	X			
3-D Cluster			X	X	X	X
Minimal cluster			X	X	X	X
Core	None					
Portfolio			X	X		
				X		
ACTUAL GOV		X				

Table 5.11 Netherlands, 21 May 1986 (76 seats needs for majority).

	PSP	PPR	PvdA	D66	CDA	GPV	SGP	RPF	VVD
Seats	1	2	52	6	54	1	3	1	27
MCW			X	X	X				
					X	X	X	X	X
4D-MCW					X	X	X	X	X
MRCW					X	X	X	X	X
4-D Cluster					X	X	X	X	X
Minimal cluster					X				X
Core	None								
Portfolio					X				
ACTUAL GOV					X				X

Table 5.13 Sweden, 18 Sept 1988 (175 votes needed to win).

	Comm	*G*	*SD*	*Centre*	*PP*	*Con*
Seats	21	20	156	42	44	66
MCW		X	X			
			X	X		
4D-MCW	None					
MRCW		X	X			
4-D Cluster	X	X	X			
Minimal cluster	X	X	X			
Core			X			
Portfolio			X			
ACTUAL GOV			X			

Table 5.14 Summarizing the performance of the various models.

Country	*Model predictions consistent with actual government*					
	MCW	*MRCW*	*Cluster*	*Min Clust.*	*Core*	*Portfolio*
Austria	Yes	No	No	No	n/a	Yes
Belgium	No	No	No	No	Yes	Yes
Denmark	No	No	No	No	n/a	No
Finland	No	No	No	No	n/a	No
Germany	Yes	Yes	Yes	Yes	n/a	Yes
Iceland	No	No	No	No	n/a	Yes
Ireland	No	No	No	No	n/a	Yes
Italy	No	No	No	No	n/a	n/a
Luxembourg	Yes	Yes	No	Yes	n/a	Yes
Netherlands	No	No	No	Yes	n/a	Yes
Norway	No	No	No	No	n/a	No
Sweden	No	No	No	No	Yes	Yes

formed did not include all predicted parties, and was a minority administration. In the case of Italy, in contrast, the center-right coalition included additional, "surplus" parties. Actual governments were thus often subsets, or supersets, of predicted governments.

It is very important to bear this in mind when comparing either the Schofield or the Laver-Shepsle approaches with these early models, therefore. The more recent game theoretic approaches set out to identify key players in the government formation game, rather than to elaborate the full membership of the government. This has the effect that both approaches typically predict subsets of the government that will form, and hence are consistent with a much larger range of potential coalitions than theories making more precise predictions. The core party approach tends to home in upon a single key player, if one exists. The portfolio allocation approach concentrates upon allocations of key portfolios. If only two portfolios are deemed salient, as in these rudimentary empirical elaborations, then at most two parties can be predicted as members of the government coalition. This does not mean that the approach predicts that the government will comprise at most two parties, but rather it means that the approach is silent on aspects of government membership other than the allocation of the two key portfolios. Nonetheless, in each practical government formation situation there is typically a large range of coalitions that *could* form, and which exclude predicted parties. Thus empirical elaboration still has an important role to play.

Within these limits, the two game theoretic models converge upon the same accurate prediction in those cases in which there is a core party in Schofield's terms. While the core party approach identified core parties only rarely, however, the portfolio allocation approach identified potential equilibrium portfolio allocations in every case but one, and was consistent with reality in eight of the eleven cases for which a prediction was made. In five cases, the portfolio allocation approach identified a single particularly strong party—one with an ideal point such that no other credible point was preferred by a legislative majority. In every one of these cases, the party identified was in fact a member of the eventual government. In six cases, two parties were identified as participants in government equilibria—in three of these cases, both parties identified were in the government. It is important to remember, however, that the game theoretic approaches that we have elaborated predict only a subset of the government that forms, and thus face an easier empirical task than traditional coalition theories.

One of the main reasons for the success of the portfolio allocation approach has to do with the way it handles what turns out to be a rather common configuration of parties in the countries under consideration. Since many experts cited the foreign affairs portfolio as being important in government formation, many of the policy spaces we use to elaborate the portfolio allocation approach combine foreign affairs and economic policy. In practice, there was quite a high correlation between estimated party positions on the finance and foreign policy dimensions, generating a series of more or less one-dimensional empirical configurations of parties in the two-dimensional portfolio allocation space. Thus, we find a range of real-world manifestations of the "Dimension Q" problem discussed in Chapter 1 and illustrated in Figure 1.5. An interesting feature of the portfolio allocation approach is that, when party configurations are "more or less" one dimensional in the Dimension Q sense, then the party controlling the median legislator on Dimension Q tends to be identified as being at the center of bargaining. If the parties were perfectly aligned on this dimension, then the core party approach would also identify the median party as being crucial. However, small departures from uni-dimensionality destroy this equilibrium in the core party model—if the median party moves off Dimension Q, then the other parties can find a point on Dimension Q that they prefer. Much larger departures from uni-dimensionality continue to imply a key role for the former "median" party under the portfolio allocation approach, however, since it takes a much larger perturbation of the system before new credible proposals enter the winset of this party. In this sense, the portfolio allocation approach appears as a more robust version of the core party model.

The three countries in which all models fail are Denmark, Finland and Norway. Interestingly, in each of these cases, this was because all models predicted a role for a particular party—the formerly agrarian Center Party in each country—that did not in fact go into government. (This is despite the fact that the Center Party has been a government participant on other occasions in each country.) In only one case, that of Italy, was it impossible for the portfolio approach to make an equilibrium prediction; this was because it predicted a "cycle" of governments, each in turn beaten by another. In effect, the portfolio allocation approach (accurately) predicts a chaotic and unstable process of government formation and maintenance in Italy.

Overall, the interesting feature of this empirical elaboration is that the models that tend to make predictions of the full membership of the government, based on rather limited theoretical criteria, tend to do worse than the models that make rather conservative predictions, based on a rather more exhaustive strategic analysis of the role of certain key players at the heart of the government formation game. The matter of which particular minor parties are added to, or subtracted from, government participation with these key players seems in some sense to be a secondary consideration. Perhaps the single most important lesson to be drawn from this discussion is that, in many countries, a small number of important actors seem to dominate the government formation process. This feature of government formation is often overlooked by earlier coalition theories, but is central to most of the more recent game theoretic approaches.

Government Formation and the Relative Importance of Different Policy Dimensions

Early policy-driven models of government formation concerned themselves with but a single dimension of policy. By implication, this dimension was assumed to be salient for all key actors, and all other potential dimensions were assumed to have no salience at all. For this reason, the relative salience of different dimensions, and the matter of whether this might vary from actor to actor, were not considered. Once multidimensional representations of policy competition became current, then the manner in which actors viewed the relationship between different policy dimensions became an important issue. Typically, all actors were assumed to view the set of salient dimensions as having the same relative importance. As we have seen in the previous chapter, however, there are in fact good empirical reasons for assuming that each actor uses a different set of relative weights for salient policy dimensions. If we retain an assumption that we have been using throughout this chapter, that the perceived distance between two points on one policy dimension does not depend upon their distance on another dimension (this is the assumption of separable preferences), then we can begin a tentative attack on the problem of estimating the impact of differential saliency weights on government formation.

Figure 5.9 shows the situation in Ireland in June 1989. (This differs from the situation analysed in Table 5.8, in that a new election had been held, resulting in a new set of party weights.) The figure replaces the circular indifference curves used to generate all predictions so far with ellipses whose axes are parallel to the basis dimensions and have relative lengths proportional to the relative weights given by the party to the dimensions in question. Thus the relative weighting given by the Labour Party to the taxation and the Northern Ireland dimensions can be seen from Appendix B to be 11.5 : 13.7, or about 0.8 : 1. This is captured by drawing Labour indifference curves, in this case the curve through Fianna Fail's ideal point, as ellipses whose axes are in the equivalent ratio. (The shorter axis is the one about which the party concerned feels more strongly. It is prepared to tolerate less movement on this, other things being equal, than on the axis about which it feels less strongly. Thus shorter distances on the more salient policy dimension are perceptually equivalent to longer distances on the less salient policy dimension.) A circular Labour indifference curve through the Fianna Fail ideal point is also shown in Figure 5.9, for comparative purposes.

From these indifference curves it can be seen that the Labour Party is more sensitive to policy distances on the taxation dimension than it is to those on the Northern Ireland dimension. Figure 5.9 shows this party-specific difference in relative weighting to be potentially very important for government formation in Ireland in 1989. If all parties are assumed to feel the same way about the importance of the policy dimensions, then Figure 5.9 shows that several proposals were in the winset of the status quo, which was a Fianna Fail minority government. Some of these, such as a Fine Gael—Labour coalition, could not be vetoed by Fianna Fail. Once the different views of key actors about the relative salience of the policy dimensions was taken into account, then the only credible proposals in the winset of the incumbent government were those that involved the participation of Fianna Fail, and could thus have been vetoed by this party, which obviously prefers its own ideal point to any alternative. On this interpretation, Fianna Fail appears to be much more powerful.

Our empirical estimates of the variation in the relative saliency weights attached by different actors to the same set of policy dimensions can be summarized in a rather straightforward manner. There are indeed differences between parties in the relative weighting of dimensions. These differences are too large to be ignored, which is the typical response of most coalition theorists. Second, these differences are not huge. The differential saliency weights illustrated in Figure 5.9 are more or less typical. These are large enough to make a difference to the predicted government when relatively knife-edge decisions are involved because key credible points are close to an indifference curve, but they are unlikely to have much impact on more robust solutions.

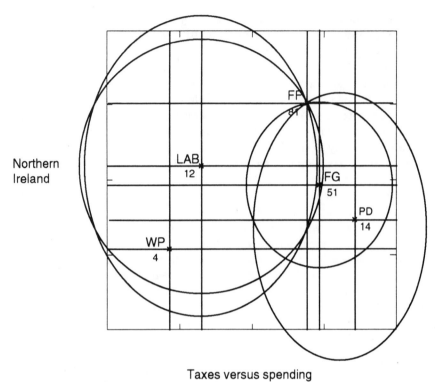

Northern
Ireland

Taxes versus spending

Figure 5.9   The impact of differential saliency weights in Ireland, 1989.

As always, the answer for those who are interested in these important and underexamined matters is to roll up their sleeves and get to work on experimenting with the effect of differences in saliency weights, using the data reported in Appendix B as sets of indicators of the orders of magnitude involved.

Conclusion

Overall, it appears to be the case that more recent game theoretic models of government formation perform rather better than those that preceded them. It must be remembered, however, that this is in large part because they are concerned to identify key actors in the government formation process, rather than to make a comprehensive prediction of the full membership of the government. The central purpose of this chapter has not been to "test" government formation theories; rather, the empirical elaborations we have presented are designed to serve as examples of the general approach that we advocate throughout the book, the essential features of which do not depend upon any particular theory.

The approach that we are promoting is grounded upon a particular way of working with theory. In particular, it has to do with the relationship between theory and data. We do not see the value of data as the raw material with which to conduct tests of various theories. For reasons outlined in the first chapter, it is probably the case that many of the theories discussed in this chapter cannot be tested, in the strict sense of the term. Many of them, for example, depend upon assuming a policy space of a certain dimensionality. Yet, as we have seen, there is no very satisfactory manner of estimating the dimensionality of any particular policy space. As we saw in earlier chapters, purely inductive empirical techniques for assessing the dimensionality of a particular data set run the risk of missing much of the point of what is interesting about the political system concerned. Alternatively, we can use a theory to tell us about the dimensionality of the relevant policy space, as Schofield suggests when he implies that systems containing what looks like a core party are probably at most two-dimensional. But the dimensionality of a particular policy space is not a particularly interesting thing in and for itself. It is only interesting to the extent that it enables us to operationalize a useful theory, so as to be able to describe the interaction between particular political actors in a non-obvious and suggestive manner. In other words, we need an estimate of the dimensionality of a given policy space in order to put a theory to work, not the other way around.

A second fundamental problem with the testing of theories such as these has to do with the type of data that we are bound to use. It is always true, of course, that theory fashions the way in which data are collected, analyzed and reported. In this important sense there can never be a truly objective scientific test of any theory. Such problems are particularly acute in relation to spatial theories of party competition, furthermore, since the notion of a policy dimension is the very epitome of an "artificial" theoretical construct. Certainly, once we move beyond crude notions of left and right of the type that structured seating arrangements in the post-revolutionary Assemblé National, we must take steps to "impose" the notion of a policy dimension on our data. We can of course estimate party positions on any policy dimension that tickles our fancy. But determining whether these dimensions are the ones that "really" structure party competition, or indeed whether they have any meaning or validity whatsoever, is quite another matter.

The fact that we cannot conduct rigorous scientific tests of many of the theories with which we have been concerned should by no means be taken to imply that the empirical elaboration of these theories is not a worthwhile exercise. On the contrary, it is our contention that the confrontation between theory and data is an essential part of the process of developing an intellectual understanding of the process being modeled. Not least, this is because the process of elaborating a particular theory on the basis of a particular empirical data set typically reveals aspects of the theories which are vague and underspecified.

In the last analysis, therefore, the most important reason for theorists to get involved in empirical research is that it takes them on an intellectual safari. The world that exists inside an ivory tower may not exactly be neat and tidy, but at least it is more or less under control. "Facts" are allowed through the door from time to time, but they are usually "stylized facts," carefully selected, shaped, smoothed and packaged in such a way as to make a particular point. Stylized facts are useful rhetorical devices, to be sure, especially if they are able to pass themselves off as being close enough to reality to be worth taking seriously. But they have no rough edges; they leave no intellectual splinters under the fingernails. In the last analysis there is no getting away from the problem that stylized facts are, quite simply, made up by the theorist to do a particular job. If they don't do the job they can easily be thrown on the scrap heap and, for this reason, can never really challenge the theory they are fashioned to serve.

The essential feature of good empirical research on the "real" world is that things are at least slightly out of control. Even before the research gets under way, the process of operationalizing key concepts forces us to anticipate the awkward shapes and sizes of what we are likely to find. Mundane but difficult decisions have to be taken about these concepts. These decisions can often seem tiresome and far removed from the commanding heights of intellectual endeavor, but being forced to consider how an abstract concept can be applied to the real world is of immense educational value. To do this, we must typically pause and reflect about the true meaning of the concept itself. Almost every theoretical concept that we set out to apply in empirical work turns out to be underspecified in some way—to be in need of serious attention from a theorist before being taken out on empirical safari. The net product of all of this may not be a real test—far too much remains under the control of the analyst. Rather the result is a state of mind, a sense of being open to the real world and a belief that a theory which cannot accommodate itself to the real world is a worse theory because of this. The real point of confronting theory with data is heuristic—it is an indispensible learning experience.

The essential purpose of this book, therefore, is to expand our understanding of party competition by setting data side by side with theory. We set out to begin building a body of data that is relevant to the concerns of those with a theoretical interest in the relationship between policy and party competition. By illustrating how these data can be applied to some of the relevant theories, by making the data available and by exhorting analysts to roll up their sleeves and experiment with them, we hope to contribute towards a state of mind that sees theory and data as interrelated.

The data presented in this book are far from being the last word on the subjects with which they deal. Indeed, their main claim to usefulness is that, in many cases, they are the first word on the subject. Our preoccupation in this chapter with government formation reflects our own particular interests. Our preoccupation throughout this book with the policy dimensions of party competition reflects the emphases of much of the mainstream theoretical literature.

In relation to this, perhaps the strongest general message to come from our expert survey is that, when asked to do so, the country specialists who supplied our data are quite prepared to nominate a wide range of policy dimensions as being important to party competition. What is more, they are quite prepared to say that different parties give different values to the importance of these dimensions. This is in some contrast to the much more simple assumptions made by most theorists. At the very least, it implies that the theoretical drive towards models of party competition set in more complex policy spaces is well-founded. It also, in rather general terms, casts some doubt over the usefulness of the notorious chaos results. One response to these, as we have seen, is to argue that the contrast between theoretical chaos and real world stability implies that the real political world is in practice very low-dimensional. An alternative response is that useful theories of party competition simply must be capable of accounting for political stability in policy spaces of high dimensionality.

When push comes to shove, of course, country specialists will always tend to think of the world as a rich and complex multidimensional sort of a place, while theorists will always be inclined to think of it as rather simple. This is as it should be, but it does not absolve these two groups of scholars from engaging each other in dialogue. Neither is right, neither is wrong, since a policy dimension is not the sort of thing that you can walk up to and kick if you begin to doubt its existence.

To describe the relationship between policy and party competition in terms of policy dimensions is no more than to use a particular theoretical language. Quite different languages could probably be used to describe the same set of problems, so the only sure test of the approach as a whole is whether it adds something to our understanding of politics. And the only sure way to find out about this is to get involved in practical political analysis.

It is for this reason above all others that we have left open so many of the questions that we have raised in the preceeding chapters. We could have taken the comfortable way out and come to a set of closed conclusions that could be cited (or not) by subsequent authors. But this would have been to undermine the entire point of the exercise. If we are subsequently cited only by people who have not played with the data themselves, we will have failed. If our discussion encourages others to go out and use the data themselves—either forgetting or contradicting all of our conclusions—we will have succeeded handsomely.

Appendix A: Methodological Matters

Response Rates

Table A1 gives the number of people written to by us and asked for judgments, by country, the number replying, and the response rate implied by this. As noted in Chapter Two, the highest response rates were in the English-speaking countries and Scandinavia. The lowest were in southern European countries, together with Switzerland, Belgium, Iceland and Japan.

Questions Asked

Table A2 provides the text of the questions asked in the questionnaire. A copy of the sixteen-page questionnaire itself, showing the layout of the scales on which respondents were asked to mark the positions of each party, is available on request from the authors.

Face Validity

Table A3 reports the positions of the parties estimated by us on the "public ownership" scale, taken on *a priori* grounds to be the scale most closely related to traditional conceptions of left and right. These are compared with party positions on the left-right scale estimated on the basis of expert surveys by Castles and Mair (1984) and by Morgan (1976), and with positions on a left-right scale estimated on the basis of the content analysis of party manifestos by Laver and Budge (1991). Only those countries for which a set of estimates was generated by at least one other study have been included in the table. As Chapter 2 reports, the correlation between the four scales was very high.

Table A1   Targets and responses in expert survey, by country.

	Targets	*Responses*	*Response rate*
	N	N	%
Ireland	50	36	72
Canada	60	28	47
Britain	75	34	45
Austria	20	8	40
Malta	18	7	39
Australia	56	21	38
Finland	38	14	37
USA	100	35	35
Israel	29	10	34
Norway	56	19	34
New Zealand	43	14	33
Sweden	64	19	30
Portugal	26	7	27
Netherlands	60	16	27
France	61	15	25
Germany	81	19	23
Greece	23	5	22
Denmark	50	10	20
Luxembourg	30	5	17
Italy	52	8	15
Belgium	46	6	13
Iceland	40	5	13
Spain	44	5	11
Switzerland	31	3	10
Japan	75	6	8
TOTAL	1228	355	29

Assessing Respondent Bias in Scale Locations

Our expert respondents were asked to score each party in the country with which they were dealing on a number of twenty-point policy scales. Obviously, our respondents were not machines; many must have had personal views about the parties upon which they were making judgments. This leaves open the possibility that our respondents gave biased answers to our questions, in the sense that their supposedly "objective" expert responses were in some systematic way affected by their own "subjective" political views. (The quotation marks are intended to remind us that all of these scales are, of course, mental artifacts. None is objective in the sense that you can walk up to it and kick it.)

We attempted to assess the possible extent of this problem by including, very close to the end of the survey form, a question that asked respondents: "Taking all aspects of party policy into account, please score each of the parties in terms of how close it is to you own personal views." Respondents were given a fifteen-

Table A2 Policy scales and other parameters estimated in expert survey.

PARTY SCALES

For scales 1–10, respondents were asked to locate the positions of both party leaders and party voters, and to rate the importance attached by the leaders of each party to each policy dimension. Respondents were asked to locate the leaders, legislators and activists of each party on scales 11–13, the leaders of each party on scales 14 and 15, and the party in general on scale 16.

1. TAXES VERSUS PUBLIC SERVICES.
   Promote raising taxes to increase public services. (1)
   Promote cutting public services to cut taxes. (20)
2. FOREIGN POLICY.
   Promote development of friendly relations with Soviet Union. (1)
   Oppose development of friendly relations with Soviet Union. (20)
3. PUBLIC OWNERSHIP.
   Promote maximum public ownership of business and industry. (1)
   Oppose all public ownership of business and industry. (20)
4. SOCIAL POLICY.
   Promote permissive policies on matters such as abortion and homosexual law. (1)
   Oppose permissive policies on matters such as abortion and homosexual law. (20)
5. THE RELIGIOUS DIMENSION.
   Strongly anticlerical. (1)
   Strongly proclerical. (20)
6. URBAN VERSUS RURAL INTERESTS.
   Promote interests of urban and industrial voters above others. (1)
   Promote interests of rural and agricultural voters above others. (20)
7. CENTRALIZATION OF DECISION MAKING.
   Promote decentralization of all decision making. (1)
   Oppose any decentralization of decision making. (20)
8. ENVIRONMENTAL POLICY.
   Support protection of environment, even at the cost of economic growth. (1)
   Support economic growth, even at the cost of damage to environment. (20)
9. OTHER SCALE 1.
   Respondent asked to interpret endpoints.
10. OTHER SCALE 2.
    Respondent asked to interpret endpoints.
11. ASSESS THE INFLUENCE THAT PARTY LEADERS, PARTY LEGISLATORS AND PARTY ACTIVISTS HAVE OVER THE FORMATION OF PARTY POLICY.
    Have no influence at all. (1)
    Have a very great influence. (20)
12. ASSESS THE INFLUENCE THAT PARTY LEADERS, PARTY LEGISLATORS AND PARTY ACTIVISTS HAVE OVER DECISIONS ABOUT PARTICIPA-TION IN GOVERNMENT.
    Have no influence at all. (1)
    Have a very great influence. (20)

Table A2 *Continued*

13. ASSESS HOW FAR INTO THE FUTURE MEMBERS OF EACH SECTION OF EACH PARTY LOOK WHEN MAKING IMPORTANT DECISIONS ABOUT THE MEMBERSHIP OF THE GOVERNMENT.
Not at all. (1)
Many years. (5)

14. FORCED TO MAKE A CHOICE, WOULD PARTY LEADERS GIVE UP POLICY OBJECTIVES IN ORDER TO GET INTO GOVERNMENT OR WOULD THEY SACRIFICE A PLACE IN GOVERNMENT IN ORDER TO MAINTAIN POLICY OBJECTIVES?
Give up place in government. (1)
Give up policy objectives. (20)

15. HOW MUCH CAN PARTY LEADERS USE GROUPS OUTSIDE THE LEGISLATURE TO PUT PRESSURE ON OTHER PARTIES?
Can often use outside groups. (1)
Can never use outside groups. (20)

16. TAKING ALL ASPECTS OF PARTY POLICY INTO ACCOUNT, SCORE EACH PARTY IN TERMS OF HOW CLOSE IT IS TO YOUR OWN PERSONAL VIEWS.
Same as respondent. (1)
Farthest from respondent. (15)

PARTY SYSTEM PARAMETERS

17. HOW MUCH IMPACT DO PARTIES IN THE PARLIAMENTARY OPPOSITION HAVE ON GOVERNMENT POLICY?
No impact. (1) High impact. (9)

18. WHAT PROPORTION OF ALL GOVERNMENTS FALL AS A RESULT OF POLICY DISPUTES BETWEEN GOVERNMENT MEMBERS?
None. (1) All. (9)

19. ARE CABINET PORTFOLIOS VALUED MORE AS REWARDS OF OFFICE OR AS MEANS TO AFFECT POLICY?
Policy. (1) Office. (9)

20. HOW OFTEN DO CABINET MEMBERS MAKE PUBLIC THEIR DISAGREEMENT WITH DECISIONS TAKEN IN CABINET WHILE REMAINING IN CABINET?
Never. (1) Always. (9)

21. HOW MUCH AUTONOMY DOES A CABINET MEMBER HAVE IN MAKING POLICY IN HER OR HIS DEPARTMENT?
Great autonomy. (1) No autonomy. (9)

22. HOW OFTEN ARE CABINET ASSIGNMENTS CHANGED DURING THE LIFETIME OF A GOVERNMENT?
Never. (1) Very often. (9)

23. PLEASE LIST THE KEY CABINET POSITIONS THAT MUST BE FILLED AS PART OF THE PROCESS OF FORMING A GOVERNMENT. PLEASE RANK THESE IN ORDER OF IMPORTANCE.

Table A3 Comparison of estimated party positions on the public ownership scale with other left right-scales.

Country	Party	Laver & Hunt	Laver & Budge	Castles & Mair	Morgan
Austria	KPÖ	3.0		0.5	
	G	7.6			
	SPÖ	9.1	−18	3.0	
	ÖVP	12.7	15	5.8	
	FPÖ	15.8	−7	6.8	
Belgium	PS	6.6	−22	2.7	32
	SP	6.8			
	ECO/AGA	8.0			
	FDF	10.3	−4	5.6	72
	PSC/CVP	14.0	−2	6.1	71
	VU	15.4	−7	6.8	83
	FB	16.0		9.8	
	PRL/PVV	18.8	18	7.7	100
Britain	PC	7.3		3.4	
	SNP	7.3		4.4	
	LAB	7.4	−39	2.3	
	DEM	12.0	−10	5.0	
	CON	18.2	29	7.8	
Denmark	DKP	2.3	−32	1.0	0
	VS	4.3	−22	0.8	7
	SF	5.5	−33	1.9	20
	G	8.2	—	—	—
	SD	8.8	−14	3.8	41
	CD	12.4	30	5.7	—
	RV	13.3	−6	4.8	62
	KRF	14.6	30	6.2	—
	KF	16.0	28	7.3	100
	RF	16.7			84
	V	17.8	18	6.7	82
	FP	19.2	26	8.7	—
Finland	DA	2.9			
	FPDL	4.8		1.8	0
	SDP	8.3		3.0	26
	G	9.7			
	P	11.9			
	A/C	12.1		5.2	58
	FRP	12.7			64
	LPP	14.5		5.6	70
	FCL	14.9			
	DPP	14.9		6.1	80
	KOK	15.1		7.2	99

Table A3 *Continued*

Country	Party	Laver & Hunt	Laver & Budge	Castles & Mair	Morgan
France	PCF	1.5		1.4	
	PS	7.7		2.6	
	MRG	10.1		3.8	
	G	11.0		3.5	
	RPR	16.1		8.2	
	UDF	16.4		6.6	
	FN	18.5		9.8	
Germany	G	9.5	−26	2.8	
	SPD	14.1	−7	3.3	
	CDU	15.2	9	6.7	
	FPD	15.4	16	5.1	
	NPD	16.7			
Iceland	DA	4.8		1.7	
	WA	7.8		3.6	
	SDP	8.2		4.9	
	PP	8.6		5.9	
	IP	10.2		8.8	
	CP	11.2		7.9	
Ireland	WP	2.9		1.8	
	LAB	6.1	−23	3.6	
	FF	11.5	10	6.3	
	FG	13.9	18	6.8	
	PD	16.5			
Italy	DP	2.9	−25	0.5	
	PC	5.9	−13	1.6	3
	G	8.9			
	PSI	10.1	−14	3.1	23
	DC	10.4	4	5.4	57
	PSDI	11.3	−13	5.4	36
	PRI	14.1	−9	4.8	42
	MSI	14.9	4	9.1	100
	PLI	16.5	3	5.9	73
Luxembourg	KPL	2.0	−41		0
	G	4.6			
	LSAP	8.0	−34		36
	CSV	14.2	−5		86
	DP	17.2	−11		93
Netherlands	CPN	1.9		0.8	5
	PSP	2.6		0.6	8
	PPR	5.4	−39	1.6	20
	PVDA	8.3	−28	2.6	27
	D'66	11.7	−22	4.4	39
	CDA	13.9	−17	5.7	51(KVP)
	VVD	16.9	15	7.4	76

Table A3 *Continued*

Country	Party	Laver & Hunt	Laver & Budge	Castles & Mair	Morgan
Norway	SF	5.4	−36	1.2	7
	LAB	8.2	−32	3.0	35
	V	10.9	−20	4.0	64
	KRF	11.4	2	6.1	69
	DLF	12.9			
	H	15.8	4	7.7	100
	FRP	19.1	40	9.4	
Spain	PCE	3.3		2.7	
	PSOE	9.4		3.6	
	CDS	10.4			
	PNN	14.4		6.7	
Sweden	CP	4.0	−39	1.2	0
	SD	9.4	−31	2.9	33
	G	11.1			
	CP	13.2	−7	5.9	65
	M	17.4	34	7.7	100

Note: Only those countries for which estimates have been generated for at least one other study have been included in this table.

point scale on which to locate all parties in relation to their own views. Contrary to what might have been expected, the response rate on this question was high. This allowed us to check, for every party in the survey, the extent to which it was possible to predict, for any given observation, the scale location of a party knowing only a respondent's self-assessed ideological distance from that party. If the scale position of a party could systematically have been predicted from respondent's ideological distance from it, we could have inferred that the expert placements of this party on this scale were systematically biased by the ideological views of the experts. If it was not possible to predict the scale positions of a given party on the basis of the ideological views of experts, then we have no basis for inferring that the scales are biased. (This does not, of course, mean that they are not biased in some way; it simply means that we have not been able to estimate statistically the extent of such bias.)

We make no claims in any of this work about the "true" policy positions of the parties. However, if our respondents do appear to be giving ideologically unbiased judgments, then this certainly suggests that a different selection of experts, with different ideological views, might well have generated the same estimates of scale positions. It implies that our results are not merely a product of our selection of experts. If our respondents appear to be giving ideologically biased judgments, then this implies the reverse, that the particular group of experts upon which we are relying is conditioning our results; that a different group of experts might well have generated different estimates. This would give real cause for concern about the whole basis of the expert survey technique.

We attempted to assess the extent of bias by regressing each expert's judgment about the scale position of a party against the expert's self-assessed ideological distance from party. We did this for every party in every country in the analysis, for the first five of the "party leader" policy scales. (These scales were related to tax cuts/public spending; foreign policy; public ownership; social policy; and anticlericalism.)

The regression model was thus, quite simply:

$$Y_{spi} = a_{sp} + b_{sp}X_{pi} + \varepsilon$$

where Y_{spi} is the location of party p on scale s by expert i, X_{pi} is expert i's self-assessed ideological distance from party p and ε is the error term. The coefficient b_{sp} can be taken as an indicator of the bias of the experts' judgments of the position of party p on scale s. If b_{sp} is zero then scale locations are unrelated to ideological distances. A positive value implies that the less an expert likes a party, the more to the right he or she places it. A negative value implies that the less an expert likes a party, the more to the left he or she places it. The constant a_{sp} can be interpreted as an estimate of the "true" position of party p on scale s in those circumstances in which there is no expert bias. This suggests that, for scales for which there is no evidence of bias, the standard error of a_{sp} can be used as an indicator of the precision of the estimates of scale positions.

Our essential task in looking for respondent bias in the location of party p on scale s is thus to assess whether b_{sp} differs significantly from zero. In statistical terms, a coefficient may, of course, not differ significantly from zero for two reasons. The first is that it is not different from zero. The second is that it does differ from zero, but we have too few observations to allow us to infer statistically that it does so. The latter possibility is clearly evident for quite a few of the countries in this analysis, where the number of responses was low. Indeed about half of the countries in our analysis are based on too few expert opinions to allow us to evaluate the possibility of expert bias with any degree of confidence, and the estimates of scale positions for these countries should be used with circumspection as a consequence. (These countries are: Austria, Belgium, Denmark, Greece, Iceland, Israel, Italy, Japan, Luxembourg, Malta, Portugal and Spain.) The other half of our countries do have sufficient opinions for us to be able to analyze these statistically for bias. (These countries are Australia, Britain, Canada, Finland, France, Germany, Ireland, the Netherlands, Norway, New Zealand, Sweden and the USA). We do not report the result of every one of the very many regressions that were estimated in order to investigate the possibility of bias in the estimates of each party on each scale in each of these countries. Table A4 reports only the 22 bias analyses that were statistically significant, at the 0.05 level, out of the 355 sets of party/scale expert judgments in the twelve party systems for which some sort of statistical analysis made sense. (Note that performing this analysis on totally unbiased random data would generate statistically significant bias coefficients, at the 0.05 level, in five percent of tests, that is in seventeen or eighteen of our 355 tests.) What is important is not so much the precise set of parameters as the general conclusions about expert bias that we can draw from these results.

For four of the countries analyzed—France, Germany, New Zealand and the USA—there was no statistically significant bias coefficient for any party for any of the scales tested. In the remaining eight—Australia, Britain, Canada, Finland, Ireland, the Netherlands, Norway and Sweden—there was some evidence of bias, though typically in only one or two scales, and then only for one or two parties. Thus, in Australia, Finland and Norway, evidence of expert bias exists for only one party for a single scale (and it should be noted that in Finland scale positions were estimated for a large number of parties). In Canada it exists for two scales,

Table A4 Analysis of respondent bias for twelve party systems.

COUNTRY (N of party scales tested)	SCALE (s)	Party (p)	a_{sp}	s.e. a_{sp}	b_{sp}	s.e. b_{sp}	adjusted r^2
Australia (20)	Social policy	LAB	5.0	0.93	0.33	0.13	.23
Britain (25)	Taxes/serv.	CON	14.5	1.18	0.22	0.09	.13
	Taxes/serv.	DEM	6.0	0.87	0.33	0.12	.18
	Taxes/serv.	PC	0.7	1.81	0.47	0.16	.27
	Pub. own.	PC	1.7	1.53	0.53	0.13	.43
	Social policy	CON	12.2	1.32	0.26	0.10	.15
	Anticlerical	CON	14.3	1.12	−0.37	0.10	.61
Canada (15)	Taxes/serv.	CON	10.9	1.18	0.23	0.10	.16
	For policy	LIB	9.9	0.89	−0.22	0.11	.13
Finland (55)	Pub. own.	FRP	20.3	3.34	−0.69	0.29	.27
Ireland (35)	Pub. own.	FF	9.6	0.94	0.19	0.09	.11
	Social policy	DSP	2.5	1.03	0.33	0.13	.22
	Social policy	WP	3.1	1.29	0.33	0.15	.11
Netherlands (50)	For policy	D66	3.6	1.44	0.86	0.28	.39
	Pub. own.	PSP	5.4	1.30	−0.28	0.12	.30
	Social policy	D66	−0.4	1.74	0.90	0.34	.32
	Social policy	SGP	12.8	2.21	0.48	0.16	.43
	Anticlerical	VVD	2.1	1.24	0.63	0.13	.64
Norway (40)	Taxes/serv.	FRP	15.1	1.41	0.24	0.10	.28
Sweden (35)	Taxes/serv.	PP	11.1	1.21	0.32	0.14	.23
	For policy	SD	9.6	1.12	−0.38	0.15	.30
	Anticlerical	CDU	23.5	2.01	−0.40	0.17	.33
France (35)	None	None					
Germany (20)	None	None					
New Zealand (15)	None	None					
USA (10)	None	None					

in each case for one party only, with estimates for Ireland and Sweden also biased only to a similarly limited degree. In only two countries, therefore, is there more extensive evidence of biased responses from our experts. In Britain, there were biased responses on four of the five tested scales, with three different parties being involved; in the Netherlands (albeit in quite a large party system) evidence of bias showed up on four scales, with four parties being involved.

Overall, there was quite a clear pattern in the bias coefficients, involving the location of right-wing parties farther to the right by those who liked them less. This is illustrated rather neatly by probably the most striking example of apparent bias in the location of a major European political party on a scale that was important to it. This is the location of the Dutch VVD (Liberal) party on the pro-versus anticlericalism scale. The estimated regression equation for the VVD was:

$$\text{Proclericalism score} = 2.1 + 0.63 \text{ (Ideological distance)} + \varepsilon : r^2 = .64$$

(Note that that the proclericalism scale ranged from 1 to 20 and the ideological distance scale from 1 to 15.) In other words, a respondent who felt very close to the VVD would have given the party a proclericalism score of 2.7; a respondent who saw the VVD as being as far away as possible would have given the party a much more proclerical score of 11.6.

The bias coefficients in the Netherlands tended to be quite a bit higher than those found in other systems. A more typical example can be found in the location of the British Conservative Party (the object of the most consistently, if modestly, biased expert judgments among the major parties in this study). On the social policy scale, for example, the estimated bias model for the British Conservatives was as follows:

$$\text{Social conservatism} = 12.2 + 0.26 \text{ (Ideological distance)} + \varepsilon : r^2 = .15$$

In other words, a respondent who felt as close as possible ideologically to the Conservatives would have located the party at 12.5 on this scale; a respondent who felt as far away as possible would have located it at 16.1. The tendency towards bias in these particular expert judgments, while statistically significant, was not very pronounced, as the r^2 value of .15 for this model indicates.

These examples illustrate the only real pattern to emerge from the bias analyses, which was for respondents to rate right-wing parties as being more right wing if they didn't like them and to rate them as being less right-wing if they did like them. There was no evidence whatsoever of a complementary tendency on the left. In general, estimated scale positions for left wing parties showed little evidence of bias.

What can we conclude from all of this? We have no precedents to go on in comparing this analysis of bias with those of other studies that have estimated party policy positions using expert judgments since, to the best of our knowledge, no such bias analysis has been conducted before. However, the very small proportion of scales that appear to have been the subject of biased expert judgments is encouraging, though it should be remembered that we have only been able to test twelve of the twenty-four countries studied in this way. While, as we said above, the data for the countries that could not be tested for bias should be used with circumspection, our analysis suggests that, if the other countries are anything like the ones we have tested, systematic expert bias in scale positions should not be a major problem. This leaves us with the problem of the imprecision of the estimates of scale position in these systems, of course, but it does suggest on the face of it that we will not be *systematically* wrong if we use the data for countries with only a small number of experts' responses on the basis that it may not be perfect, but it's the best that we've currently got.

Appendix B: Data Section

The data that follow are organised into twenty-four country reports. First, we report means and standard deviations of the scores given by our experts for the variables related to the party system as a whole. These are described in full as variables 17–22 in Table A2 above. The means and standard deviations of the rankings of cabinet positions are also given, though not all cabinet portfolios in each system are listed. We only report rankings for those portfolios listed by a substantial proportion of our respondents . Many experts ignored minor portfolios; thus while rankings for all key portfolios are reported, some less salient portfolios are not listed.

Table 3 (and when applicable Table 4) deals with data specific to individual parties. For each party in each country, it gives means and standard deviations of the "raw" judgments made by our experts on each scale. It also gives a mean standard score for each party, calculated on the basis of all judgments in relation to the scale and country in question. These figures are given for expert judgments of the positions of both party leaders and party voters, and in addition, of the importance of each policy dimension for party leaders.

The remaining section of each country report involve graphic representations of various aspects of these data. Graph 1 gives a notched box plot for each party, describing the distribution of estimates of party positions on the most salient policy dimension. (This dimension contrasts tax cuts with public spending increases.) In the centre of each plot is a short vertical line, representing the median judgment. The two vertical lines on either side of this represent the upper and lower quartiles of our expert judgments. The diagonal lines running horizontally from the median reach their maximum length at the 95 percent confidence intervals around the median. The lines and stars beyond these limits reflect outlying judgments. If the confidence intervals around the medians of two parties do not overlap, then we can be confident on the basis of our data that the two parties have different policy positions. If they do overlap, can cannot be confident on the basis of our data that the two parties have different policies. Note that this is much more likely in those countries for which we had very few expert judgments.

The remaining graphs are a set of two-dimensional plots of party policy positions. First we plot the mean positions of party leaders on the two "common" policy dimensions, those rated most salient across all countries. One of these, as we have seen, was the "tax cuts versus spending increases" dimension. The other was a "social policy" dimension that contrasted policies on matters such as abortion and homosexual law. This plot is presented in two different forms. Graph 3 is a simple two-dimensional depiction of the information, while Graph 2 is a Voronoi tessellation (also known as a Thiessen diagram). This plot is divided up into a number of areas, each of which relates to a party—the boundaries of the area define the portion of the policy space that is closer to that party than to any other party. These are the "policy domains" of each party. In addition to labelling each party with its initials, we give the share of the electorate won by the party in the election immediately before 31 December 1989. The final graph—Graph 4—plots party positions on the "tax cuts versus spending increases" dimension against the most salient "local" dimension in the country concerned. If the "tax cuts versus spending increases" dimension was the most salient, then it was plotted against the second most salient local dimension. In one or two countries, the two common dimensions are also the most salient local dimensions, and this final graph is not given. (All plots in this appendix were generated on a Macintosh SE or CX, using the Systat 5.0 statistical package.)

Australia
Table 1

	Mean	SD
Impact of opposition parties on govt policy (1=lo; 9=hi)	4.29	1.90
Prop. of govts falling on policy disputes (1=lo; 9=hi)	3.33	1.98
Cabinet portfolios as policy (1) or office (9) payoffs	5.81	1.72
Cabinet members publicize internal splits (1=lo; 9=hi)	3.57	1.80
Policy autonomy of cabinet ministers (1=hi; 9=lo)	4.67	1.62
Frequency of cabinet reshuffles (1=lo; 9=hi)	5.76	1.30

RANKING OF CABINET POSITIONS		
Treasurer	1.05	0.23
Finance	4.22	3.38
Foreign Affairs and Trade	4.19	2.71
Industry, Technology and Commerce	4.20	2.08
Environment	9.45	2.88
Defense	5.93	2.89
Transport and Communications	10.14	3.67
Primary Industries and Energy	12.00	2.83
Community Services and Health	8.50	2.62
Social Security	5.85	1.86
Attorney General	8.00	2.83
Employment, Education and Training	6.69	1.89
Industrial Relations	7.60	5.32
Administrative Services	10.50	0.71

Australia
Table 2

Party	Abbrev.
Labor Party	LAB
Liberal Party	LIB
National Party	NAT
Democrats	DEM

Australia
Table 3

Party		Increase services (1) vs cut taxes (20)			Pro friendly relations USSR (1) vs anti (20)		
		Leads	Vots	Imp.	Leads	Vots	Imp.
DEM	Mean Raws	7.71	8.57	9.95	7.10	7.50	8.44
DEM	SD Raws	2.92	2.20	2.63	2.88	2.71	3.84
DEM	Mean Scores	-1.04	-0.74	-1.01	-0.71	-0.75	-0.36
LAB	SD Raws	10.10	8.48	15.00	7.29	7.38	10.32
LAB	Mean Scores	2.70	2.27	2.87	2.17	2.22	3.50
LAB	Mean Raws	-0.45	-0.76	0.27	-0.67	-0.77	0.12
LIB	Mean Scores	15.29	14.24	16.25	12.14	12.91	11.00
LIB	Mean Raws	1.98	2.53	3.32	3.18	2.63	2.73
LIB	SD Raws	0.85	0.76	0.58	0.56	0.55	0.30
NAT	Mean Raws	14.43	14.19	14.55	13.05	14.48	9.53
NAT	SD Raws	2.48	3.03	3.91	3.31	3.22	4.95
NAT	Mean Scores	0.64	0.75	0.15	0.79	0.93	-0.08

Party		Pro public own. (1) vs anti (20)			Pro permissive social policy (1) vs anti (20)		
		Leads	Vots	Imp.	Leads	Vots	Imp.
DEM	Mean Raws	9.91	8.75	9.19	4.67	5.71	14.20
DEM	SD Raws	2.81	2.61	2.58	2.01	2.35	2.86
DEM	Mean Scores	-0.59	-0.53	-0.75	-1.05	-1.10	0.35
LAB	SD Raws	9.10	7.14	13.19	7.19	8.95	14.47
LAB	Mean Scores	2.64	2.58	2.64	2.27	2.42	3.79
LAB	Mean Raws	-0.79	-0.91	0.29	-0.57	-0.43	0.41
LIB	Mean Scores	15.76	14.62	14.14	12.52	12.71	11.80
LIB	Mean Raws	2.57	2.31	3.83	3.30	2.85	4.07
LIB	SD Raws	0.87	0.84	0.54	0.44	0.34	-0.23
NAT	Mean Raws	14.29	13.48	11.81	16.43	16.81	10.60
NAT	SD Raws	3.48	3.98	4.31	2.77	2.58	4.73
NAT	Mean Scores	0.50	0.57	-0.07	1.18	1.18	-0.51

Australia
Table 3 (cont.)

Party		Anticlerical (1) vs proclerical (20)			Pro urban interests (1) vs anti (20)		
		Leads	Vots	Imp.	Leads	Vots	Imp.
DEM	Mean Raws	8.39	8.08	6.22	6.52	6.38	7.24
DEM	SD Raws	2.53	2.35	4.45	2.36	2.58	3.18
DEM	Mean Scores	-0.76	-0.93	-0.17	-0.73	-0.71	-0.96
LAB	SD Raws	8.85	10.25	6.72	6.95	6.38	10.76
LAB	Mean Scores	2.64	2.99	4.65	2.54	2.71	2.97
LAB	Mean Raws	-0.64	-0.38	-0.06	-0.65	-0.71	-0.26
LIB	Mean Scores	13.46	13.17	7.33	9.81	9.91	11.52
LIB	Mean Raws	2.88	2.73	4.22	2.80	2.57	3.23
LIB	SD Raws	0.51	0.37	0.07	-0.12	-0.08	-0.10
NAT	Mean Raws	14.92	15.42	7.72	18.43	18.76	18.62
NAT	SD Raws	3.38	3.23	5.06	1.54	1.41	1.40
NAT	Mean Scores	0.88	0.94	0.16	1.50	1.50	1.32

Party		Pro decentralization of decisions (1) vs anti (20)			Envir. over growth (1) vs. growth over env (20)		
		Leads	Vots	Imp.	Leads	Vots	Imp.
DEM	Mean Raws	8.55	8.16	10.74	3.29	3.81	17.81
DEM	SD Raws	4.77	4.21	3.89	2.15	2.21	2.11
DEM	Mean Scores	-0.37	-0.46	-0.36	-1.29	-1.24	0.99
LAB	SD Raws	13.95	13.05	11.05	8.52	9.00	14.38
LAB	Mean Scores	3.22	3.12	3.05	1.83	2.61	1.83
LAB	Mean Raws	0.85	0.74	-0.28	-0.34	-0.27	0.15
LIB	Mean Scores	9.45	9.84	13.16	13.33	12.52	11.62
LIB	Mean Raws	3.05	2.97	3.55	2.76	2.79	3.14
LIB	SD Raws	-0.16	-0.05	0.28	0.53	0.38	-0.53
NAT	Mean Raws	8.75	9.05	13.42	16.57	16.52	11.29
NAT	SD Raws	4.29	4.42	3.99	2.38	2.91	4.70
NAT	Mean Scores	-0.32	-0.24	0.35	1.11	1.13	-0.61

Party		No influence on party policy (1) vs high (20)			No influence on partic. in govt (1) vs high (20)		
		Leads	Legs	Acts	Leads	Legs	Acts
DEM	Mean Raws	11.81	13.52	15.24	12.14	10.00	9.86
DEM	SD Raws	4.77	3.46	2.76	5.10	5.25	6.44
DEM	Mean Scores	-0.88	0.18	0.88	-0.92	-0.42	0.41
LAB	SD Raws	14.95	13.19	13.43	16.75	12.81	9.00
LAB	Mean Scores	2.85	3.22	3.11	2.84	4.89	6.18
LAB	Mean Raws	-0.02	0.09	0.43	0.24	0.25	0.25
LIB	Mean Scores	16.91	12.33	8.57	17.50	12.00	5.81
LIB	Mean Raws	1.90	4.14	3.19	2.50	3.52	4.32
LIB	SD Raws	0.51	-0.15	-0.76	0.43	0.05	-0.32
NAT	Mean Raws	16.48	12.43	9.48	16.31	12.06	6.00
NAT	SD Raws	2.16	3.49	3.09	3.20	2.82	4.31
NAT	Mean Scores	0.39	-0.12	-0.54	0.13	0.07	-0.29

Party		Do not look to future (1) vs look many years (5)			Give up office (1) vs give up policy (20)	Can use groups (1) vs not (20)	Close to resp (1) vs not (15)
		Leads	Legs	Acts			
DEM	Mean Raws	3.31	3.25	3.25	9.84	12.67	8.50
DEM	SD Raws	1.30	1.29	1.53	4.35	5.58	4.80
DEM	Mean Scores	-0.36	-0.25	-0.17	-1.11	0.65	-0.11
LAB	Mean Raws	3.74	3.67	3.63	15.37	6.62	6.40
LAB	SD Raws	0.56	0.59	0.83	3.27	4.35	3.65
LAB	Mean Scores	0.19	0.25	0.20	0.22	-0.50	-0.57
LIB	Mean Raws	3.63	3.56	3.47	16.53	8.86	8.15
LIB	SD Raws	0.50	0.51	0.77	2.44	4.81	3.63
LIB	Mean Scores	0.06	0.12	0.05	0.50	-0.08	-0.18
NAT	Mean Raws	3.63	3.33	3.32	16.11	8.91	12.85
NAT	SD Raws	0.50	0.77	0.95	2.51	4.71	3.44
NAT	Mean Scores	0.06	-0.15	-0.11	0.39	-0.07	0.86

**Australia
Graph 1**

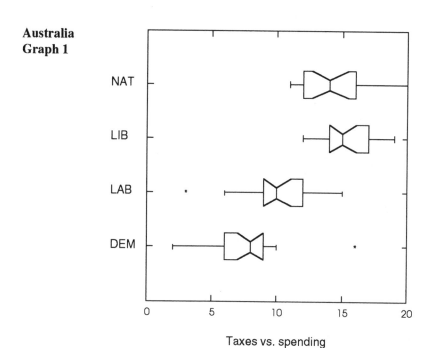

Taxes vs. spending

**Australia
Graph 2
(7/87 election %)**

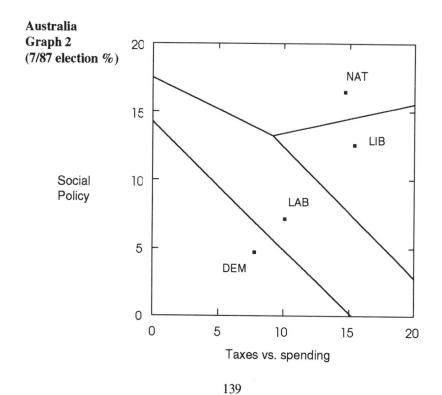

Social
Policy

Taxes vs. spending

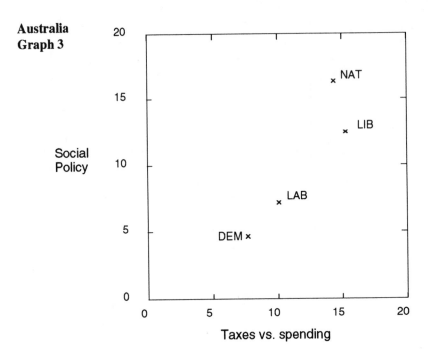

**Australia
Graph 3**

Social
Policy

Taxes vs. spending

Austria
Table 1

	Mean	SD
Impact of opposition parties on govt policy (1=lo; 9=hi)	4.14	2.12
Prop. of govts falling on policy disputes (1=lo; 9=hi)	3.50	2.14
Cabinet portfolios as policy (1) or office (9) payoffs	6.14	2.73
Cabinet members publicize internal splits (1=lo; 9=hi)	3.75	1.98
Policy autonomy of cabinet ministers (1=hi; 9=lo)	3.50	2.14
Frequency of cabinet reshuffles (1=lo; 9=hi)	4.00	1.85

RANKING OF CABINET POSITIONS

	Mean	SD
Finance	1.00	0.00
Foreign Affairs	5.67	1.53
Economic Affairs	2.25	0.50
Environment, Youth and Family	10.50	3.54
National Defense	10.00	2.65
Interior	4.00	1.41
Employment and Social Affairs	5.50	1.29
Agriculture and Forestry	8.50	3.54
Justice	9.67	1.53
Education, the Arts and Sport	8.67	0.58

Austria
Table 2

Party	Abbrev.
Socialist Party	SPO
People's Party	OVP
Freedom Party	FPO
Greens	G
Communist Party	KPO

Austria
Table 3

Party		Increase services (1) vs cut taxes (20)			Pro friendly relations USSR (1) vs anti (20)		
		Leads	Vots	Imp.	Leads	Vots	Imp.
FPO	Mean Raws	15.44	16.63	13.78	12.00	13.14	9.13
FPO	SD Raws	2.35	2.13	3.80	2.93	4.10	2.59
FPO	Mean Scores	1.02	1.23	0.03	1.07	1.06	-0.47
G	Mean Raws	7.00	6.38	10.67	6.88	7.14	9.57
G	SD Raws	1.80	2.13	4.61	2.48	2.80	3.26
G	Mean Scores	-0.72	-0.87	-0.83	-0.24	-0.27	-0.35
KPO	Mean Raws	5.25	5.67	14.71	3.57	3.67	13.50
KPO	SD Raws	3.01	2.34	3.77	3.82	3.62	5.21
KPO	Mean Scores	-1.08	-1.01	0.29	-1.08	-1.03	0.68
OVP	Mean Raws	13.56	13.00	15.56	8.75	9.00	11.63
OVP	SD Raws	4.80	4.21	1.42	3.45	4.20	3.82
OVP	Mean Scores	0.63	0.49	0.52	0.24	0.14	0.19
SPO	Mean Raws	10.67	10.13	13.89	7.38	8.14	11.25
SPO	SD Raws	2.83	2.48	2.32	2.07	2.97	3.62
SPO	Mean Scores	0.03	-0.10	0.06	-0.11	-0.05	0.09

Party		Pro public own. (1) vs anti (20)			Pro permissive social policy (1) vs anti (20)		
		Leads	Vots	Imp.	Leads	Vots	Imp.
FPO	Mean Raws	15.78	15.13	15.13	11.89	13.88	9.13
FPO	SD Raws	6.00	5.99	3.94	4.40	5.11	3.04
FPO	Mean Scores	1.06	1.02	0.33	0.64	0.73	-1.20
G	Mean Raws	7.56	7.63	10.50	4.25	5.57	16.00
G	SD Raws	2.07	1.92	4.47	2.38	2.44	1.85
G	Mean Scores	-0.39	-0.36	-0.71	-1.05	-1.02	0.56
KPO	Mean Raws	3.00	3.86	16.43	6.83	8.00	17.57
KPO	SD Raws	2.67	2.91	5.53	3.66	4.08	1.62
KPO	Mean Scores	-1.20	-1.06	0.63	-0.48	-0.51	0.96
OVP	Mean Raws	12.67	12.63	14.63	13.78	14.38	12.13
OVP	SD Raws	4.39	4.60	2.62	1.48	1.69	3.76
OVP	Mean Scores	0.51	0.56	0.22	1.06	0.84	-0.43
SPO	Mean Raws	9.11	8.00	11.88	7.00	8.38	14.75
SPO	SD Raws	2.26	2.27	3.52	1.12	2.20	2.19
SPO	Mean Scores	-0.12	-0.29	-0.40	-0.44	-0.43	0.24

Austria
Table 3 (cont.)

		Anticlerical (1) vs proclerical (20)			Pro urban interests (1) vs anti (20)		
Party		Leads	Vots	Imp.	Leads	Vots	Imp.
FPO	Mean Raws	6.13	5.86	8.29	10.88	11.17	8.67
FPO	SD Raws	2.75	1.46	4.39	3.00	2.56	2.34
FPO	Mean Scores	-0.44	-0.55	-0.23	0.42	0.49	-0.56
G	Mean Raws	7.13	7.29	6.86	9.38	9.14	11.83
G	SD Raws	2.53	1.80	3.93	3.70	3.39	2.79
G	Mean Scores	-0.22	-0.18	-0.53	0.08	0.07	0.15
KPO	Mean Raws	3.29	3.67	8.80	3.71	3.33	8.00
KPO	SD Raws	2.63	3.20	5.31	2.75	3.01	7.45
KPO	Mean Scores	-1.06	-1.11	-0.13	-1.18	-1.14	-0.71
OVP	Mean Raws	15.00	13.86	13.57	14.38	14.57	15.17
OVP	SD Raws	2.51	0.90	4.79	1.06	2.44	2.40
OVP	Mean Scores	1.49	1.52	0.88	1.20	1.20	0.90
SPO	Mean Raws	8.63	8.57	9.29	6.00	5.43	11.67
SPO	SD Raws	2.39	1.72	3.82	1.60	2.30	3.08
SPO	Mean Scores	0.10	0.16	-0.02	-0.67	-0.70	0.11

		Pro decentralization of decisions (1) vs anti (20)			Envir. over growth(1) v. growth over env (20)		
Party		Leads	Vots	Imp.	Leads	Vots	Imp.
FPO	Mean Raws	8.25	7.17	6.38	12.56	12.00	11.86
FPO	SD Raws	3.66	1.94	3.42	3.50	2.52	3.63
FPO	Mean Scores	-0.28	-0.40	-0.37	0.42	0.61	-0.48
G	Mean Raws	5.38	4.33	11.38	2.33	3.63	18.75
G	SD Raws	3.07	2.34	5.04	2.60	2.77	1.58
G	Mean Scores	-0.82	-0.92	0.57	-1.59	-1.39	1.05
KPO	Mean Raws	15.00	17.20	5.00	12.00	11.00	9.40
KPO	SD Raws	6.11	0.84	6.14	3.54	3.00	7.02
KPO	Mean Scores	0.99	1.46	-0.63	0.31	0.37	-1.03
OVP	Mean Raws	7.22	5.17	11.13	13.11	10.88	14.14
OVP	SD Raws	4.35	2.32	4.91	1.69	2.80	2.04
OVP	Mean Scores	-0.47	-0.77	0.53	0.53	0.34	0.03
SPO	Mean Raws	13.33	14.00	7.38	12.78	11.00	14.00
SPO	SD Raws	3.00	1.79	4.84	2.39	2.73	2.31
SPO	Mean Scores	0.67	0.87	-0.18	0.47	0.37	-0.01

Austria
Table 3 (cont.)

Party		No influence on party policy (1) vs high (20)			No influence on partic. in govt (1) vs high (20)		
		Leads	Legs	Acts	Leads	Legs	Acts
FPO	Mean Raws	17.11	12.25	8.89	16.25	8.86	6.00
FPO	SD Raws	1.90	3.28	3.95	3.01	3.93	4.14
FPO	Mean Scores	0.45	0.06	0.00	0.10	-0.34	-0.18
G	Mean Raws	11.00	13.63	14.00	12.25	12.57	9.75
G	SD Raws	4.54	3.02	3.78	5.85	5.06	5.90
G	Mean Scores	-1.21	0.47	1.08	-0.78	0.49	0.58
KPO	Mean Raws	18.13	14.00	5.57	15.67	6.33	2.67
KPO	SD Raws	1.46	4.24	4.50	7.34	5.13	1.97
KPO	Mean Scores	0.73	0.57	-0.71	-0.03	-0.90	-0.84
OVP	Mean Raws	14.44	10.63	8.11	17.25	10.71	7.63
OVP	SD Raws	3.50	3.42	4.14	1.83	3.99	4.93
OVP	Mean Scores	-0.27	-0.41	-0.17	0.32	0.07	0.15
SPO	Mean Raws	16.33	11.13	7.78	17.50	11.14	7.25
SPO	SD Raws	1.80	3.76	3.87	1.51	4.22	5.06
SPO	Mean Scores	0.24	-0.26	-0.24	0.38	0.17	0.08

Party		Do not look to future (1) vs look many years (5)			Give up office (1) vs give up policy (20)	Can use groups (1) vs not (20)	Close to resp (1) vs not (15)
		Leads	Legs	Acts			
FPO	Mean Raws	3.88	3.43	3.67	15.67	14.56	13.43
FPO	SD Raws	0.84	0.79	0.52	4.47	3.68	1.27
FPO	Mean Scores	-0.08	-0.06	0.14	0.60	0.74	0.81
G	Mean Raws	4.14	3.50	3.17	7.44	8.33	7.75
G	SD Raws	0.69	1.38	1.84	5.22	5.07	3.99
G	Mean Scores	0.22	0.02	-0.33	-0.93	-0.34	-0.69
KPO	Mean Raws	3.60	2.00	3.40	7.83	15.75	14.00
KPO	SD Raws	1.67	1.41	1.52	6.18	5.42	2.45
KPO	Mean Scores	-0.39	-1.50	-0.11	-0.86	0.95	0.96
OVP	Mean Raws	3.88	3.71	3.67	15.00	7.00	8.86
OVP	SD Raws	0.84	0.76	0.52	1.94	2.69	2.85
OVP	Mean Scores	-0.08	0.24	0.14	0.48	-0.57	-0.40
SPO	Mean Raws	4.13	3.71	3.67	14.67	6.33	8.88
SPO	SD Raws	0.64	0.76	0.52	2.12	4.80	3.27
SPO	Mean Scores	0.20	0.24	0.14	0.42	-0.68	-0.39

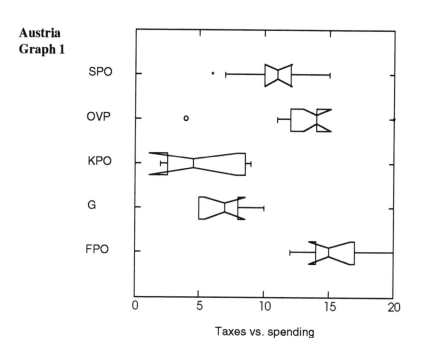

**Austria
Graph 1**

Taxes vs. spending

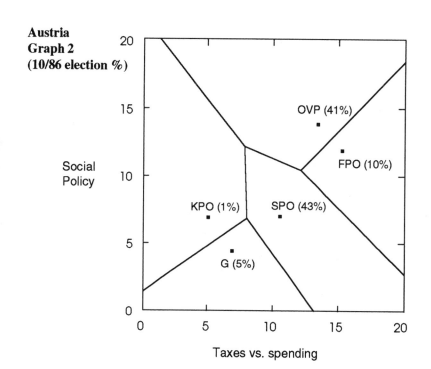

**Austria
Graph 2
(10/86 election %)**

Social
Policy

Taxes vs. spending

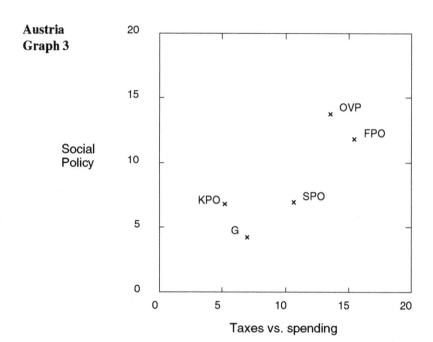

**Austria
Graph 3**

Social
Policy

Taxes vs. spending

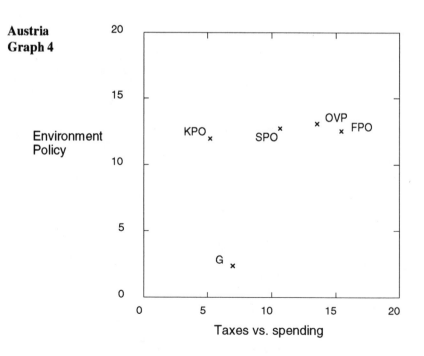

**Austria
Graph 4**

Environment
Policy

Taxes vs. spending

Belgium
Table 1

	Mean	SD
Impact of opposition parties on govt policy (1=lo; 9=hi)	2.60	1.52
Prop. of govts falling on policy disputes (1=lo; 9=hi)	8.40	0.55
Cabinet portfolios as policy (1) or office (9) payoffs	6.00	1.41
Cabinet members publicize internal splits (1=lo; 9=hi)	4.60	2.41
Policy autonomy of cabinet ministers (1=hi; 9=lo)	5.40	1.82
Frequency of cabinet reshuffles (1=lo; 9=hi)	4.60	2.07

RANKING OF CABINET POSITIONS

Finance	2.00	1.00
Foreign Affairs	4.00	1.00
Defense	7.00	1.41
Social Welfare	5.00	1.41
Justice	2.00	NA
Education	9.00	NA
Labor	5.00	NA

Belgium
Table 2

Party	Abbrev.
Flemish Christian People's Party	CVP
Francophone Christian Democrat Party	PSC
Flemish Socialist Party	SP
Francophone Socialist Party	PS
Flemish Party of Liberty and Progress	PVV
Francophone Reform Liberal Party	PRL
Flemish People's Union	VU
Francophone Democratic Front	FDF
Flemish Environmentalist Party (Agalev)	AG
Francophone Environmentalist Party (Ecolo)	ECO
Flemish Nationalist Party	FB

Belgium
Table 3

Party		Increase services (1) vs cut taxes (20)			Pro friendly relations USSR (1) vs anti (20)		
		Leads	Vots	Imp.	Leads	Vots	Imp.
AGA	Mean Raws	9.20	9.00	9.00	9.75	8.00	8.40
AGA	SD Raws	4.09	5.24	5.20	4.27	4.24	5.94
AGA	Mean Scores	-0.54	-0.67	-0.91	-0.38	-0.66	-0.55
CVP	Mean Raws	12.40	12.20	15.60	11.40	11.40	12.00
CVP	SD Raws	3.65	2.28	2.07	3.78	3.78	3.08
CVP	Mean Scores	0.16	0.04	0.36	0.02	0.07	0.20
ECO	Mean Raws	9.20	9.00	9.00	9.75	8.00	8.40
ECO	SD Raws	4.09	5.24	5.20	4.27	4.24	5.94
ECO	Mean Scores	-0.54	-0.67	-0.91	-0.38	-0.66	-0.55
FB	Mean Raws	15.00	15.00	3.00	17.00	18.33	5.00
FB	SD Raws	4.58	4.58	1.41	4.36	2.08	2.83
FB	Mean Scores	0.72	0.65	-2.06	1.39	1.55	-1.25
FDF	Mean Raws	10.75	12.00	11.25	13.00	12.50	7.00
FDF	SD Raws	3.10	3.61	4.03	2.83	2.12	4.24
FDF	Mean Scores	-0.21	-0.01	-0.47	0.41	0.30	-0.84
PRL	Mean Raws	17.00	17.80	19.20	13.40	14.20	12.20
PRL	SD Raws	2.00	0.84	0.84	3.65	3.70	4.32
PRL	Mean Scores	1.16	1.27	1.05	0.51	0.67	0.25
PS	Mean Raws	6.80	7.80	14.80	9.20	7.80	13.40
PS	SD Raws	2.95	2.49	3.56	3.03	2.59	1.14
PS	Mean Scores	-1.07	-0.93	0.21	-0.52	-0.70	0.50
PSC	Mean Raws	12.60	12.20	15.60	11.40	11.20	12.00
PSC	SD Raws	3.51	2.28	2.07	3.36	3.49	3.08
PSC	Mean Scores	0.20	0.04	0.36	0.02	0.02	0.20
PVV	Mean Raws	17.20	17.80	19.60	13.40	14.20	12.20
PVV	SD Raws	2.17	0.84	0.55	3.65	3.70	4.32
PVV	Mean Scores	1.20	1.27	1.13	0.51	0.67	0.25
SP	Mean Raws	7.00	8.20	14.40	7.40	6.60	15.80
SP	SD Raws	3.16	2.28	3.51	2.61	3.21	3.03
SP	Mean Scores	-1.03	-0.85	0.13	-0.96	-0.96	1.00
VU	Mean Raws	12.60	12.75	12.25	11.50	13.00	10.25
VU	SD Raws	2.30	2.06	4.99	5.20	6.25	6.90
VU	Mean Scores	0.20	0.16	-0.28	0.04	0.41	-0.16

Belgium
Table 3 (cont.)

Party		Pro public own. (1) vs anti (20)			Pro permissive social policy (1) vs anti (20)		
		Leads	Vots	Imp.	Leads	Vots	Imp.
AGA	Mean Raws	8.00	7.40	4.00	6.60	5.60	14.20
AGA	SD Raws	3.94	3.36	3.37	3.21	4.34	3.83
AGA	Mean Scores	-0.82	-0.85	-0.93	-0.61	-0.69	0.16
CVP	Mean Raws	14.00	14.00	10.20	18.20	15.20	15.80
CVP	SD Raws	2.35	2.45	4.55	1.30	4.09	2.39
CVP	Mean Scores	0.31	0.33	0.02	1.29	0.97	0.47
ECO	Mean Raws	8.00	7.40	4.00	6.60	5.60	14.20
ECO	SD Raws	3.94	3.36	3.37	3.21	4.34	3.83
ECO	Mean Scores	-0.82	-0.85	-0.93	-0.61	-0.69	0.16
FB	Mean Raws	16.00	17.67	9.50	19.00	19.00	12.00
FB	SD Raws	3.61	1.53	9.19	1.00	1.00	NA
FB	Mean Scores	0.68	0.98	-0.09	1.42	1.62	-0.27
FDF	Mean Raws	10.33	10.33	3.67	9.67	9.00	6.00
FDF	SD Raws	1.16	1.16	2.08	4.16	4.58	4.36
FDF	Mean Scores	-0.38	-0.33	-0.98	-0.11	-0.10	-1.43
PRL	Mean Raws	18.80	19.00	12.00	8.75	9.00	9.20
PRL	SD Raws	1.30	1.23	7.97	5.91	6.68	5.22
PRL	Mean Scores	1.21	1.22	0.30	-0.26	-0.10	-0.81
PS	Mean Raws	6.60	5.60	16.60	4.20	5.20	18.60
PS	SD Raws	2.30	1.95	4.39	1.79	1.48	1.34
PS	Mean Scores	-1.09	-1.18	1.00	-1.00	-0.76	1.01
PSC	Mean Raws	14.00	13.60	10.20	16.20	13.75	16.20
PSC	SD Raws	2.35	3.13	4.55	1.64	4.03	2.59
PSC	Mean Scores	0.31	0.26	0.02	0.96	0.72	0.55
PVV	Mean Raws	18.80	19.00	12.00	6.80	7.80	9.20
PVV	SD Raws	1.30	1.23	7.97	3.63	4.55	5.22
PVV	Mean Scores	1.21	1.22	0.30	-0.58	-0.31	-0.81
SP	Mean Raws	6.80	6.00	16.00	4.20	5.20	18.00
SP	SD Raws	3.35	2.74	5.66	1.79	1.48	1.23
SP	Mean Scores	-1.05	-1.11	0.91	-1.00	-0.76	0.90
VU	Mean Raws	15.40	15.40	6.50	16.40	14.40	8.75
VU	SD Raws	4.51	4.04	2.89	2.88	4.83	4.79
VU	Mean Scores	0.57	0.58	-0.55	0.99	0.83	-0.90

Belgium
Table 3 (cont.)

Party		Anticlerical (1) vs proclerical (20)			Pro urban interests (1) vs anti (20)		
		Leads	Vots	Imp.	Leads	Vots	Imp.
AGA	Mean Raws	10.50	10.00	4.00	12.00	12.00	11.67
AGA	SD Raws	5.75	3.74	4.24	1.00	3.61	9.24
AGA	Mean Scores	-0.35	-0.28	-0.67	0.39	0.41	0.39
CVP	Mean Raws	17.80	16.00	17.20	14.00	12.67	16.33
CVP	SD Raws	1.92	3.39	2.17	2.16	2.08	2.08
CVP	Mean Scores	1.13	0.98	1.24	0.80	0.55	1.11
ECO	Mean Raws	10.50	7.75	4.00	12.00	12.00	10.67
ECO	SD Raws	5.75	6.08	4.24	1.00	3.61	8.51
ECO	Mean Scores	-0.35	-0.76	-0.67	0.39	0.41	0.24
FB	Mean Raws	16.67	17.33	11.50	11.00	11.00	NA
FB	SD Raws	2.52	3.79	0.71	NA	NA	NA
FB	Mean Scores	0.90	1.27	0.42	0.19	0.20	NA
FDF	Mean Raws	11.00	11.00	5.67	5.67	6.00	2.00
FDF	SD Raws	4.00	1.00	5.69	5.03	5.00	NA
FDF	Mean Scores	-0.25	-0.07	-0.43	-0.91	-0.86	-1.10
PRL	Mean Raws	11.40	10.40	5.60	9.00	9.00	3.75
PRL	SD Raws	3.36	2.07	7.23	7.21	7.21	2.50
PRL	Mean Scores	-0.17	-0.20	-0.44	-0.22	-0.22	-0.83
PS	Mean Raws	6.60	6.20	8.20	5.33	6.67	8.67
PS	SD Raws	3.05	3.27	7.66	3.79	4.93	6.81
PS	Mean Scores	-1.14	-1.08	-0.06	-0.98	-0.72	-0.07
PSC	Mean Raws	17.00	15.40	17.00	15.00	14.00	16.33
PSC	SD Raws	2.92	3.85	2.12	2.71	2.94	2.08
PSC	Mean Scores	0.97	0.86	1.21	1.01	0.83	1.11
PVV	Mean Raws	11.20	10.40	5.20	8.67	9.00	3.75
PVV	SD Raws	3.49	2.07	6.38	7.10	7.21	2.50
PVV	Mean Scores	-0.21	-0.20	-0.50	-0.29	-0.22	-0.83
SP	Mean Raws	7.40	7.40	8.50	5.33	6.67	12.50
SP	SD Raws	2.51	2.51	7.94	3.79	4.93	2.12
SP	Mean Scores	-0.97	-0.83	-0.02	-0.98	-0.72	0.52
VU	Mean Raws	15.00	14.75	8.50	11.00	11.50	5.67
VU	SD Raws	3.54	3.78	6.61	0.00	0.71	4.16
VU	Mean Scores	0.56	0.72	-0.02	0.19	0.30	-0.53

Belgium
Table 3 (cont.)

Party		Pro decentralization of decisions (1) vs anti (20)			Envir. over growth (1) v. growth over env (20)		
		Leads	Vots	Imp.	Leads	Vots	Imp.
AGA	Mean Raws	3.33	1.50	20.00	2.00	1.60	20.00
AGA	SD Raws	2.52	0.71	NA	1.73	0.89	0.00
AGA	Mean Scores	-1.26	-1.51	1.19	-1.54	-1.52	1.28
CVP	Mean Raws	14.00	13.00	13.00	10.40	11.20	11.50
CVP	SD Raws	3.00	2.65	1.00	3.05	2.86	4.93
CVP	Mean Scores	0.48	0.46	-0.31	-0.05	0.16	0.11
ECO	Mean Raws	3.33	1.67	20.00	2.00	1.60	20.00
ECO	SD Raws	2.52	0.58	NA	1.73	0.89	0.00
ECO	Mean Scores	-1.26	-1.48	1.19	-1.54	-1.52	1.28
FB	Mean Raws	2.00	2.00	20.00	13.00	8.00	1.00
FB	SD Raws	NA	NA	NA	2.83	NA	NA
FB	Mean Scores	-1.48	-1.43	1.19	0.42	-0.40	-1.34
FDF	Mean Raws	7.50	7.00	7.00	10.00	10.00	5.67
FDF	SD Raws	0.71	1.41	NA	1.00	2.65	5.69
FDF	Mean Scores	-0.58	-0.57	-1.59	-0.12	-0.05	-0.70
PRL	Mean Raws	16.00	15.33	15.00	16.40	16.50	5.20
PRL	SD Raws	3.00	2.08	5.66	3.29	2.38	5.85
PRL	Mean Scores	0.80	0.87	0.12	1.02	1.08	-0.76
PS	Mean Raws	13.00	12.00	13.50	13.60	14.20	12.25
PS	SD Raws	6.56	5.00	3.54	4.39	4.44	2.06
PS	Mean Scores	0.32	0.29	-0.20	0.52	0.68	0.21
PSC	Mean Raws	15.00	14.67	15.00	10.00	11.00	11.50
PSC	SD Raws	1.73	0.58	1.41	2.35	2.74	4.93
PSC	Mean Scores	0.64	0.75	0.12	-0.12	0.12	0.11
PVV	Mean Raws	16.00	15.33	11.50	16.40	16.50	3.60
PVV	SD Raws	3.00	2.08	10.61	3.29	2.38	3.98
PVV	Mean Scores	0.80	0.87	-0.63	1.02	1.08	-0.98
SP	Mean Raws	16.00	14.50	12.67	12.20	12.00	11.00
SP	SD Raws	5.66	3.54	4.93	4.44	3.39	6.88
SP	Mean Scores	0.80	0.72	-0.38	0.28	0.30	0.04
VU	Mean Raws	9.50	7.00	17.50	12.75	12.00	4.67
VU	SD Raws	7.78	4.24	2.12	2.36	3.61	6.35
VU	Mean Scores	-0.26	-0.57	0.65	0.37	0.30	-0.84

Belgium
Table 3 (cont.)

		No influence on party policy (1) vs high (20)			No influence on partic. in govt (1) vs high (20)		
Party		Leads	Legs	Acts	Leads	Legs	Acts
AGA	Mean Raws	8.40	14.00	16.75	11.00	10.00	10.00
AGA	SD Raws	4.56	4.18	3.59	9.54	8.19	9.54
AGA	Mean Scores	-1.63	0.08	1.50	-1.42	-0.13	0.83
CVP	Mean Raws	17.40	14.40	5.00	17.80	9.80	4.25
CVP	SD Raws	1.14	2.88	2.94	1.48	4.92	3.95
CVP	Mean Scores	0.40	0.22	-0.54	0.26	-0.14	-0.27
ECO	Mean Raws	8.40	14.00	16.75	11.00	10.00	10.00
ECO	SD Raws	4.56	4.18	3.59	9.54	8.19	9.54
ECO	Mean Scores	-1.63	0.08	1.50	-1.42	-0.13	0.83
FB	Mean Raws	19.50	12.50	4.50	20.00	3.00	1.00
FB	SD Raws	0.71	9.19	4.95	NA	NA	NA
FB	Mean Scores	0.87	-0.45	-0.63	0.80	-0.47	-0.88
FDF	Mean Raws	16.50	12.50	8.50	18.00	6.50	5.00
FDF	SD Raws	0.71	0.71	6.36	2.83	7.78	5.66
FDF	Mean Scores	0.20	-0.45	0.07	0.31	-0.30	-0.12
PRL	Mean Raws	18.60	13.60	5.25	17.80	15.20	3.75
PRL	SD Raws	1.14	1.82	4.35	1.48	1.22	3.78
PRL	Mean Scores	0.67	-0.06	-0.50	0.26	1.11	-0.36
PS	Mean Raws	16.80	13.40	5.75	17.60	10.20	5.25
PS	SD Raws	2.59	1.52	4.99	1.52	5.22	4.92
PS	Mean Scores	0.27	-0.13	-0.41	0.21	-0.12	-0.08
PSC	Mean Raws	16.60	13.80	5.00	17.80	9.80	4.25
PSC	SD Raws	1.14	2.17	2.94	1.48	4.92	3.95
PSC	Mean Scores	0.22	0.01	-0.54	0.26	-0.14	-0.27
PVV	Mean Raws	18.40	14.00	6.00	17.80	10.00	5.00
PVV	SD Raws	0.89	2.55	3.56	1.48	5.05	4.62
PVV	Mean Scores	0.63	0.08	-0.37	0.26	-0.13	-0.12
SP	Mean Raws	17.20	13.80	5.75	17.60	10.20	5.25
SP	SD Raws	1.92	2.49	4.92	1.52	5.22	4.92
SP	Mean Scores	0.36	0.01	-0.41	0.21	-0.12	-0.08
VU	Mean Raws	17.25	14.00	8.50	16.50	10.25	6.75
VU	SD Raws	1.89	2.16	4.20	2.89	6.45	5.32
VU	Mean Scores	0.37	0.08	0.07	-0.06	-0.12	0.21

Belgium
Table 3 (cont.)

Party		Do not look to future (1) vs look many years (5)			Give up office (1) vs give up policy (20)	Can use groups (1) vs not (20)	Close to resp (1) vs not (15)
		Leads	Legs	Acts			
AGA	Mean Raws	4.33	4.33	4.33	6.33	15.75	3.80
AGA	SD Raws	0.58	0.58	1.16	8.39	3.20	1.64
AGA	Mean Scores	0.60	0.55	0.53	-0.30	1.37	-0.92
CVP	Mean Raws	4.25	3.75	3.75	11.50	4.00	10.50
CVP	SD Raws	0.50	1.26	0.50	7.33	1.41	3.32
CVP	Mean Scores	0.50	-0.10	-0.27	0.57	-0.73	0.61
ECO	Mean Raws	4.33	4.33	4.33	6.33	15.75	3.00
ECO	SD Raws	0.58	0.58	1.16	8.39	3.20	2.16
ECO	Mean Scores	0.60	0.55	0.53	-0.30	1.37	-1.10
FB	Mean Raws	4.00	4.00	5.00	1.00	14.00	15.00
FB	SD Raws	NA	NA	NA	0.00	8.49	0.00
FB	Mean Scores	0.19	0.18	1.44	-1.20	1.06	1.64
FDF	Mean Raws	4.00	4.33	4.33	9.67	12.00	2.67
FDF	SD Raws	1.00	0.58	1.16	5.51	1.41	1.16
FDF	Mean Scores	0.19	0.55	0.53	0.26	0.70	-1.18
PRL	Mean Raws	3.75	3.50	3.75	9.00	5.50	9.75
PRL	SD Raws	0.50	1.00	0.50	7.55	3.70	3.10
PRL	Mean Scores	-0.11	-0.39	-0.27	0.15	-0.46	0.44
PS	Mean Raws	3.50	3.50	3.75	9.50	3.75	6.50
PS	SD Raws	1.00	1.00	0.50	6.56	1.71	1.29
PS	Mean Scores	-0.42	-0.39	-0.27	0.23	-0.77	-0.30
PSC	Mean Raws	4.25	3.75	3.75	10.67	4.25	8.25
PSC	SD Raws	0.50	1.26	0.50	8.51	1.89	5.56
PSC	Mean Scores	0.50	-0.10	-0.27	0.43	-0.68	0.10
PVV	Mean Raws	3.75	3.50	3.75	6.33	5.75	9.60
PVV	SD Raws	0.50	1.00	0.50	4.73	4.11	3.36
PVV	Mean Scores	-0.11	-0.39	-0.27	-0.30	-0.42	0.41
SP	Mean Raws	3.50	3.50	3.75	7.50	4.00	6.60
SP	SD Raws	1.00	1.00	0.50	4.93	2.16	4.22
SP	Mean Scores	-0.42	-0.39	-0.27	-0.10	-0.73	-0.28
VU	Mean Raws	3.00	4.25	4.00	7.75	9.00	11.00
VU	SD Raws	1.41	0.50	1.16	1.71	4.55	2.65
VU	Mean Scores	-1.02	0.46	0.07	-0.06	0.17	0.72

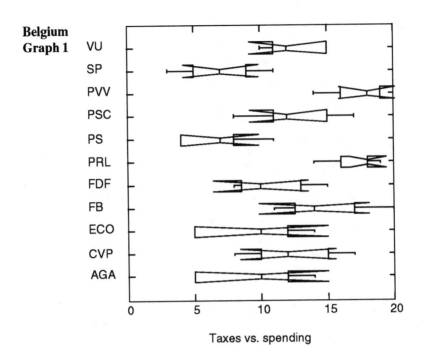

Belgium Graph 1

Taxes vs. spending

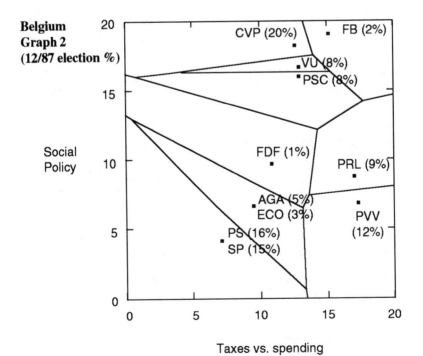

Belgium Graph 2 (12/87 election %)

Social Policy

Taxes vs. spending

**Belgium
Graph 3**

Social
Policy

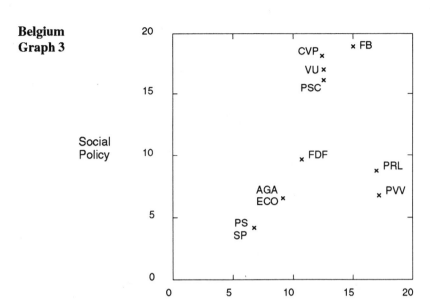

Taxes vs. spending

**Belgium
Graph 4**

Centralization
Policy

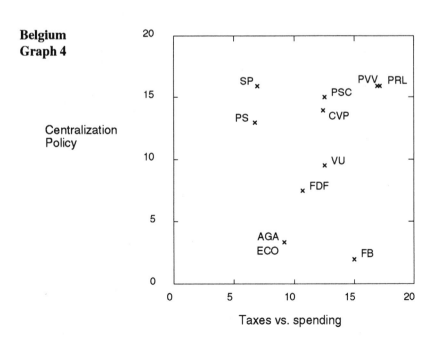

Taxes vs. spending

Britain
Table 1

	Mean	SD
Impact of opposition parties on govt policy (1=lo; 9=hi)	2.03	0.63
Prop. of govts falling on policy disputes (1=lo; 9=hi)	2.00	1.52
Cabinet portfolios as policy (1) or office (9) payoffs	5.94	1.86
Cabinet members publicize internal splits (1=lo; 9=hi)	3.94	1.94
Policy autonomy of cabinet ministers (1=hi; 9=lo)	4.36	1.67
Frequency of cabinet reshuffles (1=lo; 9=hi)	6.33	1.19

RANKING OF CABINET POSITIONS

Chancellor of the Exchequer	1.12	0.42
Foreign and Commonwealth Affairs	2.39	1.17
Environment	6.55	2.84
Defense	6.04	2.70
Transport	9.86	2.12
Energy	10.13	1.73
Health	6.56	2.25
Social Services	6.65	2.85
Agriculture, Fisheries and Food	10.08	3.45
Home Secretary	3.26	1.26
Education and Science	7.39	2.79
Employment	8.20	2.70
Trade and Industry	6.18	2.75

Britain
Table 2

Party	Abbrev.
Conservative Party	CON
Democrats (Alliance)	DEM
Labor Party	LAB
Plaid Cymru	PC
Scottish National Party	SNP

Britain
Table 3

Party		Increase services (1) vs cut taxes (20)			Pro friendly relations USSR (1) vs anti (20)		
		Leads	Vots	Imp.	Leads	Vots	Imp.
CON	Mean Raws	17.21	12.91	17.50	11.21	11.42	14.12
CON	SD Raws	2.31	2.67	2.12	3.19	3.33	4.42
CON	Mean Scores	1.64	1.39	0.90	1.23	1.15	0.81
DEM	Mean Raws	8.21	8.25	12.47	6.88	7.21	10.47
DEM	SD Raws	2.48	2.05	3.74	2.78	2.55	3.73
DEM	Mean Scores	-0.08	0.05	-0.14	-0.03	-0.13	0.03
LAB	Mean Raws	5.35	6.00	14.65	4.97	6.12	11.97
LAB	SD Raws	2.20	2.09	4.04	2.05	2.74	3.75
LAB	Mean Scores	-0.63	-0.60	0.31	-0.59	-0.46	0.35
PC	Mean Raws	5.43	6.44	9.41	5.58	6.54	5.88
PC	SD Raws	2.80	2.41	4.66	2.40	2.12	2.95
PC	Mean Scores	-0.62	-0.47	-0.78	-0.41	-0.34	-0.95
SNP	Mean Raws	5.96	6.37	10.37	5.73	6.42	7.44
SNP	SD Raws	2.47	2.12	4.51	1.95	1.92	3.24
SNP	Mean Scores	-0.51	-0.50	-0.58	-0.37	-0.37	-0.62

Party		Pro public own. (1) vs anti (20)			Pro permissive social policy (1) vs anti (20)		
		Leads	Vots	Imp.	Leads	Vots	Imp.
CON	Mean Raws	18.18	15.36	16.27	15.34	16.56	11.88
CON	SD Raws	1.59	2.40	3.08	2.64	1.97	4.92
CON	Mean Scores	1.52	1.30	1.01	1.45	1.27	-0.12
DEM	Mean Raws	12.03	11.46	9.55	6.87	8.45	13.09
DEM	SD Raws	2.19	1.92	3.61	2.39	2.54	4.18
DEM	Mean Scores	0.27	0.27	-0.44	-0.65	-0.79	0.12
LAB	Mean Raws	7.44	8.24	13.62	6.53	10.31	14.82
LAB	SD Raws	1.93	2.28	3.24	2.09	3.14	5.46
LAB	Mean Scores	-0.67	-0.58	0.44	-0.73	-0.32	0.46
PC	Mean Raws	7.30	8.33	8.39	8.96	10.85	10.93
PC	SD Raws	2.63	2.87	3.99	2.56	3.30	5.33
PC	Mean Scores	-0.70	-0.55	-0.69	-0.13	-0.18	-0.31
SNP	Mean Raws	7.33	8.15	9.07	9.56	11.39	11.21
SNP	SD Raws	2.79	2.85	3.72	1.83	2.83	4.85
SNP	Mean Scores	-0.70	-0.60	-0.54	0.02	-0.05	-0.25

Britain
Table 3 (cont.)

Party		Anticlerical (1) vs proclerical (20)			Pro urban interests (1) vs anti (20)		
		Leads	Vots	Imp.	Leads	Vots	Imp.
CON	Mean Raws	10.30	12.78	5.58	12.69	11.84	9.77
CON	SD Raws	2.06	2.33	4.10	2.41	3.46	4.37
CON	Mean Scores	-0.19	0.55	0.16	0.59	0.58	-0.03
DEM	Mean Raws	10.89	11.50	3.74	11.17	10.52	9.79
DEM	SD Raws	1.36	1.51	2.60	2.58	2.27	4.00
DEM	Mean Scores	0.06	0.06	-0.34	0.19	0.25	-0.03
LAB	Mean Raws	10.00	9.67	4.58	6.15	4.80	9.45
LAB	SD Raws	2.74	1.32	3.50	2.68	1.87	4.55
LAB	Mean Scores	-0.31	-0.66	-0.11	-1.14	-1.19	-0.11
PC	Mean Raws	11.50	11.88	5.75	12.29	11.57	11.19
PC	SD Raws	2.62	3.44	4.20	3.42	3.49	5.02
PC	Mean Scores	0.31	0.20	0.21	0.48	0.51	0.28
SNP	Mean Raws	11.25	11.00	5.38	10.21	9.13	9.52
SNP	SD Raws	3.24	3.07	3.75	3.59	3.65	4.60
SNP	Mean Scores	0.21	-0.14	0.11	-0.07	-0.10	-0.09

Party		Pro decentralization of decisions (1) vs anti (20)			Envir. over growth (1) v. growth over env (20)		
		Leads	Vots	Imp.	Leads	Vots	Imp.
CON	Mean Raws	15.61	11.91	11.67	14.68	12.38	10.79
CON	SD Raws	3.31	3.28	5.19	2.20	2.47	3.75
CON	Mean Scores	1.42	1.24	-0.55	1.32	0.99	-0.55
DEM	Mean Raws	5.26	6.27	15.28	6.50	6.09	15.52
DEM	SD Raws	2.41	2.41	3.46	2.42	2.49	3.41
DEM	Mean Scores	-0.49	-0.20	0.20	-0.78	-0.78	0.65
LAB	Mean Raws	10.21	8.63	12.39	10.12	9.94	12.94
LAB	SD Raws	3.10	2.35	4.15	2.28	3.10	3.58
LAB	Mean Scores	0.42	0.40	-0.40	0.15	0.30	0.00
PC	Mean Raws	3.52	3.89	16.21	7.07	7.00	13.10
PC	SD Raws	2.13	1.87	4.66	3.01	2.78	3.93
PC	Mean Scores	-0.81	-0.81	0.39	-0.63	-0.52	0.04
SNP	Mean Raws	3.72	3.79	16.62	8.50	8.41	12.45
SNP	SD Raws	2.59	1.79	4.65	2.60	2.99	3.79
SNP	Mean Scores	-0.77	-0.84	0.47	-0.27	-0.13	-0.13

Britain
Table 3 (cont.)

Party		No influence on party policy (1) vs high (20)			No influence on partic. in govt (1) vs high (20)		
		Leads	Legs	Acts	Leads	Legs	Acts
CON	Mean Raws	18.91	9.56	6.32	18.86	11.59	5.57
CON	SD Raws	1.55	3.73	3.84	1.56	4.24	4.56
CON	Mean Scores	1.13	-0.41	-1.23	0.84	-0.07	-0.58
DEM	Mean Raws	13.72	12.28	13.26	14.65	12.62	9.27
DEM	SD Raws	2.47	3.90	3.17	4.10	4.16	4.78
DEM	Mean Scores	-0.22	0.28	0.40	-0.06	0.16	0.15
LAB	Mean Raws	14.97	12.15	12.15	16.19	12.63	8.70
LAB	SD Raws	2.29	2.98	3.59	3.31	3.72	5.28
LAB	Mean Scores	0.10	0.25	0.14	0.27	0.16	0.04
PC	Mean Raws	12.14	10.93	13.63	11.52	11.00	9.95
PC	SD Raws	4.11	4.30	2.47	5.18	5.60	4.61
PC	Mean Scores	-0.63	-0.07	0.48	-0.73	-0.20	0.29
SNP	Mean Raws	12.21	10.96	13.44	11.76	11.30	9.85
SNP	SD Raws	3.81	4.29	2.31	4.68	5.28	4.74
SNP	Mean Scores	-0.62	-0.06	0.44	-0.67	-0.13	0.27

Party		Do not look to future (1) vs look many years (5)			Give up office(1) vs give up policy (20)	Can use groups (1) vs not (20)	Close to resp (1) vs not (15)
		Leads	Legs	Acts			
CON	Mean Raws	3.68	3.54	2.83	13.45	9.45	12.09
CON	SD Raws	0.72	0.65	1.13	4.65	5.63	4.21
CON	Mean Scores	0.18	0.22	-0.12	0.54	-0.43	0.70
DEM	Mean Raws	3.46	3.22	3.17	12.97	14.72	6.43
DEM	SD Raws	1.10	0.90	1.19	4.25	4.91	3.30
DEM	Mean Scores	-0.04	-0.10	0.15	0.44	0.48	-0.62
LAB	Mean Raws	3.61	3.50	3.21	11.48	9.37	6.97
LAB	SD Raws	0.50	0.58	1.25	4.37	4.66	3.75
LAB	Mean Scores	0.11	0.18	0.18	0.15	-0.44	-0.50
PC	Mean Raws	3.30	3.11	2.84	7.00	13.86	10.96
PC	SD Raws	1.46	1.41	1.50	3.66	6.07	3.44
PC	Mean Scores	-0.19	-0.21	-0.11	-0.75	0.34	0.43
SNP	Mean Raws	3.32	3.11	2.79	7.21	13.05	9.42
SNP	SD Raws	1.34	1.41	1.44	4.15	5.83	3.41
SNP	Mean Scores	-0.18	-0.21	-0.15	-0.71	0.19	0.07

Britain
Table 4

		Antinuclear (1) vs pronuclear (20)		
Party		Leads	Vots	Imp.
CON	Mean Raws	18.38	16.88	19.00
CON	SD Raws	2.20	2.03	0.82
DEM	Mean Raws	10.38	10.38	13.00
DEM	SD Raws	2.50	2.39	4.55
LAB	Mean Raws	6.88	11.75	12.75
LAB	SD Raws	3.36	2.43	4.86
PC	Mean Raws	5.13	7.50	13.50
PC	SD Raws	2.95	3.46	5.20
SNP	Mean Raws	6.13	8.88	12.25
SNP	SD Raws	2.47	3.80	3.40

**Britain
Graph 1**

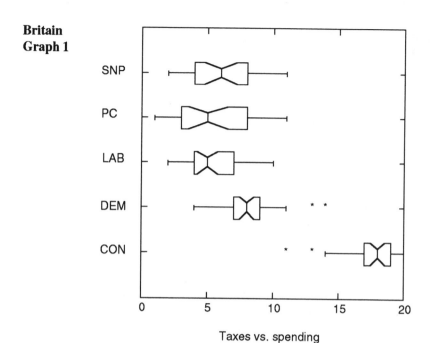

Taxes vs. spending

**Britain
Graph 2
(6/87 election %)**

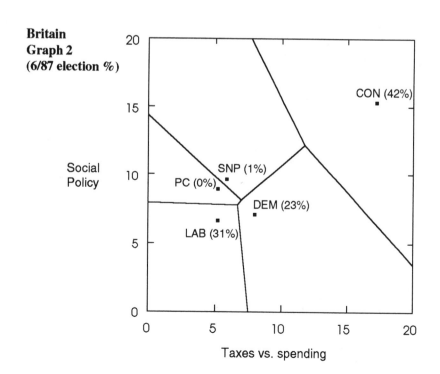

Taxes vs. spending

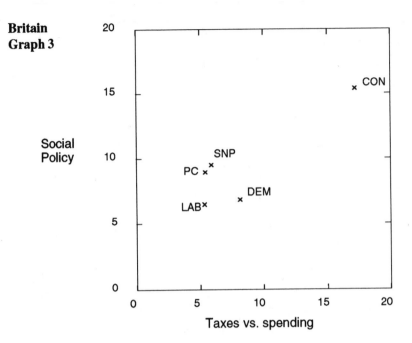

**Britain
Graph 3**

Social Policy

Taxes vs. spending

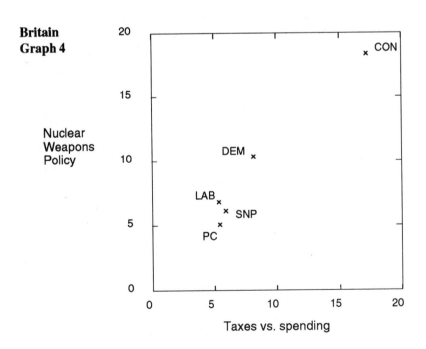

**Britain
Graph 4**

Nuclear Weapons Policy

Taxes vs. spending

Canada

Table 1

	Mean	SD
Impact of opposition parties on govt policy (1=lo; 9=hi)	3.46	1.93
Prop. of govts falling on policy disputes (1=lo; 9=hi)	2.25	1.92
Cabinet portfolios as policy (1) or office (9) payoffs	5.32	1.96
Cabinet members publicize internal splits (1=lo; 9=hi)	1.96	0.79
Policy autonomy of cabinet ministers (1=hi; 9=lo)	5.33	1.78
Frequency of cabinet reshuffles (1=lo; 9=hi)	5.63	1.39

RANKING OF CABINET POSITIONS

Finance	1.50	1.54
Treasury Board	3.85	1.34
External affairs	3.05	1.79
Trade	4.86	3.39
Environment	10.50	1.20
Defense	8.64	3.27
Transport	9.40	2.80
Energy, Mines and Resources	8.44	2.83
Health and Social Welfare	6.67	2.81
Agriculture	9.64	4.37
Justice	5.31	3.40
Labor	8.90	4.25
Communications	9.50	2.93

Canada

Table 2

Party	Abbrev.
Conservative Party	CON
Liberal Party	LIB
New Democratic Party	ND
Parti nationaliste du Quebec	PQ

Canada

Table 3

Party		Increase services (1) vs cut taxes (20)			Pro friendly relations USSR (1) vs anti (20)		
		Leads	Vots	Imp.	Leads	Vots	Imp.
CON	Mean Raws	13.58	13.00	13.72	9.77	11.77	11.29
CON	SD Raws	1.90	1.70	2.28	2.75	2.86	3.83
CON	Mean Scores	1.16	1.16	0.28	0.72	1.03	0.14
LIB	Mean Raws	9.35	9.50	11.96	8.08	7.89	11.29
LIB	SD Raws	2.28	1.36	2.54	2.04	2.09	3.69
LIB	Mean Scores	0.05	0.14	-0.20	0.11	-0.13	0.14
ND	Mean Raws	5.54	5.54	13.48	5.62	5.69	12.38
ND	SD Raws	2.18	2.18	4.75	1.92	1.89	3.47
ND	Mean Scores	-0.96	-1.01	0.22	-0.77	-0.78	0.38
PQ	Mean Raws	7.23	7.00	10.18	6.80	6.50	3.80
PQ	SD Raws	2.28	1.83	4.54	2.05	2.07	2.62
PQ	Mean Scores	-0.51	-0.59	-0.68	-0.35	-0.54	-1.58

Canada
Table 3 (cont.)

Party		Pro public own. (1) vs anti (20)			Pro permissive social policy (1) vs anti (20)		
		Leads	Vots	Imp.	Leads	Vots	Imp.
CON	Mean Raws	14.04	13.96	13.37	12.54	14.07	11.22
CON	SD Raws	2.37	2.38	3.58	2.41	2.28	2.72
CON	Mean Scores	1.13	1.12	0.18	1.13	1.14	-0.57
LIB	Mean Raws	10.04	10.14	10.93	8.67	9.67	12.89
LIB	SD Raws	2.10	2.27	2.75	1.66	1.75	2.72
LIB	Mean Scores	0.12	0.15	-0.53	0.18	0.09	-0.11
ND	Mean Raws	5.79	5.96	14.93	3.93	5.57	15.89
ND	SD Raws	2.01	1.84	2.35	2.09	2.22	3.22
ND	Mean Scores	-0.95	-0.90	0.63	-0.97	-0.89	0.73
PQ	Mean Raws	6.92	6.39	10.36	5.00	6.31	12.82
PQ	SD Raws	2.57	2.53	3.47	2.61	3.66	4.69
PQ	Mean Scores	-0.66	-0.80	-0.69	-0.71	-0.72	-0.13

Party		Anticlerical (1) vs proclerical (20)			Pro urban interests (1) vs anti (20)		
		Leads	Vots	Imp.	Leads	Vots	Imp.
CON	Mean Raws	11.00	10.43	6.68	12.20	13.26	9.91
CON	SD Raws	1.63	2.51	4.10	2.29	2.33	4.35
CON	Mean Scores	0.76	0.53	0.11	0.93	1.07	0.32
LIB	Mean Raws	10.57	11.43	6.53	8.65	8.21	7.30
LIB	SD Raws	2.07	3.26	4.65	2.13	2.30	3.28
LIB	Mean Scores	0.65	0.79	0.07	-0.19	-0.33	-0.30
ND	Mean Raws	6.57	5.71	5.16	7.90	8.11	9.35
ND	SD Raws	3.69	2.36	4.02	3.19	3.18	4.79
ND	Mean Scores	-0.43	-0.70	-0.26	-0.42	-0.36	0.18
PQ	Mean Raws	4.57	6.00	7.00	7.20	6.70	6.44
PQ	SD Raws	2.64	3.65	3.61	2.62	2.83	3.05
PQ	Mean Scores	-0.97	-0.62	0.19	-0.64	-0.74	-0.51

Canada
Table 3 (cont.)

Party		Pro decentralization of decisions (1) vs anti (20)			Envir. over growth (1) v. growth over env (20)		
		Leads	Vots	Imp.	Leads	Vots	Imp.
CON	Mean Raws	6.60	7.60	11.50	12.54	12.00	9.85
CON	SD Raws	2.47	3.19	4.97	2.38	2.40	3.79
CON	Mean Scores	-0.68	-0.59	-0.11	0.99	1.02	-0.33
LIB	Mean Raws	11.48	11.84	11.89	9.68	8.50	11.19
LIB	SD Raws	3.43	2.73	4.19	2.04	2.58	3.51
LIB	Mean Scores	0.40	0.37	-0.03	0.20	0.07	-0.01
ND	Mean Raws	12.72	12.76	11.77	5.39	5.07	13.41
ND	SD Raws	3.69	4.14	4.21	2.41	2.58	4.25
ND	Mean Scores	0.68	0.58	-0.05	-0.98	-0.85	0.53
PQ	Mean Raws	5.55	6.64	14.67	7.23	6.31	9.00
PQ	SD Raws	5.01	5.20	7.25	2.49	2.43	4.50
PQ	Mean Scores	-0.91	-0.81	0.55	-0.47	-0.52	-0.53

Party		No influence on party policy (1) vs high (20)			No influence on partic. in govt (1) vs high (20)		
		Leads	Legs	Acts	Leads	Legs	Acts
CON	Mean Raws	16.86	10.46	6.75	15.78	9.94	6.00
CON	SD Raws	2.58	4.21	3.27	4.86	4.72	4.53
CON	Mean Scores	0.50	-0.26	-0.70	0.23	-0.07	-0.28
LIB	Mean Raws	16.39	12.21	8.07	16.00	10.17	6.47
LIB	SD Raws	2.30	3.55	3.22	4.31	4.72	4.52
LIB	Mean Scores	0.35	0.20	-0.40	0.28	-0.02	-0.19
ND	Mean Raws	14.00	11.82	13.21	13.56	11.28	9.18
ND	SD Raws	2.71	3.44	3.41	4.87	4.70	5.58
ND	Mean Scores	-0.44	0.10	0.74	-0.22	0.22	0.34
PQ	Mean Raws	12.50	11.09	13.67	11.38	8.88	8.88
PQ	SD Raws	3.21	4.39	4.19	5.48	5.08	6.03
PQ	Mean Scores	-0.94	-0.09	0.84	-0.66	-0.29	0.28

Canada
Table 3 (cont.)

Party		Do not look to future (1) vs look many years (5)			Give up office(1) vs give up policy (20)	Can use groups (1) vs not (20)	Close to resp (1) vs not (15)
		Leads	Legs	Acts			
CON	Mean Raws	3.60	3.63	3.33	16.59	11.52	11.42
CON	SD Raws	0.50	0.60	0.77	3.03	4.75	3.77
CON	Mean Scores	-0.16	-0.03	-0.25	0.61	0.06	0.62
LIB	Mean Raws	3.60	3.47	3.39	16.68	12.24	7.68
LIB	SD Raws	0.50	0.61	0.78	2.53	4.55	3.52
LIB	Mean Scores	-0.16	-0.24	-0.19	0.62	0.21	-0.24
ND	Mean Raws	4.00	3.94	4.00	9.96	10.00	5.32
ND	SD Raws	0.47	0.73	0.84	4.81	4.87	2.90
ND	Mean Scores	0.48	0.40	0.49	-0.65	-0.26	-0.78
PQ	Mean Raws	3.50	3.43	3.40	6.60	11.08	12.36
PQ	SD Raws	1.20	1.27	1.52	3.37	4.76	3.67
PQ	Mean Scores	-0.32	-0.30	-0.18	-1.28	-0.03	0.84

Canada
Table 4

Party		Pro French language promotion (1) vs anti (20)			Pro trade links with US (1) vs anti (20)		
		Leads	Vots	Imp.	Leads	Vots	Imp.
CON	Mean	9.67	12.00	12.50	4.25	6.13	17.83
	SD	2.94	1.87	2.38	4.40	3.64	1.47
LIB	Mean	7.00	8.60	15.00	13.75	12.38	17.17
	SD	2.10	1.67	2.16	4.10	2.88	2.48
ND	Mean	6.83	10.00	9.25	16.25	15.50	17.67
	SD	1.60	2.53	2.75	5.12	4.66	1.86

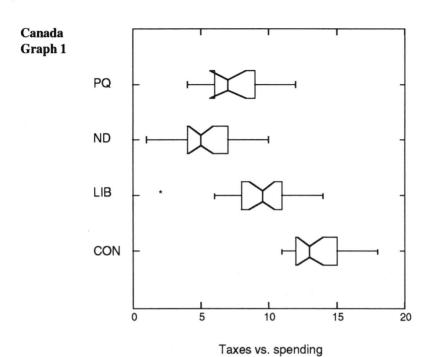

**Canada
Graph 1**

Taxes vs. spending

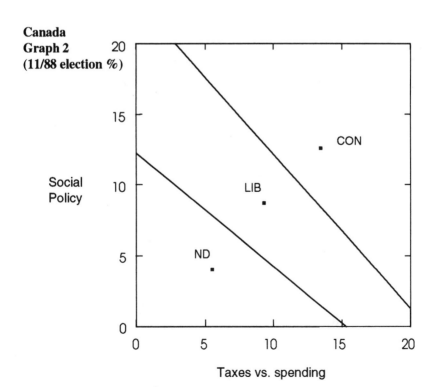

**Canada
Graph 2
(11/88 election %)**

Social
Policy

Taxes vs. spending

167

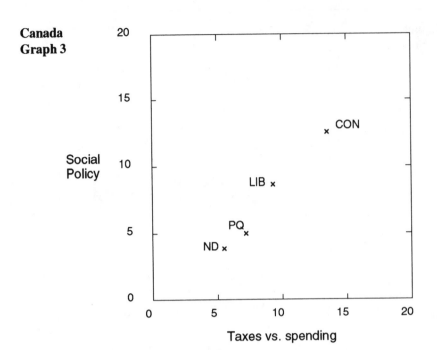

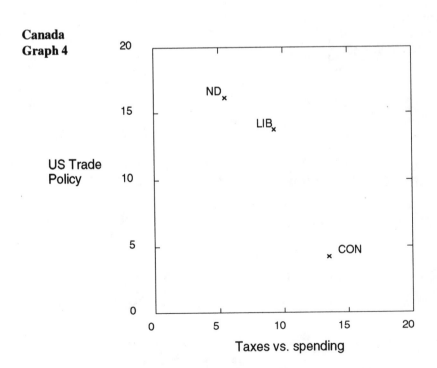

Denmark
Table 1

	Mean	SD
Impact of opposition parties on govt policy (1=lo; 9=hi)	6.50	2.27
Prop. of govts falling on policy disputes (1=lo; 9=hi)	3.80	2.04
Cabinet portfolios as policy (1) or office (9) payoffs	3.67	2.06
Cabinet members publicize internal splits (1=lo; 9=hi)	3.80	2.10
Policy autonomy of cabinet ministers (1=hi; 9=lo)	4.20	1.55
Frequency of cabinet reshuffles (1=lo; 9=hi)	5.00	1.76

RANKING OF CABINET POSITIONS

Finance	1.67	0.52
Foreign Affairs	1.67	1.21
Industry	9.00	1.73
Environment	8.75	4.03
Defense	8.00	4.36
Transport & Public works	9.50	2.12
Health	13.50	2.12
Social Affairs	5.75	4.27
Agriculture	8.80	1.64
Justice	5.17	2.14
Education	6.60	1.34
Labor	9.00	2.16
Interior	4.33	1.51
Economic affairs/Taxation	5.60	3.58

Denmark
Table 2

Party	Abbrev.
Social Democrats	SD
Conservative People's Party	KF
Socialist People's Party	SF
Liberal Party	V
Radical Liberal Party	RV
Center Democrats	CD
Progress Party	FP
Christian People's Party	KrF
Common Course	CC
Left Socialists	VS
Greens	G
Communist Party	DKP

Denmark Table 3		Increase services (1) vs cut taxes (20)			Pro friendly relations USSR (1) vs anti (20)		
Party		Leads	Vots	Imp.	Leads	Vots	Imp.
CC	Mean Raws	7.33	7.40	7.60	4.33	4.50	8.00
CC	SD Raws	4.55	4.98	3.85	3.33	3.45	2.92
CC	Mean Scores	-0.72	-0.74	-0.96	-0.87	-0.82	-0.78
CD	Mean Raws	11.78	12.63	13.75	13.89	13.56	13.29
CD	SD Raws	3.60	3.11	3.41	4.70	4.72	3.77
CD	Mean Scores	0.09	0.29	0.13	1.12	0.99	0.20
DKP	Mean Raws	3.57	3.50	10.00	1.14	1.57	15.33
DKP	SD Raws	2.64	1.87	4.47	0.38	0.79	4.32
DKP	Mean Scores	-1.40	-1.51	-0.54	-1.53	-1.41	0.58
FP	Mean Raws	19.40	17.70	19.00	13.44	13.44	4.83
FP	SD Raws	1.08	2.06	2.83	4.69	4.77	2.40
FP	Mean Scores	1.47	1.28	1.06	1.02	0.96	-1.37
G	Mean Raws	7.17	7.40	4.33	6.00	5.43	4.00
G	SD Raws	2.79	1.67	4.37	2.45	2.70	3.03
G	Mean Scores	-0.75	-0.74	-1.54	-0.52	-0.64	-1.53
KF	Mean Raws	16.00	15.67	16.00	11.25	12.25	13.86
KF	SD Raws	1.00	2.12	2.83	3.33	4.77	3.76
KF	Mean Scores	0.85	0.88	0.53	0.57	0.73	0.31
KRF	Mean Raws	12.70	12.20	11.60	10.11	10.38	7.75
KRF	SD Raws	1.89	2.25	4.72	3.37	3.70	3.62
KRF	Mean Scores	0.25	0.20	-0.25	0.33	0.35	-0.83
RF	Mean Raws	15.20	12.20	12.33	10.83	10.67	11.00
RF	SD Raws	3.63	2.95	5.92	2.71	2.34	4.34
RF	Mean Scores	0.71	0.20	-0.12	0.48	0.41	-0.22
RV	Mean Raws	12.50	12.11	14.33	7.11	8.11	14.00
RV	SD Raws	1.84	1.76	3.87	2.26	3.14	4.44
RV	Mean Scores	0.22	0.18	0.23	-0.29	-0.10	0.34
SD	Mean Raws	9.10	9.78	13.33	7.56	7.67	13.88
SD	SD Raws	1.91	1.92	5.20	2.01	2.40	3.14
SD	Mean Scores	-0.40	-0.28	0.06	-0.20	-0.19	0.31
SF	Mean Raws	6.70	6.33	12.33	4.67	4.89	18.00
SF	SD Raws	3.02	2.96	6.16	1.94	1.97	1.69
SF	Mean Scores	-0.84	-0.95	-0.12	-0.80	-0.75	1.08
V	Mean Raws	17.40	16.60	17.80	12.11	12.11	13.25
V	SD Raws	1.51	1.65	2.66	3.48	3.86	4.53
V	Mean Scores	1.11	1.07	0.85	0.75	0.70	0.20
VS	Mean Raws	3.38	3.29	8.29	4.86	4.14	17.71
VS	SD Raws	2.26	1.60	5.68	2.85	2.55	1.70
VS	Mean Scores	-1.44	-1.55	-0.84	-0.76	-0.90	1.03

Denmark Table 3 (cont.)		Pro public own. (1) vs anti (20)			Pro permissive social policy (1) vs anti (20)		
Party		Leads	Vots	Imp.	Leads	Vots	Imp.
CC	Mean Raws	3.20	4.50	10.50	6.50	7.20	11.60
CC	SD Raws	2.28	2.65	0.58	3.62	3.27	6.27
CC	Mean Scores	-1.32	-1.17	-0.13	-0.42	-0.46	0.08
CD	Mean Raws	12.43	14.86	7.83	11.22	13.00	9.38
CD	SD Raws	5.53	3.44	3.97	5.74	5.32	5.45
CD	Mean Scores	0.20	0.54	-0.67	0.36	0.50	-0.31
DKP	Mean Raws	2.33	3.67	18.00	7.33	7.50	10.80
DKP	SD Raws	2.07	2.42	2.55	3.01	3.73	7.01
DKP	Mean Scores	-1.46	-1.31	1.40	-0.28	-0.41	-0.06
FP	Mean Raws	19.25	18.63	13.86	14.00	14.70	10.38
FP	SD Raws	1.17	1.60	4.74	6.11	6.06	5.88
FP	Mean Scores	1.32	1.16	0.56	0.81	0.78	-0.13
G	Mean Raws	8.20	7.60	4.20	6.83	6.67	7.00
G	SD Raws	3.42	2.97	3.56	3.49	3.50	2.83
G	Mean Scores	-0.50	-0.66	-1.41	-0.36	-0.55	-0.72
KF	Mean Raws	16.00	17.38	12.00	11.56	11.78	9.75
KF	SD Raws	1.07	1.85	4.90	5.32	4.89	5.34
KF	Mean Scores	0.78	0.95	0.18	0.41	0.30	-0.24
KRF	Mean Raws	14.63	15.00	7.14	18.30	18.60	13.80
KRF	SD Raws	2.97	3.38	3.72	2.79	2.84	4.80
KRF	Mean Scores	0.56	0.56	-0.81	1.51	1.43	0.46
RF	Mean Raws	16.67	17.33	11.75	9.67	10.50	7.83
RF	SD Raws	1.53	1.16	4.19	2.42	3.21	3.37
RF	Mean Scores	0.89	0.95	0.13	0.10	0.09	-0.58
RV	Mean Raws	13.25	12.88	8.43	5.60	7.22	10.67
RV	SD Raws	1.98	1.96	3.69	3.84	3.46	5.61
RV	Mean Scores	0.33	0.21	-0.55	-0.57	-0.45	-0.08
SD	Mean Raws	8.75	7.00	11.29	7.00	8.33	12.56
SD	SD Raws	2.61	3.21	2.98	2.87	2.92	7.13
SD	Mean Scores	-0.41	-0.76	0.03	-0.34	-0.27	0.25
SF	Mean Raws	5.50	5.75	14.43	2.40	3.00	14.00
SF	SD Raws	2.88	2.49	2.99	1.35	1.80	7.04
SF	Mean Scores	-0.94	-0.96	0.68	-1.09	-1.15	0.50
V	Mean Raws	17.75	17.88	11.88	12.30	13.20	9.89
V	SD Raws	1.04	1.46	4.61	5.21	4.96	5.09
V	Mean Scores	1.07	1.04	0.15	0.53	0.53	-0.22
VS	Mean Raws	4.29	4.29	12.83	1.38	1.57	14.86
VS	SD Raws	2.14	2.43	5.00	1.06	1.13	5.55
VS	Mean Scores	-1.14	-1.20	0.35	-1.26	-1.39	0.65

Denmark Table 3 (cont.) Party		Anticlerical (1) vs proclerical (20)			Pro urban interests (1) vs anti (20)		
		Leads	Vots	Imp.	Leads	Vots	Imp.
CC	Mean Raws	4.00	2.00	3.00	2.00	1.67	8.33
CC	SD Raws	NA	NA	NA	0.00	0.58	8.51
CC	Mean Scores	-1.41	-1.61	-0.58	-1.34	-1.39	-0.36
CD	Mean Raws	14.50	13.50	5.67	8.20	8.00	6.83
CD	SD Raws	4.95	3.54	7.23	2.28	2.00	2.93
CD	Mean Scores	0.67	0.46	-0.16	-0.29	-0.28	-0.62
DKP	Mean Raws	4.00	2.00	2.50	1.75	2.25	11.00
DKP	SD Raws	NA	NA	0.71	0.96	1.26	8.12
DKP	Mean Scores	-1.41	-1.61	-0.66	-1.38	-1.29	0.12
FP	Mean Raws	10.00	11.33	3.00	14.60	13.00	10.88
FP	SD Raws	2.65	4.04	2.00	4.83	3.81	5.08
FP	Mean Scores	-0.22	0.07	-0.58	0.80	0.60	0.10
G	Mean Raws	12.00	12.00	1.50	11.00	10.00	11.67
G	SD Raws	NA	NA	0.71	6.38	5.35	6.35
G	Mean Scores	0.17	0.19	-0.81	0.19	0.07	0.24
KF	Mean Raws	14.00	14.25	7.75	10.00	10.00	9.71
KF	SD Raws	2.94	3.78	4.03	2.83	2.65	4.15
KF	Mean Scores	0.57	0.60	0.17	0.02	0.07	-0.11
KRF	Mean Raws	19.50	19.75	19.20	15.29	15.00	12.38
KRF	SD Raws	1.00	0.50	0.84	3.55	3.37	5.76
KRF	Mean Scores	1.66	1.58	1.96	0.91	0.95	0.36
RF	Mean Raws	10.00	8.00	5.00	12.67	11.33	11.00
RF	SD Raws	NA	NA	NA	5.51	3.22	7.81
RF	Mean Scores	-0.22	-0.53	-0.26	0.47	0.30	0.12
RV	Mean Raws	7.00	9.00	5.25	12.00	12.29	9.57
RV	SD Raws	1.73	1.73	5.25	2.45	2.56	4.72
RV	Mean Scores	-0.82	-0.35	-0.23	0.36	0.47	-0.14
SD	Mean Raws	8.67	7.33	3.00	7.00	6.00	9.00
SD	SD Raws	1.53	1.53	1.83	2.31	2.89	4.20
SD	Mean Scores	-0.49	-0.65	-0.58	-0.49	-0.63	-0.24
SF	Mean Raws	6.00	4.67	3.00	5.43	5.00	8.14
SF	SD Raws	1.00	1.16	3.37	2.88	2.77	5.11
SF	Mean Scores	-1.02	-1.13	-0.58	-0.76	-0.81	-0.39
V	Mean Raws	14.25	14.50	13.25	18.13	18.38	15.50
V	SD Raws	1.71	1.29	1.50	2.42	1.92	6.57
V	Mean Scores	0.62	0.64	1.03	1.40	1.54	0.92
VS	Mean Raws	5.50	4.00	1.33	2.20	2.60	8.60
VS	SD Raws	2.12	0.00	0.58	1.30	1.82	6.35
VS	Mean Scores	-1.12	-1.25	-0.84	-1.31	-1.23	-0.31

Denmark Table 3 (cont.)		Pro decentralization of decisions (1) vs anti (20)			Envir. over growth (1) vs growth over env (20)		
Party		Leads	Vots	Imp.	Leads	Vots	Imp.
CC	Mean Raws	13.00	13.33	8.67	12.25	13.00	6.75
CC	SD Raws	2.65	3.06	6.51	2.63	4.40	3.10
CC	Mean Scores	0.23	0.97	-0.14	0.61	0.72	-0.92
CD	Mean Raws	12.86	13.17	7.00	11.86	12.43	7.57
CD	SD Raws	3.58	2.14	6.16	1.95	1.90	2.15
CD	Mean Scores	0.22	0.93	-0.45	0.53	0.61	-0.76
DKP	Mean Raws	16.00	15.60	6.67	10.60	11.40	7.00
DKP	SD Raws	3.16	3.05	6.35	1.95	3.85	3.65
DKP	Mean Scores	0.48	1.47	-0.51	0.28	0.41	-0.87
FP	Mean Raws	9.71	9.00	7.50	15.38	15.38	6.00
FP	SD Raws	2.43	4.15	5.40	3.50	3.78	2.58
FP	Mean Scores	-0.04	0.01	-0.36	1.24	1.16	-1.07
G	Mean Raws	4.17	4.33	14.60	1.00	1.17	20.00
G	SD Raws	2.23	1.75	3.05	0.00	0.41	0.00
G	Mean Scores	-0.50	-1.02	0.98	-1.66	-1.52	1.64
KF	Mean Raws	24.50	11.86	7.13	13.63	13.50	9.88
KF	SD Raws	35.43	3.34	4.39	3.34	3.07	2.95
KF	Mean Scores	1.18	0.64	-0.43	0.89	0.81	-0.32
KRF	Mean Raws	7.71	8.57	7.00	9.38	8.75	13.13
KRF	SD Raws	2.43	3.74	3.55	3.82	4.43	4.67
KRF	Mean Scores	-0.21	-0.09	-0.45	0.03	-0.09	0.31
RF	Mean Raws	7.50	8.25	8.75	9.50	9.25	8.75
RF	SD Raws	4.44	3.10	4.50	3.70	4.50	4.99
RF	Mean Scores	-0.22	-0.16	-0.12	0.06	0.01	-0.54
RV	Mean Raws	7.14	8.67	10.38	6.00	5.25	14.38
RV	SD Raws	2.34	2.34	5.45	2.93	2.19	4.21
RV	Mean Scores	-0.25	-0.07	0.19	-0.65	-0.75	0.55
SD	Mean Raws	13.38	12.86	9.38	9.56	10.00	11.13
SD	SD Raws	3.46	2.61	4.10	2.24	2.35	2.48
SD	Mean Scores	0.26	0.86	0.00	0.07	0.15	-0.08
SF	Mean Raws	4.86	4.71	11.00	4.13	3.50	16.00
SF	SD Raws	1.95	2.43	5.66	1.13	1.07	2.45
SF	Mean Scores	-0.44	-0.94	0.30	-1.03	-1.08	0.86
V	Mean Raws	6.38	5.86	11.88	12.88	13.25	8.25
V	SD Raws	1.51	2.41	6.38	2.53	3.06	3.62
V	Mean Scores	-0.32	-0.69	0.47	0.74	0.76	-0.63
VS	Mean Raws	3.83	3.50	11.50	2.50	2.17	17.33
VS	SD Raws	1.17	1.05	6.09	0.55	0.41	2.88
VS	Mean Scores	-0.52	-1.21	0.40	-1.36	-1.33	1.12

173

Denmark Table 3 (cont.)		No influence on party policy (1) vs high (20)			No influence on partic. in govt (1) vs high (20)		
Party		Leads	Legs	Acts	Leads	Legs	Acts
CC	Mean Raws	19.20	5.60	2.00	19.00	4.00	2.00
CC	SD Raws	0.84	2.61	1.00	NA	NA	NA
CC	Mean Scores	1.03	-1.27	-1.32	0.78	-1.05	-0.68
CD	Mean Raws	18.75	10.00	4.63	16.29	7.80	2.17
CD	SD Raws	1.39	4.69	3.34	6.82	5.98	1.60
CD	Mean Scores	0.95	-0.27	-0.85	0.37	-0.40	-0.65
DKP	Mean Raws	17.83	6.60	6.33	13.00	7.50	4.00
DKP	SD Raws	1.72	3.72	6.02	8.49	4.95	1.73
DKP	Mean Scores	0.78	-1.04	-0.55	-0.13	-0.45	-0.32
FP	Mean Raws	17.33	10.38	4.50	13.20	7.25	2.60
FP	SD Raws	2.83	4.63	3.21	8.67	5.68	2.07
FP	Mean Scores	0.69	-0.18	-0.87	-0.10	-0.49	-0.57
G	Mean Raws	4.14	6.20	17.86	5.00	13.00	14.00
G	SD Raws	4.22	4.44	1.46	1.41	NA	9.54
G	Mean Scores	-1.72	-1.14	1.53	-1.34	0.50	1.46
KF	Mean Raws	15.88	12.86	7.50	16.63	9.00	4.25
KF	SD Raws	2.85	3.85	3.25	6.46	6.42	3.81
KF	Mean Scores	0.42	0.39	-0.34	0.42	-0.19	-0.28
KRF	Mean Raws	12.75	13.71	8.13	14.25	11.00	5.71
KRF	SD Raws	3.33	2.43	3.09	5.99	5.62	4.27
KRF	Mean Scores	-0.15	0.59	-0.22	0.06	0.16	-0.02
RF	Mean Raws	10.50	10.83	12.00	14.00	13.50	8.50
RF	SD Raws	3.62	2.64	4.90	2.83	3.54	9.19
RF	Mean Scores	-0.56	-0.08	0.47	0.43	0.61	1.64
RV	Mean Raws	13.78	11.88	9.56	14.33	11.50	4.67
RV	SD Raws	3.60	3.80	3.81	7.12	7.59	5.16
RV	Mean Scores	0.04	0.16	0.03	0.08	0.24	-0.20
SD	Mean Raws	15.22	12.13	8.89	15.38	9.67	5.00
SD	SD Raws	3.63	3.36	2.89	6.14	6.12	4.36
SD	Mean Scores	0.30	0.22	-0.09	0.23	-0.08	-0.14
SF	Mean Raws	11.13	14.00	14.78	8.57	11.80	10.14
SF	SD Raws	4.79	4.18	3.87	5.00	6.72	7.36
SF	Mean Scores	-0.45	0.65	0.97	-0.80	0.29	0.78
V	Mean Raws	14.56	13.38	8.44	15.38	10.17	4.63
V	SD Raws	3.32	2.67	3.40	6.39	6.18	3.82
V	Mean Scores	0.18	0.51	-0.17	0.23	0.01	-0.21
VS	Mean Raws	4.57	12.50	17.00	5.50	17.00	13.00
VS	SD Raws	3.87	4.85	3.32	2.12	1.41	8.72
VS	Mean Scores	-1.64	0.31	1.37	-1.26	1.19	1.29

Denmark
Table 3 (cont.)

Party		Do not look to future (1) vs look many years (5)			Give up office(1) vs give up policy (20)	Can use groups (1) vs not (20)	Close to resp (1) vs not (15)
		Leads	Legs	Acts			
CC	Mean Raws	4.00	4.00	4.00	5.50	11.50	14.50
CC	SD Raws	NA	NA	NA	6.36	8.35	0.58
CC	Mean Scores	0.18	0.17	0.31	-1.14	0.28	1.40
CD	Mean Raws	3.40	3.40	3.20	16.83	13.67	9.71
CD	SD Raws	0.89	0.89	0.84	3.06	5.54	2.93
CD	Mean Scores	-0.59	-0.70	-0.82	0.83	0.63	0.18
DKP	Mean Raws	4.50	4.50	4.00	3.00	5.40	12.80
DKP	SD Raws	0.71	0.71	0.00	2.83	4.83	2.17
DKP	Mean Scores	0.82	0.90	0.31	-1.58	-0.70	0.97
FP	Mean Raws	4.00	3.75	3.50	6.80	14.29	13.75
FP	SD Raws	0.82	0.50	0.58	5.26	6.42	1.49
FP	Mean Scores	0.18	-0.19	-0.40	-0.92	0.73	1.21
G	Mean Raws	4.67	4.67	4.67	1.00	10.60	8.00
G	SD Raws	0.58	0.58	0.58	0.00	6.47	3.16
G	Mean Scores	1.03	1.14	1.25	-1.93	0.14	-0.26
KF	Mean Raws	3.60	3.80	3.60	16.00	8.29	7.38
KF	SD Raws	0.55	0.45	0.55	3.25	5.09	3.20
KF	Mean Scores	-0.33	-0.12	-0.25	0.68	-0.24	-0.42
KRF	Mean Raws	3.80	3.80	3.60	13.13	14.00	9.25
KRF	SD Raws	0.45	0.45	0.55	2.85	4.80	1.98
KRF	Mean Scores	-0.08	-0.12	-0.25	0.18	0.68	0.06
RF	Mean Raws	4.00	4.00	3.50	8.50	11.75	10.25
RF	SD Raws	0.00	0.00	0.71	3.54	8.46	1.89
RF	Mean Scores	0.00	0.00	1.00	0.62	1.36	0.48
RV	Mean Raws	3.75	3.75	3.50	14.33	12.14	5.13
RV	SD Raws	0.50	0.50	0.58	2.34	5.31	3.09
RV	Mean Scores	-0.14	-0.19	-0.40	0.39	0.39	-0.99
SD	Mean Raws	3.60	3.60	3.60	16.25	4.43	5.63
SD	SD Raws	0.55	0.55	0.55	2.05	4.93	1.92
SD	Mean Scores	-0.33	-0.41	-0.25	0.73	-0.86	-0.87
SF	Mean Raws	4.00	4.00	4.40	8.75	5.43	7.38
SF	SD Raws	0.71	0.71	0.55	5.12	1.90	4.57
SF	Mean Scores	0.18	0.17	0.88	-0.58	-0.70	-0.42
V	Mean Raws	3.50	3.67	3.67	14.63	7.83	7.63
V	SD Raws	1.38	1.03	0.82	3.89	4.96	3.38
V	Mean Scores	-0.46	-0.31	-0.16	0.44	-0.31	-0.36
VS	Mean Raws	4.67	4.67	4.67	1.00	7.80	10.67
VS	SD Raws	0.58	0.58	0.58	0.00	6.61	4.13
VS	Mean Scores	1.03	1.14	1.25	-1.93	-0.32	0.42

**Denmark
Graph 1**

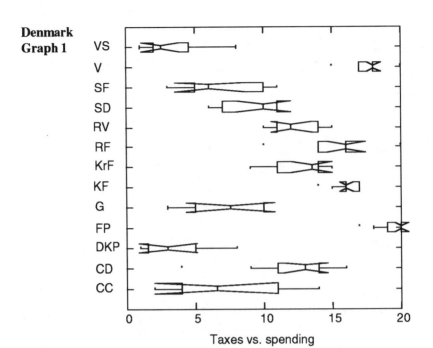

Taxes vs. spending

**Denmark
Graph 2
(5/88 election %)**

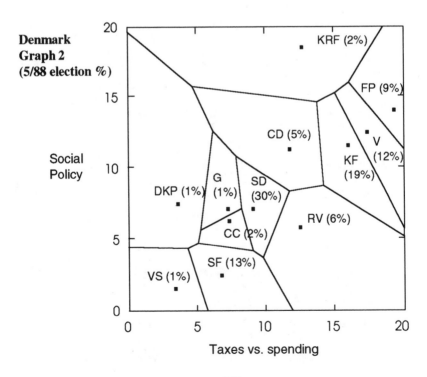

Taxes vs. spending

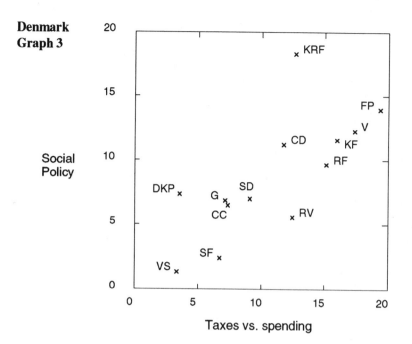

Denmark Graph 3

Social Policy

Taxes vs. spending

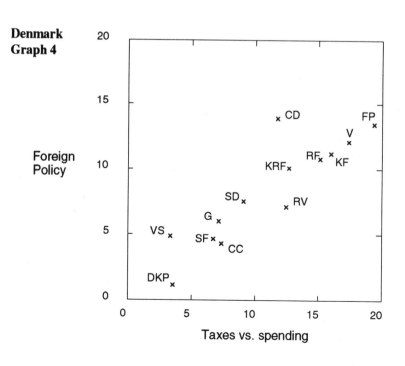

Denmark Graph 4

Foreign Policy

Taxes vs. spending

Finland
Table 1

	Mean	SD
Impact of opposition parties on govt policy (1=lo; 9=hi)	4.86	1.83
Prop. of govts falling on policy disputes (1=lo; 9=hi)	5.93	1.94
Cabinet portfolios as policy (1) or office (9) payoffs	4.64	2.34
Cabinet members publicize internal splits (1=lo; 9=hi)	4.93	1.98
Policy autonomy of cabinet ministers (1=hi; 9=lo)	3.93	1.90
Frequency of cabinet reshuffles (1=lo; 9=hi)	3.93	1.33

RANKING OF CABINET POSITIONS

Finance	1.77	0.44
Foreign Affairs	1.21	0.43
Trade and Industry	3.50	0.71
Environment	8.50	2.55
Defense	10.30	2.67
Transport and Communications	8.57	1.72
Interior	4.64	1.95
Social Affairs and Health	6.50	2.65
Agriculture and Forestry	8.83	3.04
Justice	6.22	2.59
Education	5.38	1.39
Labor	9.56	1.24

Finland
Table 2

Party	Abbrev.
Social Democrats	SDP
National Coalition	KOK
Center Party	A/C
Finnish People's Democratic Union	FPDL
Rural Party	FRP
Swedish People's Party	SPP
Democratic Alternative	DA
Greens	G
Christian League	FCL
Liberal People's Party	LPP
Pensioner's Party	P

Finland
Table 3

Party		Increase services (1) vs cut taxes (20)			Pro friendly relations USSR (1) vs anti (20)		
		Leads	Vots	Imp.	Leads	Vots	Imp.
A/C	Mean Raws	11.21	11.57	11.17	3.86	8.46	12.75
A/C	SD Raws	2.75	3.03	3.66	1.70	3.78	5.50
A/C	Mean Scores	0.28	0.18	-0.12	-0.47	-0.08	0.51
DA	Mean Raws	3.64	4.36	13.58	1.43	2.00	15.17
DA	SD Raws	2.17	2.53	4.44	1.16	1.24	5.15
DA	Mean Scores	-1.35	-1.37	0.39	-1.08	-0.60	0.94
FCL	Mean Raws	13.71	14.39	8.58	9.43	22.21	9.67
FCL	SD Raws	2.97	3.33	2.64	4.60	35.63	3.80
FCL	Mean Scores	0.81	0.78	-0.67	0.93	1.03	-0.04
FDPL	Mean Raws	4.50	5.79	13.00	2.43	3.07	13.54
FDPL	SD Raws	2.03	2.42	4.83	1.16	1.59	4.81
FDPL	Mean Scores	-1.17	-1.06	0.27	-0.83	-0.51	0.65
FRP	Mean Raws	10.43	11.15	11.82	7.64	10.64	6.92
FRP	SD Raws	2.44	2.58	3.09	3.57	3.37	4.38
FRP	Mean Scores	0.11	0.09	0.02	0.48	0.10	-0.53
G	Mean Raws	7.43	8.43	7.83	7.86	8.79	6.25
G	SD Raws	2.17	1.95	3.95	3.59	3.07	4.35
G	Mean Scores	-0.54	-0.50	-0.83	0.54	-0.05	-0.65
KOK	Mean Raws	14.29	16.14	15.33	5.46	11.07	10.33
KOK	SD Raws	2.43	2.69	5.42	2.76	4.29	5.28
KOK	Mean Scores	0.94	1.16	0.77	-0.07	0.14	0.08
LPP	Mean Raws	13.00	13.73	11.64	7.20	9.70	6.91
LPP	SD Raws	2.19	2.76	4.34	3.99	3.71	3.59
LPP	Mean Scores	0.66	0.64	-0.02	0.37	0.03	-0.53
P	Mean Raws	11.78	11.63	8.33	9.00	10.50	3.44
P	SD Raws	4.06	3.89	4.90	5.16	4.84	4.13
P	Mean Scores	0.40	0.19	-0.72	0.83	0.09	-1.15
SDP	Mean Raws	5.86	7.29	14.58	4.14	6.79	12.17
SDP	SD Raws	2.96	2.59	3.75	1.75	3.89	5.36
SDP	Mean Scores	-0.88	-0.74	0.61	-0.40	-0.21	0.41
SPP	Mean Raws	14.71	15.07	12.17	6.31	10.69	9.50
SPP	SD Raws	2.34	2.43	4.73	3.82	4.31	4.82
SPP	Mean Scores	1.03	0.93	0.09	0.15	0.10	-0.07

Finland
Table 3 (cont.)

Party		Pro public own. (1) vs anti (20)			Pro permissive social policy (1) vs anti (20)		
		Leads	Vots	Imp.	Leads	Vots	Imp.
A/C	Mean Raws	12.14	13.43	11.62	14.86	16.21	12.15
A/C	SD Raws	3.04	3.76	3.66	3.66	2.55	4.36
A/C	Mean Scores	0.23	0.32	0.07	0.80	0.86	-0.12
DA	Mean Raws	2.93	3.64	17.77	5.23	6.31	15.23
DA	SD Raws	4.80	4.50	4.99	3.37	3.15	4.29
DA	Mean Scores	-1.51	-1.44	1.35	-0.80	-0.84	0.55
FCL	Mean Raws	14.85	15.15	8.92	19.21	19.43	13.23
FCL	SD Raws	3.18	3.65	3.86	1.63	1.16	4.13
FCL	Mean Scores	0.75	0.63	-0.49	1.53	1.41	0.12
FDPL	Mean Raws	4.79	5.36	14.93	3.85	5.77	16.29
FDPL	SD Raws	3.89	3.23	3.13	3.00	3.30	4.14
FDPL	Mean Scores	-1.16	-1.13	0.76	-1.03	-0.93	0.78
FRP	Mean Raws	12.69	13.00	9.00	14.77	16.36	12.77
FRP	SD Raws	3.45	3.85	2.49	2.89	2.02	3.88
FRP	Mean Scores	0.34	0.25	-0.47	0.79	0.88	0.01
G	Mean Raws	9.69	9.83	7.54	3.71	4.00	12.77
G	SD Raws	2.43	1.99	3.60	2.23	2.32	3.61
G	Mean Scores	-0.23	-0.33	-0.78	-1.05	-1.24	0.01
KOK	Mean Raws	15.07	16.50	12.92	11.46	13.54	8.85
KOK	SD Raws	3.77	4.38	3.99	4.10	4.01	3.58
KOK	Mean Scores	0.79	0.88	0.34	0.24	0.40	-0.84
LPP	Mean Raws	14.50	15.80	9.09	6.90	8.00	11.00
LPP	SD Raws	1.84	1.69	3.15	2.77	3.09	3.10
LPP	Mean Scores	0.68	0.75	-0.45	-0.52	-0.55	-0.37
P	Mean Raws	11.88	13.38	5.63	15.88	16.13	12.78
P	SD Raws	2.17	2.50	4.34	2.10	1.81	6.00
P	Mean Scores	0.18	0.31	-1.18	0.97	0.84	0.02
SDP	Mean Raws	8.29	8.21	11.85	6.36	7.71	15.46
SDP	SD Raws	2.56	2.36	3.16	2.90	3.22	4.43
SDP	Mean Scores	-0.50	-0.62	0.12	-0.61	-0.60	0.60
SPP	Mean Raws	14.93	15.79	11.77	9.39	10.50	8.69
SPP	SD Raws	4.22	4.61	3.94	4.09	3.78	2.90
SPP	Mean Scores	0.76	0.75	0.10	-0.11	-0.12	-0.87

Finland
Table 3 (cont.)

Party		Anticlerical (1) vs proclerical (20)			Pro urban interests (1) vs anti (20)		
		Leads	Vots	Imp.	Leads	Vots	Imp.
A/C	Mean Raws	16.86	17.43	15.00	17.79	17.86	18.17
A/C	SD Raws	2.03	1.70	2.31	1.76	1.46	1.80
A/C	Mean Scores	0.94	0.93	0.94	1.77	1.75	1.53
DA	Mean Raws	2.14	2.79	6.85	6.21	5.43	9.58
DA	SD Raws	1.66	2.05	4.65	2.01	1.87	2.68
DA	Mean Scores	-1.68	-1.70	-0.53	-0.65	-0.80	-0.50
FCL	Mean Raws	19.36	19.57	19.46	11.93	11.79	8.27
FCL	SD Raws	1.15	0.76	1.13	1.39	1.48	2.57
FCL	Mean Scores	1.39	1.31	1.75	0.55	0.50	-0.81
FDPL	Mean Raws	4.64	5.57	6.36	8.29	7.93	11.46
FDPL	SD Raws	1.82	1.56	3.25	2.43	2.43	2.63
FDPL	Mean Scores	-1.23	-1.20	-0.62	-0.22	-0.29	-0.06
FRP	Mean Raws	14.86	15.93	12.46	14.21	14.50	14.67
FRP	SD Raws	2.32	1.94	4.16	2.75	3.21	3.87
FRP	Mean Scores	0.59	0.66	0.48	1.02	1.06	0.70
G	Mean Raws	7.64	7.71	4.62	8.43	7.71	9.42
G	SD Raws	2.79	2.20	3.18	2.44	2.56	3.12
G	Mean Scores	-0.70	-0.82	-0.93	-0.19	-0.33	-0.54
KOK	Mean Raws	15.07	15.79	12.62	6.71	6.93	12.73
KOK	SD Raws	2.43	2.12	2.63	3.54	3.41	2.61
KOK	Mean Scores	0.62	0.63	0.51	-0.55	-0.49	0.24
LPP	Mean Raws	10.00	11.18	6.64	4.82	4.46	10.60
LPP	SD Raws	3.16	3.28	3.38	2.75	2.16	3.75
LPP	Mean Scores	-0.28	-0.20	-0.57	-0.95	-1.00	-0.26
P	Mean Raws	14.88	15.88	8.56	9.75	9.75	7.25
P	SD Raws	1.96	1.55	4.64	3.01	3.01	3.24
P	Mean Scores	0.59	0.65	-0.22	0.09	0.08	-1.06
SDP	Mean Raws	9.64	10.00	5.54	3.21	4.21	13.83
SDP	SD Raws	1.74	1.75	2.26	2.16	3.47	4.28
SDP	Mean Scores	-0.34	-0.41	-0.77	-1.28	-1.05	0.50
SPP	Mean Raws	13.21	14.43	8.83	10.50	11.29	11.00
SPP	SD Raws	2.64	2.71	3.95	2.59	2.73	3.25
SPP	Mean Scores	0.29	0.39	-0.17	0.25	0.40	-0.17

Finland
Table 3 (cont.)

Party		Pro decentralization of decisions (1) vs anti (20)			Envir. over growth (1) vs growth over env (20)		
		Leads	Vots	Imp.	Leads	Vots	Imp.
A/C	Mean Raws	7.00	8.29	15.31	10.07	12.50	12.69
A/C	SD Raws	5.66	5.17	3.73	3.81	3.70	4.46
A/C	Mean Scores	-0.54	-0.39	1.00	0.08	0.28	0.26
DA	Mean Raws	10.36	10.36	11.08	8.50	9.79	10.92
DA	SD Raws	5.49	5.00	3.69	4.50	3.85	3.93
DA	Mean Scores	0.14	0.07	0.02	-0.25	-0.28	-0.10
FCL	Mean Raws	10.92	11.46	8.85	10.36	11.43	7.39
FCL	SD Raws	3.80	4.03	3.56	4.27	4.59	3.20
FCL	Mean Scores	0.26	0.32	-0.50	0.14	0.06	-0.82
FDPL	Mean Raws	9.36	9.71	10.43	7.14	9.86	14.29
FDPL	SD Raws	4.63	3.75	3.84	3.72	4.06	3.34
FDPL	Mean Scores	-0.06	-0.07	-0.13	-0.53	-0.27	0.59
FRP	Mean Raws	9.14	10.07	12.08	10.77	12.77	8.69
FRP	SD Raws	4.80	4.51	3.97	2.86	2.39	3.71
FRP	Mean Scores	-0.10	0.01	0.25	0.23	0.34	-0.56
G	Mean Raws	6.36	6.43	13.62	1.43	1.86	19.54
G	SD Raws	4.96	5.40	3.75	0.94	1.29	0.88
G	Mean Scores	-0.67	-0.80	0.61	-1.73	-1.93	1.66
KOK	Mean Raws	12.39	12.54	9.77	14.50	15.79	9.92
KOK	SD Raws	3.86	3.71	2.80	2.88	1.93	2.93
KOK	Mean Scores	0.55	0.55	-0.28	1.01	0.96	-0.31
LPP	Mean Raws	9.30	10.60	11.00	7.40	9.90	12.27
LPP	SD Raws	5.50	5.02	4.98	2.80	3.41	3.23
LPP	Mean Scores	-0.07	0.12	0.00	-0.48	-0.26	0.17
P	Mean Raws	11.75	11.50	5.67	12.88	13.13	4.67
P	SD Raws	2.87	2.78	4.33	2.10	2.95	3.50
P	Mean Scores	0.43	0.32	-1.23	0.67	0.41	-1.38
SDP	Mean Raws	11.57	11.00	10.85	12.07	12.79	12.62
SDP	SD Raws	4.78	2.99	3.41	3.69	3.75	3.12
SDP	Mean Scores	0.39	0.21	-0.03	0.50	0.34	0.24
SPP	Mean Raws	9.07	9.57	10.69	12.14	13.50	10.46
SPP	SD Raws	4.71	4.27	4.27	3.48	3.67	4.22
SPP	Mean Scores	-0.12	-0.10	-0.07	0.52	0.49	-0.20

Finland
Table 3 (cont.)

Party		No influence on party policy (1) vs high (20)			No influence on partic. in govt (1) vs high (20)		
		Leads	Legs	Acts	Leads	Legs	Acts
A/C	Mean Raws	16.92	12.46	7.92	17.00	14.23	6.15
A/C	SD Raws	2.63	3.23	3.42	2.24	3.90	4.12
A/C	Mean Scores	0.08	0.15	-0.20	0.47	0.39	-0.13
DA	Mean Raws	16.31	12.39	9.42	14.31	12.58	6.46
DA	SD Raws	2.87	5.19	4.54	3.66	4.64	4.98
DA	Mean Scores	0.04	0.13	0.14	-0.20	-0.01	-0.07
FCL	Mean Raws	17.15	11.92	7.00	15.92	12.46	4.83
FCL	SD Raws	4.16	5.02	3.67	3.15	3.73	4.51
FCL	Mean Scores	0.75	0.02	-0.40	0.21	-0.04	-0.41
FDPL	Mean Raws	15.92	11.54	9.58	15.31	12.69	6.92
FDPL	SD Raws	2.33	3.89	3.99	3.15	4.29	4.54
FDPL	Mean Scores	0.02	-0.07	0.18	0.05	0.02	0.03
FRP	Mean Raws	17.85	11.15	5.25	18.08	10.77	4.15
FRP	SD Raws	1.68	3.85	2.83	1.80	3.96	2.94
FRP	Mean Scores	0.14	-0.16	-0.79	0.74	-0.45	-0.55
G	Mean Raws	7.69	12.08	14.92	9.15	13.08	12.58
G	SD Raws	3.95	5.02	4.54	4.45	3.59	5.16
G	Mean Scores	-0.52	0.06	1.36	-1.48	0.11	1.22
KOK	Mean Raws	15.08	13.17	7.50	16.31	13.92	6.08
KOK	SD Raws	2.72	3.69	3.63	2.59	3.80	3.84
KOK	Mean Scores	-0.04	0.31	-0.29	0.30	0.31	-0.15
LPP	Mean Raws	11.82	9.63	10.10	12.88	11.13	10.25
LPP	SD Raws	3.66	5.04	4.28	3.87	5.54	4.20
LPP	Mean Scores	-0.25	-0.51	0.29	-0.56	-0.36	0.73
P	Mean Raws	10.50	7.40	9.29	9.60	7.50	6.80
P	SD Raws	3.55	4.62	5.71	1.52	4.51	4.76
P	Mean Scores	-0.34	-1.03	0.11	-1.37	-1.23	0.00
SDP	Mean Raws	16.85	12.15	8.92	17.15	13.15	5.69
SDP	SD Raws	3.05	4.02	3.61	3.18	4.36	4.11
SDP	Mean Scores	0.08	0.07	0.03	0.51	0.13	-0.23
SPP	Mean Raws	13.92	12.85	7.25	16.25	13.23	6.31
SPP	SD Raws	3.04	3.98	3.49	2.80	3.49	4.44
SPP	Mean Scores	-0.12	0.23	-0.34	0.29	0.15	-0.10

Finland
Table 3 (cont.)

Party		Do not look to future (1) vs look many years (5)			Give up office(1) vs give up policy (20)	Can use groups (1) vs not (20)	Close to resp (1) vs not (15)
		Leads	Legs	Acts			
A/C	Mean Raws	3.58	3.50	3.46	14.85	5.25	8.86
A/C	SD Raws	1.24	0.67	0.52	3.26	2.18	4.35
A/C	Mean Scores	0.06	0.02	0.24	0.61	-0.81	0.02
DA	Mean Raws	3.83	3.91	3.70	3.00	6.67	11.86
DA	SD Raws	1.47	1.14	1.25	2.65	4.19	3.28
DA	Mean Scores	0.26	0.40	0.50	-1.47	-0.54	0.74
FCL	Mean Raws	2.75	2.67	2.46	11.08	11.50	11.93
FCL	SD Raws	1.14	1.16	0.93	4.07	4.21	3.41
FCL	Mean Scores	-0.64	-0.76	-0.79	-0.05	0.38	0.76
FDPL	Mean Raws	3.83	3.92	3.64	8.08	5.67	7.29
FDPL	SD Raws	1.12	0.67	0.81	4.11	2.31	3.89
FDPL	Mean Scores	0.26	0.41	0.43	-0.58	-0.73	-0.36
FRP	Mean Raws	3.17	3.27	2.80	16.08	14.83	10.71
FRP	SD Raws	1.12	1.19	0.79	2.78	4.43	2.97
FRP	Mean Scores	-0.29	-0.20	-0.44	0.82	1.02	0.47
G	Mean Raws	3.67	3.67	3.46	4.00	8.58	6.29
G	SD Raws	1.16	1.23	1.21	2.61	3.68	2.84
G	Mean Scores	0.13	0.17	0.24	-1.29	-0.18	-0.60
KOK	Mean Raws	3.75	3.75	3.46	14.77	7.92	8.29
KOK	SD Raws	1.06	0.97	0.69	4.17	3.37	3.38
KOK	Mean Scores	0.20	0.25	0.24	0.59	-0.30	-0.12
LPP	Mean Raws	3.63	3.00	3.00	14.50	16.70	6.64
LPP	SD Raws	0.52	0.93	0.58	3.24	2.50	3.88
LPP	Mean Scores	0.09	-0.45	-0.23	0.55	1.38	-0.52
P	Mean Raws	2.67	2.67	2.00	11.00	15.86	12.78
P	SD Raws	1.03	1.03	1.00	2.68	4.60	2.28
P	Mean Scores	-0.71	-0.76	-1.26	-0.07	1.22	0.97
SDP	Mean Raws	3.92	3.83	3.73	12.62	4.50	4.79
SDP	SD Raws	1.44	0.94	0.65	5.28	2.32	3.26
SDP	Mean Scores	0.33	0.33	0.53	0.22	-0.96	-0.96
SPP	Mean Raws	3.50	3.58	3.00	15.77	10.83	8.07
SPP	SD Raws	1.24	1.17	0.89	3.14	3.27	3.77
SPP	Mean Scores	-0.01	0.09	-0.23	0.77	0.26	-0.17

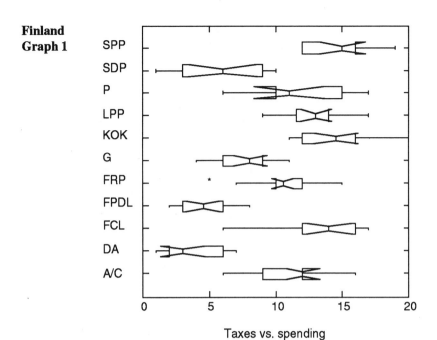

**Finland
Graph 1**

Taxes vs. spending

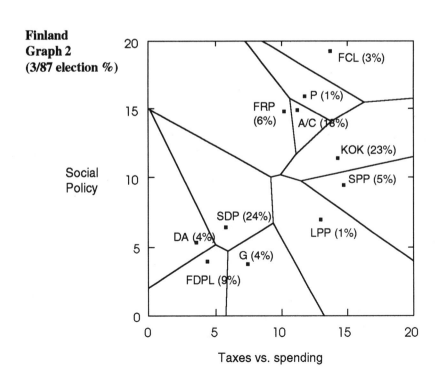

**Finland
Graph 2
(3/87 election %)**

Social
Policy

Taxes vs. spending

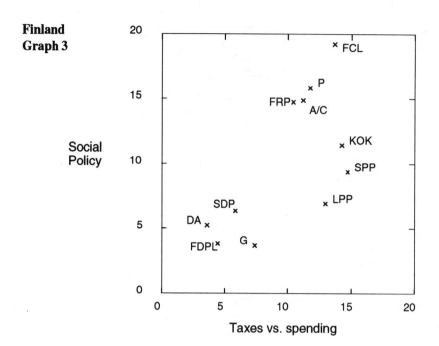

**Finland
Graph 3**

Social Policy

Taxes vs. spending

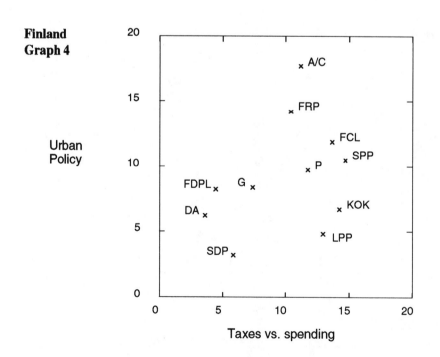

**Finland
Graph 4**

Urban Policy

Taxes vs. spending

France
Table 1   Mean   SD

	Mean	SD
Impact of opposition parties on govt policy (1=lo; 9=hi)	3.40	2.03
Prop. of govts falling on policy disputes (1=lo; 9=hi)	2.62	1.12
Cabinet portfolios as policy (1) or office (9) payoffs	6.07	1.27
Cabinet members publicize internal splits (1=lo; 9=hi)	3.40	1.50
Policy autonomy of cabinet ministers (1=hi; 9=lo)	5.50	2.03
Frequency of cabinet reshuffles (1=lo; 9=hi)	4.50	1.87

RANKING OF CABINET POSITIONS

	Mean	SD
Finance	2.36	1.91
Foreign Affairs	3.58	1.56
Industry	7.33	4.04
Environment	2.83	1.72
Defense	5.00	1.63
Transport	9.33	2.08
Interior	3.17	1.83
Health and family affairs	6.50	0.71
Social Affairs and employment	3.44	1.13
Agriculture	9.00	3.37
Justice	6.00	1.41
Education	3.00	2.24
Labor	4.75	1.71
Housing	8.00	2.83

France
Table 2

Party	Abbrev.
Socialist Party	PS
Left Radicals	MRG
Rally for the Republic	RPR
Union for French Democracy	UDF
Communist Party	PCF
National Front	FN
Greens	G

France
Table 3

Party		Increase services (1) vs cut taxes (20)			Pro friendly relations USSR (1) vs anti (20)		
		Leads	Vots	Imp.	Leads	Vots	Imp.
FN	Mean Raws	18.00	16.20	13.91	18.86	17.92	9.85
FN	SD Raws	2.07	2.86	6.28	1.51	1.66	5.76
FN	Mean Scores	1.40	1.17	0.08	1.63	1.34	-0.09
G	Mean Raws	7.50	8.91	9.42	8.70	10.80	8.00
G	SD Raws	2.54	2.17	4.58	3.95	3.99	6.20
G	Mean Scores	-0.47	-0.30	-0.92	-0.14	-0.03	-0.46
MRG	Mean Raws	8.87	9.07	10.80	8.18	9.67	7.80
MRG	SD Raws	2.26	2.37	1.93	2.71	2.92	3.49
MRG	Mean Scores	-0.22	-0.27	-0.61	-0.23	-0.24	-0.50
PCF	Mean Raws	2.13	3.13	16.60	1.14	3.14	11.77
PCF	SD Raws	1.06	1.25	4.32	0.36	1.51	5.43
PCF	Mean Scores	-1.42	-1.46	0.67	-1.46	-1.49	0.29
PS	Mean Raws	6.73	7.00	13.47	7.14	8.64	11.43
PS	SD Raws	2.58	1.93	2.85	2.32	2.87	4.55
PS	Mean Scores	-0.60	-0.69	-0.02	-0.42	-0.44	0.22
RPR	Mean Raws	14.00	14.43	15.20	11.14	13.50	11.79
RPR	SD Raws	3.44	2.56	3.47	3.28	3.39	5.31
RPR	Mean Scores	0.69	0.81	0.36	0.28	0.49	0.29
UDF	Mean Raws	13.57	14.14	13.93	10.93	12.86	10.29
UDF	SD Raws	3.08	2.11	3.85	3.00	3.23	3.81
UDF	Mean Scores	0.61	0.75	0.08	0.25	0.37	-0.01

France
Table 3 (cont.)

Party		Pro public own. (1) vs anti (20)			Pro permissive social policy (1) vs anti (20)		
		Leads	Vots	Imp.	Leads	Vots	Imp.
FN	Mean Raws	18.47	16.80	11.71	19.36	18.36	13.46
FN	SD Raws	2.10	2.62	5.44	1.01	1.99	5.09
FN	Mean Scores	1.15	1.06	-0.35	1.61	1.47	0.03
G	Mean Raws	11.00	10.40	8.00	4.15	4.08	11.31
G	SD Raws	2.21	2.37	3.65	2.88	3.29	6.40
G	Mean Scores	-0.11	-0.16	-1.12	-0.91	-1.03	-0.47
MRG	Mean Raws	10.14	10.43	12.20	5.92	6.83	12.50
MRG	SD Raws	1.46	1.79	2.39	2.50	3.01	3.37
MRG	Mean Scores	-0.25	-0.16	-0.24	-0.62	-0.55	-0.20
PCF	Mean Raws	1.47	3.07	18.33	7.60	7.67	16.21
PCF	SD Raws	0.74	2.49	1.80	3.87	3.54	4.71
PCF	Mean Scores	-1.71	-1.56	1.04	-0.34	-0.40	0.66
PS	Mean Raws	7.67	7.00	13.29	3.87	4.67	15.80
PS	SD Raws	1.99	1.81	2.37	2.03	1.99	2.43
PS	Mean Scores	-0.67	-0.81	-0.02	-0.96	-0.92	0.57
RPR	Mean Raws	16.07	15.47	14.33	14.47	14.87	12.13
RPR	SD Raws	2.55	2.10	5.02	3.07	2.88	2.67
RPR	Mean Scores	0.74	0.80	0.20	0.80	0.86	-0.28
UDF	Mean Raws	16.40	15.27	13.40	11.53	12.00	11.80
UDF	SD Raws	1.55	1.98	5.04	3.44	2.95	2.18
UDF	Mean Scores	0.80	0.77	0.01	0.31	0.36	-0.36

France
Table 3 (cont.)

Party		Anticlerical (1) vs proclerical (20)			Pro urban interests (1) vs anti (20)		
		Leads	Vots	Imp.	Leads	Vots	Imp.
FN	Mean Raws	16.85	14.92	13.73	11.63	9.75	8.00
FN	SD Raws	4.10	4.19	4.22	3.46	3.11	5.40
FN	Mean Scores	1.17	0.91	0.61	0.39	0.07	-0.29
G	Mean Raws	9.70	9.56	5.09	12.22	11.67	10.27
G	SD Raws	1.70	2.13	2.59	5.22	5.50	5.66
G	Mean Scores	-0.10	-0.16	-1.09	0.53	0.54	0.18
MRG	Mean Raws	6.18	6.82	9.44	8.75	8.71	8.64
MRG	SD Raws	2.56	2.79	3.64	1.17	1.50	3.85
MRG	Mean Scores	-0.72	-0.70	-0.23	-0.26	-0.19	-0.16
PCF	Mean Raws	3.29	4.29	9.92	5.22	5.11	9.55
PCF	SD Raws	2.02	2.40	5.92	3.42	2.62	5.01
PCF	Mean Scores	-1.23	-1.21	-0.14	-1.07	-1.07	0.03
PS	Mean Raws	5.86	7.00	9.57	7.00	6.44	8.90
PS	SD Raws	2.74	2.66	5.00	3.16	3.21	4.53
PS	Mean Scores	-0.78	-0.67	-0.21	-0.66	-0.75	-0.11
RPR	Mean Raws	14.21	14.29	12.31	13.11	12.89	11.09
RPR	SD Raws	2.46	2.49	4.72	3.98	1.62	5.30
RPR	Mean Scores	0.70	0.78	0.33	0.73	0.84	0.35
UDF	Mean Raws	15.07	14.86	13.43	11.63	11.88	9.27
UDF	SD Raws	2.34	2.21	3.72	2.67	1.96	4.43
UDF	Mean Scores	0.86	0.90	0.55	0.39	0.59	-0.03

France
Table 3 (cont.)

Party		Pro decentralization of decisions (1) vs anti (20)			Envir. over growth (1) vs growth over env (20)		
		Leads	Vots	Imp.	Leads	Vots	Imp.
FN	Mean Raws	14.31	13.00	7.83	16.17	15.50	3.82
FN	SD Raws	3.75	2.63	5.11	1.90	2.20	1.89
FN	Mean Scores	0.97	1.00	-0.77	0.85	1.06	-1.00
G	Mean Raws	4.39	4.39	14.17	1.86	1.79	19.46
G	SD Raws	5.25	5.28	5.70	1.66	1.05	1.13
G	Mean Scores	-0.88	-0.86	0.54	-1.75	-1.57	1.74
MRG	Mean Raws	5.83	5.67	12.09	9.00	8.55	11.50
MRG	SD Raws	2.52	2.50	3.11	2.41	3.08	3.06
MRG	Mean Scores	-0.61	-0.58	0.11	-0.45	-0.27	0.35
PCF	Mean Raws	11.64	9.86	9.43	14.93	12.54	5.69
PCF	SD Raws	5.56	4.91	4.57	5.48	5.65	3.59
PCF	Mean Scores	0.47	0.32	-0.44	0.62	0.49	-0.67
PS	Mean Raws	5.07	5.27	13.31	10.57	7.93	10.85
PS	SD Raws	2.28	2.15	5.02	3.06	3.52	4.20
PS	Mean Scores	-0.75	-0.67	0.36	-0.17	-0.39	0.23
RPR	Mean Raws	13.20	12.20	11.50	15.00	13.21	6.92
RPR	SD Raws	3.67	2.65	4.09	2.08	2.08	3.01
RPR	Mean Scores	0.76	0.83	-0.02	0.64	0.62	-0.46
UDF	Mean Raws	8.79	8.13	12.85	13.07	10.93	8.14
UDF	SD Raws	3.47	3.16	3.53	2.46	2.37	3.82
UDF	Mean Scores	-0.06	-0.05	0.26	0.29	0.19	-0.24

France
Table 3 (cont.)

Party		No influence on party policy (1) vs high (20)			No influence on partic. in govt (1) vs high (20)		
		Leads	Legs	Acts	Leads	Legs	Acts
FN	Mean Raws	18.77	4.82	6.83	14.63	3.20	5.67
FN	SD Raws	1.24	4.40	3.71	6.23	2.17	4.18
FN	Mean Scores	0.85	-1.02	-0.37	0.00	-1.34	-0.27
G	Mean Raws	8.92	5.38	16.25	6.29	8.00	10.00
G	SD Raws	5.27	5.83	4.22	5.31	6.87	7.03
G	Mean Scores	-1.44	-0.92	1.38	-1.52	-0.41	0.79
MRG	Mean Raws	11.67	14.25	6.17	14.60	13.20	5.64
MRG	SD Raws	3.03	3.44	4.00	5.46	4.57	3.17
MRG	Mean Scores	-0.80	0.70	-0.49	-0.01	0.60	-0.28
PCF	Mean Raws	18.60	6.36	9.00	16.57	7.25	6.64
PCF	SD Raws	1.60	3.97	6.30	5.24	4.69	4.38
PCF	Mean Scores	0.81	-0.74	0.04	0.35	-0.55	-0.03
PS	Mean Raws	15.27	13.08	12.00	17.00	11.83	8.46
PS	SD Raws	2.63	3.82	4.05	1.83	4.02	3.21
PS	Mean Scores	0.03	0.49	0.59	0.43	0.34	0.42
RPR	Mean Raws	17.13	11.86	6.53	15.85	10.18	5.77
RPR	SD Raws	1.64	3.33	3.56	4.96	3.57	2.92
RPR	Mean Scores	0.47	0.26	-0.42	0.22	0.02	-0.24
UDF	Mean Raws	14.07	14.57	5.40	13.54	12.64	5.92
UDF	SD Raws	3.24	3.44	2.29	4.89	4.41	2.87
UDF	Mean Scores	-0.25	0.76	-0.63	-0.20	0.50	-0.21

France
Table 3 (cont.)

Party		Do not look to future (1) vs look many years (5)			Give up office(1) vs give up policy (20)	Can use groups (1) vs not (20)	Close to resp (1) vs not (15)
		Leads	Legs	Acts			
FN	Mean Raws	3.11	2.88	2.89	8.13	11.71	14.62
FN	SD Raws	1.27	1.25	1.36	5.41	5.77	0.96
FN	Mean Scores	-0.43	-0.41	-0.36	-0.44	0.26	1.08
G	Mean Raws	3.78	3.57	4.22	8.25	11.00	6.58
G	SD Raws	1.48	1.27	1.39	6.84	5.42	3.83
G	Mean Scores	0.26	0.19	0.75	-0.42	0.14	-0.92
MRG	Mean Raws	3.22	3.00	2.89	13.60	15.00	9.82
MRG	SD Raws	0.97	1.41	1.27	4.88	6.33	2.75
MRG	Mean Scores	-0.31	-0.30	-0.36	0.63	0.83	-0.12
PCF	Mean Raws	3.92	3.60	3.36	7.64	3.20	12.54
PCF	SD Raws	0.79	1.17	1.21	6.09	4.57	3.05
PCF	Mean Scores	0.40	0.22	0.03	-0.53	-1.23	0.56
PS	Mean Raws	3.73	3.50	3.46	12.36	10.40	6.77
PS	SD Raws	0.65	1.08	1.04	2.62	4.17	3.90
PS	Mean Scores	0.20	0.13	0.11	0.39	0.03	-0.88
RPR	Mean Raws	3.36	3.40	3.36	11.20	10.70	11.62
RPR	SD Raws	0.81	1.08	1.03	3.52	3.68	2.76
RPR	Mean Scores	-0.17	0.04	0.03	0.16	0.08	0.33
UDF	Mean Raws	3.46	3.40	3.09	10.70	11.20	9.69
UDF	SD Raws	0.82	1.08	1.04	4.22	4.39	2.98
UDF	Mean Scores	-0.08	0.04	-0.19	0.06	0.17	-0.15

France
Table 4

Party		Pro immigration (1) vs anti (20)			pro EEC (1) vs anti (20)		
		Leads	Vots	Imp.	Leads	Vots	Imp.
FN	Mean	20.00	20.00	20.00	16.20	15.00	10.33
	SD	0.00	0.00	0.00	3.03	3.46	4.51
G	Mean	2.50	2.75	4.67	5.50	5.25	11.33
	SD	1.00	1.71	5.51	3.32	1.71	2.89
MRG	Mean	7.00	9.75	6.67	6.50	7.75	12.00
	SD	2.16	3.86	3.51	1.73	0.96	3.46
PCF	Mean	6.75	11.60	9.75	18.60	16.00	13.00
	SD	2.99	1.52	4.57	1.14	2.35	2.65
PS	Mean	4.80	7.80	9.75	5.00	5.60	14.00
	SD	1.64	2.59	3.40	1.41	1.82	0.00
RPR	Mean	13.60	16.00	16.00	12.60	11.80	11.33
	SD	2.61	2.35	1.83	4.34	4.09	2.31
UDF	Mean	12.80	14.60	13.25	4.60	5.60	16.00
	SD	0.00	0.00	0.00	2.41	1.82	4.00

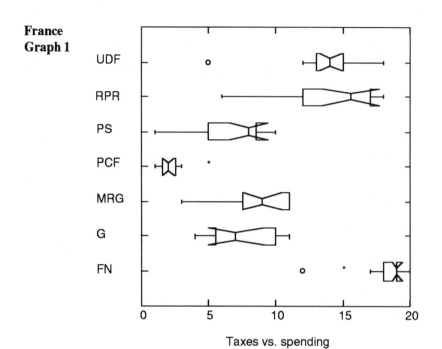

France Graph 1

Taxes vs. spending

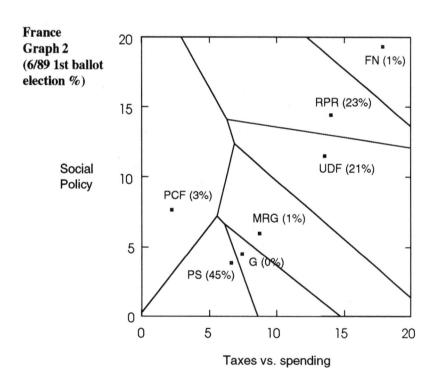

France Graph 2 (6/89 1st ballot election %)

Social Policy

Taxes vs. spending

**France
Graph 3**

Social
Policy

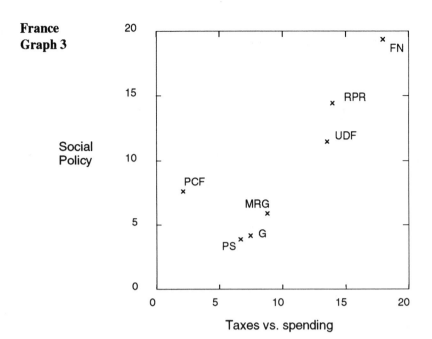

Taxes vs. spending

**France
Graph 4**

Public
Ownership
Policy

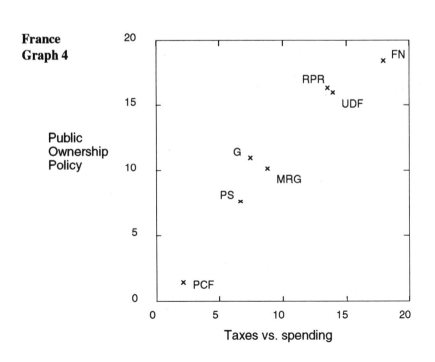

Taxes vs. spending

195

Germany
Table 1

	Mean	SD
Impact of opposition parties on govt policy (1=lo; 9=hi)	3.47	1.68
Prop. of govts falling on policy disputes (1=lo; 9=hi)	4.11	2.37
Cabinet portfolios as policy (1) or office (9) payoffs	4.53	2.14
Cabinet members publicize internal splits (1=lo; 9=hi)	4.00	2.11
Policy autonomy of cabinet ministers (1=hi; 9=lo)	4.61	1.79
Frequency of cabinet reshuffles (1=lo; 9=hi)	4.11	1.60

RANKING OF CABINET POSITIONS

Finance	2.13	1.19
Foreign Affairs	1.79	1.25
Economics	4.90	1.85
Environment	8.83	3.66
Defense	4.55	2.02
Transport	11.00	1.00
Interior	3.27	1.27
Youth, family, women and health affairs	7.33	2.52
Labor and social affairs	4.67	1.67
Food, agriculture and forestry	8.75	1.26
Justice	6.33	1.51
Education and Science	14.50	0.71

Germany
Table 2

Party	Abbrev.
Christian Democratic Union	CDU
Christian Social Union	CSU
Social Democratic Party	SDP
Free Democratic Party	FDP
Greens	G

Germany
Table 3

Party		Increase services (1) vs cut taxes (20)			Pro friendly relations USSR (1) vs anti (20)		
		Leads	Vots	Imp.	Leads	Vots	Imp.
CDU	Mean Raws	13.53	12.74	13.94	9.83	11.06	12.44
CDU	SD Raws	2.37	2.02	2.73	2.96	2.75	3.83
CDU	Mean Scores	0.59	0.45	0.36	0.48	0.58	0.11
FPD	Mean Raws	15.68	16.05	15.24	6.61	7.72	13.80
FPD	SD Raws	2.67	2.74	3.15	2.06	2.27	4.14
FPD	Mean Scores	1.01	1.16	0.68	-0.22	-0.12	0.40
G	Mean Raws	5.21	5.90	9.77	4.00	4.00	9.75
G	SD Raws	2.84	2.73	3.72	2.11	2.50	4.25
G	Mean Scores	-1.04	-1.03	-0.67	-0.78	-0.91	-0.47
NPD	Mean Raws	13.25	12.38	9.00	16.36	16.55	9.00
NPD	SD Raws	4.50	3.20	4.76	2.50	3.05	6.68
NPD	Mean Scores	0.54	0.37	-0.86	1.90	1.74	-0.63
SPD	Mean Raws	6.53	7.26	12.47	4.61	5.39	13.19
SPD	SD Raws	1.90	1.76	3.57	1.54	1.82	4.23
SPD	Mean Scores	-0.78	-0.74	-0.01	-0.65	-0.61	0.27

Party		Pro public own. (1) vs anti (20)			Pro permissive social policy (1) vs anti (20)		
		Leads	Vots	Imp.	Leads	Vots	Imp.
CDU	Mean Raws	13.56	12.87	11.31	14.42	14.58	13.41
CDU	SD Raws	1.75	1.36	2.98	2.34	2.29	2.83
CDU	Mean Scores	0.39	0.37	-0.02	0.95	0.95	0.05
FPD	Mean Raws	17.38	16.53	12.25	6.84	7.74	10.59
FPD	SD Raws	1.71	2.33	3.17	2.63	2.28	3.28
FPD	Mean Scores	1.22	1.22	0.27	-0.33	-0.31	-0.77
G	Mean Raws	7.13	7.07	10.94	2.90	3.63	14.65
G	SD Raws	2.42	2.15	3.49	3.96	4.13	2.40
G	Mean Scores	-1.01	-0.96	-0.14	-1.00	-1.07	0.40
NPD	Mean Raws	13.71	13.00	10.67	18.00	17.11	12.17
NPD	SD Raws	3.73	3.95	1.37	1.00	1.17	3.87
NPD	Mean Scores	0.43	0.41	-0.23	1.55	1.41	-0.32
SPD	Mean Raws	8.13	7.80	11.31	6.68	8.16	14.77
SPD	SD Raws	2.25	2.15	3.59	3.73	3.50	3.60
SPD	Mean Scores	-0.79	-0.79	-0.02	-0.36	-0.24	0.44

Germany
Table 3 (cont.)

Party		Anticlerical (1) vs proclerical (20)			Pro urban interests (1) vs anti (20)		
		Leads	Vots	Imp.	Leads	Vots	Imp.
CDU	Mean Raws	15.00	15.18	11.69	12.18	12.00	12.53
CDU	SD Raws	2.00	1.85	4.21	2.43	2.07	3.04
CDU	Mean Scores	1.36	1.39	0.88	0.75	0.88	0.51
FPD	Mean Raws	6.59	6.88	7.13	7.82	7.13	9.13
FPD	SD Raws	2.83	2.62	3.78	2.48	2.17	2.56
FPD	Mean Scores	-0.46	-0.46	-0.20	-0.37	-0.43	-0.46
G	Mean Raws	4.41	4.35	6.13	8.65	8.13	10.40
G	SD Raws	2.87	2.55	3.91	4.47	4.03	3.46
G	Mean Scores	-0.94	-1.02	-0.44	-0.16	-0.17	-0.10
NPD	Mean Raws	10.33	11.17	7.83	13.56	12.86	11.43
NPD	SD Raws	3.08	1.94	4.17	3.09	3.02	5.91
NPD	Mean Scores	0.35	0.49	-0.04	1.10	1.11	0.20
SPD	Mean Raws	8.35	8.59	7.06	6.18	5.81	10.53
SPD	SD Raws	2.55	2.06	3.02	1.59	1.91	2.92
SPD	Mean Scores	-0.08	-0.08	-0.22	-0.80	-0.79	-0.06

Party		Pro decentralization of decisions (1) vs anti (20)			Envir. over growth (1) vs growth over env (20)		
		Leads	Vots	Imp.	Leads	Vots	Imp.
CDU	Mean Raws	9.88	9.71	10.50	12.58	12.79	12.41
CDU	SD Raws	2.71	2.78	2.66	2.50	2.57	3.32
CDU	Mean Scores	0.10	0.06	-0.17	0.71	0.67	-0.40
FPD	Mean Raws	11.06	11.13	11.25	11.68	11.68	12.18
FPD	SD Raws	2.72	3.20	2.60	3.38	3.62	3.15
FPD	Mean Scores	0.38	0.39	0.08	0.53	0.45	-0.46
G	Mean Raws	5.31	5.06	12.00	2.00	2.68	18.82
G	SD Raws	5.13	4.99	3.71	1.00	2.24	1.02
G	Mean Scores	-1.00	-1.02	0.33	-1.44	-1.35	1.18
NPD	Mean Raws	10.50	11.29	10.71	13.71	14.29	8.71
NPD	SD Raws	4.63	4.03	3.59	3.95	3.82	2.81
NPD	Mean Scores	0.24	0.42	-0.10	0.95	0.97	-1.31
SPD	Mean Raws	11.06	11.06	10.44	8.32	8.74	14.88
SPD	SD Raws	2.90	3.21	2.61	2.03	3.09	2.78
SPD	Mean Scores	0.38	0.37	-0.19	-0.15	-0.14	0.21

Germany
Table 3 (cont.)

Party		No influence on party policy (1) vs high (20)			No influence on partic. in govt (1) vs high (20)		
		Leads	Legs	Acts	Leads	Legs	Acts
CDU	Mean Raws	15.16	12.33	8.89	16.33	12.89	7.83
CDU	SD Raws	2.32	2.83	4.11	2.11	3.74	4.68
CDU	Mean Scores	0.34	0.26	-0.27	0.43	0.11	-0.21
FPD	Mean Raws	15.39	12.11	8.63	16.41	12.77	7.11
FPD	SD Raws	2.36	3.13	3.88	2.21	4.56	4.24
FPD	Mean Scores	0.40	0.20	-0.32	0.45	0.08	-0.35
G	Mean Raws	9.53	10.68	13.58	11.06	11.89	11.72
G	SD Raws	4.22	4.08	5.55	4.22	3.76	5.58
G	Mean Scores	-1.12	-0.21	0.69	-0.98	-0.15	0.56
NPD	Mean Raws	16.67	7.60	7.78	14.67	13.00	8.00
NPD	SD Raws	3.35	4.78	4.94	5.01	2.65	5.10
NPD	Mean Scores	0.73	-1.08	-0.50	-0.02	0.14	-0.17
SPD	Mean Raws	14.05	11.58	10.79	15.22	12.28	9.06
SPD	SD Raws	2.72	3.10	4.18	2.80	3.68	4.91
SPD	Mean Scores	0.05	0.05	0.12	0.13	-0.05	0.04

Party		Do not look to future (1) vs look many years (5)			Give up office(1) vs give up policy (20)	Can use groups (1) vs not (20)	Close to resp (1) vs not (15)
		Leads	Legs	Acts			
CDU	Mean Raws	4.00	3.87	3.29	14.27	10.00	9.88
CDU	SD Raws	0.61	0.74	0.99	2.60	3.53	3.16
CDU	Mean Scores	0.13	0.09	0.01	0.62	0.02	0.23
FPD	Mean Raws	3.88	3.80	3.33	15.06	10.94	7.61
FPD	SD Raws	0.70	0.86	0.98	3.07	4.41	2.77
FPD	Mean Scores	-0.03	0.01	0.06	0.79	0.23	-0.32
G	Mean Raws	3.63	3.64	3.21	5.53	9.50	9.00
G	SD Raws	0.89	0.93	1.05	3.34	5.34	3.92
G	Mean Scores	-0.36	-0.17	-0.06	-1.25	-0.09	0.02
NPD	Mean Raws	3.25	3.25	2.25	11.00	12.50	15.00
NPD	SD Raws	1.50	1.71	1.50	2.94	5.13	0.00
NPD	Mean Scores	-0.84	-0.61	-1.00	-0.08	0.58	1.46
SPD	Mean Raws	4.24	4.00	3.53	10.56	8.06	5.67
SPD	SD Raws	0.56	0.78	0.92	2.99	3.69	3.34
SPD	Mean Scores	0.43	0.24	0.25	-0.18	-0.42	-0.79

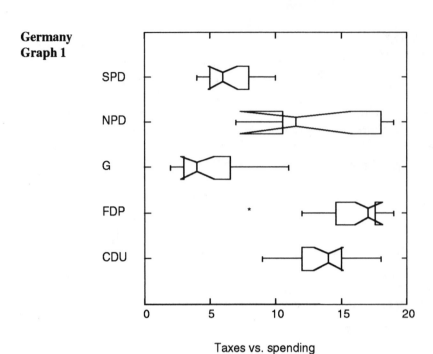

Germany Graph 1

Taxes vs. spending

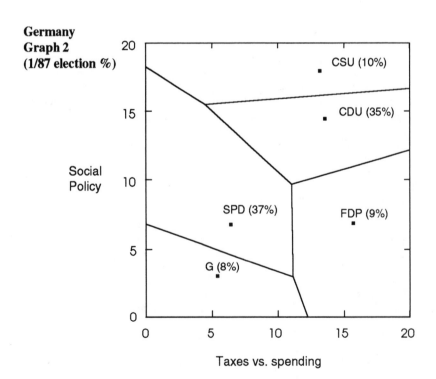

Germany Graph 2 (1/87 election %)

Taxes vs. spending

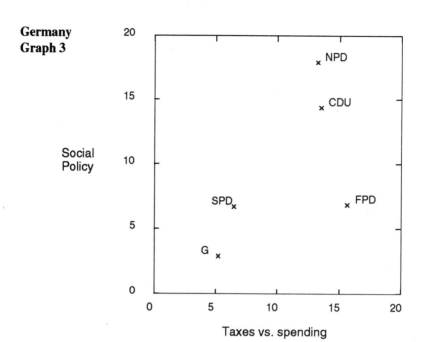

Germany
Graph 3

Social
Policy

Taxes vs. spending

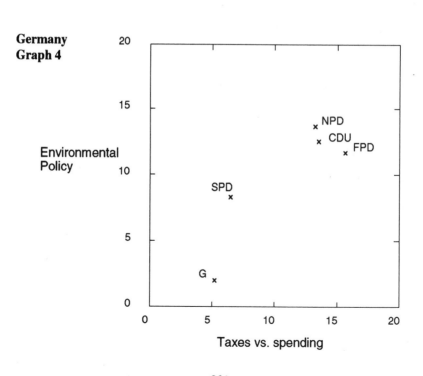

Germany
Graph 4

Environmental
Policy

Taxes vs. spending

Greece
Table 1

	Mean	SD
Impact of opposition parties on govt policy (1=lo; 9=hi)	2.20	0.45
Prop. of govts falling on policy disputes (1=lo; 9=hi)	1.20	0.45
Cabinet portfolios as policy (1) or office (9) payoffs	8.00	0.71
Cabinet members publicize internal splits (1=lo; 9=hi)	2.80	2.39
Policy autonomy of cabinet ministers (1=hi; 9=lo)	6.20	2.49
Frequency of cabinet reshuffles (1=lo; 9=hi)	8.40	0.89

RANKING OF CABINET POSITIONS		
National Economy	2.00	0.82
Foreign Affairs	3.25	1.71
Finance	7.00	4.00
Interior	8.00	3.56
Defense	3.25	1.50
Health, Welfare and Social services	7.00	1.41
Agriculture	10.50	6.36
Justice	7.00	5.20
National Education and Religion	7.00	0.00
Labor	9.67	2.08

Greece
Table 2

Party	Abbrev.
Pan-Hellenic Socialist Movement	PASOK
New Democracy	ND
Communist Party	KKE
Communist Party of the Interior	KKEes

Greece
Table 3

Party		Increase services (1) vs cut taxes (20)			Pro friendly relations USSR (1) vs anti (20)		
		Leads	Vots	Imp.	Leads	Vots	Imp.
KKE	Mean Raws	5.00	5.00	11.50	1.00	1.00	16.40
KKE	SD Raws	4.36	5.29	8.19	0.00	0.00	2.07
KKE	Mean Scores	-0.71	-0.67	-0.08	-1.03	-1.17	0.18
KKEes	Mean Raws	6.67	7.00	11.25	4.80	5.40	12.80
KKEes	SD Raws	2.89	3.61	7.93	2.59	2.07	6.42
KKEes	Mean Scores	-0.39	-0.31	-0.11	0.00	-0.32	-0.63
ND	Mean Raws	15.67	15.33	14.00	8.80	14.60	14.40
ND	SD Raws	2.89	4.04	8.68	4.03	0.55	4.62
ND	Mean Scores	1.35	1.22	0.26	1.09	1.46	-0.27
PASOK	Mean Raws	7.33	7.33	11.50	4.60	7.20	18.80
PASOK	SD Raws	3.06	3.51	7.59	1.82	1.30	0.84
PASOK	Mean Scores	-0.26	-0.25	-0.08	-0.05	0.03	0.72

Greece
Table 3 (cont.)

Party		Pro public own. (1) vs anti (20)			Pro permissive social policy (1) vs anti (20)		
		Leads	Vots	Imp.	Leads	Vots	Imp.
KKE	Mean Raws	2.60	2.50	14.00	7.75	8.25	5.00
KKE	SD Raws	1.14	1.29	6.78	4.43	5.56	4.32
KKE	Mean Scores	-1.13	-1.18	0.20	0.02	-0.05	-0.39
KKEes	Mean Raws	7.80	8.00	11.25	2.00	2.50	9.25
KKEes	SD Raws	1.92	1.63	6.24	0.82	0.58	6.24
KKEes	Mean Scores	-0.08	-0.10	-0.26	-0.99	-0.99	0.53
ND	Mean Raws	14.60	15.50	15.75	13.75	15.75	5.50
ND ·	SD Raws	4.10	1.29	4.57	6.08	3.95	4.44
ND	Mean Scores	1.29	1.38	0.49	1.08	1.17	-0.28
PASOK	Mean Raws	7.80	8.00	10.25	7.00	7.75	7.50
PASOK	SD Raws	1.92	2.94	6.80	3.37	4.65	3.87
PASOK	Mean Scores	-0.08	-0.10	-0.43	-0.11	-0.13	0.15

Party		Anticlerical (1) vs proclerical (20)			Pro urban interests (1) vs anti (20)		
		Leads	Vots	Imp.	Leads	Vots	Imp.
KKE	Mean Raws	4.40	3.20	5.80	7.00	5.50	5.00
KKE	SD Raws	2.51	1.92	4.82	3.56	2.89	6.16
KKE	Mean Scores	-0.80	-0.88	-0.38	-0.72	-0.71	-0.17
KKEes	Mean Raws	5.80	4.40	6.20	7.25	6.25	4.50
KKEes	SD Raws	3.03	1.95	3.96	2.75	4.57	5.20
KKEes	Mean Scores	-0.54	-0.69	-0.30	-0.66	-0.53	-0.25
ND	Mean Raws	16.60	18.00	8.80	11.75	9.00	5.50
ND	SD Raws	2.41	0.71	4.60	3.59	1.83	7.14
ND	Mean Scores	1.41	1.49	0.27	0.35	0.12	-0.09
PASOK	Mean Raws	8.40	9.20	9.40	14.75	13.25	9.25
PASOK	SD Raws	3.44	2.95	5.18	3.10	2.63	7.93
PASOK	Mean Scores	-0.07	0.08	0.41	1.03	1.13	0.51

Greece
Table 3 (cont.)

Party		Pro decentralization of decisions (1) vs anti (20)			Envir. over growth (1) vs growth over env (20)		
		Leads	Vots	Imp.	Leads	Vots	Imp.
KKE	Mean Raws	10.75	9.80	11.25	9.50	9.00	8.40
KKE	SD Raws	5.12	4.71	0.96	2.38	3.92	6.58
KKE	Mean Scores	0.23	0.40	-0.52	-0.05	0.03	-0.17
KKEes	Mean Raws	3.50	3.00	14.50	5.50	5.00	12.20
KKEes	SD Raws	1.00	0.71	2.08	3.11	3.46	6.76
KKEes	Mean Scores	-1.05	-1.06	0.66	-1.13	-1.01	0.44
ND	Mean Raws	13.00	10.80	10.50	12.50	11.00	8.80
ND	SD Raws	4.76	4.15	2.38	3.00	2.94	6.34
ND	Mean Scores	0.63	0.61	-0.80	0.76	0.55	-0.10
PASOK	Mean Raws	10.50	8.20	14.50	11.25	10.50	8.40
PASOK	SD Raws	6.56	4.32	3.00	2.63	2.89	6.84
PASOK	Mean Scores	0.19	0.05	0.66	0.42	0.42	-0.17

Party		No influence on party policy (1) vs high (20)			No influence on partic. in govt (1) vs high (20)		
		Leads	Legs	Acts	Leads	Legs	Acts
KKE	Mean Raws	17.20	6.60	8.20	18.75	6.50	6.00
KKE	SD Raws	3.11	5.41	4.66	1.89	3.32	3.92
KKE	Mean Scores	-0.41	-0.16	0.03	-0.02	-0.30	0.01
KKEes	Mean Raws	16.20	9.80	12.40	16.50	14.00	9.50
KKEes	SD Raws	2.05	5.59	2.70	1.92	4.32	5.45
KKEes	Mean Scores	-0.84	0.48	0.93	-1.27	1.02	0.77
ND	Mean Raws	19.20	8.60	4.20	19.40	8.40	3.40
ND	SD Raws	0.45	5.90	2.05	0.89	7.13	2.07
ND	Mean Scores	0.45	0.24	-0.83	0.35	0.03	-0.55
PASOK	Mean Raws	20.00	4.60	7.40	20.00	4.80	5.60
PASOK	SD Raws	0.00	2.07	5.23	0.00	3.70	5.55
PASOK	Mean Scores	0.80	-0.56	-0.14	0.68	-0.60	-0.08

Greece
Table 3 (cont.)

Party		Do not look to future (1) vs look many years (5)			Give up office(1) vs give up policy (20)	Can use groups (1) vs not (20)	Close to resp (1) vs not (15)
		Leads	Legs	Acts			
KKE	Mean Raws	4.33	4.33	4.00	11.20	3.40	13.75
KKE	SD Raws	0.58	0.58	0.00	4.15	2.07	1.89
KKE	Mean Scores	0.90	0.80	0.84	-0.74	-0.71	0.63
KKEes	Mean Raws	4.00	4.00	4.00	10.80	13.60	7.00
KKEes	SD Raws	1.00	1.00	0.00	2.68	5.94	3.46
KKEes	Mean Scores	0.60	0.53	0.84	-0.82	1.11	-1.02
ND	Mean Raws	2.80	2.75	2.50	17.80	7.40	11.25
ND	SD Raws	1.10	1.26	1.00	3.35	3.78	5.68
ND	Mean Scores	-0.45	-0.50	-0.63	0.67	0.01	0.02
PASOK	Mean Raws	2.80	2.75	2.50	18.80	4.50	12.75
PASOK	SD Raws	1.10	1.26	1.00	1.10	3.79	0.96
PASOK	Mean Scores	-0.45	-0.50	-0.63	0.89	-0.51	0.38

**Greece
Graph 1**

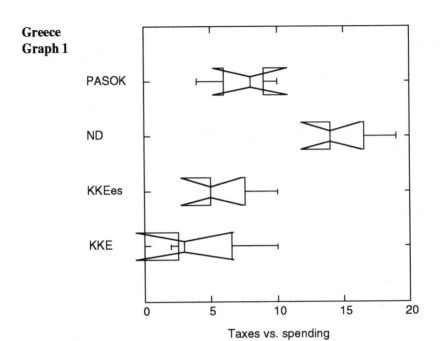

Taxes vs. spending

**Greece
Graph 2
(11/89 election %)**

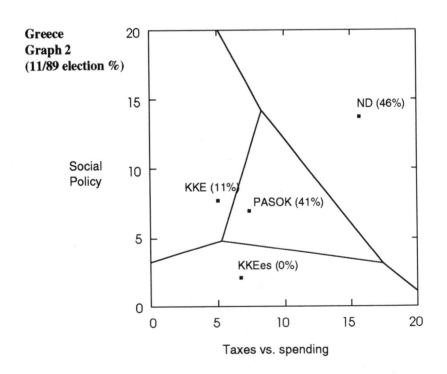

Taxes vs. spending

**Greece
Graph 3**

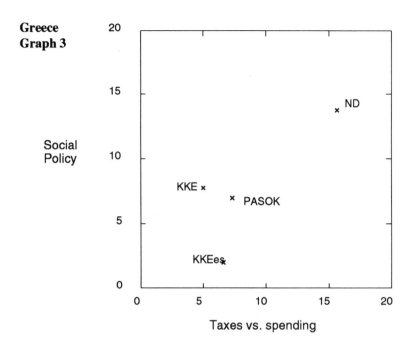

Social
Policy

Taxes vs. spending

**Greece
Graph 4**

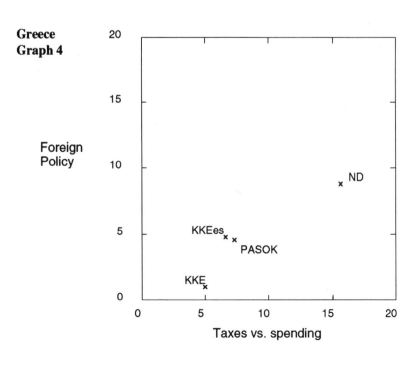

Foreign
Policy

Taxes vs. spending

Iceland
Table 1

	Mean	SD
Impact of opposition parties on govt policy (1=lo; 9=hi)	4.80	2.68
Prop. of govts falling on policy disputes (1=lo; 9=hi)	6.20	0.84
Cabinet portfolios as policy (1) or office (9) payoffs	6.00	1.00
Cabinet members publicize internal splits (1=lo; 9=hi)	6.40	0.55
Policy autonomy of cabinet ministers (1=hi; 9=lo)	3.60	2.19
Frequency of cabinet reshuffles (1=lo; 9=hi)	2.40	0.89

RANKING OF CABINET POSITIONS

Finance	1.40	0.55
Foreign Affairs	1.60	0.55
Industry	6.50	3.00
Health	6.20	0.45
Social Affairs	7.75	2.63
Fisheries	3.40	0.55
Commerce and Justice	8.00	2.00
Education	6.80	1.10

Iceland
Table 2

Party	Abbrev.
People's Alliance	PA
Social Democratic Party	SDP
Progressive Party	PP
Citizens' Party	CP
Independence Party	IP
Women's Alliance	WA

Iceland
Table 3

Party		Increase services (1) vs cut taxes (20)			Pro friendly relations USSR (1) vs anti (20)		
		Leads	Vots	Imp.	Leads	Vots	Imp.
CP	Mean Raws	15.00	16.20	15.00	11.00	10.40	8.50
CP	SD Raws	3.74	3.03	2.45	5.66	6.19	2.65
CP	Mean Scores	1.15	1.27	0.80	0.85	0.74	-0.83
IP	Mean Raws	13.80	14.40	13.60	9.40	9.20	15.25
IP	SD Raws	2.68	1.52	2.88	4.34	4.92	2.22
IP	Mean Scores	0.94	0.96	0.48	0.50	0.47	0.81
PA	Mean Raws	2.60	2.60	11.80	2.60	3.40	15.50
PA	SD Raws	0.89	0.55	5.50	1.52	0.89	4.36
PA	Mean Scores	-1.08	-1.10	0.06	-0.98	-0.83	0.87
PP	Mean Raws	8.80	9.40	10.00	6.60	6.80	12.00
PP	SD Raws	2.59	2.07	2.24	2.70	2.49	2.58
PP	Mean Scores	0.04	0.09	-0.37	-0.11	-0.07	0.02
SDP	Mean Raws	7.80	7.60	10.40	8.40	8.40	13.25
SDP	SD Raws	5.45	4.72	3.44	5.55	4.98	1.71
SDP	Mean Scores	-0.14	-0.23	-0.27	0.28	0.29	0.32
WA	Mean Raws	3.60	3.20	8.60	4.60	4.40	7.00
WA	SD Raws	1.52	1.79	5.94	1.14	1.34	2.94
WA	Mean Scores	-0.90	-0.99	-0.69	-0.54	-0.61	-1.19

Party		Pro public own. (1) vs anti (20)			Pro permissive social policy (1) vs anti (20)		
		Leads	Vots	Imp.	Leads	Vots	Imp.
CP	Mean Raws	11.20	11.40	13.60	13.50	16.00	11.20
CP	SD Raws	7.66	8.39	3.78	4.95	2.83	5.40
CP	Mean Scores	0.56	0.53	0.48	1.16	1.22	-0.52
IP	Mean Raws	10.20	10.20	14.00	11.50	14.00	11.00
IP	SD Raws	7.56	7.66	3.32	4.95	2.83	2.65
IP	Mean Scores	0.35	0.29	0.59	0.78	0.88	-0.58
PA	Mean Raws	4.80	6.60	11.80	2.50	3.50	16.00
PA	SD Raws	2.39	3.29	3.63	0.71	2.12	1.87
PA	Mean Scores	-0.75	-0.41	-0.01	-0.91	-0.93	0.71
PP	Mean Raws	8.60	8.00	12.00	9.50	11.50	10.60
PP	SD Raws	3.51	4.18	2.83	3.54	0.71	2.97
PP	Mean Scores	0.03	-0.14	0.05	0.41	0.45	-0.68
SDP	Mean Raws	8.20	7.40	11.00	6.00	7.00	13.40
SDP	SD Raws	3.11	3.13	2.65	0.00	2.83	2.51
SDP	Mean Scores	-0.05	-0.25	-0.23	-0.25	-0.33	0.04
WA	Mean Raws	7.80	8.60	8.60	1.00	1.50	17.20
WA	SD Raws	1.10	1.52	4.45	0.00	0.71	2.28
WA	Mean Scores	-0.14	-0.02	-0.88	-1.19	-1.28	1.02

Iceland
Table 3 (cont.)

Party		Anticlerical (1) vs proclerical (20)			Pro urban interests (1) vs anti (20)		
		Leads	Vots	Imp.	Leads	Vots	Imp.
CP	Mean Raws	NA	NA	1.50	8.80	9.80	10.40
CP	SD Raws	NA	NA	0.71	5.36	5.45	3.51
CP	Mean Scores	NA	NA	0.00	-0.04	0.13	-0.34
IP	Mean Raws	NA	NA	1.50	8.40	8.40	13.60
IP	SD Raws	NA	NA	0.71	5.32	5.51	5.27
IP	Mean Scores	NA	NA	0.00	-0.12	-0.14	0.39
PA	Mean Raws	NA	NA	1.50	9.60	9.60	12.50
PA	SD Raws	NA	NA	0.71	4.22	4.56	1.92
PA	Mean Scores	NA	NA	0.00	0.13	0.09	0.14
PP	Mean Raws	NA	NA	1.50	11.20	11.60	17.25
PP	SD Raws	NA	NA	0.71	7.98	8.47	0.50
PP	Mean Scores	NA	NA	0.00	0.47	0.49	1.22
SDP	Mean Raws	NA	NA	1.50	7.40	7.40	10.40
SDP	SD Raws	NA	NA	0.71	2.88	2.88	3.51
SDP	Mean Scores	NA	NA	0.00	-0.33	-0.34	-0.34
WA	Mean Raws	NA	NA	1.50	8.40	8.00	8.40
WA	SD Raws	NA	NA	0.71	2.88	3.54	4.72
WA	Mean Scores	NA	NA	0.00	-0.12	-0.22	-0.79

Party		Pro decentralization of decisions (1) vs anti (20)			Envir. over growth (1) vs growth over env (20)		
		Leads	Vots	Imp.	Leads	Vots	Imp.
CP	Mean Raws	5.80	5.20	10.20	11.60	11.80	11.60
CP	SD Raws	3.90	4.32	5.36	5.32	5.54	5.37
CP	Mean Scores	-0.47	-0.50	0.13	0.76	0.79	-0.52
IP	Mean Raws	8.20	7.40	11.40	10.60	10.60	13.00
IP	SD Raws	5.81	5.55	5.77	4.67	4.67	4.95
IP	Mean Scores	0.16	0.06	0.42	0.54	0.52	-0.19
PA	Mean Raws	10.20	10.00	7.20	6.60	7.00	15.60
PA	SD Raws	2.28	2.45	1.10	3.91	4.90	2.19
PA	Mean Scores	0.68	0.72	-0.59	-0.36	-0.28	0.42
PP	Mean Raws	8.60	8.00	9.00	8.20	7.60	14.00
PP	SD Raws	3.65	4.30	3.00	3.56	2.70	5.10
PP	Mean Scores	0.26	0.21	-0.16	0.00	-0.15	0.05
SDP	Mean Raws	8.20	7.60	8.60	8.80	9.20	12.80
SDP	SD Raws	1.92	2.30	2.97	2.59	2.05	4.92
SDP	Mean Scores	0.16	0.11	-0.26	0.14	0.21	-0.24
WA	Mean Raws	4.60	4.80	11.60	3.40	3.40	15.80
WA	SD Raws	3.13	3.03	5.13	2.19	1.52	2.39
WA	Mean Scores	-0.78	-0.60	0.46	-1.08	-1.09	0.47

Iceland
Table 3 (cont.)

Party		No influence on party policy (1) vs high (20)			No influence on partic. in govt (1) vs high (20)		
		Leads	Legs	Acts	Leads	Legs	Acts
CP	Mean Raws	16.80	12.00	10.20	17.00	13.80	9.40
CP	SD Raws	1.10	5.79	5.36	0.71	1.64	4.78
CP	Mean Scores	0.74	-0.21	-0.32	0.64	0.36	-0.43
IP	Mean Raws	14.20	14.00	9.40	16.00	14.00	9.80
IP	SD Raws	2.95	3.08	3.36	1.41	1.87	2.59
IP	Mean Scores	0.15	0.32	-0.50	0.41	0.42	-0.32
PA	Mean Raws	15.00	14.40	12.80	14.80	12.80	11.20
PA	SD Raws	2.35	2.41	4.97	3.19	2.49	3.35
PA	Mean Scores	0.33	0.43	0.29	0.13	0.07	0.05
PP	Mean Raws	14.40	13.60	9.80	15.40	12.00	9.60
PP	SD Raws	4.78	3.21	2.95	3.78	3.67	2.88
PP	Mean Scores	0.20	0.21	-0.41	0.27	-0.17	-0.37
SDP	Mean Raws	14.60	13.40	10.40	15.20	12.40	10.40
SDP	SD Raws	1.52	2.30	2.51	2.49	2.88	2.07
SDP	Mean Scores	0.24	0.16	-0.27	0.23	-0.05	-0.16
WA	Mean Raws	6.20	9.40	16.80	7.00	10.40	15.60
WA	SD Raws	3.83	3.91	2.28	4.30	6.23	3.85
WA	Mean Scores	-1.66	-0.91	1.21	-1.68	-0.64	1.22

Party		Do not look to future (1) vs look many years (5)			Give up office(1) vs give up policy (20)	Can use groups (1) vs not (20)	Close to resp (1) vs not (15)
		Leads	Legs	Acts			
CP	Mean Raws	3.40	3.20	3.20	17.60	16.00	14.20
CP	SD Raws	0.55	1.30	1.79	2.07	1.73	1.10
CP	Mean Scores	-0.73	-1.06	-0.60	0.79	1.50	0.98
IP	Mean Raws	3.80	4.00	4.00	12.60	5.80	7.20
IP	SD Raws	0.45	0.00	1.23	3.91	3.49	5.54
IP	Mean Scores	0.07	0.21	0.05	-0.10	-0.67	-0.58
PA	Mean Raws	3.80	4.00	4.00	13.00	5.20	10.80
PA	SD Raws	0.45	0.00	1.23	6.25	1.10	4.55
PA	Mean Scores	0.07	0.21	0.05	-0.03	-0.79	0.22
PP	Mean Raws	3.80	4.00	4.00	16.20	7.20	8.00
PP	SD Raws	0.45	0.00	1.23	3.70	2.17	1.87
PP	Mean Scores	0.07	0.21	0.05	0.54	-0.37	-0.40
SDP	Mean Raws	3.60	3.80	3.80	15.00	9.00	6.40
SDP	SD Raws	0.55	0.45	1.30	3.87	3.46	2.88
SDP	Mean Scores	-0.33	-0.11	-0.11	0.33	0.01	-0.76
WA	Mean Raws	4.20	4.20	4.60	4.60	10.40	12.20
WA	SD Raws	0.45	0.45	0.55	2.61	5.37	4.66
WA	Mean Scores	0.86	0.53	0.54	-1.53	0.31	0.54

**Iceland
Graph 1**

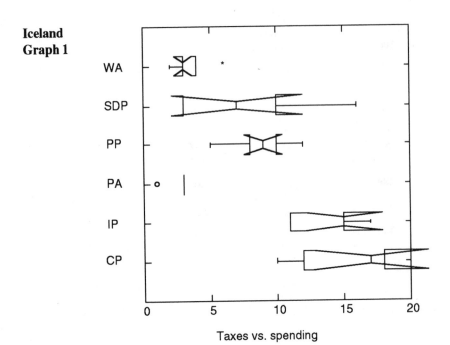

Taxes vs. spending

**Iceland
Graph 2
(4/87 election %)**

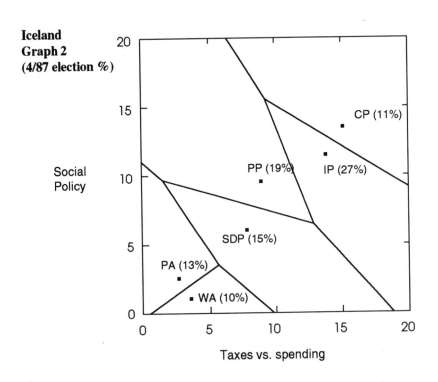

Taxes vs. spending

212

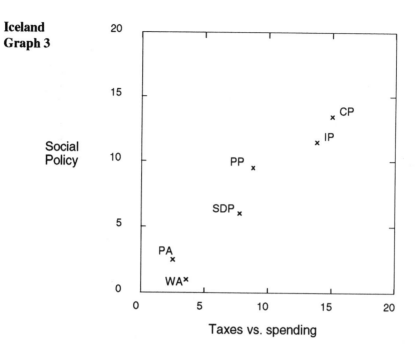

**Iceland
Graph 3**

Social
Policy

Taxes vs. spending

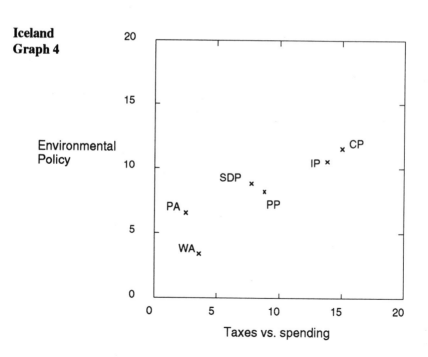

**Iceland
Graph 4**

Environmental
Policy

Taxes vs. spending

Ireland
Table 1

	Mean	SD
Impact of opposition parties on govt policy (1=lo; 9=hi)	4.06	1.97
Prop. of govts falling on policy disputes (1=lo; 9=hi)	3.38	1.65
Cabinet portfolios as policy (1) or office (9) payoffs	6.56	1.69
Cabinet members publicize internal splits (1=lo; 9=hi)	3.03	1.38
Policy autonomy of cabinet ministers (1=hi; 9=lo)	4.50	1.58
Frequency of cabinet reshuffles (1=lo; 9=hi)	4.41	1.67

RANKING OF CABINET POSITIONS

	Mean	SD
Finance	1.14	0.45
Foreign Affairs	4.47	2.70
Industry and Commerce	3.52	2.15
Environment	6.87	2.63
Defense	11.07	3.33
Transport	9.57	2.30
Energy	8.53	3.44
Health	6.64	2.04
Social Welfare	7.71	3.02
Agriculture	4.67	2.50
Justice	6.29	2.56
Education	7.64	2.40
Labor	7.35	2.91

Ireland
Table 2

Party	Abbrev.
Fianna Fail	FF
Fine Gael	FG
Labor Party	LAB
Workers Party	WP
Progressive Democrats	PD
Sinn Fein	SF
Democratic Socialist Party	DSP

Ireland

Party		Increase services (1) vs cut taxes (20)			Pro friendly relations USSR (1) vs anti (20)		
Table 3		Leads	Vots	Imp.	Leads	Vots	Imp.
DSP	Mean Raws	4.80	4.80	14.13	4.42	5.06	6.84
DSP	SD Raws	2.63	2.48	5.68	3.06	3.73	4.29
DSP	Mean Scores	-0.94	-0.95	0.10	-0.60	-0.67	-0.24
FF	Mean Raws	13.82	11.68	13.49	9.00	10.76	7.76
FF	SD Raws	2.39	1.63	3.22	2.94	3.93	4.98
FF	Mean Scores	0.71	0.42	-0.03	0.48	0.54	-0.07
FG	Mean Raws	14.68	14.18	14.64	10.15	11.76	8.33
FG	SD Raws	2.57	1.78	2.51	3.38	3.81	5.27
FG	Mean Scores	0.86	0.92	0.20	0.75	0.75	0.04
LAB	Mean Raws	6.53	7.00	13.72	5.89	6.21	8.70
LAB	SD Raws	2.05	2.19	4.64	2.49	2.62	4.79
LAB	Mean Scores	-0.62	-0.51	0.02	-0.26	-0.43	0.11
PD	Mean Raws	17.12	16.58	17.25	10.88	11.96	7.39
PD	SD Raws	1.76	2.15	2.20	3.89	4.29	5.17
PD	Mean Scores	1.31	1.40	0.71	0.92	0.80	-0.14
SF	Mean Raws	6.31	6.15	6.56	5.40	6.74	8.73
SF	SD Raws	2.88	3.06	5.26	3.25	3.54	7.44
SF	Mean Scores	-0.66	-0.68	-1.39	-0.37	-0.32	0.11
WP	Mean Raws	4.35	4.65	14.25	2.19	3.88	8.91
WP	SD Raws	2.21	2.36	5.63	1.60	2.46	5.50
WP·	Mean Scores	-1.02	-0.98	0.12	-1.13	-0.92	0.15

Ireland
Table 3 (cont.)

Party		Pro public own. (1) vs anti (20)			Pro permissive social policy (1) vs anti (20)		
		Leads	Vots	Imp.	Leads	Vots	Imp.
DSP	Mean Raws	3.88	4.29	16.08	4.88	5.92	16.65
DSP	SD Raws	2.19	2.14	3.27	2.52	2.90	2.89
DSP	Mean Scores	-0.90	-0.87	0.57	-1.00	-0.98	0.71
FF	Mean Raws	11.50	11.13	10.41	16.15	16.76	11.50
FF	SD Raws	2.00	2.12	2.77	3.14	2.32	4.85
FF	Mean Scores	0.49	0.45	-0.71	1.40	1.30	-0.39
FG	Mean Raws	13.88	13.72	11.53	11.59	13.18	11.72
FG	SD Raws	2.69	2.23	3.03	2.91	2.52	3.56
FG	Mean Scores	0.93	0.95	-0.46	0.43	0.55	-0.35
LAB	Mean Raws	6.09	6.09	15.66	7.50	8.64	15.66
LAB	SD Raws	1.78	2.16	2.30	2.85	3.18	3.68
LAB	Mean Scores	-0.50	-0.52	0.47	-0.44	-0.41	0.50
PD	Mean Raws	16.52	16.29	15.20	10.12	10.93	12.14
PD	SD Raws	2.45	1.90	3.28	3.08	3.01	3.69
PD	Mean Scores	1.41	1.44	0.37	0.12	0.07	-0.26
SF	Mean Raws	4.96	5.63	8.89	9.78	11.30	9.55
SF	SD Raws	2.62	3.18	5.69	4.10	4.74	5.88
SF	Mean Scores	-0.70	-0.61	-1.06	0.04	0.15	-0.81
WP	Mean Raws	2.91	3.36	17.22	5.79	6.36	15.78
WP	SD Raws	1.69	1.73	2.31	3.14	3.12	3.70
WP	Mean Scores	-1.08	-1.05	0.82	-0.80	-0.89	0.52

Ireland
Table 3 (cont.)

Party		Anticlerical (1) vs proclerical (20)			Pro urban interests (1) vs anti (20)		
		Leads	Vots	Imp.	Leads	Vots	Imp.
DSP	Mean Raws	3.92	4.56	13.08	4.44	4.56	12.04
DSP	SD Raws	2.53	2.47	5.58	3.19	2.93	5.24
DSP	Mean Scores	-1.12	-1.16	0.60	-0.89	-0.91	0.28
FF	Mean Raws	15.06	16.00	10.79	12.59	13.00	10.34
FF	SD Raws	2.67	2.34	5.07	2.48	2.43	3.88
FF	Mean Scores	1.30	1.27	0.12	1.10	1.14	-0.08
FG	Mean Raws	12.32	13.62	9.70	11.53	11.79	10.31
FG	SD Raws	2.52	2.44	3.60	2.09	2.03	3.46
FG	Mean Scores	0.71	0.77	-0.11	0.84	0.85	-0.09
LAB	Mean Raws	7.88	8.38	9.81	7.29	7.74	11.13
LAB	SD Raws	2.43	2.64	4.14	2.24	2.11	3.27
LAB	Mean Scores	-0.26	-0.35	-0.08	-0.20	-0.14	0.09
PD	Mean Raws	9.70	10.58	11.03	8.24	8.00	10.47
PD	SD Raws	2.71	2.42	3.97	2.78	2.85	4.06
PD	Mean Scores	0.14	0.12	0.17	0.04	-0.08	-0.06
SF	Mean Raws	8.00	9.93	7.12	8.15	8.81	5.96
SF	SD Raws	4.40	4.67	4.63	3.61	3.29	4.25
SF	Mean Scores	-0.23	-0.02	-0.65	0.01	0.12	-1.02
WP	Mean Raws	4.94	5.53	10.00	3.47	3.41	14.13
WP	SD Raws	2.56	2.15	5.15	2.42	2.00	4.96
WP	Mean Scores	-0.89	-0.95	-0.04	-1.13	-1.19	0.73

Ireland
Table 3 (cont.)

Party		Pro decentralization of decisions (1) vs anti (20)			Envir. over growth (1) vs growth over env (20)		
		Leads	Vots	Imp.	Leads	Vots	Imp.
DSP	Mean Raws	8.25	8.53	6.14	9.50	10.00	8.96
DSP	SD Raws	5.13	3.98	4.93	3.47	3.77	4.45
DSP	Mean Scores	-0.69	-0.40	0.01	-0.78	-0.65	0.20
FF	Mean Raws	14.14	11.50	5.18	14.48	14.31	6.70
FF	SD Raws	4.27	3.62	3.87	2.20	2.09	4.04
FF	Mean Scores	0.52	0.40	-0.21	0.75	0.64	-0.31
FG	Mean Raws	13.41	11.10	5.25	12.97	13.00	7.83
FG	SD Raws	3.69	3.19	3.71	2.29	2.41	3.93
FG	Mean Scores	0.37	0.29	-0.19	0.28	0.25	-0.05
LAB	Mean Raws	10.14	8.80	7.04	10.25	10.68	9.77
LAB	SD Raws	4.21	3.16	4.60	2.82	3.09	4.45
LAB	Mean Scores	-0.30	-0.33	0.21	-0.55	-0.45	0.38
PD	Mean Raws	11.64	10.25	6.46	13.07	12.82	8.32
PD	SD Raws	3.87	3.06	4.50	2.43	2.83	4.36
PD	Mean Scores	0.01	0.06	0.08	0.31	0.19	0.06
SF	Mean Raws	10.94	9.18	6.00	10.65	11.94	5.78
SF	SD Raws	4.87	4.11	4.77	2.29	2.67	4.25
SF	Mean Scores	-0.14	-0.23	-0.02	-0.43	-0.07	-0.52
WP	Mean Raws	11.67	10.37	6.68	12.03	11.76	8.83
WP	SD Raws	6.12	4.36	4.97	4.02	4.24	4.76
WP	Mean Scores	0.01	0.09	0.13	-0.01	-0.12	0.17

Ireland

Table 3 (cont.)

Party		No influence on party policy (1) vs high (20)			No influence on partic. in govt (1) vs high (20)		
		Leads	Legs	Acts	Leads	Legs	Acts
DSP	Mean Raws	14.68	12.68	12.77	13.17	9.20	9.17
DSP	SD Raws	4.63	5.47	4.15	5.63	6.63	5.66
DSP	Mean Scores	-0.22	0.11	0.53	-0.43	-0.42	0.11
FF	Mean Raws	17.64	10.67	8.03	18.13	11.03	6.31
FF	SD Raws	1.58	3.43	3.78	1.66	5.00	4.67
FF	Mean Scores	0.67	-0.37	-0.62	0.64	-0.06	-0.43
FG	Mean Raws	16.06	11.67	8.36	17.16	11.88	6.78
FG	SD Raws	1.90	3.50	3.22	2.26	4.35	4.60
FG	Mean Scores	0.20	-0.13	-0.54	0.43	0.11	-0.34
LAB	Mean Raws	12.52	13.52	12.55	13.34	12.38	11.28
LAB	SD Raws	2.74	2.54	2.98	3.53	3.61	4.56
LAB	Mean Scores	-0.87	0.31	0.48	-0.39	0.21	0.51
PD	Mean Raws	15.48	13.78	10.81	16.35	12.71	8.50
PD	SD Raws	2.53	2.92	3.45	3.67	4.30	5.03
PD	Mean Scores	0.03	0.38	0.06	0.26	0.28	-0.02
SF	Mean Raws	16.19	9.28	10.68	11.63	7.93	9.31
SF	SD Raws	3.63	6.57	5.01	7.38	6.34	6.71
SF	Mean Scores	0.24	-0.71	0.02	-0.76	-0.68	0.14
WP	Mean Raws	15.16	12.84	11.68	13.57	11.18	9.43
WP	SD Raws	3.71	4.05	4.09	5.17	5.28	5.08
WP.	Mean Scores	-0.07	0.15	0.27	-0.34	-0.03	0.16

Ireland
Table 3 (cont.)

Party		Do not look to future (1) vs look many years (5)			Give up office(1) vs give up policy (20)	Can use groups (1) vs not (20)	Close to resp (1) vs not (15)
		Leads	Legs	Acts			
DSP	Mean Raws	3.47	3.39	3.56	5.82	17.29	7.13
DSP	SD Raws	1.43	1.24	1.42	3.14	2.60	3.94
DSP	Mean Scores	-0.20	-0.13	0.03	-0.88	1.18	-0.51
FF	Mean Raws	3.45	3.17	3.03	15.31	7.81	10.39
FF	SD Raws	0.96	1.05	1.33	4.48	4.44	3.66
FF	Mean Scores	-0.22	-0.33	-0.37	0.82	-0.64	0.27
FG	Mean Raws	3.68	3.43	3.28	14.21	10.09	8.94
FG	SD Raws	0.79	0.86	1.13	3.81	4.42	3.79
FG	Mean Scores	-0.01	-0.08	-0.18	0.62	-0.20	-0.08
LAB	Mean Raws	3.77	3.83	4.03	12.85	9.16	6.93
LAB	SD Raws	0.56	0.60	1.00	3.85	3.76	3.05
LAB	Mean Scores	0.08	0.29	0.39	0.38	-0.38	-0.56
PD	Mean Raws	3.72	3.52	3.32	12.94	12.72	11.07
PD	SD Raws	0.75	0.75	1.06	3.94	4.31	3.97
PD	Mean Scores	0.03	0.00	-0.15	0.39	0.30	0.43
SF	Mean Raws	3.47	3.13	3.42	3.73	10.77	13.13
SF	SD Raws	1.78	1.78	1.84	3.54	6.75	3.60
SF	Mean Scores	-0.20	-0.37	-0.07	-1.25	-0.07	0.92
WP	Mean Raws	4.15	4.04	4.04	6.44	11.60	7.70
WP	SD Raws	1.26	1.11	1.40	3.46	4.65	3.83
WP	Mean Scores	0.43	0.48	0.39	-0.76	0.09	-0.38

Ireland
Table 4

Pro British presence in Northern Ireland (1) vs. anti (20)

Party		Leads	Vots	Imp.
DSP	Mean	3.69	6.46	12.38
	SD	3.90	4.65	6.30
FF	Mean	15.09	15.59	16.53
	SD	2.78	2.68	2.29
FG	Mean	9.64	10.95	13.33
	SD	3.17	3.07	3.33
LAB	Mean	10.91	12.71	11.53
	SD	3.22	3.00	4.24
PD	Mean	7.33	8.95	12.20
	SD	2.80	2.62	4.93
SF	Mean	19.68	19.50	19.50
	SD	0.82	1.04	1.16
WP	Mean	5.45	9.36	11.21
	SD	3.76	3.71	5.81

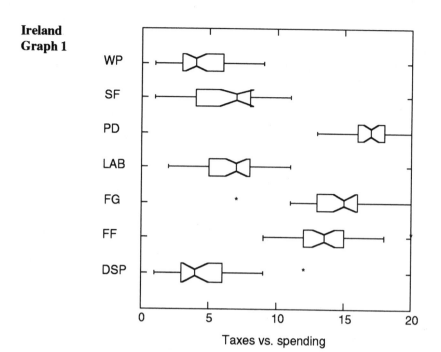

Ireland Graph 1

Taxes vs. spending

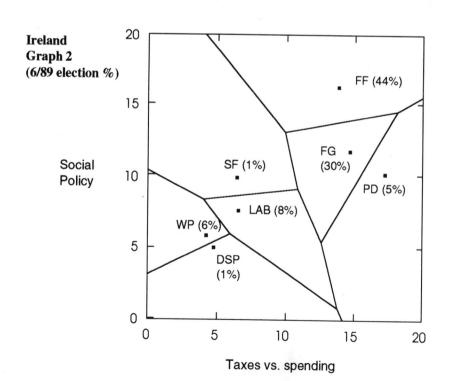

Ireland Graph 2 (6/89 election %)

FF (44%)

FG (30%)

SF (1%)

PD (5%)

LAB (8%)

WP (6%)

DSP (1%)

Social Policy

Taxes vs. spending

Ireland Graph 3

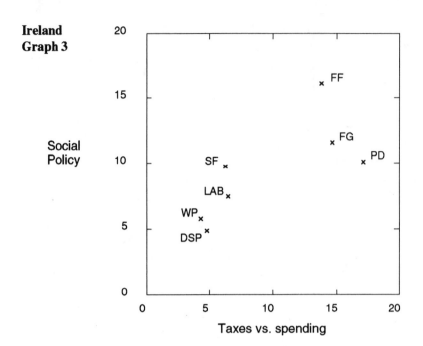

Ireland Graph 4

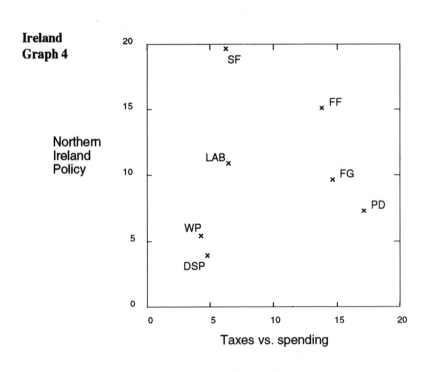

Israel
Table 1

	Mean	SD
Impact of opposition parties on govt policy (1=lo; 9=hi)	2.22	0.83
Prop. of govts falling on policy disputes (1=lo; 9=hi)	3.89	2.62
Cabinet portfolios as policy (1) or office (9) payoffs	6.44	1.88
Cabinet members publicize internal splits (1=lo; 9=hi)	7.67	1.41
Policy autonomy of cabinet ministers (1=hi; 9=lo)	3.25	1.83
Frequency of cabinet reshuffles (1=lo; 9=hi)	2.63	1.30

RANKING OF CABINET POSITIONS		
Finance	2.13	0.64
Foreign Affairs	2.63	0.74
Interior	5.80	1.92
Industry and Trade	6.00	1.41
Defense	1.25	0.46
Housing	7.67	1.15
Health	10.00	3.74
Labor and Social Affairs	9.50	0.71
Agriculture	7.67	2.80
Justice	6.00	2.00
Education	5.17	1.60

Israel
Table 2

Party	Abbrev.
Likud	LIK
Labor	LAB
Liberal Party	LIB
Shas	SHAS
Agudat Israel	AG
National Religious Party	NRP
Hadash (Democratic Front)	COM

Israel
Table 3

Party		Increase services (1) vs cut taxes (20)			Pro friendly relations USSR (1) vs anti (20)		
		Leads	Vots	Imp.	Leads	Vots	Imp.
AG	Mean Raws	9.00	9.50	3.00	10.75	11.25	4.14
AG	SD Raws	2.71	1.73	3.52	1.50	2.63	2.67
AG	Mean Scores	-0.08	0.01	-0.91	0.86	0.67	-1.11
COM	Mean Raws	3.14	5.00	14.00	1.00	1.63	17.67
COM	SD Raws	2.41	2.16	4.24	0.00	1.19	2.73
COM	Mean Scores	-1.35	-1.24	1.12	-1.70	-1.41	0.82
LAB	Mean Raws	8.29	8.71	11.13	6.75	6.13	15.63
LAB	SD Raws	2.14	1.50	2.80	0.89	1.36	5.66
LAB	Mean Scores	-0.23	-0.21	0.59	-0.19	-0.44	0.53
LIB	Mean Raws	14.50	13.00	10.00	7.25	8.80	15.83
LIB	SD Raws	1.92	1.63	3.54	2.50	6.02	6.40
LIB	Mean Scores	1.12	0.98	0.39	-0.06	0.14	0.56
LIK	Mean Raws	14.14	13.33	10.25	10.00	11.38	15.75
LIK	SD Raws	2.61	3.39	4.23	2.20	3.02	5.80
LIK	Mean Scores	1.05	1.07	0.43	0.67	0.70	0.55
NRP	Mean Raws	9.75	9.75	3.33	10.00	11.00	11.63
NRP	SD Raws	4.11	3.78	3.50	1.23	2.55	6.00
NRP	Mean Scores	0.09	0.08	-0.84	0.67	0.62	-0.04
SHAS	Mean Raws	8.50	9.00	3.00	10.50	11.25	4.25
SHAS	SD Raws	2.65	1.83	3.42	1.29	2.63	2.77
SHAS	Mean Scores	-0.19	-0.13	-0.91	0.80	0.67	-1.09

Israel
Table 3 (cont.)

Party		Pro public own. (1) vs anti (20)			Pro permissive social policy (1) vs anti (20)		
		Leads	Vots	Imp.	Leads	Vots	Imp.
AG	Mean Raws	13.00	13.00	4.13	19.89	19.89	10.00
AG	SD Raws	2.45	2.12	3.27	0.33	0.33	6.93
AG	Mean Scores	0.39	0.37	-1.06	1.02	1.00	-0.28
COM	Mean Raws	1.63	2.88	16.88	4.29	5.71	12.67
COM	SD Raws	0.92	2.48	3.31	2.69	5.50	5.57
COM	Mean Scores	-1.66	-1.59	1.05	-1.29	-1.02	0.24
LAB	Mean Raws	7.89	8.78	13.89	7.00	6.11	12.75
LAB	SD Raws	1.90	2.17	2.03	2.40	2.15	3.66
LAB	Mean Scores	-0.53	-0.45	0.56	-0.89	-0.97	0.25
LIB	Mean Raws	16.33	15.83	16.83	4.71	3.43	11.00
LIB	SD Raws	2.42	3.66	1.94	2.87	1.99	6.12
LIB	Mean Scores	0.99	0.91	1.05	-1.23	-1.35	-0.09
LIK	Mean Raws	16.33	16.00	12.56	13.00	13.22	10.88
LIK	SD Raws	2.50	2.29	3.78	2.29	2.59	1.96
LIK	Mean Scores	0.99	0.95	0.34	0.00	0.05	-0.11
NRP	Mean Raws	11.40	11.00	6.13	18.67	18.56	11.50
NRP	SD Raws	3.21	3.74	3.87	1.23	1.51	5.35
NRP	Mean Scores	0.10	-0.02	-0.73	0.84	0.81	0.01
SHAS	Mean Raws	11.80	12.20	4.13	19.67	19.44	11.50
SHAS	SD Raws	1.10	1.30	3.27	0.50	0.73	6.87
SHAS	Mean Scores	0.17	0.21	-1.06	0.99	0.94	0.01

Israel
Table 3 (cont.)

Party		Anticlerical (1) vs proclerical (20)			Pro urban interests (1) vs anti (20)		
		Leads	Vots	Imp.	Leads	Vots	Imp.
AG	Mean Raws	20.00	20.00	19.88	5.00	3.00	3.00
AG	SD Raws	0.00	0.00	0.35	1.41	1.41	1.79
AG	Mean Scores	1.10	1.12	0.87	-0.87	-1.18	-0.76
COM	Mean Raws	3.00	4.29	8.75	7.75	7.00	9.33
COM	SD Raws	1.41	3.35	6.90	4.86	5.10	2.08
COM	Mean Scores	-1.34	-1.12	-1.44	-0.29	-0.25	0.47
LAB	Mean Raws	8.38	6.50	11.50	15.33	13.20	13.17
LAB	SD Raws	1.77	1.07	2.45	1.86	1.79	6.01
LAB	Mean Scores	-0.57	-0.80	-0.87	1.29	1.18	1.22
LIB	Mean Raws	2.17	2.17	17.17	4.75	5.33	6.75
LIB	SD Raws	0.98	1.17	1.47	2.22	2.31	6.29
LIB	Mean Scores	-1.46	-1.42	0.31	-0.92	-0.64	-0.03
LIK	Mean Raws	13.13	13.00	11.00	7.83	7.80	9.17
LIK	SD Raws	1.55	2.83	3.02	3.55	2.49	4.07
LIK	Mean Scores	0.11	0.13	-0.98	-0.28	-0.07	0.44
NRP	Mean Raws	17.25	17.00	18.88	13.00	12.00	5.00
NRP	SD Raws	2.12	2.00	0.84	1.41	0.00	3.16
NRP	Mean Scores	0.70	0.70	0.66	0.80	0.90	-0.37
SHAS	Mean Raws	19.75	19.38	19.63	6.50	3.50	3.00
SHAS	SD Raws	0.46	1.41	0.52	0.71	0.71	1.27
SHAS	Mean Scores	1.06	1.04	0.82	-0.55	-1.06	-0.76

Israel
Table 3 (cont.)

Party		Pro decentralization of decisions (1) vs anti (20)			Envir. over growth (1) vs growth over env (20)		
		Leads	Vots	Imp.	Leads	Vots	Imp.
AG	Mean Raws	11.50	12.50	6.00	18.00	18.00	3.50
AG	SD Raws	3.54	4.95	2.83	NA	NA	2.74
AG	Mean Scores	0.28	0.63	-0.47	0.75	0.91	-0.80
COM	Mean Raws	9.00	8.33	10.00	5.00	5.00	7.00
COM	SD Raws	2.65	2.08	3.46	NA	NA	2.12
COM	Mean Scores	-0.30	-0.36	0.97	-1.78	-1.34	0.22
LAB	Mean Raws	14.00	11.00	6.00	15.00	12.33	8.00
LAB	SD Raws	3.56	1.63	1.63	3.16	3.22	3.37
LAB	Mean Scores	0.86	0.27	-0.47	0.17	-0.07	0.51
LIB	Mean Raws	3.33	3.00	10.00	8.00	4.00	10.00
LIB	SD Raws	0.58	1.00	3.46	5.20	2.83	3.74
LIB	Mean Scores	-1.61	-1.63	0.97	-1.19	-1.51	1.09
LIK	Mean Raws	10.00	10.25	6.00	17.25	16.33	7.71
LIK	SD Raws	3.46	3.59	1.63	0.96	1.53	2.14
LIK	Mean Scores	-0.07	0.10	-0.47	0.61	0.62	0.42
NRP	Mean Raws	14.00	14.50	7.00	18.00	18.00	4.17
NRP	SD Raws	0.00	0.71	1.41	NA	NA	2.14
NRP	Mean Scores	0.86	1.11	-0.11	0.75	0.91	-0.61
SHAS	Mean Raws	11.00	12.00	6.00	18.00	18.00	3.67
SHAS	SD Raws	4.24	5.66	2.83	NA	NA	2.58
SHAS	Mean Scores	0.16	0.51	-0.47	0.75	0.91	-0.76

Israel
Table 3 (cont.)

Party		No influence on party policy (1) vs high (20)			No influence on partic. in govt (1) vs high (20)		
		Leads	Legs	Acts	Leads	Legs	Acts
AG	Mean Raws	11.67	9.13	4.13	12.22	7.11	3.89
AG	SD Raws	7.83	6.69	2.85	7.07	4.11	3.95
AG	Mean Scores	-0.50	-0.41	-0.77	-0.43	-0.59	-0.63
COM	Mean Raws	16.38	10.50	9.29	11.71	10.67	8.83
COM	SD Raws	3.82	6.38	3.82	5.50	3.78	4.62
COM	Mean Scores	0.40	-0.13	0.50	-0.53	0.21	0.42
LAB	Mean Raws	16.33	12.13	8.00	16.56	10.00	8.11
LAB	SD Raws	2.96	2.90	3.78	2.74	3.64	4.70
LAB	Mean Scores	0.39	0.21	0.18	0.39	0.06	0.27
LIB	Mean Raws	16.00	14.67	9.50	15.86	14.00	8.43
LIB	SD Raws	2.76	3.20	4.76	3.02	5.42	5.09
LIB	Mean Scores	0.33	0.72	0.56	0.26	0.95	0.34
LIK	Mean Raws	16.22	12.63	8.00	17.63	10.50	9.13
LIK	SD Raws	3.19	2.77	3.07	1.77	3.55	4.67
LIK	Mean Scores	0.37	0.31	0.18	0.60	0.17	0.48
NRP	Mean Raws	13.11	10.71	7.83	14.75	9.50	6.25
NRP	SD Raws	4.49	5.19	3.97	5.31	4.47	4.50
NRP	Mean Scores	-0.22	-0.08	0.14	0.05	-0.06	-0.13
SHAS	Mean Raws	11.11	8.75	5.00	12.78	7.78	4.44
SHAS	SD Raws	6.79	5.06	4.24	6.76	4.35	4.16
SHAS	Mean Scores	-0.61	-0.48	-0.56	-0.33	-0.44	-0.51

Israel
Table 3 (cont.)

Party		Do not look to future (1) vs look many years (5)			Give up office(1) vs give up policy (20)	Can use groups (1) vs not (20)	Close to resp (1) vs not (15)
		Leads	Legs	Acts			
AG	Mean Raws	3.33	3.50	3.67	11.50	8.50	13.50
AG	SD Raws	1.37	1.00	1.16	4.18	6.32	2.00
AG	Mean Scores	-0.16	-0.42	0.10	0.07	0.04	0.69
COM	Mean Raws	5.00	4.50	4.50	2.00	10.83	12.83
COM	SD Raws	0.00	0.71	0.71	1.73	7.83	4.02
COM	Mean Scores	1.16	0.99	1.00	-1.84	0.44	0.54
LAB	Mean Raws	3.17	3.75	3.50	15.17	4.50	3.75
LAB	SD Raws	1.33	0.50	0.58	2.04	2.51	1.04
LAB	Mean Scores	-0.30	-0.07	-0.08	0.81	-0.66	-1.47
LIB	Mean Raws	3.75	4.00	4.00	7.50	8.50	5.17
LIB	SD Raws	0.50	0.00	0.00	4.51	8.10	3.37
LIB	Mean Scores	0.17	0.28	0.46	-0.73	0.04	-1.15
LIK	Mean Raws	3.50	3.75	3.00	13.17	8.17	11.50
LIK	SD Raws	1.38	0.50	0.82	1.47	5.38	2.07
LIK	Mean Scores	-0.03	-0.07	-0.62	0.40	-0.02	0.25
NRP	Mean Raws	3.50	3.75	3.33	14.00	8.50	12.00
NRP	SD Raws	1.52	0.96	1.53	1.90	4.32	3.67
NRP	Mean Scores	-0.03	-0.07	-0.26	0.57	0.04	0.36
SHAS	Mean Raws	3.33	3.75	3.67	12.00	9.00	13.25
SHAS	SD Raws	1.37	0.96	1.16	4.15	6.20	1.83
SHAS	Mean Scores	-0.16	-0.07	0.10	0.17	0.13	0.63

Israel
Table 4

Pro territorial compromise
for peace (1) vs. anti (20)

Party		Leads	Vots	Imp.
AG	Mean	9.14	10.86	9.33
	SD	4.14	3.44	5.85
COM	Mean	1.17	1.17	18.20
	SD	0.41	0.41	2.49
LAB	Mean	7.29	7.57	18.17
	SD	1.89	1.27	1.47
LIB	Mean	3.40	3.80	18.50
	SD	0.89	1.30	0.58
LIK	Mean	15.71	15.43	18.17
	SD	2.93	2.57	1.47
NRP	Mean	16.29	16.29	18.00
	SD	2.14	2.43	1.26
SHAS	Mean	10.86	13.29	11.83
	SD	3.53	2.81	6.24

**Israel
Graph 1**

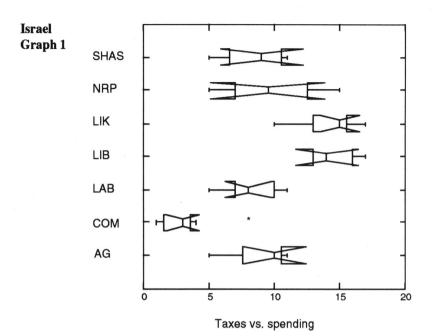

Taxes vs. spending

**Israel
Graph 2
(11/88 election %)**

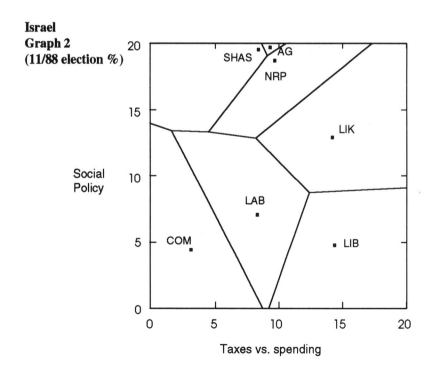

Taxes vs. spending

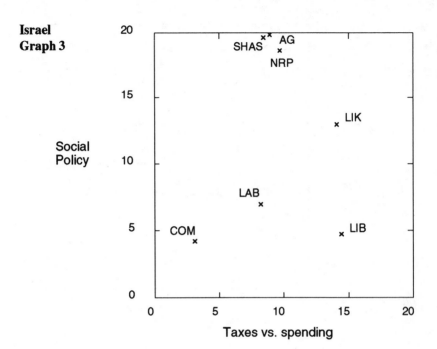

**Israel
Graph 3**

Social
Policy

Taxes vs. spending

Italy
Table 1

	Mean	SD
Impact of opposition parties on govt policy (1=lo; 9=hi)	7.13	1.55
Prop. of govts falling on policy disputes (1=lo; 9=hi)	6.38	2.45
Cabinet portfolios as policy (1) or office (9) payoffs	7.75	1.16
Cabinet members publicize internal splits (1=lo; 9=hi)	8.13	0.64
Policy autonomy of cabinet ministers (1=hi; 9=lo)	3.75	2.12
Frequency of cabinet reshuffles (1=lo; 9=hi)	4.00	2.45

RANKING OF CABINET POSITIONS

Finance	3.75	1.26
Treasury	1.33	0.82
Foreign Affairs	3.00	2.10
Industry	9.00	4.24
Interior	2.60	0.89
Defense	5.00	0.82
Transport	10.00	7.07
Health	7.50	4.95
Agriculture and Forests	7.00	1.41
Justice	9.33	4.04
Education	5.33	2.08

Italy
Table 2

Party	Abbrev.
Communist Party	PCI
Socialist Party	PSI
Social Democratic Party	PSDI
Republican Party	PRI
Christian Democratic Party	DC
Liberal Party	PLI
Italian Social Movement	MSI
Proletarian Democracy	DP
Greens	G
Radical Party	PR

Italy
Table 3

Party		Increase services (1) vs cut taxes (20)			Pro friendly relations USSR (1) vs anti (20)		
		Leads	Vots	Imp.	Leads	Vots	Imp.
DC	Mean Raws	11.00	10.00	11.57	9.86	11.43	14.14
DC	SD Raws	3.22	3.96	5.16	2.91	3.55	3.63
DC	Mean Scores	0.29	0.13	0.02	-0.04	0.28	0.23
DP	Mean Raws	1.43	2.29	9.50	4.00	3.00	11.80
DP	SD Raws	0.54	2.22	7.40	2.65	1.83	4.44
DP	Mean Scores	-1.48	-1.18	-0.35	-1.11	-1.23	-0.34
G	Mean Raws	6.40	6.40	12.40	7.20	7.00	10.25
G	SD Raws	2.79	2.97	4.10	3.19	2.61	3.59
G	Mean Scores	-0.56	-0.48	0.16	-0.53	-0.51	-0.71
MSI	Mean Raws	14.57	14.00	10.17	19.57	19.57	15.60
MSI	SD Raws	3.60	5.16	4.02	0.79	1.13	4.98
MSI	Mean Scores	0.95	0.81	-0.23	1.75	1.74	0.59
PCI	Mean Raws	3.00	2.86	11.71	3.71	3.00	12.71
PCI	SD Raws	0.82	1.95	7.23	2.63	1.63	3.95
PCI.	Mean Scores	-1.19	-1.08	0.04	-1.17	-1.23	-0.12
PLI	Mean Raws	16.29	17.71	14.57	14.86	15.29	14.57
PLI	SD Raws	1.60	1.70	6.37	2.61	3.25	4.28
PLI	Mean Scores	1.26	1.44	0.54	0.88	0.97	0.34
PR	Mean Raws	8.00	7.40	11.00	9.17	9.33	12.00
PR	SD Raws	2.24	2.07	3.81	4.17	3.67	3.08
PR	Mean Scores	-0.27	-0.31	-0.09	-0.16	-0.09	-0.29
PRI	Mean Raws	14.00	15.14	14.14	10.17	10.14	14.17
PRI	SD Raws	2.38	2.48	6.49	2.64	1.95	4.36
PRI	Mean Scores	0.84	1.01	0.47	0.02	0.05	0.24
PSDI	Mean Raws	9.43	8.14	8.20	12.17	11.71	12.00
PSDI	SD Raws	4.54	4.56	5.89	3.82	4.35	4.65
PSDI	Mean Scores	-0.01	-0.18	-0.58	0.39	0.33	-0.29
PSI	Mean Raws	9.14	7.00	10.29	9.29	7.57	13.29
PSI	SD Raws	3.29	3.61	5.47	3.45	1.72	4.57
PSI	Mean Scores	-0.06	-0.38	-0.21	-0.14	-0.41	0.02

Italy
Table 3 (cont.)

Party		Pro public own. (1) vs anti (20)			Pro permissive social policy (1) vs anti (20)		
		Leads	Vots	Imp.	Leads	Vots	Imp.
DC	Mean Raws	10.38	10.38	12.25	17.00	17.75	16.00
DC	SD Raws	2.20	3.16	3.41	1.93	2.05	3.63
DC	Mean Scores	-0.04	-0.03	-0.13	1.44	1.50	0.61
DP	Mean Raws	2.88	3.00	16.14	3.00	3.00	16.25
DP	SD Raws	1.46	1.77	2.41	1.29	1.16	3.78
DP	Mean Scores	-1.61	-1.45	0.95	-0.85	-0.95	0.66
G	Mean Raws	8.86	9.00	8.80	3.57	3.29	9.67
G	SD Raws	3.89	4.18	2.68	3.16	3.15	2.31
G	Mean Scores	-0.36	-0.30	-1.08	-0.76	-0.90	-0.80
MSI	Mean Raws	14.88	16.63	13.71	19.50	18.50	13.60
MSI	SD Raws	5.03	2.39	3.40	0.76	1.51	6.43
MSI	Mean Scores	0.89	1.17	0.28	1.85	1.63	0.07
PCI	Mean Raws	5.88	4.75	13.63	5.25	7.00	14.17
PCI	SD Raws	2.17	1.75	3.29	1.39	2.00	4.22
PCI	Mean Scores	-0.98	-1.11	0.25	-0.49	-0.29	0.20
PLI	Mean Raws	16.50	17.38	14.25	7.63	9.63	10.83
PLI	SD Raws	2.33	1.77	3.99	3.07	3.25	3.66
PLI	Mean Scores	1.23	1.32	0.43	-0.10	0.15	-0.54
PR	Mean Raws	10.86	10.57	9.00	1.71	1.57	12.50
PR	SD Raws	1.95	2.51	3.16	1.50	1.13	5.07
PR .	Mean Scores	0.06	0.01	-1.03	-1.07	-1.19	-0.17
PRI	Mean Raws	14.13	14.25	13.00	7.00	8.14	12.20
PRI	SD Raws	2.59	2.12	3.06	2.20	1.86	4.44
PRI	Mean Scores	0.74	0.72	0.08	-0.20	-0.10	-0.24
PSDI	Mean Raws	11.29	11.29	11.71	9.29	10.29	12.75
PSDI	SD Raws	3.04	3.45	2.93	4.79	3.90	6.40
PSDI	Mean Scores	0.15	0.15	-0.28	0.18	0.26	-0.11
PSI	Mean Raws	10.13	7.63	12.71	6.25	5.88	13.33
PSI	SD Raws	2.17	1.92	3.15	2.12	1.55	4.27
PSI	Mean Scores	-0.10	-0.56	0.00	-0.32	-0.47	0.02

Italy
Table 3 (cont.)

Party		Anticlerical (1) vs proclerical (20)			Pro urban interests (1) vs anti (20)		
		Leads	Vots	Imp.	Leads	Vots	Imp.
DC	Mean Raws	17.25	17.50	17.50	14.80	13.00	13.60
DC	SD Raws	3.24	2.83	2.20	1.48	1.87	1.67
DC	Mean Scores	1.64	1.73	0.92	1.68	1.30	1.28
DP	Mean Raws	2.75	2.88	12.20	5.00	3.80	7.50
DP	SD Raws	1.67	1.96	5.63	3.74	2.95	3.87
DP	Mean Scores	-1.06	-0.90	-0.21	-0.76	-0.91	-0.14
G	Mean Raws	5.20	5.20	9.25	7.75	7.20	10.00
G	SD Raws	3.27	2.95	6.99	5.38	6.22	7.26
G	Mean Scores	-0.60	-0.48	-0.84	-0.08	-0.09	0.44
MSI	Mean Raws	16.00	16.38	17.33	11.20	11.80	10.00
MSI	SD Raws	3.42	2.88	2.34	3.11	2.95	5.48
MSI	Mean Scores	1.41	1.52	0.88	0.78	1.01	0.44
PCI	Mean Raws	7.13	5.13	12.75	5.80	4.80	6.83
PCI	SD Raws	2.10	2.42	3.24	2.68	2.95	3.87
PCI	Mean Scores	-0.25	-0.49	-0.10	-0.56	-0.67	-0.30
PLI	Mean Raws	7.33	6.29	12.13	7.60	8.00	6.67
PLI	SD Raws	2.42	1.25	4.58	3.13	2.71	3.45
PLI	Mean Scores	-0.21	-0.29	-0.23	-0.12	0.10	-0.34
PR	Mean Raws	3.14	3.29	13.67	5.20	5.00	8.20
PR	SD Raws	2.12	2.36	7.06	2.95	3.00	4.32
PR	Mean Scores	-0.99	-0.82	0.10	-0.71	-0.62	0.02
PRI	Mean Raws	7.57	5.88	10.75	7.20	7.25	6.33
PRI	SD Raws	1.99	2.03	4.80	2.78	2.75	3.45
PRI	Mean Scores	-0.16	-0.36	-0.52	-0.21	-0.08	-0.41
PSDI	Mean Raws	8.71	9.43	11.83	8.80	8.75	7.17
PSDI	SD Raws	3.20	3.74	2.99	2.86	2.50	3.60
PSDI	Mean Scores	0.05	0.28	-0.29	0.18	0.28	-0.22
PSI	Mean Raws	7.13	5.25	13.00	7.20	6.25	6.50
PSI	SD Raws	2.23	1.49	2.83	2.17	2.06	3.08
PSI	Mean Scores	-0.25	-0.47	-0.04	-0.21	-0.32	-0.38

Italy
Table 3 (cont.)

Party		Pro decentralization of decisions (1) vs anti (20)			Envir. over growth (1) vs growth over env (20)		
		Leads	Vots	Imp.	Leads	Vots	Imp.
DC	Mean Raws	12.25	10.88	10.43	13.00	13.50	10.25
DC	SD Raws	1.17	3.60	1.90	2.78	1.77	3.54
DC	Mean Scores	0.52	0.44	-0.50	0.60	0.72	-0.40
DP	Mean Raws	5.83	3.86	14.17	5.00	5.38	15.67
DP	SD Raws	4.62	1.57	5.38	4.41	4.21	5.24
DP	Mean Scores	-0.66	-0.86	0.40	-0.84	-0.86	0.61
G	Mean Raws	2.20	2.33	13.20	1.17	1.50	20.00
G	SD Raws	1.30	1.37	6.46	0.41	0.84	0.00
G	Mean Scores	-1.32	-1.14	0.17	-1.54	-1.61	1.42
MSI	Mean Raws	17.50	16.63	12.71	14.25	14.75	6.29
MSI	SD Raws	2.39	2.26	5.65	3.24	2.44	3.35
MSI	Mean Scores	1.48	1.49	0.05	0.83	0.96	-1.14
PCI	Mean Raws	6.50	5.63	13.86	6.75	7.75	14.14
PCI	SD Raws	2.67	1.30	3.98	3.73	3.28	4.67
PCI	Mean Scores	-0.53	-0.53	0.33	-0.53	-0.40	0.33
PLI	Mean Raws	12.00	11.71	13.50	14.63	14.63	9.14
PLI	SD Raws	4.73	5.99	3.94	2.72	2.62	5.08
PLI	Mean Scores	0.48	0.59	0.24	0.89	0.93	-0.61
PR	Mean Raws	3.17	2.83	12.50	2.14	2.86	17.43
PR	SD Raws	1.94	1.84	4.59	1.46	1.68	1.81
PR	Mean Scores	-1.15	-1.05	0.00	-1.36	-1.35	0.94
PRI	Mean Raws	9.86	10.71	12.00	14.13	13.00	9.71
PRI	SD Raws	5.55	5.25	3.74	1.25	2.39	4.96
PRI	Mean Scores	0.08	0.41	-0.12	0.80	0.62	-0.50
PSDI	Mean Raws	10.71	9.43	10.17	12.00	12.25	10.29
PSDI	SD Raws	3.15	3.95	1.94	3.42	1.83	3.99
PSDI	Mean Scores	0.24	0.17	-0.56	0.42	0.47	-0.40
PSI	Mean Raws	9.86	8.38	12.57	10.63	9.50	12.88
PSI	SD Raws	4.49	4.10	3.74	3.38	3.07	3.09
PSI	Mean Scores	0.08	-0.03	0.02	0.17	-0.06	0.09

Italy
Table 3 (cont.)

Party		No influence on party policy (1) vs high (20)			No influence on partic. in govt (1) vs high (20)		
		Leads	Legs	Acts	Leads	Legs	Acts
DC	Mean Raws	16.50	15.38	7.00	18.38	13.25	4.25
DC	SD Raws	3.55	3.78	3.34	2.26	5.06	3.73
DC	Mean Scores	0.12	0.39	-0.39	0.26	0.16	-0.37
DP	Mean Raws	15.00	12.57	12.50	18.00	12.33	9.75
DP	SD Raws	4.34	3.36	3.42	2.71	4.73	6.70
DP	Mean Scores	-0.28	-0.30	0.88	0.12	-0.03	0.77
G	Mean Raws	13.17	12.17	14.50	13.75	9.40	11.20
G	SD Raws	6.15	2.04	3.02	6.19	3.44	6.80
G	Mean Scores	-0.77	-0.40	1.34	-1.36	-0.63	1.08
MSI	Mean Raws	17.75	13.63	8.38	18.75	12.60	3.40
MSI	SD Raws	2.38	4.75	3.78	0.96	5.81	3.21
MSI	Mean Scores	0.45	-0.04	-0.07	0.39	0.02	-0.55
PCI	Mean Raws	16.75	12.13	9.50	18.13	12.13	7.00
PCI	SD Raws	2.61	4.82	2.83	2.10	6.18	5.21
PCI	Mean Scores	0.18	-0.41	0.19	0.17	-0.07	0.20
PLI	Mean Raws	16.25	16.43	6.29	17.75	13.75	5.00
PLI	SD Raws	3.81	3.05	3.30	2.71	5.04	3.82
PLI	Mean Scores	0.05	0.64	-0.55	0.04	0.26	-0.22
PR	Mean Raws	15.83	11.50	12.20	15.60	9.40	8.40
PR	SD Raws	4.02	5.05	6.02	3.78	3.78	6.35
PR	Mean Scores	-0.06	-0.56	0.81	-0.72	-0.63	0.49
PRI	Mean Raws	15.50	15.00	6.50	18.13	13.63	5.13
PRI	SD Raws	3.55	3.46	2.83	2.10	5.24	3.68
PRI	Mean Scores	-0.15	0.29	-0.50	0.17	0.23	-0.19
PSDI	Mean Raws	15.00	15.00	6.00	17.50	13.38	5.13
PSDI	SD Raws	4.16	4.28	3.16	2.88	4.93	4.02
PSDI	Mean Scores	-0.28	0.29	-0.62	-0.05	0.18	-0.19
PSI	Mean Raws	18.00	13.50	6.00	18.50	12.63	4.88
PSI	SD Raws	2.51	4.75	3.16	1.69	4.93	3.44
PSI ·	Mean Scores	0.52	-0.07	-0.62	0.30	0.03	-0.24

Italy
Table 3 (cont.)

Party		Do not look to future (1) vs look many years (5)			Give up office(1) vs give up policy (20)	Can use groups (1) vs not (20)	Close to resp (1) vs not (15)
		Leads	Legs	Acts			
DC	Mean Raws	3.00	2.67	2.67	15.14	4.29	10.13
DC	SD Raws	0.00	0.82	0.52	4.53	2.06	2.59
DC	Mean Scores	-0.33	-0.52	-0.32	0.64	-0.55	0.38
DP	Mean Raws	3.00	3.00	2.75	6.60	8.00	9.57
DP	SD Raws	0.00	0.00	0.50	7.99	4.36	4.54
DP	Mean Scores	-0.33	-0.03	-0.18	-0.84	0.33	0.26
G	Mean Raws	3.33	3.33	3.25	6.60	6.00	4.67
G	SD Raws	0.58	0.58	1.26	6.84	4.52	2.25
G	Mean Scores	0.26	0.46	0.61	-0.84	-0.15	-0.82
MSI	Mean Raws	3.00	3.00	2.75	12.80	14.00	15.00
MSI	SD Raws	0.00	0.00	0.50	4.92	4.18	0.00
MSI	Mean Scores	-0.33	-0.03	-0.18	0.23	1.75	1.45
PCI	Mean Raws	4.00	3.71	3.33	9.17	3.57	4.13
PCI	SD Raws	0.82	0.76	1.03	2.93	1.99	3.64
PCI	Mean Scores	1.42	1.03	0.75	-0.40	-0.72	-0.93
PLI	Mean Raws	2.83	2.67	2.67	12.14	6.71	9.88
PLI	SD Raws	0.41	0.82	0.52	4.45	4.50	4.26
PLI	Mean Scores	-0.62	-0.52	-0.32	0.12	0.02	0.33
PR	Mean Raws	3.33	3.00	3.00	6.40	4.20	8.00
PR	SD Raws	0.58	0.00	0.00	2.07	2.78	2.71
PR	Mean Scores	0.26	-0.03	0.22	-0.88	-0.57	-0.08
PRI	Mean Raws	3.00	3.00	2.83	12.29	7.83	4.63
PRI	SD Raws	0.00	0.00	0.41	3.64	3.49	2.39
PRI	Mean Scores	-0.33	-0.03	-0.05	0.14	0.29	-0.82
PSDI	Mean Raws	2.83	2.67	2.67	15.00	7.60	11.38
PSDI	SD Raws	0.41	0.82	0.52	6.56	3.29	2.20
PSDI	Mean Scores	-0.62	-0.52	-0.32	0.61	0.23	0.66
PSI	Mean Raws	3.29	3.14	2.83	14.29	6.14	5.63
PSI	SD Raws	0.49	0.69	0.41	5.41	3.39	4.60
PSI	Mean Scores	0.17	0.18	-0.05	0.49	-0.11	-0.61

**Italy
Graph 1**

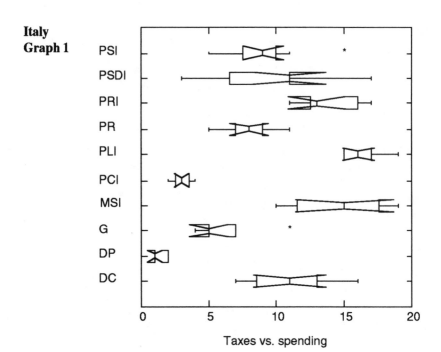

Taxes vs. spending

**Italy
Graph 2
(6/87 election %)**

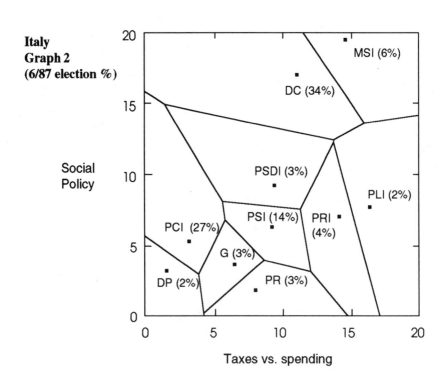

Social
Policy

Taxes vs. spending

**Italy
Graph 3**

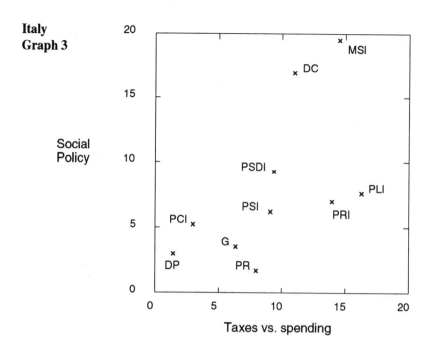

Social
Policy

Taxes vs. spending

**Italy
Graph 4**

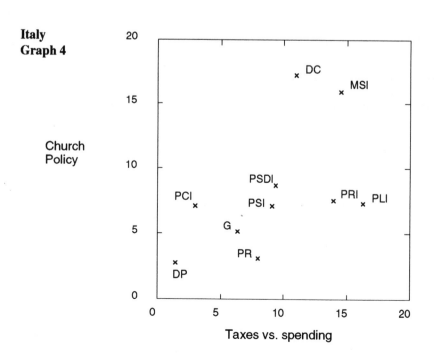

Church
Policy

Taxes vs. spending

Japan
Table 1

	Mean	SD
Impact of opposition parties on govt policy (1=lo; 9=hi)	2.67	0.82
Prop. of govts falling on policy disputes (1=lo; 9=hi)	2.80	1.92
Cabinet portfolios as policy (1) or office (9) payoffs	6.60	1.67
Cabinet members publicize internal splits (1=lo; 9=hi)	2.33	1.03
Policy autonomy of cabinet ministers (1=hi; 9=lo)	4.50	2.17
Frequency of cabinet reshuffles (1=lo; 9=hi)	6.00	2.10

RANKING OF CABINET POSITIONS

Finance	1.17	0.41
Foreign Affairs	2.33	0.52
International Trade and Industry	3.33	1.03
Environment	11.50	4.95
Defense	6.50	2.12
Transport	7.67	2.52
Health and Welfare	8.50	3.54
Agriculture	7.00	3.00
Justice	9.00	4.36
Education	9.25	4.35
Labor	12.33	3.51
Economic Planning Agency	6.50	0.71
Home Affairs	5.67	2.89

Japan
Table 2

Party	Abbrev.
Liberal Democratic Party	LDP
Socialist Party	SOC
Clean Government Party	CGP
Communist Party	COM
Democratic Socialist Party	DSP
New Liberal Club	NLC
Social Democratic Foundation	SDF

Japan
Table 3

Party		Increase services (1) vs cut taxes (20)			Pro friendly relations USSR (1) vs anti (20)		
		Leads	Vots	Imp.	Leads	Vots	Imp.
CGP	Mean Raws	7.00	7.33	15.00	6.80	8.20	8.67
CGP	SD Raws	1.73	2.08	2.00	3.49	3.42	5.13
CGP	Mean Scores	-0.25	-0.25	-0.14	-0.09	0.09	-0.53
COM	Mean Raws	2.00	3.67	17.25	4.17	3.83	11.20
COM	SD Raws	1.00	3.06	2.63	1.84	1.72	4.32
COM	Mean Scores	-1.21	-1.24	0.71	-0.64	-0.82	-0.05
DSP	Mean Raws	9.33	9.33	14.75	9.33	9.80	9.83
DSP	SD Raws	0.58	1.16	2.50	2.07	1.64	4.79
DSP	Mean Scores	0.20	0.30	-0.23	0.44	0.42	-0.31
LDP	Mean Raws	17.00	13.00	13.80	13.67	14.33	15.17
LDP	SD Raws	2.65	1.73	3.70	3.93	3.56	4.88
LDP	Mean Scores	1.68	1.29	-0.58	1.35	1.36	0.72
SDF	Mean Raws	10.50	11.00	15.00	6.67	7.33	11.33
SDF	SD Raws	0.71	0.00	2.65	4.93	4.62	6.51
SDF	Mean Scores	0.43	0.75	-0.14	-0.12	-0.09	-0.02
SOC	Mean Raws	4.67	6.00	16.40	2.33	3.33	12.33
SOC	SD Raws	1.53	2.65	2.07	1.75	2.50	5.68
SOC	Mean Scores	-0.70	-0.61	0.39	-1.02	-0.92	0.17

Japan
Table 3 (cont.)

Party		Pro public own. (1) vs anti (20)			Pro permissive social policy (1) vs anti (20)		
		Leads	Vots	Imp.	Leads	Vots	Imp.
CGP	Mean Raws	12.67	13.33	7.60	9.00	9.00	13.00
CGP	SD Raws	2.88	3.62	3.05	5.66	5.66	2.94
CGP	Mean Scores	0.44	0.46	-0.78	0.30	0.30	0.13
COM	Mean Raws	1.67	2.83	17.60	7.00	7.00	16.50
COM	SD Raws	1.03	2.14	2.51	2.83	2.83	0.71
COM	Mean Scores	-1.39	-1.38	1.14	-0.30	-0.30	1.07
DSP	Mean Raws	11.60	12.33	10.00	8.50	8.50	12.33
DSP	SD Raws	3.51	3.83	2.35	4.95	4.95	2.31
DSP	Mean Scores	0.26	0.28	-0.32	0.15	0.15	-0.05
LDP	Mean Raws	18.60	18.00	6.00	5.00	5.00	7.75
LDP	SD Raws	1.34	2.12	4.76	NA	NA	3.59
LDP	Mean Scores	1.42	1.28	-1.09	-0.90	-0.90	-1.29
SDF	Mean Raws	12.67	13.00	12.67	11.00	11.00	13.00
SDF	SD Raws	2.08	2.65	5.03	NA	NA	2.83
SDF	Mean Scores	0.44	0.40	0.19	0.90	0.90	0.13
SOC	Mean Raws	6.00	7.17	15.40	7.50	7.50	14.75
SOC	SD Raws	2.10	2.40	2.61	3.54	3.54	2.63
SOC	Mean Scores	-0.67	-0.62	0.72	-0.15	-0.15	0.60

Japan
Table 3 (cont.)

Party		Anticlerical (1) vs proclerical (20)			Pro urban interests (1) vs anti (20)		
		Leads	Vots	Imp.	Leads	Vots	Imp.
CGP	Mean Raws	17.60	19.33	15.40	7.60	8.00	11.00
CGP	SD Raws	4.34	1.16	4.28	2.30	1.58	2.35
CGP	Mean Scores	1.16	1.41	0.83	-0.15	-0.04	-0.01
COM	Mean Raws	3.40	1.75	9.33	3.80	3.60	10.50
COM	SD Raws	4.34	0.96	7.23	1.64	1.14	3.00
COM	Mean Scores	-1.03	-1.13	-0.62	-0.95	-0.98	-0.16
DSP	Mean Raws	9.80	9.75	11.25	6.67	6.20	11.00
DSP	SD Raws	3.35	4.27	0.96	2.73	3.19	2.16
DSP	Mean Scores	-0.04	0.03	-0.16	-0.35	-0.42	-0.01
LDP	Mean Raws	15.00	15.50	11.80	16.60	15.60	13.40
LDP	SD Raws	3.87	3.11	4.76	1.67	2.19	5.51
LDP	Mean Scores	0.76	0.86	-0.03	1.72	1.59	0.72
SDF	Mean Raws	9.50	10.00	10.67	3.67	3.00	8.00
SDF	SD Raws	2.12	NA	0.58	2.08	2.00	2.65
SDF	Mean Scores	-0.09	0.07	-0.30	-0.97	-1.11	-0.92
SOC	Mean Raws	4.80	3.75	11.40	9.83	10.17	11.00
SOC	SD Raws	3.90	2.06	3.78	2.64	2.23	2.12
SOC	Mean Scores	-0.82	-0.84	-0.13	0.31	0.43	-0.01

Japan
Table 3 (cont.)

Party		Pro decentralization of decisions (1) vs anti (20)			Envir. over growth (1) vs growth over env (20)		
		Leads	Vots	Imp.	Leads	Vots	Imp.
CGP	Mean Raws	8.50	8.50	10.50	8.20	7.80	10.00
CGP	SD Raws	1.73	1.73	1.92	1.30	0.84	4.58
CGP	Mean Scores	-0.02	-0.02	-0.28	-0.08	0.05	-0.10
COM	Mean Raws	7.00	7.75	12.00	4.60	3.80	11.67
COM	SD Raws	6.96	8.54	3.61	2.07	2.17	2.52
COM	Mean Scores	-0.31	-0.16	0.25	-0.83	-0.85	0.35
DSP	Mean Raws	9.50	9.50	10.00	10.33	9.50	8.33
DSP	SD Raws	1.92	2.38	1.41	3.08	2.67	1.53
DSP	Mean Scores	0.18	0.18	-0.46	0.36	0.43	-0.55
LDP	Mean Raws	13.50	12.75	11.60	17.00	14.80	7.00
LDP	SD Raws	5.69	4.72	3.58	2.45	3.70	2.83
LDP	Mean Scores	0.95	0.81	0.11	1.74	1.62	-0.91
SDF	Mean Raws	3.33	3.33	9.67	4.67	4.33	14.50
SDF	SD Raws	1.53	2.31	4.16	0.58	0.58	2.12
SDF	Mean Scores	-1.03	-1.03	-0.58	-0.82	-0.73	1.11
SOC	Mean Raws	8.80	8.40	13.20	5.50	4.33	12.50
SOC	SD Raws	5.54	5.55	1.79	2.07	1.63	3.87
SOC	Mean Scores	0.04	-0.04	0.68	-0.64	-0.73	0.57

Japan
Table 3 (cont.)

Party		No influence on party policy (1) vs high (20)			No influence on partic. in govt (1) vs high (20)		
		Leads	Legs	Acts	Leads	Legs	Acts
CGP	Mean Raws	16.83	11.80	10.50	13.20	8.80	7.60
CGP	SD Raws	2.93	3.27	5.01	7.79	6.65	6.54
CGP	Mean Scores	0.24	-0.45	0.01	0.12	-0.21	-0.01
COM	Mean Raws	17.57	13.86	10.57	11.20	8.00	8.00
COM	SD Raws	3.65	3.85	5.06	9.39	6.71	6.93
COM	Mean Scores	0.46	0.08	0.02	-0.17	-0.35	0.07
DSP	Mean Raws	15.00	12.50	11.43	10.00	8.60	6.00
DSP	SD Raws	1.73	3.56	2.99	6.12	6.88	5.00
DSP	Mean Scores	-0.30	-0.27	0.21	-0.34	-0.25	-0.33
LDP	Mean Raws	15.33	15.33	5.67	16.60	14.00	7.20
LDP	SD Raws	6.12	5.82	3.72	4.72	3.32	2.49
LDP	Mean Scores	-0.21	0.45	-1.03	0.62	0.64	-0.09
SDF	Mean Raws	15.00	14.25	11.50	15.00	14.00	12.00
SDF	SD Raws	1.63	2.06	5.75	1.73	2.65	1.73
SDF	Mean Scores	-0.30	0.18	0.22	0.39	0.64	0.86
SOC	Mean Raws	16.00	13.50	12.86	9.20	8.80	6.80
SOC	SD Raws	2.58	4.23	3.85	7.53	7.56	5.40
SOC	Mean Scores	-0.01	-0.02	0.52	-0.46	-0.21	-0.17

Japan
Table 3 (cont.)

Party		Do not look to future (1) vs look many years (5)			Give up office(1) vs give up policy (20)	Can use groups (1) vs not (20)	Close to resp (1) vs not (15)
		Leads	Legs	Acts			
CGP	Mean Raws	4.25	4.25	4.00	11.20	7.00	12.67
CGP	SD Raws	0.50	0.50	0.00	4.87	3.92	2.94
CGP	Mean Scores	0.15	0.15	0.42	0.19	-0.23	0.56
COM	Mean Raws	5.00	5.00	3.20	3.40	8.60	14.33
COM	SD Raws	0.00	0.00	2.05	2.51	7.09	1.03
COM	Mean Scores	0.95	0.95	-0.19	-1.13	0.07	0.97
DSP	Mean Raws	4.00	4.00	4.00	12.80	7.75	8.50
DSP	SD Raws	0.00	0.00	0.00	3.42	1.50	3.08
DSP	Mean Scores	-0.12	-0.12	0.42	0.46	-0.09	-0.44
LDP	Mean Raws	2.80	2.80	2.20	17.17	10.20	10.50
LDP	SD Raws	1.30	1.30	1.30	2.48	7.69	2.95
LDP	Mean Scores	-1.40	-1.40	-0.95	1.20	0.36	0.04
SDF	Mean Raws	4.25	4.25	4.00	9.00	9.33	6.00
SDF	SD Raws	0.50	0.50	0.00	3.61	2.08	4.58
SDF	Mean Scores	0.15	0.15	0.42	-0.18	0.20	-1.05
SOC	Mean Raws	4.40	4.40	3.60	5.00	6.60	7.83
SOC	SD Raws	0.55	0.55	1.52	3.54	7.13	5.00
SOC	Mean Scores	0.31	0.31	0.12	-0.86	-0.30	-0.60

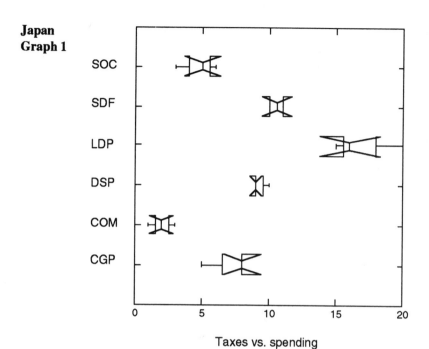

Japan Graph 1

SOC
SDF
LDP
DSP
COM
CGP

Taxes vs. spending

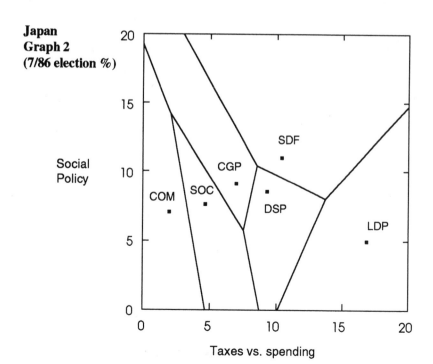

Japan Graph 2 (7/86 election %)

Social Policy

COM
SOC
CGP
SDF
DSP
LDP

Taxes vs. spending

**Japan
Graph 3**

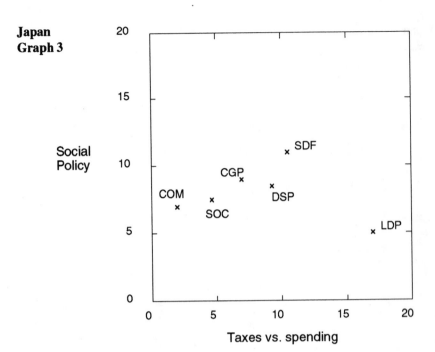

**Japan
Graph 4**

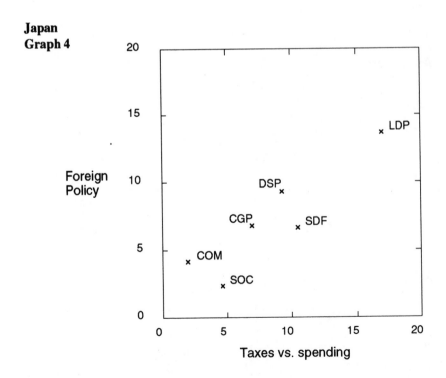

Luxembourg
Table 1

	Mean	SD
Impact of opposition parties on govt policy (1=lo; 9=hi)	4.00	1.41
Prop. of govts falling on policy disputes (1=lo; 9=hi)	4.00	2.55
Cabinet portfolios as policy (1) or office (9) payoffs	5.00	2.55
Cabinet members publicize internal splits (1=lo; 9=hi)	2.20	1.64
Policy autonomy of cabinet ministers (1=hi; 9=lo)	3.60	0.55
Frequency of cabinet reshuffles (1=lo; 9=hi)	3.20	2.28

RANKING OF CABINET POSITIONS

Finance	1.67	0.58
Foreign Affairs	1.33	0.58
Environment	5.00	0.00
Transport	6.50	0.71
Health	8.00	NA
Social Welfare	6.00	4.24
Agriculture	6.50	0.71
Justice	4.00	NA
Education	4.00	1.00

Luxembourg
Table 2

Party	Abbrev.
Christian Social Party	CSP
Communist Party	KPL
Democratic Party	DP
Green Alternative	G
Socialist Party	LSAP

Luxembourg
Table 3

Party		Pro public own. (1) vs anti (20)			Pro permissive social policy (1) vs anti (20)		
		Leads	Vots	Imp.	Leads	Vots	Imp.
CSV	Mean Raws	14.20	13.80	7.00	18.20	16.20	14.00
CSV	SD Raws	3.77	3.49	4.90	2.05	2.78	1.58
CSV	Mean Scores	0.79	0.78	-0.63	1.77	1.61	0.21
DP	Mean Raws	17.20	16.40	6.60	6.40	8.60	10.20
DP	SD Raws	3.42	2.51	6.58	2.61	3.05	3.03
DP	Mean Scores	1.27	1.21	-0.70	-0.18	0.23	-0.67
G	Mean Raws	4.60	4.60	13.80	2.40	2.60	8.00
G	SD Raws	2.51	2.97	5.12	1.52	1.82	6.16
G	Mean Scores	-0.73	-0.74	0.45	-0.84	-0.87	-1.19
KPL	Mean Raws	2.00	1.80	17.40	5.60	3.40	16.60
KPL	SD Raws	1.00	0.84	2.07	3.78	2.51	1.52
KPL	Mean Scores	-1.14	-1.20	1.03	-0.31	-0.72	0.82
LSAP	Mean Raws	8.00	8.80	10.00	4.80	6.00	15.60
LSAP	SD Raws	1.23	2.59	5.66	1.30	2.12	1.52
LSAP	Mean Scores	-0.19	-0.05	-0.15	-0.44	-0.25	0.59

Party		Increase services (1) vs cut taxes (20)			Pro friendly relations USSR (1) vs anti (20)		
		Leads	Vots	Imp.	Leads	Vots	Imp.
CSV	Mean Raws	9.20	10.00	12.00	8.40	10.80	12.25
CSV	SD Raws	1.64	2.65	3.37	2.07	2.95	4.19
CSV	Mean Scores	0.35	0.24	-0.17	0.59	0.87	0.30
DP	Mean Raws	14.20	17.40	12.25	8.80	11.20	13.00
DP	SD Raws	2.95	2.07	6.40	1.92	0.84	5.03
DP	Mean Scores	1.46	1.56	-0.11	0.71	0.97	0.46
G	Mean Raws	4.80	6.00	12.50	6.00	5.50	6.75
G	SD Raws	2.49	4.00	9.19	3.46	2.89	3.50
G	Mean Scores	-0.62	-0.47	-0.05	-0.12	-0.44	-0.88
KPL	Mean Raws	2.80	2.60	13.67	1.60	2.00	10.25
KPL	SD Raws	1.92	2.07	2.89	1.34	1.41	5.32
KPL	Mean Scores	-1.06	-1.07	0.24	-1.43	-1.31	-0.13
LSAP	Mean Raws	7.00	7.20	13.25	7.20	6.60	12.00
LSAP	SD Raws	2.35	1.79	0.96	2.17	1.82	4.69
LSAP	Mean Scores	-0.13	-0.26	0.13	0.23	-0.17	0.25

Luxembourg
Table 3 (cont.)

Party		Pro decentralization of decisions (1) vs anti (20)			Envir. over growth (1) vs growth over env (20)		
		Leads	Vots	Imp.	Leads	Vots	Imp.
CSV	Mean Raws	13.50	11.50	4.50	12.20	12.20	12.80
CSV	SD Raws	3.54	2.12	2.52	1.79	1.30	1.30
CSV	Mean Scores	0.49	0.30	-0.33	0.52	0.34	0.04
DP	Mean Raws	12.00	9.00	6.50	13.20	14.80	12.20
DP	SD Raws	7.07	4.24	4.44	4.49	4.97	4.76
DP	Mean Scores	0.19	-0.28	0.27	0.71	0.79	-0.09
G	Mean Raws	4.00	4.00	6.75	1.40	2.20	18.25
G	SD Raws	2.83	2.83	4.43	0.55	1.79	1.71
G	Mean Scores	-1.36	-1.44	0.34	-1.44	-1.39	1.17
KPL	Mean Raws	15.50	15.00	6.25	11.40	12.80	7.60
KPL	SD Raws	2.12	0.00	3.86	4.51	6.06	3.91
KPL	Mean Scores	0.88	1.11	0.19	0.38	0.44	-1.04
LSAP	Mean Raws	10.00	11.50	4.00	8.40	9.20	13.40
LSAP	SD Raws	2.83	2.12	1.63	4.83	3.70	5.27
LSAP	Mean Scores	-0.19	0.30	-0.48	-0.17	-0.18	0.16

Party		Anticlerical (1) vs proclerical (20)			Pro urban interests (1) vs anti (20)		
		Leads	Vots	Imp.	Leads	Vots	Imp.
CSV	Mean Raws	18.80	16.20	12.80	11.80	13.20	10.20
CSV	SD Raws	2.17	2.17	6.38	2.28	2.68	4.71
CSV	Mean Scores	1.82	1.65	1.30	1.06	1.16	0.41
DP	Mean Raws	5.40	7.80	6.00	8.80	9.40	9.40
DP	SD Raws	1.95	2.39	2.74	4.92	4.93	4.16
DP	Mean Scores	-0.26	0.12	-0.11	0.32	0.37	0.23
G	Mean Raws	4.00	4.80	3.40	6.40	6.20	7.80
G	SD Raws	2.83	3.49	1.82	3.21	4.03	5.07
G	Mean Scores	-0.48	-0.43	-0.64	-0.27	-0.29	-0.11
KPL	Mean Raws	1.60	1.60	5.00	3.00	2.00	6.00
KPL	SD Raws	0.89	0.89	4.30	1.23	1.41	5.61
KPL	Mean Scores	-0.85	-1.02	-0.31	-1.10	-1.15	-0.50
LSAP	Mean Raws	5.60	5.40	5.40	7.50	7.00	8.20
LSAP	SD Raws	1.82	2.07	2.19	1.73	0.82	4.32
LSAP	Mean Scores	-0.23	-0.32	-0.23	0.00	-0.12	-0.03

Luxembourg
Table 3 (cont.)

Party		No influence on party policy (1) vs high (20)			No influence on partic. in govt (1) vs high (20)		
		Leads	Legs	Acts	Leads	Legs	Acts
CSV	Mean Raws	17.40	13.80	9.20	17.20	13.80	10.40
CSV	SD Raws	1.14	3.96	3.27	2.28	2.28	3.65
CSV	Mean Scores	-0.15	0.37	-0.38	0.36	0.26	-0.32
DP	Mean Raws	17.60	16.00	8.00	18.00	13.60	8.60
DP	SD Raws	1.34	1.87	3.32	1.41	3.05	2.51
DP	Mean Scores	-0.14	0.93	-0.63	0.58	0.21	-0.72
G	Mean Raws	11.00	8.60	15.40	11.00	9.00	17.00
G	SD Raws	4.00	2.79	3.44	6.56	6.08	3.61
G	Mean Scores	-0.33	-0.94	0.93	-1.31	-1.07	1.13
KPL	Mean Raws	12.60	11.00	9.20	15.00	12.00	11.33
KPL	SD Raws	5.69	5.15	6.69	4.36	5.29	7.64
KPL	Mean Scores	0.87	-0.33	-0.38	-0.23	-0.24	-0.12
LSAP	Mean Raws	13.80	12.20	13.20	15.80	14.00	13.80
LSAP	SD Raws	1.92	1.10	2.59	2.17	1.87	2.78
LSAP	Mean Scores	-0.25	-0.03	0.47	-0.02	0.32	0.43

Party		Do not look to future (1) vs look many years (5)			Give up office(1) vs give up policy (20)	Can use groups (1) vs not (20)	Close to resp (1) vs not (15)
		Leads	Legs	Acts			
CSV	Mean Raws	4.00	3.75	3.25	14.60	6.40	5.80
CSV	SD Raws	0.82	0.50	0.96	2.30	1.52	2.78
CSV	Mean Scores	0.33	0.43	0.29	0.54	-0.90	-0.63
DP	Mean Raws	3.75	3.75	3.25	17.20	12.20	5.60
DP	SD Raws	0.50	0.50	0.96	1.64	2.59	1.14
DP	Mean Scores	0.11	0.43	0.29	0.98	0.61	-0.68
G	Mean Raws	2.50	2.00	2.00	2.67	13.75	11.25
G	SD Raws	2.12	1.41	1.41	2.08	3.40	2.36
G	Mean Scores	-0.98	-1.29	-0.88	-1.44	1.01	0.69
KPL	Mean Raws	2.50	2.00	2.00	3.67	12.00	15.00
KPL	SD Raws	2.12	1.41	1.41	1.53	2.16	0.00
KPL	Mean Scores	-0.98	-1.29	-0.88	-1.28	0.55	1.60
LSAP	Mean Raws	4.25	3.75	3.25	12.00	6.20	6.20
LSAP	SD Raws	0.50	0.50	0.96	3.39	1.48	2.17
LSAP	Mean Scores	0.55	0.43	0.29	0.11	-0.95	-0.53

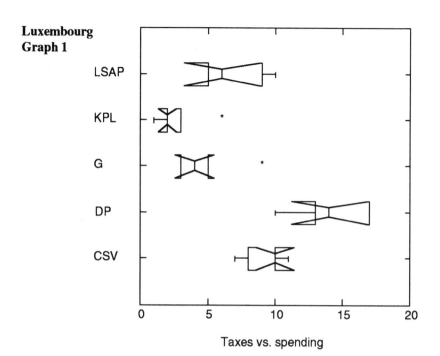

Luxembourg Graph 1

Taxes vs. spending

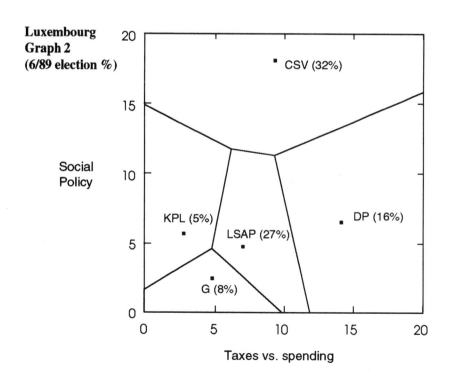

Luxembourg Graph 2 (6/89 election %)

CSV (32%)

KPL (5%)

DP (16%)

LSAP (27%)

Social Policy

G (8%)

Taxes vs. spending

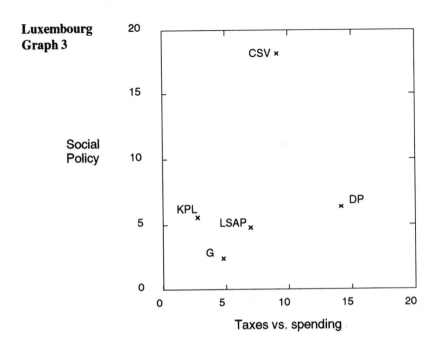

Luxembourg Graph 3

Social Policy

Taxes vs. spending

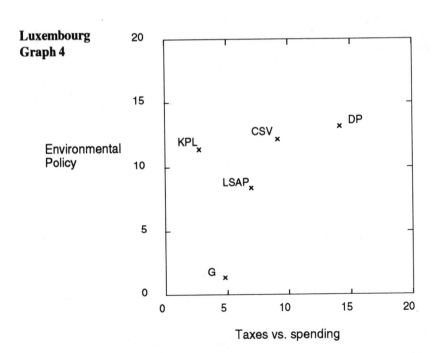

Luxembourg Graph 4

Environmental Policy

Taxes vs. spending

Malta
Table 1

	Mean	SD
Impact of opposition parties on govt policy (1=lo; 9=hi)	3.29	1.70
Prop. of govts falling on policy disputes (1=lo; 9=hi)	1.14	0.38
Cabinet portfolios as policy (1) or office (9) payoffs	5.43	1.81
Cabinet members publicize internal splits (1=lo; 9=hi)	1.57	0.79
Policy autonomy of cabinet ministers (1=hi; 9=lo)	4.43	1.81
Frequency of cabinet reshuffles (1=lo; 9=hi)	3.86	0.90

RANKING OF CABINET POSITIONS

Finance	3.40	2.51
Foreign Affairs	1.60	0.89
Industry	6.50	2.12
Interior	2.40	1.14
Housing	8.50	4.95
Social Policy	4.20	1.48
Justice	2.50	0.71
Education	4.17	1.72

Malta
Table 2

Party	Abbrev.
Labor Party	LAB
Nationalist Party	NAT

Malta
Table 3

Party		Increase services (1) vs cut taxes (20)			Pro friendly relations USSR (1) vs anti (20)		
		Leads	Vots	Imp.	Leads	Vots	Imp.
LAB	Mean Raws	6.33	4.40	14.20	5.43	9.14	12.86
LAB	SD Raws	5.65	2.30	2.17	2.07	3.63	4.56
LAB	Mean Scores	-0.50	-0.82	0.75	-0.56	-0.39	-0.10
NAT	Mean Raws	11.00	12.80	9.80	10.43	13.14	13.71
NAT	SD Raws	1.67	3.03	1.64	4.96	5.93	4.11
NAT	Mean Scores	0.50	0.82	-0.75	0.56	0.39	0.10

Party		Pro public own. (1) vs anti (20)			Pro permissive social policy (1) vs anti (20)		
		Leads	Vots	Imp.	Leads	Vots	Imp.
LAB	Mean Raws	8.86	9.57	13.14	5.43	9.29	14.14
LAB	SD Raws	4.81	2.51	3.81	1.51	5.71	4.49
LAB	Mean Scores	-0.01	-0.12	0.24	-0.92	-0.58	0.17
NAT	Mean Raws	9.00	10.67	11.50	16.71	15.86	12.57
NAT	SD Raws	4.73	5.89	2.43	2.14	3.44	5.06
NAT	Mean Scores	0.02	0.14	-0.27	0.92	0.58	-0.17

Malta
Table 3 (cont.)

Party		Anticlerical (1) vs proclerical (20)			Pro urban interests (1) vs anti (20)		
		Leads	Vots	Imp.	Leads	Vots	Imp.
LAB	Mean Raws	4.43	7.86	11.86	10.00	9.40	8.60
LAB	SD Raws	1.99	2.97	3.24	5.15	3.91	2.88
LAB·	Mean Scores	-0.89	-0.76	-0.54	-0.05	-0.13	-0.03
NAT	Mean Raws	15.71	15.00	16.00	10.40	10.40	8.80
NAT	SD Raws	3.04	3.11	3.32	3.91	3.91	5.31
NAT	Mean Scores	0.89	0.76	0.54	0.05	0.13	0.03

Party		Pro decentralization of decisions (1) vs anti (20)			Envir. over growth (1) vs growth over env (20)		
		Leads	Vots	Imp.	Leads	Vots	Imp.
LAB	Mean Raws	15.17	11.60	11.14	12.00	11.00	15.17
LAB	SD Raws	5.85	6.19	7.99	6.27	5.51	5.35
LAB	Mean Scores	0.60	0.29	0.17	-0.08	0.00	0.24
NAT	Mean Raws	7.00	8.60	9.00	12.86	11.00	12.83
NAT	SD Raws	5.18	4.22	4.36	4.56	5.39	4.54
NAT	Mean Scores	-0.60	-0.29	-0.17	0.08	0.00	-0.24

Party		No influence on party policy (1) vs high (20)			No influence on partic. in govt (1) vs high (20)		
		Leads	Legs	Acts	Leads	Legs	Acts
LAB	Mean Raws	17.43	14.33	11.14	17.71	14.50	10.86
LAB	SD Raws	3.55	5.89	4.49	2.98	5.24	5.76
LAB	Mean Scores	0.48	-0.02	-0.04	0.32	-0.04	0.00
NAT	Mean Raws	13.86	14.50	11.43	15.71	14.83	10.86
NAT	SD Raws	3.19	4.09	4.12	3.25	4.62	4.53
NAT	Mean Scores	-0.48	0.02	0.04	-0.32	0.04	0.00

Party		Do not look to future (1) vs look many years (5)			Give up office(1) vs give up	Can use groups (1) vs	Close to resp (1) vs
		Leads	Legs	Acts			
LAB	Mean Raws	4.14	4.00	3.57	11.83	5.57	11.29
LAB	SD Raws	0.38	0.63	0.98	6.59	6.78	3.73
LAB	Mean Scores	-0.17	-0.13	-0.07	-0.07	-0.57	0.40
NAT	Mean Raws	4.29	4.17	3.71	12.50	12.43	7.33
NAT	SD Raws	0.49	0.75	1.11	2.26	2.44	4.93
NAT	Mean Scores	0.17	0.13	0.07	0.07	0.57	-0.46

**Malta
Graph 1**

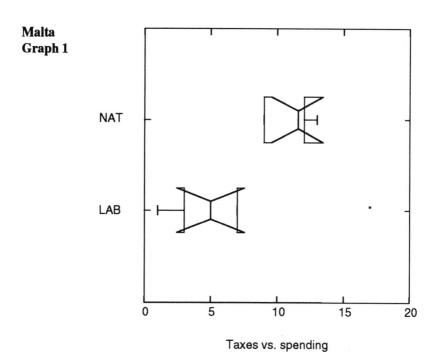

Taxes vs. spending

**Malta
Graph 2
(5/87 election %)**

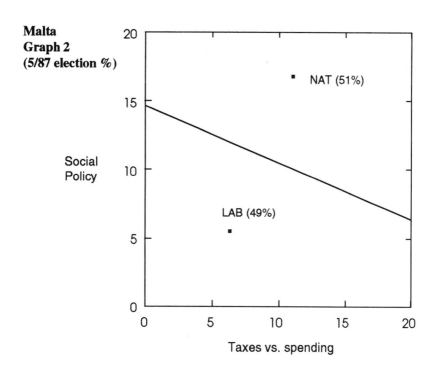

Taxes vs. spending

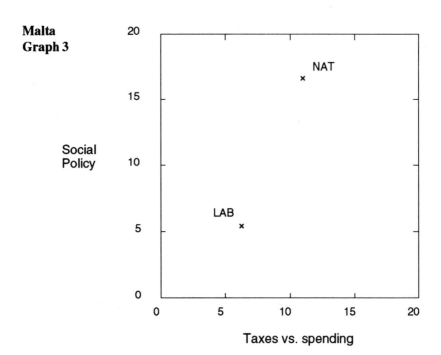

Malta Graph 3

Social Policy

Taxes vs. spending

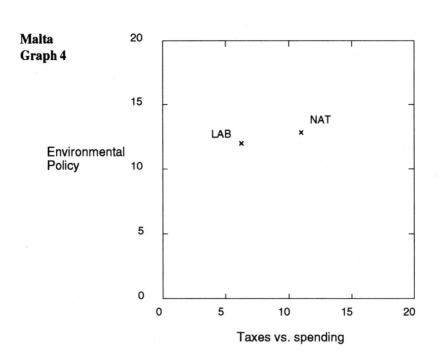

Malta Graph 4

Environmental Policy

Taxes vs. spending

Netherlands
Table 1

	Mean	SD
Impact of opposition parties on govt policy (1=lo; 9=hi)	3.60	1.99
Prop. of govts falling on policy disputes (1=lo; 9=hi)	5.60	2.06
Cabinet portfolios as policy (1) or office (9) payoffs	3.20	1.37
Cabinet members publicize internal splits (1=lo; 9=hi)	5.07	2.19
Policy autonomy of cabinet ministers (1=hi; 9=lo)	3.60	1.59
Frequency of cabinet reshuffles (1=lo; 9=hi)	2.33	0.49

RANKING OF CABINET POSITIONS

Finance	1.36	0.63
Foreign Affairs	4.38	1.85
Economic Affairs	3.15	0.99
Home Affairs	4.67	2.02
Housing & Environment	6.75	3.30
Defense	8.00	2.80
Transport & Public Works	9.75	2.12
Welfare, Health & Culture	8.17	2.14
Employment & Social Security	2.55	1.13
Agriculture & Fisheries	9.13	2.70
Justice	7.00	2.40
Education & Science	6.45	1.51

Netherlands
Table 2

Party	Abbrev.
Christian Democratic Appeal	CDA
Labor Party	PvdA
People's Party for Freedom and Democracy	VVD
Democrats '66	D66
Political Reformed Party	SGP
Radical Political Party	PPR
Pacifist Socialist Party	PSP
Reformed Political Union	GPV
Reformed Political Federation	RPF
Communist Party	CPN

Netherlands
Table 3

Party		Increase services (1) vs cut taxes (20)			Pro friendly relations USSR (1) vs anti (20)		
		Leads	Vots	Imp.	Leads	Vots	Imp.
CDA	Mean Raws	13.57	13.86	13.77	9.29	10.14	11.69
CDA	SD Raws	1.95	2.63	4.64	3.25	2.60	2.69
CDA	Mean Scores	0.56	0.42	0.22	-0.01	0.09	-0.07
CPN	Mean Raws	1.85	2.77	14.82	2.50	1.67	15.55
CPN	SD Raws	0.99	1.96	6.27	2.24	1.44	3.56
CPN	Mean Scores	-1.31	-1.32	0.39	-1.18	-1.29	0.76
D66	Mean Raws	10.36	12.00	12.00	7.79	7.93	12.31
D66	SD Raws	1.39	2.57	5.15	2.16	1.86	3.79
D66	Mean Scores	0.05	0.13	-0.06	-0.27	-0.27	0.06
GPV	Mean Raws	14.83	16.25	6.91	15.67	16.58	7.64
GPV	SD Raws	2.55	3.08	5.47	3.17	3.32	4.18
GPV	Mean Scores	0.77	0.80	-0.87	1.10	1.14	-0.94
PPR	Mean Raws	3.00	3.92	13.73	3.75	3.25	16.10
PPR	SD Raws	1.53	2.43	5.68	1.71	1.49	1.79
PPR	Mean Scores	-1.12	-1.14	0.21	-0.97	-1.03	0.88
PSP	Mean Raws	2.23	3.08	13.55	3.42	3.17	16.36
PSP	SD Raws	1.17	1.80	5.84	2.07	1.75	2.50
PSP	Mean Scores	-1.25	-1.27	0.18	-1.03	-1.05	0.93
PvdA	Mean Raws	5.79	8.43	15.08	6.00	6.14	13.23
PvdA	SD Raws	2.16	2.62	5.41	2.15	1.99	4.09
PvdA	Mean Scores	-0.68	-0.43	0.43	-0.58	-0.56	0.26
RPF	Mean Raws	16.17	16.92	7.91	16.58	17.42	7.73
RPF	SD Raws	2.48	2.64	6.11	3.06	2.75	4.10
RPF	Mean Scores	0.98	0.91	-0.72	1.26	1.28	-0.92
SGP	Mean Raws	16.00	17.36	7.82	16.58	17.08	7.55
SGP	SD Raws	2.70	2.77	6.10	3.12	2.75	4.28
SGP	Mean Scores	0.95	0.98	-0.73	1.26	1.22	-0.96
VVD	Mean Raws	17.36	18.21	16.92	12.07	12.71	12.15
VVD	SD Raws	1.95	1.85	5.16	3.05	3.50	3.41
VVD	Mean Scores	1.17	1.11	0.72	0.48	0.51	0.03

Netherlands
Table 3 (cont.)

Party		Pro public own. (1) vs anti (20)			Pro permissive social policy (1) vs anti (20)		
		Leads	Vots	Imp.	Leads	Vots	Imp.
CDA	Mean Raws	13.85	13.91	9.90	14.80	15.60	14.79
CDA	SD Raws	2.73	2.21	3.28	2.08	1.84	3.02
CDA	Mean Scores	0.41	0.35	-0.11	0.74	0.73	-0.16
CPN	Mean Raws	1.91	1.20	17.00	2.69	4.08	17.82
CPN	SD Raws	1.38	0.63	3.74	2.43	2.69	3.76
CPN	Mean Scores	-1.52	-1.53	1.29	-0.85	-0.83	0.56
D66	Mean Raws	11.69	12.46	8.73	3.93	4.40	15.14
D66	SD Raws	2.21	1.75	4.45	2.37	2.50	2.35
D66	Mean Scores	0.06	0.13	-0.35	-0.69	-0.79	-0.07
GPV	Mean Raws	17.20	18.33	6.22	19.15	19.77	14.00
GPV	SD Raws	1.87	1.58	3.77	1.41	0.44	5.94
GPV	Mean Scores	0.95	1.00	-0.84	1.32	1.30	-0.34
PPR	Mean Raws	5.36	4.80	13.00	2.08	3.00	17.46
PPR	SD Raws	1.80	2.30	2.10	1.89	2.24	3.64
PPR	Mean Scores	-0.96	-1.00	0.50	-0.93	-0.98	0.47
PSP	Mean Raws	2.55	2.50	14.00	1.39	2.08	18.17
PSP	SD Raws	1.86	2.01	3.21	0.77	1.38	1.59
PSP	Mean Scores	-1.42	-1.34	0.70	-1.02	-1.10	0.64
PvdA	Mean Raws	8.31	7.82	11.18	4.00	6.13	16.07
PvdA	SD Raws	2.32	2.36	4.19	1.89	1.85	3.69
PvdA	Mean Scores	-0.49	-0.55	0.14	-0.68	-0.55	0.15
RPF	Mean Raws	17.27	18.10	6.88	19.31	19.85	14.82
RPF	SD Raws	1.68	1.45	4.12	1.44	0.38	5.47
RPF	Mean Scores	0.96	0.97	-0.71	1.34	1.31	-0.15
SGP	Mean Raws	17.64	18.60	6.22	19.39	19.92	14.00
SGP	SD Raws	1.91	1.58	3.77	1.45	0.28	5.94
SGP	Mean Scores	1.02	1.04	-0.84	1.35	1.32	-0.34
VVD	Mean Raws	16.92	18.00	12.91	6.13	8.13	13.00
VVD	SD Raws	2.22	1.61	5.32	2.92	3.36	3.64
VVD	Mean Scores	0.91	0.95	0.48	-0.40	-0.28	-0.57

Netherlands
Table 3 (cont.)

Party		Anticlerical (1) vs proclerical (20)			Pro urban interests (1) vs anti (20)		
		Leads	Vots	Imp.	Leads	Vots	Imp.
CDA	Mean Raws	15.39	15.58	12.69	13.29	14.71	9.22
CDA	SD Raws	2.22	1.62	5.63	1.70	1.50	5.24
CDA	Mean Scores	0.67	0.67	0.35	0.80	0.80	0.52
CPN	Mean Raws	3.09	2.09	5.55	2.60	2.60	4.86
CPN	SD Raws	2.51	1.38	4.89	0.89	1.52	3.53
CPN	Mean Scores	-1.08	-1.20	-0.67	-1.27	-1.28	-0.42
D66	Mean Raws	6.31	6.25	5.82	6.67	7.00	5.44
D66	SD Raws	3.25	2.73	4.14	2.58	1.58	3.71
D66	Mean Scores	-0.63	-0.62	-0.63	-0.48	-0.52	-0.29
GPV	Mean Raws	20.00	20.00	17.82	16.00	17.25	8.63
GPV	SD Raws	0.00	0.00	5.65	2.00	2.75	5.88
GPV	Mean Scores	1.33	1.28	1.08	1.32	1.24	0.39
PPR	Mean Raws	6.46	7.00	7.09	6.20	7.80	5.00
PPR	SD Raws	2.66	4.12	4.74	2.59	3.63	3.30
PPR	Mean Scores	-0.61	-0.52	-0.45	-0.57	-0.38	-0.38
PSP	Mean Raws	2.55	2.18	5.18	3.00	3.40	4.75
PSP	SD Raws	1.81	1.25	4.02	1.00	1.52	3.28
PSP	Mean Scores	-1.16	-1.18	-0.72	-1.19	-1.14	-0.44
PvdA	Mean Raws	7.31	7.42	6.00	6.50	5.80	6.33
PvdA	SD Raws	2.14	2.31	3.92	1.52	2.59	4.24
PvdA	Mean Scores	-0.48	-0.46	-0.60	-0.51	-0.73	-0.10
RPF	Mean Raws	19.73	20.00	18.64	16.25	17.50	8.50
RPF	SD Raws	0.91	0.00	3.01	2.50	3.00	5.68
RPF	Mean Scores	1.29	1.28	1.20	1.37	1.28	0.37
SGP	Mean Raws	20.00	20.00	18.91	15.75	17.00	8.63
SGP	SD Raws	0.00	0.00	2.17	1.50	2.58	5.88
SGP	Mean Scores	1.33	1.28	1.24	1.28	1.19	0.39
VVD	Mean Raws	7.31	7.27	5.62	8.83	9.80	6.33
VVD	SD Raws	3.38	3.20	3.73	1.94	1.30	4.24
VVD	Mean Scores	-0.48	-0.48	-0.66	-0.06	-0.04	-0.10

Netherlands
Table 3 (cont.)

Party		Pro decentralization of decisions (1) vs anti (20)			Envir. over growth (1) vs growth over env (20)		
		Leads	Vots	Imp.	Leads	Vots	Imp.
CDA	Mean Raws	9.67	9.38	7.00	10.00	9.13	13.43
CDA	SD Raws	3.08	4.03	4.69	3.82	4.24	4.64
CDA	Mean Scores	-0.14	0.06	0.23	0.52	0.43	-0.15
CPN	Mean Raws	12.14	8.71	4.25	6.00	5.08	13.42
CPN	SD Raws	6.15	6.53	3.41	5.29	4.36	4.48
CPN	Mean Scores	0.38	-0.08	-0.35	-0.27	-0.40	-0.16
D66	Mean Raws	5.13	5.29	9.80	4.54	4.39	16.21
D66	SD Raws	3.04	2.81	5.85	2.18	2.29	2.36
D66	Mean Scores	-1.10	-0.81	0.82	-0.56	-0.55	0.44
GPV	Mean Raws	14.14	12.29	3.88	10.00	10.15	10.08
GPV	SD Raws	3.08	2.56	3.68	4.00	3.96	4.38
GPV	Mean Scores	0.80	0.67	-0.43	0.52	0.64	-0.87
PPR	Mean Raws	5.83	4.67	5.00	2.08	1.67	18.83
PPR	SD Raws	3.97	3.98	4.38	2.28	0.89	1.53
PPR	Mean Scores	-0.95	-0.94	-0.20	-1.05	-1.11	1.00
PSP	Mean Raws	9.57	7.71	5.00	2.00	1.54	18.58
PSP	SD Raws	6.27	6.45	4.38	2.20	0.66	1.51
PSP	Mean Scores	-0.16	-0.29	-0.20	-1.06	-1.13	0.95
PvdA	Mean Raws	10.89	8.13	7.80	6.07	6.00	16.00
PvdA	SD Raws	2.71	2.36	5.12	3.90	2.90	2.00
PvdA	Mean Scores	0.12	-0.21	0.40	-0.26	-0.22	0.40
RPF	Mean Raws	14.00	12.83	3.88	10.67	10.33	10.08
RPF	SD Raws	3.16	3.43	3.68	4.70	4.40	4.38
RPF	Mean Scores	0.77	0.79	-0.43	0.65	0.68	-0.87
SGP	Mean Raws	14.00	12.71	3.88	10.62	10.46	10.08
SGP	SD Raws	2.94	2.81	3.68	3.89	4.05	4.38
SGP	Mean Scores	0.77	0.76	-0.43	0.64	0.70	-0.87
VVD	Mean Raws	9.00	9.29	6.80	10.93	10.67	14.21
VVD	SD Raws	3.50	4.68	5.01	5.04	4.66	4.42
VVD	Mean Scores	-0.28	0.04	0.19	0.70	0.75	0.01

Netherlands
Table 3 (cont.)

Party		No influence on party policy (1) vs high (20)			No influence on partic. in govt (1) vs high (20)		
		Leads	Legs	Acts	Leads	Legs	Acts
CDA	Mean Raws	17.53	12.07	7.07	17.39	14.00	5.57
CDA	SD Raws	1.51	5.33	3.20	1.98	4.84	4.18
CDA	Mean Scores	0.61	-0.16	-0.52	0.69	0.30	-0.50
CPN	Mean Raws	13.25	12.64	15.17	9.88	9.33	10.00
CPN	SD Raws	5.85	4.50	3.61	7.34	7.37	7.48
CPN	Mean Scores	-0.28	-0.05	0.75	-0.51	-0.43	0.19
D66	Mean Raws	11.21	11.15	13.86	14.75	12.54	12.69
D66	SD Raws	4.32	4.08	4.93	3.75	4.75	4.50
D66	Mean Scores	-0.70	-0.35	0.55	0.27	0.07	0.62
GPV	Mean Raws	18.58	15.27	3.92	12.43	11.43	4.29
GPV	SD Raws	1.31	4.96	2.94	8.26	8.66	4.50
GPV	Mean Scores	0.83	0.49	-1.02	-0.10	-0.10	-0.71
PPR	Mean Raws	10.73	11.50	17.36	8.22	10.40	13.78
PPR	SD Raws	3.95	4.63	1.80	5.04	6.17	5.47
PPR	Mean Scores	-0.80	-0.28	1.10	-0.77	-0.26	0.79
PSP	Mean Raws	9.25	9.70	18.33	5.38	6.67	11.38
PSP	SD Raws	4.88	5.17	1.56	4.63	6.80	9.05
PSP	Mean Scores	-1.11	-0.64	1.25	-1.23	-0.84	0.41
PvdA	Mean Raws	12.47	13.20	14.80	14.39	15.07	12.07
PvdA	SD Raws	3.93	4.41	3.03	4.75	4.53	5.53
PvdA	Mean Scores	-0.44	0.07	0.70	0.21	0.47	0.52
RPF	Mean Raws	18.50	14.18	3.67	12.71	11.71	4.50
RPF	SD Raws	1.51	5.79	2.90	8.48	8.90	4.72
RPF	Mean Scores	0.81	0.27	-1.05	-0.06	-0.06	-0.67
SGP	Mean Raws	18.92	15.46	3.58	12.71	11.71	4.00
SGP	SD Raws	1.24	5.07	2.91	8.48	8.90	4.51
SGP	Mean Scores	0.90	0.52	-1.07	-0.06	-0.06	-0.75
VVD	Mean Raws	15.27	13.40	6.67	16.69	13.86	5.85
VVD	SD Raws	3.22	4.53	3.33	2.25	4.80	4.28
VVD	Mean Scores	0.14	0.11	-0.58	0.58	0.28	-0.46

Netherlands
Table 3 (cont.)

Party		Do not look to future (1) vs look many years (5)			Give up office(1) vs give up policy (20)	Can use groups (1) vs not (20)	Close to resp (1) vs not (15)
		Leads	Legs	Acts			
CDA	Mean Raws	4.00	3.90	3.60	14.77	6.20	8.00
CDA	SD Raws	1.16	1.10	1.08	4.07	3.55	4.33
CDA	Mean Scores	0.21	0.25	0.19	1.03	-0.83	-0.30
CPN	Mean Raws	3.67	3.50	3.33	2.78	10.91	11.08
CPN	SD Raws	1.37	1.23	1.21	2.77	5.67	2.81
CPN	Mean Scores	-0.07	-0.11	-0.07	-0.81	-0.02	0.39
D66	Mean Raws	3.78	3.67	3.44	12.39	14.87	4.86
D66	SD Raws	1.09	1.00	1.01	4.39	3.89	1.66
D66	Mean Scores	0.02	0.04	0.04	0.66	0.67	-1.01
GPV	Mean Raws	3.67	3.50	3.33	1.78	16.27	13.17
GPV	SD Raws	1.37	1.23	1.21	1.39	4.38	2.82
GPV	Mean Scores	-0.07	-0.11	-0.07	-0.96	0.91	0.86
PPR	Mean Raws	3.71	3.57	3.29	4.44	10.64	8.75
PPR	SD Raws	1.25	1.13	1.11	2.35	5.14	3.05
PPR	Mean Scores	-0.03	-0.04	-0.12	-0.55	-0.07	-0.13
PSP	Mean Raws	3.67	3.50	3.33	2.11	11.73	9.67
PSP	SD Raws	1.37	1.23	1.21	1.54	5.57	4.03
PSP	Mean Scores	-0.07	-0.11	-0.07	-0.91	0.12	0.07
PvdA	Mean Raws	3.60	3.50	3.40	11.29	5.73	4.21
PvdA	SD Raws	1.43	1.35	0.97	4.86	2.84	1.93
PvdA	Mean Scores	-0.13	-0.11	-0.01	0.50	-0.91	-1.15
RPF	Mean Raws	3.67	3.50	3.33	2.38	15.40	13.50
RPF	SD Raws	1.37	1.23	1.21	1.77	4.33	3.18
RPF	Mean Scores	-0.07	-0.11	-0.07	-0.87	0.76	0.93
SGP	Mean Raws	3.67	3.50	3.33	1.78	16.27	13.83
SGP	SD Raws	1.37	1.23	1.21	1.39	4.38	2.08
SGP	Mean Scores	-0.07	-0.11	-0.07	-0.96	0.91	1.01
VVD	Mean Raws	3.90	3.80	3.50	15.92	6.47	8.36
VVD	SD Raws	1.10	1.03	0.97	3.33	2.53	4.24
VVD	Mean Scores	0.13	0.16	0.09	1.21	-0.79	-0.22

Netherlands
Table 4

		Anti nuclear weapon deployment (1) vs pro (20)		
Party		Leads	Vots	Imp.
CDA	Mean	13.80	13.00	9.50
	SD	2.05	2.00	6.86
CPN	Mean	1.80	2.60	18.50
	SD	1.30	2.30	1.91
D66	Mean	9.60	8.60	11.50
	SD	1.34	1.95	7.33
GPV	Mean	18.00	17.60	8.50
	SD	1.22	1.95	5.80
PPR	Mean	1.20	1.40	19.25
	SD	0.45	0.55	0.96
PSP	Mean	1.00	1.00	19.75
	SD	0.00	0.00	0.50
PvdA	Mean	5.40	5.40	17.00
	SD	1.95	1.34	1.15
RPF	Mean	19.00	18.20	8.50
	SD	1.00	1.64	5.80
SGP	Mean	18.60	18.80	8.50
	SD	0.89	1.10	5.80
VVD	Mean	18.20	17.40	15.25
	SD	1.79	1.52	3.20

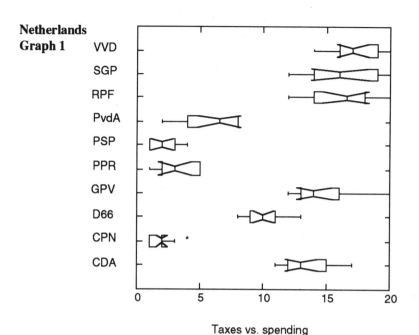

Netherlands Graph 1

Taxes vs. spending

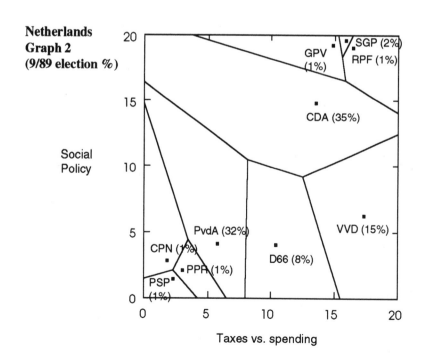

Netherlands Graph 2 (9/89 election %)

Social Policy

Taxes vs. spending

**Netherlands
Graph 3**

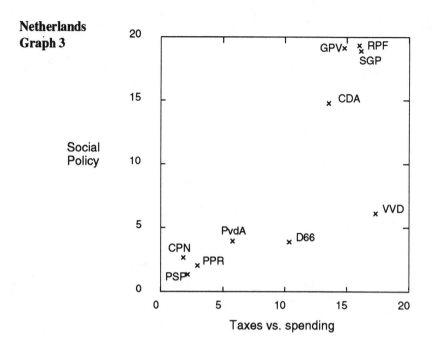

Social
Policy

Taxes vs. spending

**Netherlands
Graph 4**

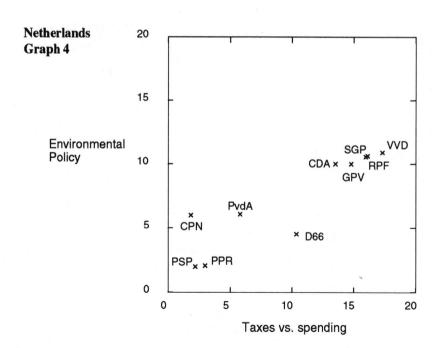

Environmental
Policy

Taxes vs. spending

New Zealand
Table 1

	Mean	SD
Impact of opposition parties on govt policy (1=lo; 9=hi)	3.29	1.77
Prop. of govts falling on policy disputes (1=lo; 9=hi)	3.54	1.94
Cabinet portfolios as policy (1) or office (9) payoffs	5.00	1.52
Cabinet members publicize internal splits (1=lo; 9=hi)	3.50	1.83
Policy autonomy of cabinet ministers (1=hi; 9=lo)	4.64	1.34
Frequency of cabinet reshuffles (1=lo; 9=hi)	5.46	1.76

RANKING OF CABINET POSITIONS

Finance	1.15	0.38
Foreign Affairs	4.45	1.92
Overseas Trade	3.80	1.87
Environment	11.75	3.40
Defense	10.71	3.25
Transport	7.50	0.71
Health	6.00	3.28
Social Welfare	6.00	2.57
Agriculture	9.57	2.51
Justice	8.22	3.35
Education	5.73	2.28
Labor	4.86	2.67
Internal Affairs	11.67	1.53
Housing	13.50	2.12
Maori affairs	8.38	2.07

New Zealand
Table 2

Party	Abbrev.
Democrats	DEM
Labor Party	LAB
National Party	NAT

New Zealand
Table 3

Party		Increase services (1) vs cut taxes (20)			Pro friendly relations USSR (1) vs anti (20)		
		Leads	Vots	Imp.	Leads	Vots	Imp.
DEM	Mean Raws	9.46	9.64	14.56	9.11	11.22	8.22
DEM	SD Raws	3.64	4.55	2.46	3.26	3.07	4.58
DEM	Mean Scores	-0.66	-0.07	-0.39	-0.06	0.16	-0.60
LAB	Mean Raws	13.79	13.79	16.39	11.69	13.77	11.92
LAB	SD Raws	1.97	3.14	2.18	2.78	2.98	4.27
LAB	Mean Scores	0.63	0.82	0.24	0.72	0.79	0.18
NAT	Mean Raws	11.23	6.15	15.75	6.83	6.58	12.33
NAT	SD Raws	3.11	2.58	3.77	1.85	1.88	4.85
NAT	Mean Scores	-0.13	-0.82	0.03	-0.74	-0.98	0.26

New Zealand
Table 3 (cont.)

Party		Pro public own. (1) vs anti (20)			Pro permissive social policy (1) vs anti (20)		
		Leads	Vots	Imp.	Leads	Vots	Imp.
DEM	Mean Raws	11.78	12.30	10.89	12.20	13.70	11.78
DEM	SD Raws	4.38	3.56	2.98	3.49	3.16	3.15
DEM	Mean Scores	-0.47	0.28	-0.40	0.28	0.40	-0.44
LAB	Mean Raws	14.71	13.93	12.64	14.00	14.71	13.29
LAB	SD Raws	3.02	2.81	3.61	2.11	2.40	3.56
LAB	Mean Scores	0.34	0.63	0.07	0.73	0.64	-0.04
NAT	Mean Raws	13.31	6.92	13.15	7.15	7.77	14.77
NAT	SD Raws	3.38	3.90	4.34	2.41	3.06	4.15
NAT	Mean Scores	-0.05	-0.90	0.20	-0.99	-1.00	0.35

Party		Anticlerical (1) vs proclerical (20)			Pro urban interests (1) vs anti (20)		
		Leads	Vots	Imp.	Leads	Vots	Imp.
DEM	Mean Raws	11.50	12.75	5.11	13.67	13.33	14.33
DEM	SD Raws	2.52	2.87	3.10	3.24	2.92	1.58
DEM	Mean Scores	0.31	0.40	0.00	0.51	0.47	0.20
LAB	Mean Raws	11.80	12.80	6.09	14.57	14.57	14.21
LAB	SD Raws	0.84	2.17	5.50	2.38	3.18	3.38
LAB	Mean Scores	0.47	0.42	0.23	0.69	0.71	0.17
NAT	Mean Raws	9.60	10.00	4.18	5.85	5.31	12.46
NAT	SD Raws	1.52	1.23	3.34	2.76	2.56	4.67
NAT	Mean Scores	-0.72	-0.75	-0.23	-1.10	-1.09	-0.32

Party		Pro decentralization of decisions (1) vs anti (20)			Envir. over growth (1) vs growth over env (20)		
		Leads	Vots	Imp.	Leads	Vots	Imp.
DEM	Mean Raws	9.63	8.00	12.11	11.11	11.56	11.22
DEM	SD Raws	4.69	4.04	2.15	2.89	3.05	3.03
DEM	Mean Scores	0.12	-0.10	0.14	-0.02	0.38	-0.25
LAB	Mean Raws	10.17	8.36	11.85	12.69	12.77	10.92
LAB	SD Raws	2.52	3.56	2.73	1.89	2.52	2.22
LAB	Mean Scores	0.27	0.00	0.05	0.53	0.69	-0.36
NAT	Mean Raws	7.91	8.60	11.25	9.58	5.92	13.39
NAT	SD Raws	3.15	3.84	3.62	3.03	2.23	2.50
NAT	Mean Scores	-0.38	0.07	-0.16	-0.56	-1.03	0.54

New Zealand
Table 3 (cont.)

Party		No influence on party policy (1) vs high (20)			No influence on partic. in govt (1) vs high (20)		
		Leads	Legs	Acts	Leads	Legs	Acts
DEM	Mean Raws	13.56	11.57	11.67	13.00	10.50	6.17
DEM	SD Raws	3.58	5.03	4.03	4.20	4.68	4.79
DEM	Mean Scores	-0.66	-0.49	0.49	-1.01	-0.52	-0.14
LAB	Mean Raws	16.00	13.86	8.14	16.82	12.18	6.82
LAB	SD Raws	2.11	3.88	3.53	1.47	2.71	4.54
LAB	Mean Scores	0.25	0.09	-0.38	0.34	0.00	0.01
NAT	Mean Raws	15.85	14.15	9.92	16.46	13.09	7.09
NAT	SD Raws	2.19	3.39	4.21	2.07	2.74	4.44
NAT	Mean Scores	0.19	0.17	0.06	0.21	0.28	0.07

Party		Do not look to future (1) vs look many years (5)			Give up office(1) vs give up policy (20)	Can use groups (1) vs not (20)	Close to resp (1) vs not (15)
		Leads	Legs	Acts			
DEM	Mean Raws	4.33	4.17	4.00	14.00	17.75	12.22
DEM	SD Raws	1.03	0.98	1.16	5.66	1.91	3.53
DEM	Mean Scores	0.94	0.87	0.40	-0.04	1.39	0.33
LAB	Mean Raws	3.33	3.33	3.27	14.73	5.92	12.33
LAB	SD Raws	0.49	0.65	1.10	4.82	2.35	3.85
LAB	Mean Scores	-0.45	-0.19	-0.25	0.11	-0.73	0.36
NAT	Mean Raws	3.64	3.27	3.55	13.70	8.92	8.33
NAT	SD Raws	0.51	0.65	1.13	5.06	4.08	3.80
NAT	Mean Scores	-0.03	-0.27	-0.01	-0.10	-0.19	-0.61

New Zealand
Table 4

Party		Pro nuclear weapon free zone (1) vs. anti (20)		
		Leads	Vots	Imp.
DEM	Mean	6.25	7.00	11.67
	SD	2.50	2.58	0.58
LAB	Mean	6.00	3.67	15.40
	SD	2.97	1.75	1.95
NAT	Mean	15.17	14.67	13.80
	SD	1.83	2.42	2.17

**New Zealand
Graph 1**

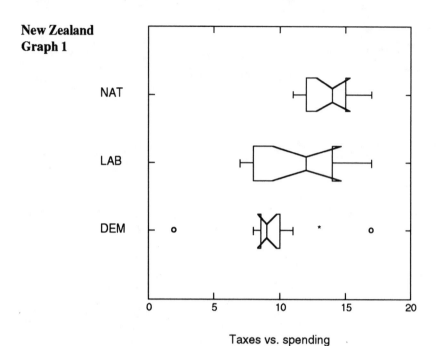

Taxes vs. spending

**New Zealand
Graph 2
(8/87 election %)**

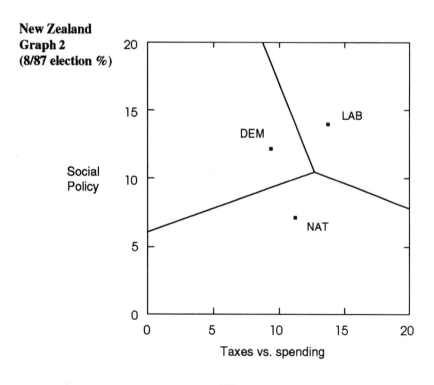

Taxes vs. spending

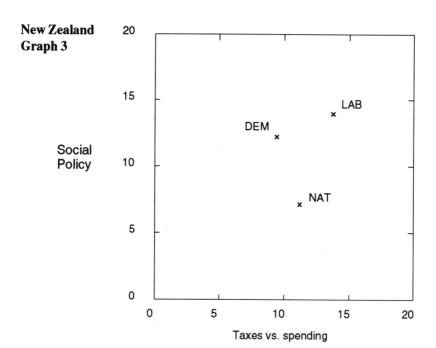

New Zealand Graph 3

Social Policy

Taxes vs. spending

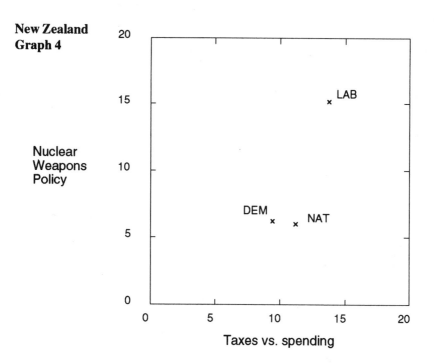

New Zealand Graph 4

Nuclear Weapons Policy

Taxes vs. spending

Norway
Table 1

	Mean	SD
Impact of opposition parties on govt policy (1=lo; 9=hi)	6.76	1.39
Prop. of govts falling on policy disputes (1=lo; 9=hi)	3.24	1.75
Cabinet portfolios as policy (1) or office (9) payoffs	2.75	1.29
Cabinet members publicize internal splits (1=lo; 9=hi)	2.71	1.10
Policy autonomy of cabinet ministers (1=hi; 9=lo)	4.35	1.37
Frequency of cabinet reshuffles (1=lo; 9=hi)	4.50	1.51

RANKING OF CABINET POSITIONS

	Mean	SD
Finance	1.56	0.81
Foreign Affairs	2.13	1.81
Industry	5.30	3.68
Environment	9.70	3.40
Defense	10.33	1.87
Trade and Shipping	9.71	3.09
Petroleum and Energy	6.13	2.90
Communications	7.25	2.87
Health and Social Affairs	4.31	2.24
Agriculture	9.62	1.98
Justice	7.78	2.86
Church and Education	6.69	2.95
Local Government and Labor	3.50	0.71
Consumer Affairs and Government Administration	7.13	3.60

Norway
Table 2

Party	Abbrev.
Labor Party	A
Conservatives	H
Christian People's Party	KRF
Center Party	SP
Socialist Left Party	SF
Progress Party	FRP
Liberals	V
Liberal People's Party	DLF

Norway
Table 3

Party		Increase services (1) vs cut taxes (20)			Pro friendly relations USSR (1) vs anti (20)		
		Leads	Vots	Imp.	Leads	Vots	Imp.
A	Mean Raws	6.37	7.26	13.61	6.28	6.24	11.53
A	SD Raws	2.19	2.18	3.66	2.14	2.05	3.76
A	Mean Scores	-0.85	-0.79	0.22	-0.67	-0.72	0.04
DLF	Mean Raws	11.56	12.00	11.33	9.75	10.13	11.13
DLF	SD Raws	0.73	1.31	2.29	1.58	1.64	2.80
DLF	Mean Scores	0.26	0.27	-0.26	0.18	0.14	-0.05
FRP	Mean Raws	18.39	18.22	17.94	14.63	15.44	10.06
FRP	SD Raws	1.34	1.77	4.45	2.96	3.18	5.25
FRP	Mean Scores	1.72	1.65	1.14	1.37	1.31	-0.27
H	Mean Raws	14.32	14.79	16.17	11.82	12.24	13.53
H	SD Raws	1.83	1.81	3.50	3.17	3.77	4.80
H	Mean Scores	0.85	0.89	0.76	0.68	0.60	0.46
KRF	Mean Raws	9.58	10.05	9.22	10.06	10.69	8.65
KRF	SD Raws	2.06	1.96	3.72	3.36	3.96	4.03
KRF	Mean Scores	-0.17	-0.17	-0.71	0.25	0.26	-0.57
SF	Mean Raws	4.06	4.50	12.22	3.94	3.81	17.29
SF	SD Raws	1.70	2.23	4.85	1.98	1.76	3.35
SF	Mean Scores	-1.35	-1.40	-0.08	-1.24	-1.26	1.25
SP	Mean Raws	9.74	10.47	10.44	9.38	10.56	8.41
SP	SD Raws	2.21	2.07	3.29	2.94	3.08	3.28
SP	Mean Scores	-0.13	-0.07	-0.45	0.09	0.23	-0.62
V	Mean Raws	9.41	9.83	9.33	7.00	7.31	10.00
V	SD Raws	1.97	1.72	2.38	1.70	2.44	3.20
V	Mean Scores	-0.20	-0.22	-0.69	-0.49	-0.48	-0.28

Norway
Table 3 (cont.)

Party		Pro public own. (1) vs anti (20)			Pro permissive social policy (1) vs anti (20)		
		Leads	Vots	Imp.	Leads	Vots	Imp.
A	Mean Raws	8.17	7.77	13.56	6.33	7.44	16.33
A	SD Raws	1.72	1.44	3.26	2.14	2.12	3.90
A	Mean Scores	-0.85	-0.95	0.28	-0.75	-0.66	0.67
DLF	Mean Raws	12.88	12.75	9.67	10.86	11.67	10.78
DLF	SD Raws	1.55	0.89	3.20	1.07	2.07	2.22
DLF	Mean Scores	0.22	0.16	-0.53	0.12	0.14	-0.56
FRP	Mean Raws	19.12	18.82	17.00	11.18	11.81	12.69
FRP	SD Raws	1.22	1.43	4.18	4.43	5.19	5.39
FRP	Mean Scores	1.65	1.51	1.00	0.19	0.17	-0.14
H	Mean Raws	15.83	16.50	15.44	9.94	10.61	12.44
H	SD Raws	1.62	1.51	3.47	3.40	3.79	3.79
H	Mean Scores	0.90	0.99	0.67	-0.05	-0.06	-0.19
KRF	Mean Raws	11.39	11.47	7.94	18.44	18.67	14.67
KRF	SD Raws	1.20	1.28	2.98	1.20	1.33	4.63
KRF	Mean Scores	-0.12	-0.13	-0.89	1.59	1.46	0.30
SF	Mean Raws	5.44	5.41	15.00	3.61	4.22	15.64
SF	SD Raws	2.09	1.87	3.62	1.79	2.46	4.68
SF	Mean Scores	-1.48	-1.48	0.58	-1.28	-1.26	0.51
SP	Mean Raws	12.33	12.94	9.82	13.61	14.78	10.75
SP	SD Raws	2.11	2.46	3.96	2.20	2.42	4.27
SP	Mean Scores	0.10	0.20	-0.50	0.66	0.73	-0.57
V	Mean Raws	10.94	10.82	8.00	8.22	8.65	12.17
V	SD Raws	0.94	1.24	2.83	3.19	2.98	3.38
V	Mean Scores	-0.22	-0.27	-0.87	-0.39	-0.43	-0.26

Norway
Table 3 (cont.)

Party		Anticlerical (1) vs proclerical (20)			Pro urban interests (1) vs anti (20)		
		Leads	Vots	Imp.	Leads	Vots	Imp.
A	Mean Raws	8.65	8.82	7.29	7.72	7.17	11.22
A	SD Raws	2.06	2.53	3.72	2.32	1.92	2.94
A	Mean Scores	-0.65	-0.59	-0.48	-0.57	-0.65	-0.30
DLF	Mean Raws	12.75	12.50	9.63	10.22	9.63	10.78
DLF	SD Raws	2.32	2.07	3.42	1.79	1.69	3.87
DLF	Mean Scores	0.23	0.19	-0.05	-0.09	-0.19	-0.41
FRP	Mean Raws	9.19	9.25	5.88	4.25	4.75	11.40
FRP	SD Raws	3.67	4.03	4.00	2.62	2.98	4.78
FRP	Mean Scores	-0.53	-0.50	-0.74	-1.24	-1.10	-0.26
H	Mean Raws	13.35	12.65	10.18	5.39	5.22	10.33
H	SD Raws	3.16	2.85	4.71	2.00	2.39	3.53
H	Mean Scores	0.36	0.23	0.05	-1.02	-1.01	-0.51
KRF	Mean Raws	18.53	18.71	18.82	14.72	15.06	12.44
KRF	SD Raws	1.84	1.86	1.19	2.27	2.07	3.65
KRF	Mean Scores	1.47	1.51	1.63	0.77	0.82	-0.02
SF	Mean Raws	5.47	5.59	7.40	11.06	9.83	11.65
SF	SD Raws	2.63	2.40	4.55	2.98	3.07	3.57
SF	Mean Scores	-1.33	-1.28	-0.46	0.07	-0.16	-0.20
SP	Mean Raws	14.94	15.13	10.94	18.61	19.28	17.78
SP	SD Raws	2.14	2.25	3.90	2.33	0.96	4.41
SP	Mean Scores	0.70	0.75	0.19	1.51	1.60	1.22
V	Mean Raws	11.18	10.65	8.41	12.72	13.17	13.44
V	SD Raws	1.98	2.18	4.69	3.03	2.55	3.00
V	Mean Scores	-0.11	-0.20	-0.27	0.39	0.46	0.22

Norway
Table 3 (cont.)

Party		Pro decentralization of decisions (1) vs anti (20)			Envir. over growth (1) vs growth over env (20)		
		Leads	Vots	Imp.	Leads	Vots	Imp.
A	Mean Raws	11.75	11.13	10.82	12.56	13.18	12.59
A	SD Raws	4.06	3.65	4.38	2.98	2.51	2.83
A	Mean Scores	0.67	0.62	-0.26	0.59	0.64	-0.02
DLF	Mean Raws	8.75	8.50	10.88	10.89	11.75	11.75
DLF	SD Raws	1.58	1.41	4.09	4.05	4.40	4.83
DLF	Mean Scores	0.00	0.00	-0.24	0.29	0.37	-0.19
FRP	Mean Raws	7.64	7.79	14.19	17.86	17.29	6.56
FRP	SD Raws	5.21	4.81	4.55	1.99	3.02	4.00
FRP	Mean Scores	-0.25	-0.17	0.55	1.54	1.41	-1.24
H	Mean Raws	11.44	10.69	11.12	14.28	14.00	9.41
H	SD Raws	2.58	2.77	3.79	3.46	2.43	2.81
H	Mean Scores	0.60	0.51	-0.19	0.90	0.79	-0.67
KRF	Mean Raws	8.81	8.60	9.77	8.59	8.56	11.60
KRF	SD Raws	2.86	3.20	4.02	2.09	2.04	3.36
KRF	Mean Scores	0.01	0.02	-0.51	-0.13	-0.23	-0.22
SF	Mean Raws	9.00	9.14	12.56	3.50	4.61	16.12
SF	SD Raws	5.34	4.66	3.83	1.15	3.01	3.57
SF	Mean Scores	0.05	0.15	0.16	-1.04	-0.98	0.69
SP	Mean Raws	5.69	5.38	13.31	6.50	8.11	14.71
SP	SD Raws	4.47	4.65	3.84	2.28	3.05	3.22
SP	Mean Scores	-0.69	-0.74	0.34	-0.50	-0.32	0.41
V	Mean Raws	6.88	6.81	12.18	2.41	3.47	17.82
V	SD Raws	4.35	4.28	3.81	0.87	3.28	4.23
V	Mean Scores	-0.42	-0.40	0.07	-1.23	-1.19	1.04

Norway
Table 3 (cont.)

Party		No influence on party policy (1) vs high (20)			No influence on partic. in govt (1) vs high (20)		
		Leads	Legs	Acts	Leads	Legs	Acts
A	Mean Raws	16.71	12.69	11.20	16.43	13.31	8.14
A	SD Raws	1.86	3.01	3.69	2.53	3.30	4.15
A	Mean Scores	0.72	0.04	0.13	0.46	0.17	-0.06
DLF	Mean Raws	12.67	10.00	10.00	12.43	9.00	6.50
DLF	SD Raws	3.46	7.81	5.18	3.74	5.00	3.62
DLF	Mean Scores	-0.41	-0.58	-0.15	-0.66	-0.99	-0.45
FRP	Mean Raws	17.60	12.50	7.31	16.15	12.82	7.15
FRP	SD Raws	3.40	5.68	4.59	3.63	3.34	4.34
FRP	Mean Scores	0.97	0.00	-0.77	0.39	0.04	-0.30
H	Mean Raws	15.35	15.07	8.73	17.07	14.08	7.36
H	SD Raws	2.67	3.58	3.43	1.49	3.40	3.37
H	Mean Scores	0.35	0.59	-0.44	0.65	0.37	-0.25
KRF	Mean Raws	13.81	12.85	10.14	14.86	13.58	8.86
KRF	SD Raws	2.48	2.85	3.53	2.93	2.81	3.92
KRF	Mean Scores	-0.08	0.08	-0.12	0.02	0.24	0.11
SF	Mean Raws	11.44	11.64	13.88	11.77	12.08	10.54
SF	SD Raws	3.78	3.78	4.18	3.77	2.91	5.25
SF	Mean Scores	-0.75	-0.20	0.74	-0.85	-0.16	0.50
SP	Mean Raws	13.00	13.62	10.80	15.00	14.23	8.31
SP	SD Raws	2.39	2.87	4.21	2.66	2.68	3.95
SP	Mean Scores	-0.31	0.25	0.03	0.06	0.42	-0.02
V	Mean Raws	11.69	5.20	12.31	13.00	9.40	9.64
V	SD Raws	3.26	4.38	3.71	4.29	4.90	4.72
V	Mean Scores	-0.68	-1.69	0.38	-0.50	-0.88	0.29

Norway
Table 3 (cont.)

Party		Do not look to future (1) vs look many years (5)			Give up office(1) vs give up policy (20)	Can use groups (1) vs not (20)	Close to resp (1) vs not (15)
		Leads	Legs	Acts			
A	Mean Raws	3.90	4.00	3.57	13.25	4.69	4.33
A	SD Raws	0.99	0.58	0.79	2.79	3.24	2.19
A	Mean Scores	0.53	0.33	0.25	0.49	-1.00	-0.96
DLF	Mean Raws	3.50	3.67	3.33	11.25	16.00	8.83
DLF	SD Raws	0.84	0.58	0.58	3.15	1.55	3.13
DLF	Mean Scores	0.11	-0.10	-0.07	0.04	1.14	0.12
FRP	Mean Raws	2.70	3.00	2.71	10.67	15.79	13.93
FRP	SD Raws	0.95	1.00	0.95	5.01	3.58	3.20
FRP	Mean Scores	-0.73	-0.97	-0.90	-0.10	1.10	1.33
H	Mean Raws	3.80	4.14	3.71	13.31	7.44	9.36
H	SD Raws	1.14	0.69	0.76	3.79	3.39	3.10
H	Mean Scores	0.43	0.52	0.44	0.51	-0.48	0.24
KRF	Mean Raws	3.50	4.00	3.57	11.81	8.56	10.33
KRF	SD Raws	0.85	0.58	0.79	4.31	2.45	3.02
KRF	Mean Scores	0.11	0.33	0.25	0.17	-0.27	0.47
SF	Mean Raws	3.00	3.43	3.29	6.00	13.47	6.27
SF	SD Raws	0.94	0.98	0.49	2.56	4.24	3.83
SF	Mean Scores	-0.41	-0.41	-0.13	-1.16	0.66	-0.50
SP	Mean Raws	3.40	3.86	3.29	10.47	5.50	9.13
SP	SD Raws	0.84	0.38	0.49	4.45	3.41	2.90
SP	Mean Scores	0.01	0.15	-0.13	-0.14	-0.85	0.19
V	Mean Raws	3.40	3.83	3.57	11.77	13.50	5.14
V	SD Raws	0.70	0.75	0.79	4.13	3.53	2.41
V	Mean Scores	0.01	0.12	0.25	0.16	0.67	-0.77

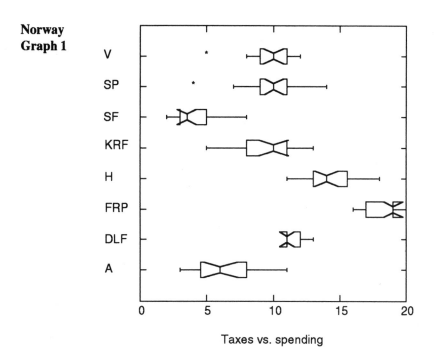

**Norway
Graph 1**

Taxes vs. spending

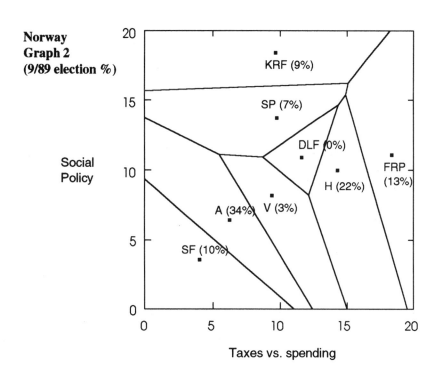

**Norway
Graph 2
(9/89 election %)**

Social
Policy

Taxes vs. spending

**Norway
Graph 3**

Social
Policy

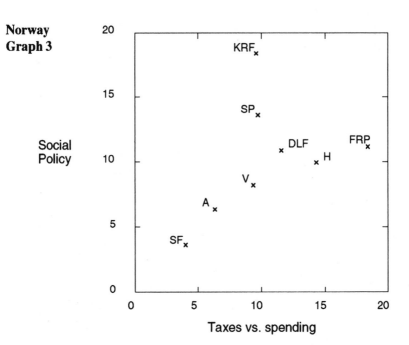

Taxes vs. spending

Portugal
Table 1

	Mean	SD
Impact of opposition parties on govt policy (1=lo; 9=hi)	4.29	2.14
Prop. of govts falling on policy disputes (1=lo; 9=hi)	4.14	2.48
Cabinet portfolios as policy (1) or office (9) payoffs	5.86	1.35
Cabinet members publicize internal splits (1=lo; 9=hi)	5.00	1.83
Policy autonomy of cabinet ministers (1=hi; 9=lo)	5.57	2.64
Frequency of cabinet reshuffles (1=lo; 9=hi)	5.86	1.07

RANKING OF CABINET POSITIONS		
Finance	1.00	0.00
Foreign Affairs	4.71	2.69
Industry and Energy	5.33	2.42
Interior	7.00	2.45
Defense	5.25	4.57
Health	5.80	1.64
Agriculture, Fisheries and Food	7.60	2.07
Education	4.00	1.90
Employment and Social Security	5.67	1.63

Portugal
Table 2

Party	Abbrev.
Socialist Party	PSP
Democratic Intervention	DI
Social Democrats	PSD
Center Social Democrats	CDS
Communist Party	PCP
Democratic Renewal Party	PRD
Democratic Movement	MDP
Popular Democratic Union	UDP
Revolutionary Socialist Party	PSR
Christian Democratic Party	PDC
Greens	G

Portugal
Table 3

Party		Increase services (1) vs cut taxes (20)			Pro friendly relations USSR (1) vs anti (20)		
		Leads	Vots	Imp.	Leads	Vots	Imp.
CDS	Mean Raws	17.00	17.29	15.00	15.86	17.43	12.29
CDS	SD Raws	2.24	2.98	3.92	3.81	2.88	2.87
CDS	Mean Scores	1.29	1.36	0.41	1.23	1.31	0.26
DI	Mean Raws	8.00	10.00	19.00	2.00	2.00	20.00
DI	SD Raws	NA	NA	NA	NA	NA	NA
DI	Mean Scores	-0.29	0.08	1.32	-1.21	-1.17	1.82
G	Mean Raws	5.00	6.00	6.00	5.00	4.00	1.00
G	SD Raws	4.24	5.66	7.07	NA	NA	0.00
G	Mean Scores	-0.82	-0.62	-1.63	-0.68	-0.85	-2.03
MDP	Mean Raws	7.00	7.50	17.00	3.00	3.00	11.50
MDP	SD Raws	2.83	3.54	1.41	0.00	0.00	12.02
MDP	Mean Scores	-0.47	-0.35	0.87	-1.03	-1.01	0.10
PCP	Mean Raws	3.43	3.57	12.86	1.14	1.57	13.71
PCP	SD Raws	2.57	2.99	5.90	0.38	1.51	6.05
PCP	Mean Scores	-1.10	-1.04	-0.07	-1.36	-1.24	0.55
PDC	Mean Raws	17.33	17.00	13.67	16.33	17.33	9.33
PDC	SD Raws	3.79	5.20	4.73	1.53	2.08	4.04
PDC	Mean Scores	1.35	1.31	0.11	1.31	1.30	-0.34
PRD	Mean Raws	9.83	9.00	12.40	9.00	8.83	10.80
PRD	SD Raws	0.75	1.10	3.91	2.83	3.97	3.49
PRD	Mean Scores	0.03	-0.09	-0.18	0.02	-0.07	-0.05
PSD	Mean Raws	14.00	13.33	12.40	13.00	13.33	10.50
PSD	SD Raws	2.76	2.34	4.10	3.63	2.88	2.43
PSD	Mean Scores	0.76	0.67	-0.18	0.72	0.65	-0.11
PSP	Mean Raws	8.75	8.13	11.63	7.88	8.38	12.00
PSP	SD Raws	2.87	2.30	2.97	3.09	2.83	3.69
PSP	Mean Scores	-0.16	-0.24	-0.35	-0.18	-0.15	0.20
PSR	Mean Raws	4.00	4.00	14.67	6.67	6.00	10.50
PSR	SD Raws	4.36	5.20	4.04	3.06	5.57	2.12
PSR	Mean Scores	-1.00	-0.96	0.34	-0.39	-0.53	-0.11
UDP	Mean Raws	4.00	4.00	14.67	7.00	7.00	6.67
UDP	SD Raws	5.20	5.20	3.51	3.00	6.00	4.16
UDP	Mean Scores	-1.00	-0.96	0.34	-0.33	-0.37	-0.88

Portugal
Table 3 (cont.)

Party		Pro public own. (1) vs anti (20)			Pro permissive social policy (1) vs anti (20)		
		Leads	Vots	Imp.	Leads	Vots	Imp.
CDS	Mean Raws	18.14	18.71	16.86	18.17	18.67	12.14
CDS	SD Raws	2.34	1.11	2.19	1.60	1.21	5.37
CDS	Mean Scores	1.38	1.46	0.26	1.44	1.47	-0.50
DI	Mean Raws	1.00	1.00	20.00	1.00	1.00	19.00
DI	SD Raws	NA	NA	NA	NA	NA	NA
DI	Mean Scores	-1.18	-1.21	1.05	-1.16	-1.27	0.94
G	Mean Raws	2.00	2.00	8.50	1.00	1.00	10.00
G	SD Raws	1.41	1.41	10.61	0.00	0.00	12.73
G	Mean Scores	-1.03	-1.06	-1.87	-1.16	-1.27	-0.95
MDP	Mean Raws	2.00	3.00	18.00	3.00	4.50	18.50
MDP	SD Raws	0.00	1.41	NA	2.83	4.95	0.71
MDP	Mean Scores	-1.03	-0.91	0.55	-0.86	-0.73	0.84
PCP	Mean Raws	1.14	1.86	18.86	2.67	4.33	16.43
PCP	SD Raws	0.38	0.90	1.46	1.63	2.66	4.47
PCP	Mean Scores	-1.16	-1.08	0.76	-0.91	-0.76	0.40
PDC	Mean Raws	18.33	18.67	15.00	20.00	19.33	10.67
PDC	SD Raws	2.08	2.31	6.08	0.00	1.16	7.64
PDC	Mean Scores	1.41	1.45	-0.22	1.72	1.57	-0.81
PRD	Mean Raws	8.60	8.80	13.80	9.20	9.80	14.80
PRD	SD Raws	2.19	2.68	3.11	2.68	3.27	2.78
PRD	Mean Scores	-0.05	-0.04	-0.52	0.08	0.09	0.06
PSD	Mean Raws	13.83	13.33	15.00	12.40	12.60	13.17
PSD	SD Raws	2.04	2.73	3.23	1.95	1.14	3.60
PSD	Mean Scores	0.74	0.65	-0.22	0.57	0.53	-0.28
PSP	Mean Raws	9.50	9.00	14.00	8.00	8.86	14.38
PSP·	SD Raws	1.93	1.51	3.07	2.08	2.34	3.38
PSP	Mean Scores	0.09	-0.01	-0.47	-0.10	-0.06	-0.03
PSR	Mean Raws	3.33	3.33	18.33	2.67	2.67	18.00
PSR	SD Raws	4.04	4.04	2.08	2.89	2.89	1.73
PSR	Mean Scores	-0.84	-0.86	0.63	-0.91	-1.01	0.73
UDP	Mean Raws	2.67	2.67	17.67	2.00	2.00	17.33
UDP	SD Raws	2.89	2.89	3.22	1.73	1.73	2.89
UDP	Mean Scores	-0.93	-0.96	0.46	-1.01	-1.12	0.59

Portugal
Table 3 (cont.)

Party		Anticlerical (1) vs proclerical (20)			Pro urban interests (1) vs anti (20)		
		Leads	Vots	Imp.	Leads	Vots	Imp.
CDS	Mean Raws	19.29	19.29	16.67	16.50	17.33	13.17
CDS	SD Raws	0.76	0.95	2.34	1.98	2.07	3.87
CDS	Mean Scores	1.46	1.46	1.51	1.34	1.34	0.57
DI	Mean Raws	1.00	1.00	3.00	3.00	3.00	9.00
DI	SD Raws	NA	NA	NA	NA	NA	NA
DI	Mean Scores	-1.23	-1.26	-0.88	-1.32	-1.25	-0.31
G	Mean Raws	1.50	1.50	2.00	8.50	8.00	14.00
G	SD Raws	0.71	0.71	1.41	9.19	9.90	5.66
G	Mean Scores	-1.16	-1.18	-1.05	-0.23	-0.34	0.74
MDP	Mean Raws	2.00	2.00	3.50	7.00	7.00	11.00
MDP	SD Raws	1.41	1.41	0.71	4.24	4.24	NA
MDP	Mean Scores	-1.09	-1.11	-0.79	-0.53	-0.52	0.11
PCP	Mean Raws	2.71	3.00	4.83	7.00	6.80	10.83
PCP	SD Raws	1.25	2.08	4.62	3.24	3.42	6.24
PCP	Mean Scores	-0.98	-0.96	-0.56	-0.53	-0.56	0.08
PDC	Mean Raws	20.00	20.00	16.33	17.00	17.33	15.00
PDC	SD Raws	0.00	0.00	3.51	4.36	4.62	4.58
PDC	Mean Scores	1.57	1.56	1.45	1.44	1.34	0.95
PRD	Mean Raws	9.00	10.00	6.60	9.80	9.60	8.80
PRD	SD Raws	2.12	1.41	2.51	1.79	2.30	3.11
PRD	Mean Scores	-0.05	0.08	-0.25	0.02	-0.06	-0.35
PSD	Mean Raws	13.50	13.33	8.40	10.80	12.00	9.20
PSD	SD Raws	1.52	1.63	4.98	1.79	2.55	4.09
PSD	Mean Scores	0.61	0.57	0.07	0.22	0.38	-0.27
PSP	Mean Raws	9.63	9.50	7.57	8.29	8.57	10.43
PSP	SD Raws	1.19	1.41	3.51	2.06	2.30	5.35
PSP	Mean Scores	0.04	0.01	-0.08	-0.28	-0.24	-0.01
PSR	Mean Raws	3.00	3.00	4.33	4.50	4.00	6.67
PSR	SD Raws	3.46	3.46	4.16	3.54	4.24	4.16
PSR	Mean Scores	-0.94	-0.96	-0.64	-1.02	-1.07	-0.80
UDP	Mean Raws	2.00	2.00	4.00	2.67	2.33	6.67
UDP	SD Raws	1.73	1.73	3.61	2.08	2.31	3.51
UDP	Mean Scores	-1.09	-1.11	-0.70	-1.38	-1.37	-0.80

Portugal
Table 3 (cont.)

Party		Pro decentralization of decisions (1) vs anti (20)			Envir. over growth (1) vs growth over env (20)		
		Leads	Vots	Imp.	Leads	Vots	Imp.
CDS	Mean Raws	12.50	12.20	11.00	13.83	14.50	7.67
CDS	SD Raws	3.08	4.03	4.42	2.56	2.67	3.08
CDS	Mean Scores	0.33	0.52	-0.30	1.09	1.00	-0.70
DI	Mean Raws	20.00	20.00	8.00	3.00	3.00	9.00
DI	SD Raws	NA	NA	NA	NA	NA	NA
DI	Mean Scores	1.71	1.87	-0.89	-1.27	-1.32	-0.37
G	Mean Raws	1.00	1.00	10.00	1.00	1.00	20.00
G	SD Raws	0.00	0.00	12.73	0.00	0.00	0.00
G	Mean Scores	-1.79	-1.41	-0.50	-1.71	-1.73	2.38
MDP	Mean Raws	11.50	11.50	14.00	4.50	6.00	8.00
MDP	SD Raws	12.02	12.02	7.07	3.54	5.66	2.83
MDP	Mean Scores	0.14	0.40	0.29	-0.95	-0.72	-0.62
PCP	Mean Raws	13.83	11.83	13.33	5.83	7.33	13.17
PCP	SD Raws	6.21	6.56	6.06	3.19	3.62	3.06
PCP	Mean Scores	0.58	0.46	0.15	-0.66	-0.45	0.67
PDC	Mean Raws	15.33	13.00	9.00	15.33	17.00	6.67
PDC	SD Raws	5.51	6.08	8.89	3.06	4.36	3.51
PDC	Mean Scores	0.85	0.66	-0.70	1.42	1.50	-0.95
PRD	Mean Raws	8.20	6.60	15.20	8.60	9.60	10.50
PRD	SD Raws	2.59	3.98	2.39	1.52	1.14	2.52
PRD	Mean Scores	-0.47	-0.45	0.52	-0.05	0.01	0.01
PSD	Mean Raws	11.60	7.00	13.40	12.60	13.60	10.80
PSD	SD Raws	2.88	4.06	3.78	1.14	1.52	1.79
PSD	Mean Scores	0.16	-0.38	0.17	0.82	0.82	0.08
PSP	Mean Raws	8.57	6.86	13.29	9.86	9.86	11.00
PSP	SD Raws	2.30	3.24	2.81	0.90	1.86	1.29
PSP	Mean Scores	-0.40	-0.40	0.15	0.22	0.06	0.13
PSR	Mean Raws	8.67	8.67	12.67	4.00	4.00	9.67
PSR	SD Raws	6.81	6.81	6.03	2.65	2.65	6.43
PSR	Mean Scores	-0.38	-0.09	0.02	-1.05	-1.12	-0.20
UDP	Mean Raws	9.00	9.33	11.67	5.00	5.00	9.33
UDP	SD Raws	6.93	7.23	7.02	3.00	3.00	5.86
UDP	Mean Scores	-0.32	0.03	-0.17	-0.84	-0.92	-0.29

Portugal
Table 3 (cont.)

Party		No influence on party policy (1) vs high (20)			No influence on partic. in govt (1) vs high (20)		
		Leads	Legs	Acts	Leads	Legs	Acts
CDS	Mean Raws	15.86	10.29	7.71	14.86	11.43	6.83
CDS	SD Raws	2.61	3.90	3.20	3.53	4.28	2.64
CDS	Mean Scores	-0.02	0.20	0.05	-0.10	0.49	0.16
DI	Mean Raws	13.00	10.00	5.00	18.00	4.00	3.00
DI	SD Raws	NA	NA	NA	NA	NA	NA
DI	Mean Scores	-0.83	0.14	-0.50	0.64	-0.91	-0.72
G	Mean Raws	10.50	4.50	15.00	10.00	4.50	18.00
G	SD Raws	7.78	0.71	7.07	7.07	0.71	NA
G	Mean Scores	-1.54	-0.87	1.54	-1.24	-0.81	2.73
MDP	Mean Raws	16.00	5.00	4.00	16.00	4.00	2.00
MDP	SD Raws	2.83	1.41	0.00	NA	0.00	0.00
MDP	Mean Scores	0.03	-0.78	-0.70	0.17	-0.91	-0.95
PCP	Mean Raws	19.43	6.71	3.71	16.86	6.57	3.43
PCP	SD Raws	0.79	4.61	3.86	7.01	5.16	3.95
PCP	Mean Scores	1.00	-0.46	-0.76	0.37	-0.42	-0.62
PDC	Mean Raws	15.67	4.00	5.00	15.50	5.00	4.00
PDC	SD Raws	5.13	4.24	5.66	3.54	5.66	4.24
PDC	Mean Scores	-0.07	-0.96	-0.50	0.05	-0.72	-0.49
PRD	Mean Raws	14.80	11.60	8.40	15.40	9.60	7.60
PRD	SD Raws	3.35	5.73	5.32	4.22	5.94	4.34
PRD	Mean Scores	-0.32	0.44	0.19	0.03	0.15	0.34
PSD	Mean Raws	17.00	9.17	7.83	15.83	9.67	7.17
PSD	SD Raws	2.10	5.27	4.71	3.76	4.76	4.75
PSD.	Mean Scores	0.31	-0.01	0.08	0.13	0.16	0.24
PSP	Mean Raws	14.14	13.88	11.13	15.63	12.13	8.38
PSP	SD Raws	3.08	5.41	4.85	3.16	4.85	3.38
PSP	Mean Scores	-0.51	0.86	0.75	0.08	0.62	0.52
PSR	Mean Raws	16.00	8.00	5.00	13.67	8.50	3.00
PSR	SD Raws	4.58	9.90	4.00	4.04	10.61	2.83
PSR	Mean Scores	0.03	-0.23	-0.50	-0.38	-0.06	-0.72
UDP	Mean Raws	16.33	5.00	5.67	14.33	5.50	2.50
UDP	SD Raws	4.04	5.66	4.16	3.79	6.36	2.12
UDP	Mean Scores	0.12	-0.78	-0.37	-0.22	-0.63	-0.83

Portugal
Table 3 (cont.)

Party		Do not look to future (1) vs look many years (5)			Give up office(1) vs give up policy (20)	Can use groups (1) vs not (20)	Close to resp (1) vs not (15)
		Leads	Legs	Acts			
CDS	Mean Raws	3.40	2.75	3.25	13.86	13.14	11.14
CDS	SD Raws	0.55	0.50	0.50	3.02	4.30	3.53
CDS	Mean Scores	0.25	-0.20	0.36	0.59	0.19	0.32
DI	Mean Raws	3.00	3.00	3.00	11.00	20.00	15.00
DI	SD Raws	NA	NA	NA	NA	NA	NA
DI	Mean Scores	-0.21	0.08	0.05	0.01	1.27	1.19
G	Mean Raws	3.00	3.00	3.00	6.00	13.50	14.00
G	SD Raws	NA	NA	NA	7.07	6.36	NA
G	Mean Scores	-0.21	0.08	0.05	-1.01	0.25	0.96
MDP	Mean Raws	3.00	3.00	3.00	10.50	18.00	13.00
MDP	SD Raws	NA	NA	NA	0.71	2.83	2.83
MDP	Mean Scores	-0.21	0.08	0.05	-0.09	0.95	0.74
PCP	Mean Raws	4.00	3.75	3.25	8.86	3.00	12.14
PCP	SD Raws	0.71	0.50	0.50	4.22	2.08	3.76
PCP	Mean Scores	0.93	0.91	0.36	-0.43	-1.40	0.54
PDC	Mean Raws	2.00	2.00	2.00	7.00	20.00	11.67
PDC	SD Raws	1.41	1.41	1.41	4.58	0.00	4.16
PDC	Mean Scores	-1.34	-1.03	-1.22	-0.81	1.27	0.43
PRD	Mean Raws	3.00	3.00	3.00	14.00	15.20	8.20
PRD	SD Raws	0.00	0.00	0.00	2.45	2.95	2.86
PRD	Mean Scores	-0.21	0.08	0.05	0.62	0.51	-0.35
PSD	Mean Raws	3.50	3.33	3.33	13.50	10.67	7.00
PSD	SD Raws	0.58	1.16	0.58	3.56	2.73	3.85
PSD	Mean Scores	0.36	0.45	0.47	0.52	-0.20	-0.62
PSP	Mean Raws	3.50	3.20	3.40	13.75	7.00	4.25
PSP	SD Raws	0.55	0.84	0.55	3.88	4.21	3.24
PSP	Mean Scores	0.36	0.30	0.55	0.57	-0.78	-1.24
PSR	Mean Raws	2.00	2.00	2.00	4.67	19.67	12.67
PSR	SD Raws	1.41	1.41	1.41	5.51	0.58	2.08
PSR	Mean Scores	-1.34	-1.03	-1.22	-1.28	1.21	0.66
UDP	Mean Raws	2.00	2.00	2.00	5.33	19.33	13.33
UDP	SD Raws	1.41	1.41	1.41	4.93	0.58	0.58
UDP	Mean Scores	-1.34	-1.03	-1.22	-1.15	1.16	0.81

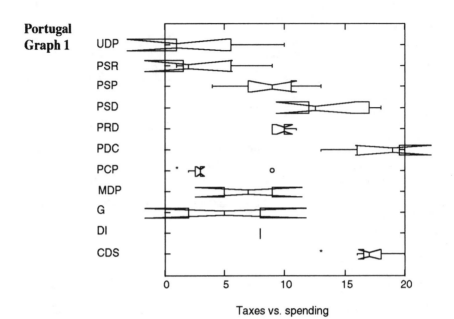

Portugal Graph 1

Taxes vs. spending

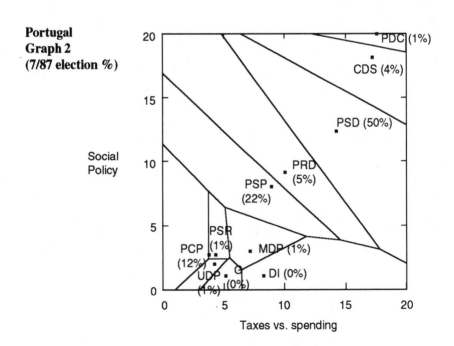

Portugal Graph 2 (7/87 election %)

PDC (1%)

CDS (4%)

PSD (50%)

PRD (5%)

PSP (22%)

PSR (1%)

PCP (12%)

MDP (1%)

UDP (1%)

G (0%)

DI (0%)

Social Policy

Taxes vs. spending

**Portugal
Graph 3**

Social
Policy

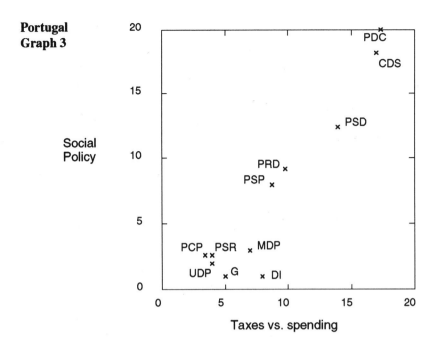

Taxes vs. spending

**Portugal
Graph 4**

Public
Ownership
Policy

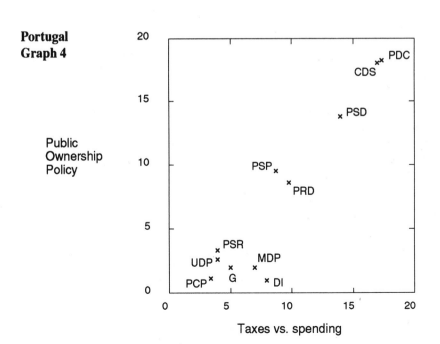

Taxes vs. spending

Spain
Table 1

	Mean	SD
Impact of opposition parties on govt policy (1=lo; 9=hi)	2.00	0.00
Prop. of govts falling on policy disputes (1=lo; 9=hi)	2.20	1.64
Cabinet portfolios as policy (1) or office (9) payoffs	4.75	1.50
Cabinet members publicize internal splits (1=lo; 9=hi)	1.80	1.30
Policy autonomy of cabinet ministers (1=hi; 9=lo)	5.25	1.89
Frequency of cabinet reshuffles (1=lo; 9=hi)	2.40	0.55

RANKING OF CABINET POSITIONS

Economy, Finance and Trade	1.33	0.58
Foreign Affairs	6.50	3.54
Interior	3.00	0.00
Public Administration	8.50	7.78
Defense	4.50	3.54
Justice	6.50	6.36

Spain
Table 2

Party	Abbrev.
Socialist Party	PSOE
Popular Coalition	CP
Democratic and Social Center	CDS
Convergence and Unity	CiU
United Left	IU
Basque Nationalist Party	EAJ-PNV
Herri Batsuna	HB
Communist Unity	MUC
Democratic Reformist Party	PRD

Spain
Table 3

Party		Increase services (1) vs cut taxes (20)			Pro friendly relations USSR (1) vs anti (20)		
		Leads	Vots	Imp.	Leads	Vots	Imp.
CDS	Mean Raws	9.40	9.60	10.80	8.60	8.60	11.00
CDS	SD Raws	1.67	1.52	2.68	1.14	2.41	3.08
CDS	Mean Scores	0.16	-0.04	-0.36	-0.03	0.02	-0.09
CIU	Mean Raws	11.00	15.20	14.80	11.80	11.80	9.75
CIU	SD Raws	4.69	1.64	1.92	1.30	2.28	3.86
CIU	Mean Scores	0.51	1.00	0.53	0.76	0.77	-0.38
CP	Mean Raws	14.60	16.20	15.80	13.60	13.80	13.60
CP	SD Raws	1.82	2.59	2.78	2.07	2.28	4.16
CP	Mean Scores	1.29	1.19	0.76	1.20	1.24	0.51
EAJ-PNV	Mean Raws	11.80	13.40	10.80	11.40	12.00	7.60
EAJ-PNV	SD Raws	2.39	1.52	5.72	2.07	2.45	4.34
EAJ-PNV	Mean Scores	0.68	0.67	-0.36	0.66	0.82	-0.87
HB	Mean Raws	6.75	6.00	5.00	5.50	4.25	5.33
HB	SD Raws	3.59	3.56	4.32	4.44	3.40	5.13
HB	Mean Scores	-0.42	-0.71	-1.67	-0.79	-1.00	-1.39
IU	Mean Raws	3.20	3.40	14.00	3.60	4.40	14.20
IU	SD Raws	1.30	1.34	4.18	1.95	2.19	2.17
IU	Mean Scores	-1.20	-1.19	0.35	-1.25	-0.97	0.65
MUC	Mean Raws	2.33	3.00	15.33	4.00	4.00	15.00
MUC	SD Raws	0.58	0.00	1.53	2.65	2.65	2.65
MUC	Mean Scores	-1.39	-1.27	0.65	-1.15	-1.06	0.83
PRD	Mean Raws	13.00	18.00	10.00	13.00	12.00	15.00
PRD	SD Raws	NA	NA	NA	NA	NA	NA
PRD	Mean Scores	0.94	1.52	-0.54	1.05	0.82	0.83
PSOE	Mean Raws	6.60	6.60	13.00	7.80	6.60	12.60
PSOE	SD Raws	2.07	2.79	2.35	2.17	1.67	2.97
PSOE	Mean Scores	-0.45	-0.60	0.13	-0.22	-0.45	0.28

Spain
Table 3 (cont.)

Party		Pro public own. (1) vs anti (20)			Pro permissive social policy (1) vs anti (20)		
		Leads	Vots	Imp.	Leads	Vots	Imp.
CDS	Mean Raws	10.40	10.00	8.00	7.20	7.60	13.20
CDS	SD Raws	1.14	1.23	3.94	1.48	3.36	3.63
CDS	Mean Scores	-0.02	0.01	-0.65	-0.18	-0.07	-0.10
CIU	Mean Raws	14.80	15.00	9.00	10.40	10.20	11.40
CIU	SD Raws	0.84	2.00	2.00	2.88	2.78	1.82
CIU	Mean Scores	0.87	0.96	-0.42	0.40	0.38	-0.54
CP	Mean Raws	16.60	15.20	13.80	17.20	16.60	10.80
CP	SD Raws	1.67	3.27	3.27	1.92	1.82	5.07
CP	Mean Scores	1.23	0.99	0.71	1.63	1.49	-0.69
EAJ-PNV	Mean Raws	14.40	14.60	6.60	13.80	15.20	12.40
EAJ-PNV	SD Raws	0.89	0.89	2.79	3.77	1.92	2.61
EAJ-PNV	Mean Scores	0.79	0.88	-0.98	1.01	1.25	-0.30
HB	Mean Raws	6.00	5.50	6.67	3.50	2.50	13.25
HB	SD Raws	2.94	3.32	5.51	2.52	1.00	7.09
HB	Mean Scores	-0.90	-0.85	-0.97	-0.85	-0.95	-0.09
IU	Mean Raws	4.00	3.60	15.00	2.40	2.40	17.80
IU	SD Raws	1.58	1.52	2.00	0.89	0.89	1.48
IU	Mean Scores	-1.30	-1.21	0.99	-1.05	-0.97	1.03
MUC	Mean Raws	3.33	2.67	16.00	2.33	2.33	15.67
MUC	SD Raws	1.53	0.58	0.00	1.53	1.53	5.86
MUC	Mean Scores	-1.44	-1.39	1.22	-1.06	-0.98	0.51
PRD	Mean Raws	16.00	18.00	13.00	6.00	5.00	16.00
PRD	SD Raws	NA	NA	NA	NA	NA	NA
PRD	Mean Scores	1.11	1.53	0.52	-0.40	-0.52	0.59
PSOE	Mean Raws	9.40	7.80	11.20	6.00	4.40	14.60
PSOE	SD Raws	1.82	1.79	1.64	1.41	1.82	1.14
PSOE	Mean Scores	-0.22	-0.41	0.10	-0.40	-0.62	0.24

Spain
Table 3 (cont.)

Party		Anticlerical (1) vs proclerical (20)			Pro urban interests (1) vs anti (20)		
		Leads	Vots	Imp.	Leads	Vots	Imp.
CDS	Mean Raws	9.60	9.80	5.50	11.00	8.50	5.50
CDS	SD Raws	2.07	2.59	3.79	1.41	2.12	3.54
CDS	Mean Scores	-0.09	0.06	-0.45	0.56	-0.02	-0.41
CIU	Mean Raws	11.40	12.80	7.60	7.50	8.00	7.50
CIU	SD Raws	1.67	3.03	3.13	4.95	4.24	6.36
CIU	Mean Scores	0.32	0.65	0.05	-0.34	-0.16	0.03
CP	Mean Raws	16.20	15.80	11.20	14.50	13.00	9.00
CP	SD Raws	2.17	1.79	4.44	0.71	1.41	8.49
CP	Mean Scores	1.40	1.24	0.91	1.46	1.25	0.36
EAJ-PNV	Mean Raws	15.40	15.60	9.80	12.50	13.00	11.00
EAJ-PNV	SD Raws	1.67	1.14	5.22	0.71	1.41	1.41
EAJ-PNV	Mean Scores	1.22	1.20	0.58	0.95	1.25	0.80
HB	Mean Raws	6.50	5.00	8.25	9.00	10.00	6.50
HB	SD Raws	3.32	3.16	4.57	0.00	1.41	4.95
HB	Mean Scores	-0.79	-0.88	0.21	0.05	0.41	-0.19
IU	Mean Raws	5.60	4.60	5.80	4.50	4.00	4.00
IU	SD Raws	1.34	1.14	4.60	0.71	0.00	1.41
IU	Mean Scores	-0.99	-0.96	-0.38	-1.11	-1.29	-0.74
MUC	Mean Raws	5.00	3.00	4.33	8.00	6.00	3.00
MUC	SD Raws	3.00	1.73	1.53	NA	NA	NA
MUC	Mean Scores	-1.13	-1.28	-0.72	-0.21	-0.72	-0.96
PRD	Mean Raws	10.00	7.00	3.00	3.00	6.00	14.00
PRD	SD Raws	NA	NA	NA	NA	NA	NA
PRD	Mean Scores	0.00	-0.49	-1.04	-1.49	-0.72	1.45
PSOE	Mean Raws	7.60	6.40	6.00	6.00	6.00	7.00
PSOE	SD Raws	1.67	1.95	2.55	2.83	2.83	5.66
PSOE	Mean Scores	-0.54	-0.61	-0.33	-0.72	-0.72	-0.08

Spain
Table 3 (cont.)

Party		Pro decentralization of decisions (1) vs anti (20)			Envir. over growth (1) vs growth over env (20)		
		Leads	Vots	Imp.	Leads	Vots	Imp.
CDS	Mean Raws	7.80	10.00	13.40	8.40	7.75	10.75
CDS	SD Raws	1.92	3.16	2.61	2.61	3.20	5.91
CDS	Mean Scores	0.43	0.73	-0.82	-0.22	-0.22	0.10
CIU	Mean Raws	3.60	3.80	18.20	12.75	12.50	8.60
CIU	SD Raws	2.30	1.79	1.64	1.26	1.73	4.10
CIU	Mean Scores	-0.50	-0.63	0.71	0.70	0.79	-0.34
CP	Mean Raws	13.60	14.40	13.20	16.00	16.00	5.80
CP	SD Raws	2.88	2.88	3.03	2.00	1.41	2.17
CP	Mean Scores	1.71	1.69	-0.89	1.38	1.53	-0.92
EAJ-PNV	Mean Raws	2.60	3.00	18.60	11.25	11.75	8.80
EAJ-PNV	SD Raws	1.52	1.41	1.52	2.75	2.63	4.21
EAJ-PNV	Mean Scores	-0.72	-0.81	0.84	0.38	0.63	-0.30
HB	Mean Raws	1.00	1.25	20.00	2.33	3.00	16.00
HB	SD Raws	0.00	0.50	0.00	1.53	1.73	2.00
HB	Mean Scores	-1.08	-1.19	1.29	-1.49	-1.22	1.17
IU	Mean Raws	4.40	5.60	15.60	4.80	4.25	14.60
IU	SD Raws	2.30	2.07	2.88	0.84	2.06	2.61
IU	Mean Scores	-0.32	-0.24	-0.12	-0.97	-0.96	0.89
MUC	Mean Raws	3.00	4.33	15.67	4.67	4.67	10.33
MUC	SD Raws	2.00	2.31	2.52	2.52	2.08	7.64
MUC	Mean Scores	-0.63	-0.52	-0.10	-1.00	-0.87	0.01
PRD	Mean Raws	3.00	8.00	14.00	13.00	11.00	2.00
PRD	SD Raws	NA	NA	NA	NA	NA	NA
PRD	Mean Scores	-0.63	0.29	-0.63	0.75	0.47	-1.70
PSOE	Mean Raws	9.40	8.80	14.20	10.80	7.25	11.40
PSOE	SD Raws	3.65	2.17	1.92	3.77	2.87	2.61
PSOE	Mean Scores	0.78	0.46	-0.57	0.29	-0.32	0.23

Spain
Table 3 (cont.)

Party		No influence on party policy (1) vs high (20)			No influence on partic. in govt (1) vs high (20)		
		Leads	Legs	Acts	Leads	Legs	Acts
CDS	Mean Raws	5.20	7.80	2.60	19.60	5.20	2.40
CDS	SD Raws	0.39	3.90	0.55	0.55	3.63	0.89
CDS	Mean Scores	1.06	-0.15	-1.12	0.81	-0.25	-0.86
CIU	Mean Raws	17.67	11.20	7.00	18.80	8.00	6.40
CIU	SD Raws	1.16	2.78	3.16	1.10	3.94	3.65
CIU	Mean Scores	-0.14	0.64	-0.28	0.54	0.44	0.12
CP	Mean Raws	17.40	11.80	5.80	18.40	8.40	5.40
CP	SD Raws	1.14	3.96	3.27	0.89	4.93	3.78
CP	Mean Scores	-0.15	0.78	-0.51	0.41	0.53	-0.13
EAJ-PNV	Mean Raws	13.33	9.40	13.40	16.00	8.00	9.20
EAJ-PNV	SD Raws	2.52	1.34	3.36	1.58	4.24	3.42
EAJ-PNV	Mean Scores	-0.27	0.22	0.95	-0.38	0.44	0.81
HB	Mean Raws	13.75	6.75	15.75	12.67	6.75	9.75
HB	SD Raws	0.50	5.56	0.96	4.73	6.29	7.23
HB	Mean Scores	-0.26	-0.40	1.40	-1.49	0.13	0.94
IU	Mean Raws	15.60	6.00	12.75	14.00	4.20	7.50
IU	SD Raws	1.34	2.16	3.30	2.55	1.48	2.38
IU	Mean Scores	-0.20	-0.58	0.83	-1.05	-0.49	0.39
MUC	Mean Raws	17.00	1.33	8.00	16.33	1.33	4.33
MUC	SD Raws	2.65	0.58	6.25	4.73	0.58	3.51
MUC	Mean Scores	-0.16	-1.67	-0.08	-0.27	-1.19	-0.39
PRD	Mean Raws	13.00	18.00	2.00	18.00	2.00	3.00
PRD	SD Raws	NA	NA	NA	NA	NA	NA
PRD	Mean Scores	-0.29	2.23	-1.23	0.28	-1.03	-0.72
PSOE	Mean Raws	18.60	7.80	5.60	19.20	6.80	3.40
PSOE	SD Raws	0.55	1.30	2.61	0.84	3.11	1.14
PSOE	Mean Scores	-0.11	-0.15	-0.54	0.67	0.14	-0.62

Spain
Table 3 (cont.)

Party		Do not look to future (1) vs look many years (5)			Give up office(1) vs give up policy (20)	Can use groups (1) vs not (20)	Close to resp (1) vs not (15)
		Leads	Legs	Acts			
CDS	Mean Raws	3.75	3.33	3.25	16.60	15.20	7.80
CDS	SD Raws	0.50	0.58	0.96	2.41	3.11	2.39
CDS	Mean Scores	-0.41	-0.45	-0.59	0.90	1.16	-0.32
CIU	Mean Raws	4.50	4.67	4.50	14.00	8.00	7.00
CIU	SD Raws	0.58	0.58	0.58	2.12	3.74	2.65
CIU	Mean Scores	0.47	0.86	0.61	0.47	-0.14	-0.53
CP	Mean Raws	3.75	3.67	3.25	13.00	8.00	11.20
CP	SD Raws	0.50	0.58	0.96	3.54	2.55	1.30
CP	Mean Scores	-0.41	-0.12	-0.59	0.31	-0.14	0.59
EAJ-PNV	Mean Raws	4.25	4.33	4.25	13.00	6.80	10.60
EAJ-PNV	SD Raws	0.50	0.58	0.50	4.18	4.27	1.67
EAJ-PNV	Mean Scores	0.18	0.53	0.37	0.31	-0.36	0.43
HB	Mean Raws	3.75	2.67	3.25	1.50	2.00	15.00
HB	SD Raws	1.89	2.08	2.06	1.00	1.41	0.00
HB	Mean Scores	-0.41	-1.10	-0.59	-1.59	-1.23	1.60
IU	Mean Raws	4.33	4.00	4.50	4.80	4.40	7.20
IU	SD Raws	0.58	0.00	0.58	3.27	3.44	4.21
IU	Mean Scores	0.28	0.20	0.61	-1.04	-0.80	-0.48
MUC	Mean Raws	4.00	3.00	4.00	7.33	15.33	11.67
MUC	SD Raws	0.00	1.41	NA	10.12	5.51	3.22
MUC	Mean Scores	-0.12	-0.78	0.13	-0.63	1.19	0.71
PRD	Mean Raws	5.00	4.00	4.00	19.00	19.00	5.00
PRD	SD Raws	NA	NA	NA	NA	NA	NA
PRD	Mean Scores	1.07	0.20	0.13	1.30	1.85	-1.07
PSOE	Mean Raws	4.25	4.33	4.00	13.80	9.80	4.60
PSOE	SD Raws	0.96	0.58	0.82	1.92	4.09	0.89
PSOE	Mean Scores	0.18	0.53	0.13	0.44	0.18	-1.17

Spain
Graph 1

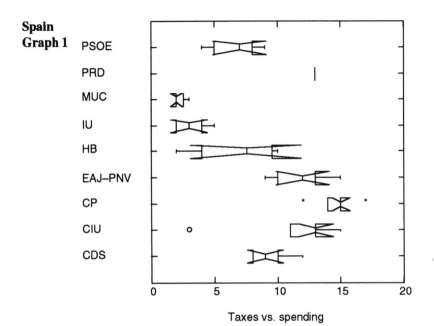

Taxes vs. spending

Spain
Graph 2
(10/89 election %)

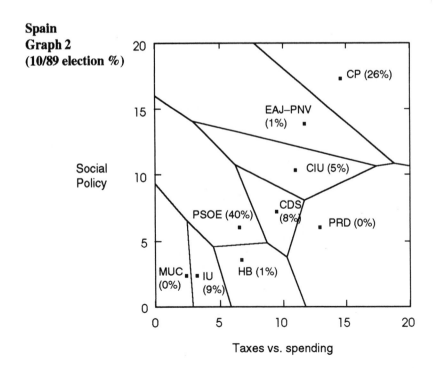

Taxes vs. spending

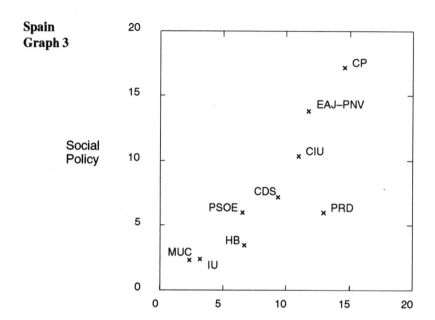

**Spain
Graph 3**

Social
Policy

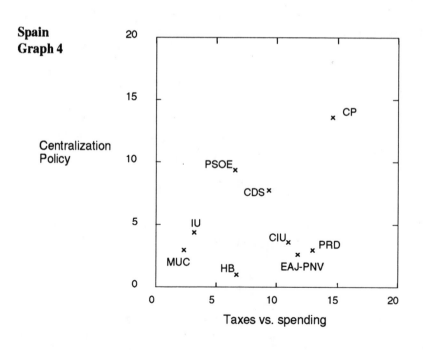

**Spain
Graph 4**

Centralization
Policy

Taxes vs. spending

Sweden
Table 1

	Mean	SD
Impact of opposition parties on govt policy (1=lo; 9=hi)	5.16	1.57
Prop. of govts falling on policy disputes (1=lo; 9=hi)	4.35	2.50
Cabinet portfolios as policy (1) or office (9) payoffs	2.84	1.30
Cabinet members publicize internal splits (1=lo; 9=hi)	2.11	0.58
Policy autonomy of cabinet ministers (1=hi; 9=lo)	4.78	1.77
Frequency of cabinet reshuffles (1=lo; 9=hi)	5.11	1.37

RANKING OF CABINET POSITIONS

Finance	1.00	0.00
Foreign Affairs	2.86	1.21
Industry	6.00	3.54
Defense	6.14	2.12
Environment and Energy	4.75	1.71
Housing	11.67	0.58
Health and Social Affairs	3.56	1.33
Agriculture	13.00	1.00
Justice	8.50	4.80
Education and Cultural Affairs	6.00	2.45
Labor and Equality Affairs	3.75	1.71
Transport and Communications	12.67	1.53

Sweden
Table 2

Party	Abbrev.
Social Democrats	SD
Moderate Unity Party	M
People's Party	PP
Center Party	CP
Christian Democratic Union	CDU
Communist Left	COM
Greens	G

Sweden
Table 3

Party		Increase services (1) vs cut taxes (20)			Pro friendly relations USSR (1) vs anti (20)		
		Leads	Vots	Imp.	Leads	Vots	Imp.
CDU	Mean Raws	12.21	12.29	11.15	10.67	12.00	7.42
CDU	SD Raws	1.93	2.16	2.97	2.64	2.63	3.90
CDU	Mean Scores	0.42	0.40	-0.50	0.33	0.36	-0.63
COM	Mean Raws	3.58	4.95	13.18	4.38	5.13	10.50
COM	SD Raws	1.87	1.84	4.98	2.28	2.68	4.43
COM	Mean Scores	-1.42	-1.44	-0.05	-1.34	-1.40	0.06
CP	Mean Raws	10.84	11.53	12.77	10.31	11.75	9.00
CP	SD Raws	1.34	1.26	2.93	2.44	2.38	3.48
CP	Mean Scores	0.13	0.21	-0.14	0.24	0.29	-0.28
G	Mean Raws	7.41	8.44	7.86	8.69	9.46	8.62
G	SD Raws	2.58	2.03	3.39	1.80	1.20	4.05
G	Mean Scores	-0.60	-0.56	-1.22	-0.19	-0.29	-0.36
M	Mean Raws	17.00	16.28	18.44	13.80	15.20	15.07
M	SD Raws	1.65	1.99	1.86	2.88	2.88	3.88
M	Mean Scores	1.43	1.40	1.11	1.17	1.17	1.09
PP	Mean Raws	13.63	13.26	15.82	11.50	12.63	9.50
PP	SD Raws	2.01	1.41	2.86	2.13	2.09	3.67
PP	Mean Scores	0.72	0.65	0.53	0.56	0.52	-0.16
SD	Mean Raws	7.63	8.42	13.41	7.00	8.44	10.75
SD	SD Raws	3.06	2.34	4.27	2.42	2.78	4.16
SD	Mean Scores	-0.56	-0.57	0.00	-0.64	-0.55	0.12

Sweden
Table 3 (cont.)

Party		Pro public own. (1) vs anti (20)			Pro permissive social policy (1) vs anti (20)		
		Leads	Vots	Imp.	Leads	Vots	Imp.
CDU	Mean Raws	13.85	14.25	10.14	16.92	18.00	13.43
CDU	SD Raws	1.52	2.01	4.02	3.17	1.92	3.90
CDU	Mean Scores	0.40	0.45	-0.52	1.56	1.51	0.25
COM	Mean Raws	3.95	5.47	14.00	4.00	5.81	14.35
COM	SD Raws	2.22	2.17	5.05	1.97	1.68	5.40
COM	Mean Scores	-1.71	-1.59	0.30	-1.00	-1.24	0.43
CP	Mean Raws	13.21	13.63	12.12	11.69	13.94	12.71
CP	SD Raws	1.75	2.09	3.35	3.36	2.21	4.20
CP	Mean Scores	0.27	0.31	-0.10	0.52	0.59	0.11
G	Mean Raws	11.13	11.31	6.73	6.08	8.08	8.87
G	SD Raws	2.06	2.44	2.99	2.84	2.23	4.58
G	Mean Scores	-0.18	-0.23	-1.25	-0.59	-0.73	-0.63
M	Mean Raws	17.44	17.44	17.06	12.20	14.27	9.25
M	SD Raws	1.79	1.65	3.55	3.75	2.46	4.64
M	Mean Scores	1.17	1.20	0.95	0.63	0.67	-0.56
PP	Mean Raws	15.47	14.90	14.82	6.75	10.56	11.59
PP	SD Raws	2.46	2.40	3.56	2.98	2.87	4.95
PP	Mean Scores	0.75	0.60	0.47	-0.46	-0.17	-0.10
SD	Mean Raws	9.42	9.95	12.50	6.63	9.13	14.35
SD	SD Raws	1.84	2.30	2.73	2.39	2.53	5.87
SD	Mean Scores	-0.54	-0.55	-0.02	-0.48	-0.49	0.43

Sweden
Table 3 (cont.)

Party		Anticlerical (1) vs proclerical (20)			Pro urban interests (1) vs anti (20)		
		Leads	Vots	Imp.	Leads	Vots	Imp.
CDU	Mean Raws	18.55	18.36	18.00	12.53	12.40	10.15
CDU	SD Raws	1.64	1.80	2.12	2.23	1.96	3.29
CDU	Mean Scores	0.53	1.38	1.71	0.58	0.51	-0.04
COM	Mean Raws	3.71	4.57	4.18	6.11	6.28	7.77
COM	SD Raws	2.37	2.50	3.70	3.29	3.56	4.34
COM	Mean Scores	-0.76	-1.53	-0.82	-0.76	-0.87	-0.50
CP	Mean Raws	14.50	14.43	11.00	16.42	16.42	17.00
CP	SD Raws	1.95	2.14	4.06	1.95	2.19	1.66
CP	Mean Scores	0.17	0.55	0.43	1.39	1.42	1.27
G	Mean Raws	9.50	9.67	3.87	13.88	13.65	14.13
G	SD Raws	2.51	1.44	1.77	2.21	2.21	4.70
G	Mean Scores	-0.26	-0.46	-0.88	0.86	0.79	0.72
M	Mean Raws	15.00	15.14	10.25	7.00	8.11	7.94
M	SD Raws	2.32	2.28	4.11	3.77	2.97	4.70
M	Mean Scores	0.22	0.70	0.29	-0.58	-0.45	-0.46
PP	Mean Raws	18.00	12.39	9.13	6.95	7.58	7.13
PP	SD Raws	27.20	2.73	4.10	2.17	1.77	4.05
PP	Mean Scores	0.48	0.12	0.08	-0.59	-0.57	-0.62
SD	Mean Raws	9.00	9.43	6.00	6.11	6.95	8.35
SD	SD Raws	1.92	2.71	2.65	2.08	2.51	3.72
SD	Mean Scores	-0.30	-0.51	-0.49	-0.77	-0.71	-0.38

Sweden
Table 3 (cont.)

Party		Pro decentralization of decisions (1) vs anti (20)			Envir. over growth (1) vs growth over env (20)		
		Leads	Vots	Imp.	Leads	Vots	Imp.
CDU	Mean Raws	7.69	8.00	10.54	7.40	8.67	14.14
CDU	SD Raws	1.80	1.78	2.99	2.95	2.64	2.69
CDU	Mean Scores	-0.31	-0.17	-0.31	-0.34	-0.18	0.08
COM	Mean Raws	9.56	9.00	9.65	6.26	7.16	15.82
COM	SD Raws	4.31	4.38	3.97	3.94	3.11	2.01
COM	Mean Scores	0.12	0.10	-0.51	-0.55	-0.49	0.45
CP	Mean Raws	5.94	6.06	16.53	6.17	6.94	16.94
CP	SD Raws	3.28	3.23	2.04	2.36	2.62	2.10
CP	Mean Scores	-0.72	-0.68	1.04	-0.57	-0.53	0.69
G	Mean Raws	4.69	4.81	15.13	1.88	2.82	19.31
G	SD Raws	3.81	3.56	4.61	1.11	1.33	1.25
G	Mean Scores	-1.02	-1.00	0.73	-1.36	-1.39	1.22
M	Mean Raws	11.77	11.31	10.13	15.89	15.17	8.29
M	SD Raws	2.93	2.89	4.33	2.59	2.85	3.98
M	Mean Scores	0.64	0.70	-0.40	1.23	1.17	-1.21
PP	Mean Raws	10.28	9.50	11.29	13.00	12.37	10.44
PP	SD Raws	3.34	2.66	3.95	2.81	2.69	3.57
PP	Mean Scores	0.29	0.23	-0.14	0.69	0.59	-0.74
SD	Mean Raws	12.56	11.44	10.00	13.16	12.74	12.11
SD	SD Raws	3.22	2.12	3.43	3.37	3.84	3.23
SD	Mean Scores	0.83	0.74	-0.43	0.72	0.67	-0.37

Sweden
Table 3 (cont.)

Party		No influence on party policy (1) vs high (20)			No influence on partic. in govt (1) vs high (20)		
		Leads	Legs	Acts	Leads	Legs	Acts
CDU	Mean Raws	14.23	7.71	8.83	15.27	12.60	6.91
CDU	SD Raws	3.56	6.18	3.93	2.57	4.99	3.24
CDU	Mean Scores	0.01	-1.15	-0.39	-0.05	-0.31	-0.19
COM	Mean Raws	14.31	12.38	10.69	14.69	13.73	8.33
COM	SD Raws	2.92	3.24	3.30	3.72	3.62	4.34
COM	Mean Scores	0.03	0.21	0.11	-0.22	0.02	0.15
CP	Mean Raws	13.69	11.80	10.88	16.29	13.75	7.44
CP	SD Raws	3.26	2.18	2.85	2.44	3.09	4.41
CP	Mean Scores	-0.15	0.04	0.16	0.25	0.03	-0.06
G	Mean Raws	9.57	12.43	13.71	10.23	13.77	11.23
G	SD Raws	3.86	3.84	3.27	2.59	3.42	4.53
G	Mean Scores	-1.29	0.22	0.93	-1.50	0.03	0.84
M	Mean Raws	15.44	11.93	9.13	16.75	13.88	6.56
M	SD Raws	2.28	2.58	3.56	2.72	3.18	3.37
M	Mean Scores	0.34	0.08	-0.31	0.38	0.06	-0.27
PP	Mean Raws	15.50	12.67	9.19	16.47	13.69	6.94
PP	SD Raws	2.97	2.13	3.66	2.43	2.96	3.73
PP	Mean Scores	0.36	0.29	-0.30	0.30	0.01	-0.18
SD	Mean Raws	16.13	10.69	9.63	17.12	13.81	6.88
SD	SD Raws	2.63	3.52	3.67	3.10	3.64	4.57
SD	Mean Scores	0.54	-0.28	-0.18	0.48	0.05	-0.19

Sweden
Table 3 (cont.)

Party		Do not look to future (1) vs look many years (5)			Give up office(1) vs give up policy (20)	Can use groups (1) vs not (20)	Close to resp (1) vs not (15)
		Leads	Legs	Acts			
CDU	Mean Raws	3.75	3.50	3.13	7.91	13.79	11.75
CDU	SD Raws	1.17	1.20	1.13	3.33	5.24	2.26
CDU	Mean Scores	-0.16	-0.38	-0.25	-0.33	0.67	0.63
COM	Mean Raws	3.91	4.10	3.46	5.73	13.65	8.56
COM	SD Raws	1.14	0.74	1.13	3.11	4.68	4.40
COM	Mean Scores	0.02	0.32	0.06	-0.78	0.65	-0.20
CP	Mean Raws	3.67	3.67	3.33	12.60	8.00	9.69
CP	SD Raws	0.65	0.65	1.07	3.80	3.57	2.36
CP	Mean Scores	-0.25	-0.19	-0.06	0.64	-0.37	0.09
G	Mean Raws	3.44	3.63	3.56	4.75	9.79	8.79
G	SD Raws	1.51	1.30	1.33	3.44	6.46	3.93
G	Mean Scores	-0.50	-0.24	0.15	-0.98	-0.05	-0.14
M	Mean Raws	4.17	3.92	3.50	9.86	8.56	11.81
M	SD Raws	0.58	0.79	1.09	5.29	4.72	4.28
M	Mean Scores	0.30	0.11	0.10	0.07	-0.27	0.64
PP	Mean Raws	3.92	3.75	3.42	13.13	12.29	8.38
PP	SD Raws	0.67	0.75	1.08	3.30	3.80	3.44
PP	Mean Scores	0.02	-0.09	0.02	0.74	0.40	-0.25
SD	Mean Raws	4.25	4.08	3.33	10.94	4.88	6.94
SD	SD Raws	0.45	0.67	1.07	4.51	4.51	3.45
SD	Mean Scores	0.39	0.31	-0.06	0.29	-0.94	-0.63

**Sweden
Graph 1**

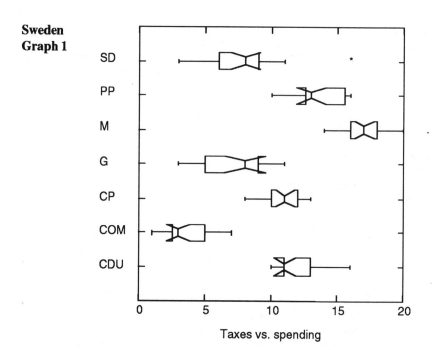

Taxes vs. spending

**Sweden
Graph 2
(9/88 election %)**

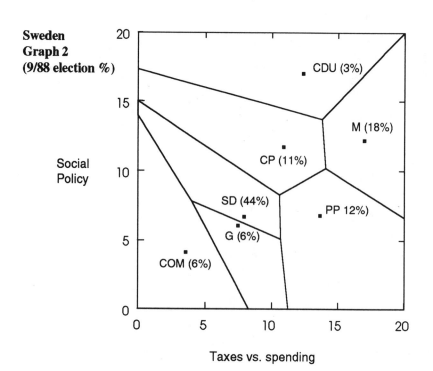

Social
Policy

Taxes vs. spending

**Sweden
Graph 3**

Social
Policy

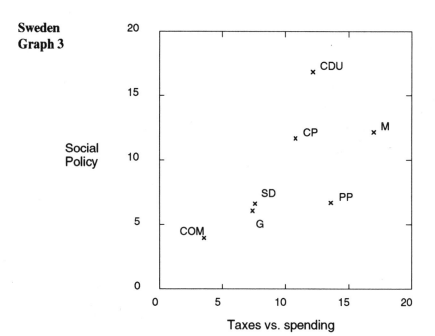

Taxes vs. spending

**Sweden
Graph 4**

Public
Ownership
Policy

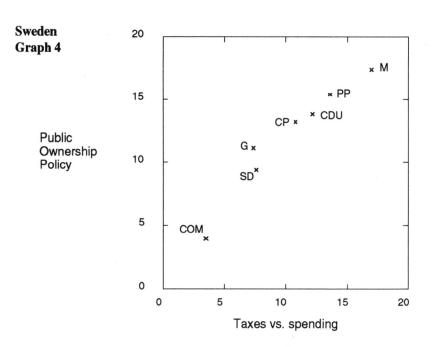

Taxes vs. spending

United States
Table 1

	Mean	SD
Impact of opposition parties on govt policy (1=lo; 9=hi)	6.12	1.92
Prop. of govts falling on policy disputes (1=lo; 9=hi)	1.65	1.23
Cabinet portfolios as policy (1) or office (9) payoffs	5.47	1.98
Cabinet members publicize internal splits (1=lo; 9=hi)	3.75	1.78
Policy autonomy of cabinet ministers (1=hi; 9=lo)	4.13	1.73
Frequency of cabinet reshuffles (1=lo; 9=hi)	5.90	1.70

RANKING OF CABINET POSITIONS

Treasury	2.81	1.17
State	1.27	0.63
Interior	7.50	2.32
Commerce	7.43	2.99
Defense	2.36	1.05
Transport	9.00	2.83
Energy	8.14	2.73
Housing and Urban Development	9.00	3.83
Health and Human Services	5.38	1.54
Agriculture	8.20	2.20
Attorney General	4.17	0.94
Education	8.13	2.47
Labor	8.00	2.92

United States
Table 2

Party	Abbrev.
Democratic Party	DEM
Republican Party	REP

United States
Table 3

Party		Increase services (1) vs cut taxes (20)			Pro friendly relations USSR (1) vs anti (20)		
		Leads	Vots	Imp.	Leads	Vots	Imp.
DEM	Mean Raws	6.34	8.51	12.91	6.52	7.09	10.97
DEM	SD Raws	1.91	2.20	3.70	2.99	2.75	3.36
DEM	Mean Scores	-0.91	-0.75	-0.28	-0.55	-0.58	-0.26
REP	Mean Raws	15.71	13.60	15.00	10.85	11.46	12.79
REP	SD Raws	2.32	2.33	3.61	3.62	3.37	3.47
REP	Mean Scores	0.91	0.75	0.28	0.55	0.58	0.26

United States
Table 3 (cont.)

Party		Pro public own. (1) vs anti (20)			Pro permissive social policy (1) vs anti (20)		
		Leads	Vots	Imp.	Leads	Vots	Imp.
DEM	Mean Raws	13.03	12.86	5.06	6.03	8.31	14.80
DEM	SD Raws	3.63	3.75	4.82	2.43	2.17	3.97
DEM	Mean Scores	-0.64	-0.58	-0.10	-0.89	-0.78	0.14
REP	Mean Raws	17.97	17.18	6.06	15.80	14.69	13.74
REP	SD Raws	2.13	2.16	5.55	2.42	2.83	3.29
REP	Mean Scores	0.64	0.58	0.10	0.89	0.78	-0.14

Party		Anticlerical (1) vs proclerical (20)			Pro urban interests (1) vs anti (20)		
		Leads	Vots	Imp.	Leads	Vots	Imp.
DEM	Mean Raws	9.33	10.33	4.64	7.00	6.52	7.29
DEM	SD Raws	2.96	2.29	4.17	2.56	2.14	5.21
DEM	Mean Scores	-0.70	-0.64	-0.24	-0.77	-0.77	0.03
REP	Mean Raws	14.44	14.67	7.21	12.44	11.85	7.03
REP	SD Raws	2.19	2.96	5.96	1.95	2.21	4.69
REP	Mean Scores	0.70	0.64	0.24	0.77	0.77	-0.03

Party		Pro decentralization of decisions (1) vs anti (20)			Envir. over growth (1) vs growth over env (20)		
		Leads	Vots	Imp.	Leads	Vots	Imp.
DEM	Mean Raws	12.33	11.27	8.44	7.23	7.86	13.62
DEM	SD Raws	3.08	2.45	4.82	3.07	2.44	3.13
DEM	Mean Scores	0.69	0.56	-0.17	-0.77	-0.59	0.46
REP	Mean Raws	6.60	7.87	10.09	14.34	11.80	10.18
REP	SD Raws	2.96	2.66	4.55	2.81	2.97	3.59
REP	Mean Scores	-0.69	-0.56	0.17	0.77	0.59	-0.46

United States
Table 3 (cont.)

Party		No influence on party policy (1) vs high (20)			No influence on partic. in govt (1) vs high (20)		
		Leads	Legs	Acts	Leads	Legs	Acts
DEM	Mean Raws	11.03	15.00	11.24	9.15	10.46	10.00
DEM	SD Raws	5.56	4.05	3.69	6.01	6.64	5.00
DEM	Mean Scores	-0.12	0.16	0.05	-0.03	0.05	0.09
REP	Mean Raws	12.35	13.77	10.91	9.54	9.85	9.15
REP	SD Raws	5.97	3.67	3.28	5.88	6.74	4.20
REP	Mean Scores	0.12	-0.16	-0.05	0.03	-0.05	-0.09

Party		Do not look to future (1) vs look many years (5)			Give up office(1) vs give up policy (20)	Can use groups (1) vs not (20)	Close to resp (1) vs not (15)
		Leads	Legs	Acts			
DEM	Mean Raws	3.65	3.44	3.52	14.21	10.13	7.92
DEM	SD Raws	0.78	0.79	0.90	3.78	4.57	4.69
DEM	Mean Scores	-0.08	0.03	-0.08	-0.04	-0.05	-0.51
REP	Mean Raws	3.78	3.39	3.65	14.50	10.58	12.81
REP	SD Raws	0.85	0.78	0.83	3.11	5.04	3.85
REP	Mean Scores	0.08	-0.03	0.08	0.04	0.05	0.49

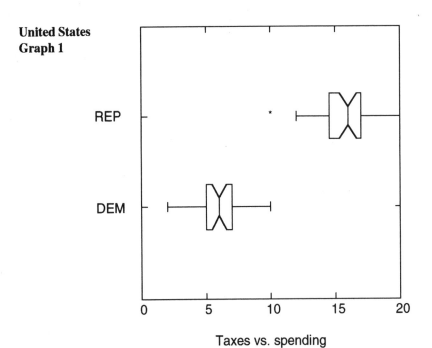

**United States
Graph 1**

REP

DEM

Taxes vs. spending

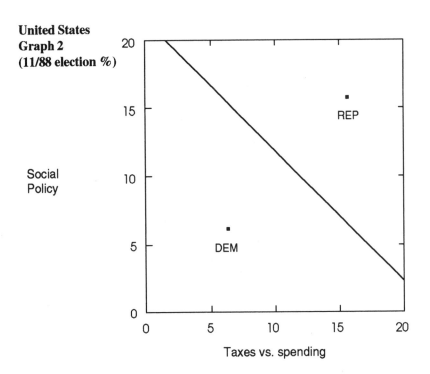

**United States
Graph 2
(11/88 election %)**

Social
Policy

REP

DEM

Taxes vs. spending

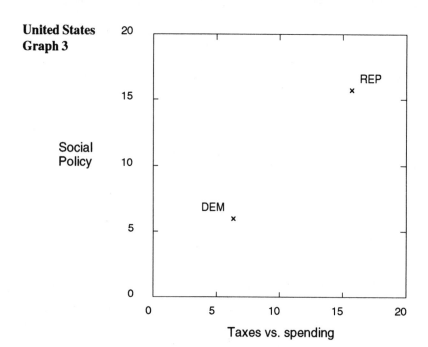

**United States
Graph 3**

Social
Policy

Taxes vs. spending

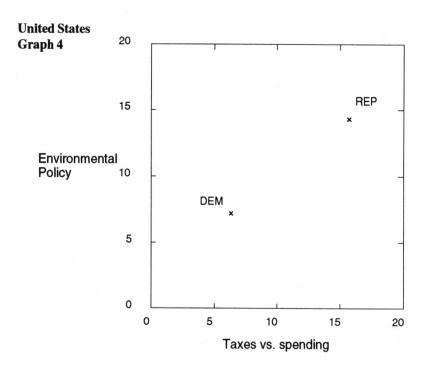

**United States
Graph 4**

Environmental
Policy

Taxes vs. spending

References

Austen-Smith, D., and Banks, J. 1988. Elections, coalitions and legislative outcomes. In *American Political Science Review*, 82, 405–422.

——, 1990. Stable portfolio allocations. *American Political Science Review*, 84, 891–906.

Axelrod, R. 1970. *Conflict of Interest*. Chicago: Markham.

Bergman, T., and Strom, K. 1989. *Electoral commitments and budget priorities in Sweden*. Berlin: ECPR Manifesto Research Group Conference on Party Programs and Government Expenditures.

Browne, E., and Feste, K. 1975. Qualitative Dimensions of Coalition Payoffs: Evidence for European Party Governments 1945–70. *American Behavioral Scientist*, 18, 530–556.

Browne, E., and Franklin, M. 1973. Aspects of Coalition Payoffs in European Parliamentary Democracies. In *American Political Science Review*, 67, 453–69.

Browne, E., and Frendreis, J. 1980. Allocating Coalition Payoffs by Conventional Norm: An Assessment of the Evidence for Cabinet Coalition Situations. In *American Journal of Political Science*, 24, 753–768.

Browne, E., and Dreijmanis, J. 1982. *Government Coalitions in Western Democracies*. New York: Longman.

Bruneau, T., and MacCleod, A. 1986. *Politics in Contemporary Portugal*. Boulder, Col: Lynne Rienner.

Budge, I., and Hofferbert, R. 1990. Mandates and policy outputs: US party platforms and Federal expenditures, 1948–1985. In *American Political Science Review*,

Budge, I., and Keman, H. 1990. *How party government works: testing a theory of formation, functioning and termination in 20 democracies*. Oxford: Oxford University Press.

Budge, I., Robertson, D., and Hearl, D. 1987. *Ideology, Strategy and Party Change*. Cambridge: Cambridge University Press.

Campbell, A., Converse, P., Miller, W., and Stokes, D. 1964. *The American Voter*. New York: Wiley.

Carlyle, T. 1871. *French Revolution, Vol 1*. London: Chapman and Hall.

Castles, F., and Mair, P. 1984. Left-Right Political Scales: Some Expert Judgements. *European Journal of Political Research*, 12, 83–88.

De Swaan, A. 1973. *Coalition Theories and Cabinet Formation*. Amsterdam: Elsevier.

Dodd, L. C. 1976. *Coalitions in Parliamentary Government*. Princeton: Princeton University Press.

Downs, A. 1957. *An Economic Theory of Democracy*. New York: Harper and Row.

Franklin, M., and Mackie, T. 1984. Reassessing the importance of size and ideology for the formation of governing coalitions in parliamentary democracies. In *American Journal of Political Science, 28*, 671–92.

Gallagher, M., Laver, M., and Mair, P. 1991. *Representative Government in Western Europe*. New York: McGraw Hill.

Grofman, B. 1982. A Dynamic Model of Protocoalition Formation in Ideological n— space. In *Behavioural Science, 27*, 77–90.

Hofferbert, R., and Klingemann, H.-D. 1989. *The policy impact of party programs and government declarations in the Federal Republic of Germany*. Berlin: ECPR Manifesto Research Group Conference on Party Programs and Government Expenditures.

Inglehart, R., and Klingemann, H.-D. 1976. Party Identification, Ideological Preference and the Left-Right Dimensions Among Western Mass Publics. In I. Budge, I. Crewe, and D. Farlie, eds., *Party Identification and Beyond: Representations of Voting and Party Competition*. London: Wiley.

Keman, H. 1989. *Party programs and policy making in the Netherlands: the paradox of coalescence and confrontation 1948–1986*. Berlin: ECPR Manifesto Research Group Conference on Party Programs and Government Expenditures.

Laver, M. 1989. Party competition and party system change: the interaction of coalition bargaining and electoral competition. In *Journal of Theoretical Politics, 2*.

Laver, M., and Budge, I., eds, 1992. *Party Policy and Coalition Government*. London: Macmillan.

Laver, M., and Mitchell, P. 1989. *Party policy and government spending in Ireland, 1957–87*. Mimeo, University College Galway.

Laver, M., and Schofield, N. 1990. *Multiparty Government: the Politics of Coalition in Europe*. Oxford: Oxford University Press.

Laver, M., and Shepsle, K. 1990a. Coalitions and cabinet government. In *American Political Science Review*, 84, 873–890.

————. 1990b. Government coalitions and intraparty politics. In *British Journal of Political Science,* 20, 489–507.

Leiserson, M. 1966. *Coalitions in politics.* PhD, Yale University.

Luebbert, G. 1986. *Comparative Democracy: Policy Making and Governing Coalitions in Europe and Israel.* New York: Columbia University Press.

McKelvey, R. D. 1976. Intransitivities in multidimensional voting models and some implications for agenda control. In *Journal of Economic Theory,* 12, 472–482.

————. 1979. General conditions for global intransitivities in formal voting models. *Econometrica,* 47, 1085–1111.

McKelvey, R. D., and Schofield, N. 1987. Generalised symmetry conditions at a core point. In *Econometrica,* 55, 923–933.

————. 1986. Structural instability of the core. In *Journal of Mathematical Economics,* 15, 179–198.

Morgan, M.-J. 1976. *The modelling of governmental coalition formation: a policy-based approach with interval measurement.* PhD, University of Michigan.

Sani, G., and Sartori, G. 1983. Polarization, Fragmentation and Competition in Western Democracies. In Daalder, H., and Mair, P. eds., *Western European Party Systems.* London: Sage.

Schofield, N. 1983. Generic instability of majority rule. In *Review of Economic Studies,* 50, 696–705.

————. 1986. Existence of a structurally stable equilibrium for a non-collegial voting rule. In *Public Choice,* 51, 267–284,

————. 1990. *An empirical analysis of the conditions for stable coalition government.* University of Rochester: Paper presented at conference in honour of William Riker, October 12–13, 1990.

Shepsle, K. 1979. Institutional arrangements and equilibrium in multidimensional voting models. In *American Journal of Political Science,* 23, 27–60.

Shepsle, K., and Weingast, B. 1981. Structure induced equilibrium and legislative choice. In *Public Choice,* 37, 503–519.

————. 1987. The institutional foundations of committee power. In *American Political Science Review,* 81, 85–104.

Taylor, M., and Laver, M. 1973. Government coalitions in Western Europe. In *European Journal of Political Research,* 1, 205–248.

Index